CENTRAL AMERICA

TOP SIGHTS, AUTHENTIC EXPERIENCES

Ashley Harrell, Isabel Albiston, Ray Bartlett,
Celeste Brash, Stuart Butler, Paul Clammer, Steve Fallon,
Anna Kaminski, Brian Kluepfel, Carolyn McCarthy

Contents

Plan Your Trip

Central America's
Top 18...............................4
Need to Know................ 22
Hotspots For.................. 24

Essential Central
America 26
Month by Month............ 28
Get Inspired................... 31

Itineraries 32
Family Travel................. 38

Mexico's Yucatán & Chiapas   41

Mérida   42

Mérida's
Museums.................... 44
Mérida's
Regional Cuisine 46
Uxmal Ruins.............. 48
Cenotes 52
Sights............................55
Activities......................56
Tours 56
Shopping 57
Eating...........................58
Drinking & Nightlife...... 61

Chichén Itzá   64

Visiting the Site 66
Valladolid 74

Palenque   78

Visiting the Site 80
Palenque 86

Guatemala   89

Antigua   90

Spanish & Salsa 92
Visiting Volcanoes.... 94
Splendor in
the Ruins 96
Sights............................98
Activities.....................102
Tours 102

Shopping 103
Eating...........................104
Drinking & Nightlife....108
Entertainment............ 110

Lago de Atitlán   112

Lake Communities... 114
Volcán San Pedro 118
Panajachel 120

Tikal   126

Visiting the Site 128
Uaxactún 134
Flores &
Santa Elena 136
El Remate 138

Belize   141

Northern Cayes   142

Belize Barrier Reef ... 144
The Blue Hole 148
Ambergris Caye
& San Pedro 150
Caye Caulker 155

El Salvador   161

Ruta de las Flores   162

Coffee along
the Flower Route 164
Driving Tour:
Ruta de las Flores... 166
Juayúa 168
Apaneca 168

Ataco 170
Ahuachapán............... 170

Honduras   173

Copán   174

Visiting the Site 176
Copán Ruinas.............180

Bay Islands   184

Diving &
Snorkeling 186
Roatán 191
Utila 193

Nicaragua   197

Granada   198

Volcán
Mombacho 200
Pueblos Blancos..... 202
Colonial Explorer
Walking Tour 206
Sights........................... 208
Tours 209
Courses 211
Shopping 211
Eating........................... 212
Drinking & Nightlife ... 213

Isla de Ometepe   216

Outdoor Activities ... 218
Moyogalpa 223

CUBA

Isla de la
Juventud

CAYMAN
ISLANDS
(UK)

JAMAICA

RN CAYES
42

4
aja

illo

Caribbean
Sea

Laguna de
Caratasca

Bilwi
(Puerto Cabezas)

a

NICARAGUA
agalpa

oaco
GUA

El Rama

Pearl
Lagoon

Bluefields

ago de
caragua

San
Carlos

El Castillo

Tortuguero

COSTA
RICA

Puerto
Limón

BOCAS
DEL TORO
p310

Colón

PANAMA CITY
p284

untarenas
SAN JOSÉ

Quepos

Golfo de
los Mosquitos

Bahía de
Panamá

p266

San Vito

Boquete

David

PANAMA

Penonomé

La Palma

QUÍ PROVINCE p324

Golfo de
Chiriquí

Santiago

Chitré

Golfo de
Panamá

Yaviza

Santa
Catalina

COLOMBIA

Welcome to Central America

With cerulean seas and verdant forests, magnificent Maya ruins and smoking volcanoes, Central America is like a tropical fairy tale – except all of it is real.

Central America's seven countries plus Mexico's Yucatán and Chiapas states equal 300-plus volcanoes, two expansive tropical coasts and one giant adventure playground. And while the region may take up less space than Texas, its rich mix of people and cultures has created a diverse and dynamic society.

Maya civilizations once sprawled from Mexico to Honduras, leaving behind ruins in five present-day countries where visitors can still step back and connect with an ancient and mysterious past. The Spanish left their mark throughout with colonial plazas, fervent beauty contests and silent hours of siesta. African culture permeates the Caribbean coast, from the Congo rebel traditions to lip-smacking *rondón* seafood gumbo.

What's more, Central America's natural environs are simply awe-inspiring, and your adventures here will be limited only by your will. Zip through rainforest canopies, swim alongside sea turtles or trek to sublime cloud-forest vistas. Scuba dive with whale sharks, snorkel the world's second-largest coral reef or set sail among virgin isles. And whether you prefer the chilled-out vibes on the Caribbean coast or the monster swells over on the Pacific shores, Central America offers just about any sun-soaked experience that your inner beach bum desires. Hello, paradise.

...visitors can still step back and connect with an ancient and mysterious past.

El Palacio (p83) at Palenque, Mexico
JAN WLODARCZYK/ALAMY STOCK PHOTO ©

MÉRIDA p42

CHICHÉN ITZÁ p64

PALENQUE p78

TIKAL p126

NORTHE p

BELIZE

BAY ISLANDS p18

COPÁN p174

LAGO DE ATITLÁN p112

ANTIGUA p90

RUTA DE LAS FLORES p162

GRANADA p198

ISLA DE OMETEPE p216

VOLCÁN ARENAL p250

MONTEVERDE p230

MANUEL ANTONI

CHIRI

N
0 ———— 200 km
0 ———— 100 miles

Gulf of
Mexico

Río
Lagartos

Cancún

Valladolid

Playa del
Carmen

Isla
Cozumel

Campeche

Tulum

Yucatán
Peninsula

MEXICO

MEXICO

Chetumal

Corozal

Ambergris Caye
San Pedro
Caye Caulker

Orange
Walk

Belize City

Tuxtla
Gutiérrez

San Cristóbal
de las Casas

Bethel

Flores

BELMOPAN

BELIZE

Dangriga

Placencia

Punta
Gorda

Gulf of
Honduras

Utila

Roatán

Guar

La Ceiba

Tru

San Pedro
Sula

Presa la
Angostura

La Mesilla

GUATEMALA

Cobán

Lago de
Izabal

Río Dulce

HONDURAS

Huehuetenango

Chichicastenango

Chiquimula

Gracias

Comayagua

Quetzaltenango

GUATEMALA
CITY

Santa Ana

TEGUCIGALPA

SAN SALVADOR

EL SALVADOR

San
Miguel

La Union

Somoto

Jinoteg

Estelí

Ma

Chinandega

Lago de
Managua

E

León

MANA

Masaya

Rivas

Liberia

PACIFIC
OCEAN

N

Playa Santo Domingo
& Santa Cruz 223
Around Volcán
Maderas 226

Costa Rica   229

Monteverde   230

**Bosque Nuboso
Monteverde** 232
Coffee Tours 236
Canopy Tours 238
Monteverde
& Santa Elena 241

Volcán Arenal   250

**Parque Nacional
Volcán Arenal** 252
Hot Springs 256
La Fortuna 258

El Castillo 264

Manuel Antonio   266

**Parque Nacional
Manuel Antonio** 268
Wildlife-Watching 272
Quepos 274
Manuel Antonio 278

Panama   283

Panama City   284

Casco Viejo 286
Panama Canal 288
**Panama Rainforest
Discovery Center** 292
Isla Taboga 294
**Panamá Viejo
Walking Tour** 296
Sights......................... 299

Activities.....................301
Tours 301
Shopping 303
Eating 304
Drinking & Nightlife 307
Entertainment........... 308

Bocas del Toro   310

Surfing 312
Isla Colón &
Bocas Town 314
Isla Bastimentos 320
Isla San Cristobal 322
Isla Carenero 322

Chiriquí Province   324

**Parque Nacional
Volcán Barú** 326
**Chiriquí
Coffee Farms** 330
Boquete......................332

In Focus

Central America
Today 340
History 342
People & Society 350
Arts & Culture 353
Outdoor Activities 356

Survival Guide

Directory A–Z 361
Transport 370
Language....................376
Index 378
Symbols &
Map Key..................... 384

Tent-making bats, Costa Rica (p229)
NATURE PICTURE LIBRARY/ALAMY STOCK PHOTO ®

Plan Your Trip
Central America's Top 18

Lago de Atitlán, Guatemala

Central America's most picturesque crater lake

Possibly the single most beautiful destination in Guatemala, Atitlán
(p112) elicits poetic outbursts from even the most seasoned traveler. The lake is ringed by volcanoes and villages such as Santiago
Atitlán, with its thriving indigenous culture, and San Marcos La
Laguna, humming with cosmic energy. Kayaking and hiking make
a longer stay worthwhile. Above: Lago de Atitlán and Volcán de San Pedro
(p118); right: Tzutujil woman wearing traditional hat

1

Northern Cayes, Belize

Belize's ultimate tropical-island getaways

Take a plunge into warm waters, discover kitesurfing or explore Belize's barrier reef in the Northern Cayes (p142). Relaxed Caye Caulker seduces everyone from backpackers to families with its laid-back atmosphere, refreshing lack of cars and heaping plates of grilled lobster. Ambergris Caye is for days of snorkeling the reef, kayaking the lagoon and dining and happening nightlife. Top: Hammocks on Caye Caulker; bottom: diving in Belize Barrier Reef (p144)

2

Bocas del Toro, Panama

A dreamy Caribbean island chain

'It's all good,' say the relaxed locals on Bocas del Toro (p310). Pedal to the beach on a bike, hum to improvised calypso on Isla Bastimentos and laze over dinner in a thatched hut on the waterfront. Accommodations options include cheap digs, stunning jungle lodges and luxury resorts on outer islands. Surfers hit the breaks, but there's also snorkeling among dazzling corals and oversized starfish, or volunteering opportunities to help nesting sea turtles.

3

Mérida, Mexico's Yucatán & Chiapas

The Yucatán Peninsula's undisputed cultural capital

This large but manageable city (p42) has a beautifully maintained colonial heart. It's veined with narrow cobbled streets and dotted with sunny plazas, with a wealth of museums and galleries, and some of the best food in the region. Just out of town are wildlife reserves, graceful haciendas, and jungle-shrouded cenotes to swim in. Further afield, little-visited Maya sites allow you to step back in time without the crowds. Plaza Grande, Mérida

Isla de Ometepe, Nicaragua

Lago de Nicaragua's twin volcano centerpiece

Home to archaeological remains, waterfalls, monkeys and birdlife, Isla de Ometepe (p216) is also a hot spot for activity-seekers. Take to the volcanoes, ziplines and lush hillsides cut by walking tracks, or kayak, bike and climb your way through this lost paradise. At the heart of the island's charms are the cool hostels, camping areas and peaced-out traveler scenes. Customize your experience, from high-end luxury lodges to groovy-groupie hippie huts. View from atop Volcán Maderas (p219)

DAVID CAYLESS/GETTY IMAGES ©

Volcán Arenal, Costa Rica

Iconic volcano and bubbling hot springs

While the molten night views are gone, this mighty, perfectly conical giant (p250) is still considered active and worthy of a pilgrimage. Whether shrouded in mist or bathed in sunshine, Arenal has several beautiful trails to explore, and at its base you're just a short drive away from its many hot springs, in which sore muscles are destined to be soothed. Even better, some of these springs are free, and any local can point the way.

Tikal, Guatemala

Guatemala's remarkably restored jungle temples

You'll marvel at these temples' monumental size and architectural brilliance, particularly in the early morning at the Gran Plaza in Tikal (p126). It's a testament to the cultural and artistic heights scaled by this jungle civilization, which thrived for some 16 centuries. A highlight is the sky-high vantage provided by towering Templo IV, on the west edge of the precinct. Equally compelling is the abundance of wildlife.

7

Bay Islands, Honduras

A backpacker's Honduran island dream

Imagine swimming in turquoise waters off white-sand beaches, then sipping a sundowner – but on a backpacking budget. Well, Honduras' Bay Islands (p184) offer that opportunity. Blessed with a fascinating British and buccaneering heritage, today these islands are renowned for their coral reefs and scuba diving. Search for the world's biggest fish, the whale shark, off Utila island, or explore shipwrecks in Roatán. Then feast on surf-fresh seafood and investigate the lively bar scenes. Roatán Island (p186)

Panama City, Panama

Panama's seaside and high-octane capital

Think crowds, casinos and a stacked skyline of shimmering glass and steel towers. This city (p284) of nearly a million people sits within striking distance of one of the world's great marvels of engineering, the Panama Canal, and also features the atmospheric colonial architecture of Casco Viejo. It's incongruous, yet appealing – and undeniably authentic. Oh, and the lush rainforest and sandy beaches (Pacific and Caribbean) are just a short day trip away. Far left: Panama City skyline; left: street scene, Casco Viejo (p286)

MADRUGADA VERDE/SHUTTERSTOCK ©

RICHARD MASCHMEYER/ROBERTHARDING/GETTY IMAGES ©

ANTON_IVANOV/SHUTTERSTOCK ©

Palenque, Mexico's Chiapas

Some of the Maya world's finest ruins

In Palenque (p78) pyramids rise above jungle treetops and howler monkeys sound off like monsters in the dense canopy. Wander the maze-like Palacio, scale the stone staircase of the Templo de las Inscripciones and survey the sprawling ruins. Then head downhill, following the Otolum River and its pretty waterfalls, and finish by visiting Palenque's museum. Top: Palace and observatory; bottom left: relief from Templo XIX; bottom right: howler monkey

10

Monteverde, Costa Rica

A pristine expanse of forest

Monteverde (p230) is a sprawling expanse of villages, farms and nature reserves. Bosque Nuboso Monteverde (Monteverde Cloud Forest) is a mysterious Neverland shrouded in mist, dangling with mossy vines, and sprouting with oversized ferns and magnificent bromeliads, home to more than 400 species of bird, including the elusive quetzal.

Red Bridge, Bosque Nuboso Monteverde (p232)

11

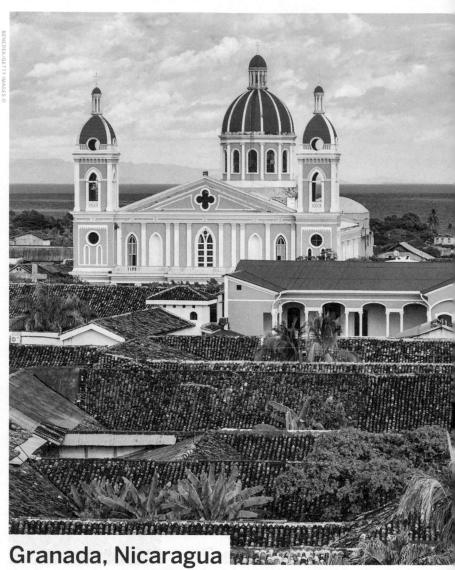

Granada, Nicaragua

Nicaragua's most vibrant colonial gem

Granada (p198) is a town of palpable magnetism. At the heart of the city's charms are the picture-perfect cobblestone streets and polychromatic colonial homes, and a lilting air that brings the city's spirited past into present-day focus. Trips here begin and end on foot; simply dawdling from gallery to restaurant to colonial church can take up the better part of a day. Nearby, islands, volcanoes and villages await further exploration. Granada Cathedral

12

WALKABOUT PHOTO GUIDES/SHUTTERSTOCK ©

Copán, Honduras

Stunning Maya site in a lovely location

Copán's location in an idyllic river valley, home to scarlet macaws and surrounded by pine-forested hills, is simply sublime. The site itself (p174) is also very special indeed, with a towering hieroglyphic stairway and a great plaza dotted with imposing, fabulously carved stelae and altars. When you've had your fill of exploring Maya temples, you'll find the charming little neighboring town of Copán Ruinas a delightful base.

13

ONDREJ PROSICKY/SHUTTERSTOCK ©

Chiriquí Province, Panama

Cloud forest and coffee farms galore

Equal parts adventure hub and mountain retreat, the Chiriquí Province (p324) is a magnet for expats, retirees and travelers of all stripes. Birdwatchers comb the forest for a glimpse of the resplendent quetzal, while adrenaline addicts head to Boquete, a major hub for rafting and kayaking. Coffee farms dot the countryside, with tours showing the process from leaf to cup. Fuel up, and you're ready for the next adventure. Resplendent quetzal

14

ROBERTO A SANCHEZ/GETTY IMAGES ©

KRYSSIA CAMPOS/GETTY IMAGES ©

FRANCOIS JOSEPH BERGER/
GETTY IMAGES ©

Antigua, Guatemala

Eat, party and learn Spanish in style

With mammoth volcanic peaks and coffee-covered slopes as a backdrop for the scattered remnants of Spanish occupation, the former capital of Guatemala (p90) makes an appealing setting for learning Spanish. Nowhere else in the country packs in such a great culinary and nightlife scene, along with fabulous souvenir shopping, a sweet central plaza and picture-postcard vistas. Top: Downtown Antigua; bottom left: Maya women at a market; bottom right: enchilada

15

Manuel Antonio, Costa Rica

Alive with the calls of the wild

Although droves of visitors pack Parque Nacional Manuel Antonio (p266), the country's most popular (and smallest) national park remains an absolute gem. Capuchin monkeys share tropical white-sand beaches with dive-bombing brown pelicans, and sleepy sloths dangle adorably over its trails. It's a perfect place to introduce curious youngsters to the wonders of the rainforest; indeed, you may start to feel like a kid again yourself. Capuchin monkeys

16

17

Ruta de las Flores, El Salvador

A charming drive through bucolic hills

Winding through coffee plantations and mountain villages, and traversing the volcanic Apaneca Range, the Flower Route (p162) is packed with waterfalls, food fairs and hiking trails. Stop off to savor the local caffeine at a cafe or tour a *finca* (farm) to get the lowdown on coffee growing in El Salvador. Bathing in Los Chorros de Calera waterfall (p168)

MICKAEL ROUZE/SHUTTERSTOCK ©

MATYAS REHAK/SHUTTERSTOCK ©

DE AGOSTINI/ARCHIVIO J
LANGE/GETTY IMAGES ©

18

Chichén Itzá, Mexico's Yucatán

Mexico's most popular Maya sight

From the imposing, monolithic El Castillo pyramid (where the shadow of the plumed serpent god Kukulcán creeps down the staircase during the spring and autumn equinoxes) to the Sacred Cenote and curiously designed El Caracol, the legacy of Maya astronomers at Chichén Itzá (p64) will blow your mind. Admire the Platform of Skulls and the stone carvings at the Temple of Warriors, or come back at night for the sound-and-light show.

Plan Your Trip
Need to Know

When to Go

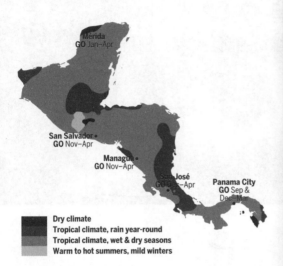

Mérida
GO Jan–Apr

San Salvador •
GO Nov–Apr

Managua •
GO Nov–Apr

San José
GO Dec–Apr

Panama City
GO Sep &
Dec–Mar

- Dry climate
- Tropical climate, rain year-round
- Tropical climate, wet & dry seasons
- Warm to hot summers, mild winters

High Season (mid-Dec–mid-Apr)

- Dry season throughout most of the region.
- High hotel demand; rates rise 25% to 50%.
- Many more tourists in popular destinations.

High Season Peak (holidays)

- Includes Christmas, New Year and Easter week.
- Hotel rates may be up to double the normal rates.
- Resorts, festival towns and beaches are crowded with national vacationers.

Low Season (mid-Apr–early Dec)

- Rainy season in most of the region; hurricane season between June and November.
- Places can still be enjoyed – check regional climates.
- Accommodations and resorts are better priced.

Currency

Belize: Belize dollar (BZ$); Costa Rica: colón (₡), US dollar (US$); El Salvador: US dollar; Guatemala: quetzal (Q); Honduras: lempira (L); Mexico: peso (M$); Nicaragua: córdoba (C$), US dollar; Panama: balboa (B/.), US dollar.

Languages

Spanish, English

Visas

Generally not required for under 90 days. Belize issues 30-day visas. The Centro America 4 (CA-4) agreement allows 90 days in Guatemala, Nicaragua, Honduras and El Salvador.

Money

ATMs are common, except in remote areas. Midrange and high-end businesses accept credit cards.

Cell Phones

Cell phones are widely used. You can purchase a local cell phone in a kiosk for as little as US$20, or a prepaid SIM card for around US$5.

Time

Central Standard Time (GMT/UTC minus six hours)

Daily Costs

Budget: Less than US$50

- Dorm bed: US$10–15
- Set meals or street food: US$4–8
- Public transport: US$5–15

Midrange: US$50–180

- Double room in a midrange hotel: US$30–60
- Restaurant meals: US$8–20
- Park fees or surf lessons: US$8–25

Top End: More than US$180

- Double room in a high-end hotel, resort or lodge: US$60–140
- Guided hikes and tours: US$30–60

Useful Websites

Planeta (www.planeta.com) Regional articles, events, reference material and links, with an emphasis on sustainable travel.

Tico Times (www.ticotimes.net) Based in Costa Rica, a long-standing online newspaper covering Central America news and culture.

Lonely Planet (www.lonelyplanet.com/central-america) Destination information, hotel bookings, traveler forum and more.

Top Tips

- Learn as much Spanish as you can – even just basic phrases. It can't hurt, and it might very well help you bond with the locals.
- Pack half the clothes that you think you'll need: laundry service is cheap in the region.
- Visit local *mercados* (markets) – not just to eat fresh food cheaply, but also to sample a lively slice of local life.
- Be aware that Belize, Costa Rica and Mexico are significantly more expensive than other parts of the region. The cheapest places to travel here are Guatemala, Honduras, El Salvador and Nicaragua.

- Relax and bring a good book with you wherever you go; Central Americans are rarely in a hurry and it helps to go with the flow.
- When visiting indigenous communities, ask permission to take photos, particularly of children, and dress more modestly than beachwear.

Getting Around

Buses are the cheapest and most accessible way to get around, particularly along the Pan-American Hwy (also called the Panamericana or Interamericana), which runs through all the countries except Belize.

Air Because of the region's skinny stature, a flight can save several hours of backtracking. Each country has at least one international airport, as well as regional and charter flights via national airlines.

Boat Various types of boats serve islands and some borders.

Bus The main form of regional transport, from comfortable, air-conditioned, long-haul buses to run-down former school buses.

Car & Motorcycle Rentals are usually not allowed to cross international borders.

Train Limited to the Panama City–Colón route in Panama, and a basic commuter service in Costa Rica's Central Valley.

For more on **getting around**, see p371

Plan Your Trip
Hotspots for...

History

Time travel has never been so easy! Visiting Central America's Maya ruins and colonial cities will transport you back to bygone eras of the region's mysterious past.

MEUNIERD/SHUTTERSTOCK ©

Tikal, Guatemala (p126)
This regional superstar features soaring, jungle-shrouded temples.

Best Vantage Point
Climb to the top of
Templo IV.

Copán, Honduras (p174)
A temple acropolis with incredibly intricate Maya carvings.

Best Vantage Point
Park yourself at the
Hieroglyphic Stairway.

Mérida, Mexico (p42)
One of the Americas' largest colonial-era *centro históricos*.

Best Vantage Point
Wandering around the
Plaza Grande.

Wildlife-watching

Thanks largely to conservation efforts, Central America's air, land and sea still teem with wild creatures. Visitors will encounter them often, and should tread lightly.

MARTIN MECNAROWSKI/SHUTTERSTOCK ©

Isla Bastimentos, Panama (p320)
From July to August, four turtle species hatch on the north shore.

What to Spot
Baby turtles scrambling to
the sea.

Belize Barrier Reef, Belize (p144)
The Western Hemisphere's finest reef makes Belize a fish-spying paradise.

What to Spot
Stingrays and nurse sharks
abound.

Monteverde, Costa Rica (p230)
Monteverde is the Costa Rican cloud forest at its dreamiest.

What to Spot
Peep at keel-billed toucans
and motmots.

Outdoor Adventure

Whether you're zipping through a canopy, poking around a sharky reef or hiking the slopes of a volcano, Central America is synonymous with adrenaline.

SIMON DANNHAUER/SHUTTERSTOCK ©

The Blue Hole, Belize (p148)
Swim with stalactites and reef sharks in this giant sinkhole.

Tour Operator
Dive in with Long Caye Diving Services (p149).

San Pedro, Guatemala (p118)
A hike here rewards with gorgeous views of Lago de Atitlán.

Tour Operator
Climb volcanoes with experts from Geo Travel (p119).

Parque Nacional Manuel Antonio, Costa Rica (p268)
Easy access to rafting, canopy tours and adventure parks.

Tour Operator
Ride a river with Unique Tours (p274).

Coffee

Coffee is all the rage on the isthmus, and you can visit any number of crisp-aired mountain towns to learn the process and sample the beans.

©MORGAN ARNOLD/GETTY IMAGES ©

Antigua, Guatemala (p90)
Coffee-covered hills give this town a picturesque backdrop.

Best Cup of Joe
Growers lead tours at De la Gente (p103).

Lago de Yojoa, Honduras (p183)
Some of the country's best coffee is grown near this scenic oasis.

Best Cup of Joe
El Dorao Cafe (p183) is as local as it gets.

Monteverde, Costa Rica (p230)
Discover Costa Rica's golden beans on local coffee tours.

Best Cup of Joe
Sample the goods at Café de Monteverde (p236).

Plan Your Trip
Essential Central America

MICHAEL BOYNY/LOOK-FOTO/GETTY IMAGES ©

Activities

Offering two dramatic and diverse coastlines of warm sand, salty swells and abundant marine life, Central America lures all types of ocean lovers, be they scuba divers or surfers, paddleboarders or anglers. Meanwhile, the inland terrain is studded with mountains and volcanoes begging to be explored on foot, by bike or on horseback, and the tropical rainforests are rich with birds and wildlife. Raging rivers ideal for rafting plunge through picturesque canyons, crisscrossing the region. Adventure awaits!

Shopping

Souvenirs, handicrafts, woodwork and locally made arts and crafts are popular buys all over Central America, but the folk art in Guatemala, Nicaragua and Mexico are particularly coveted. For the best deals on indigenous pieces such as the gorgeous textiles woven throughout Guatemala, ceremonial masks of the Boruca people in Costa Rica and *molas* (handmade women's clothing) from the Guna tribe in Panama, visit the villages themselves. Mountain towns (particularly in Guatemala, Costa Rica and Honduras) produce and sell excellent coffee, and you'll also find a wide variety of affordable items in Zona Libres (tax-free zones) and urban malls in large cities.

Eating

Central America may not be known as a culinary destination, with beans and rice tending to dominate the plate, but an amalgam of cultures, fertile soils, varied climates and expansive shorelines have resulted in some seriously delicious dishes. The Caribbean side of the isthmus tends to work with more spice and coconut milk, with excellent results, but those looking for a true foodie's paradise should make for Mexico.

VLAD ISPAS/SHUTTERSTOCK ©

Drinking & Nightlife

In backpacker towns and touristy islands around Central America, there's no shortage of bars and nightclubs, and capitals like Panama City and San José also feature high-end cocktail bars and trendy microbreweries. Admission and cover charges are generally reasonable, though upscale clubs try to out-price any unwanted clientele. In more remote areas, the nighttime scene is considerably more laid-back, but rest assured that every beach town on the isthmus has at least one local bar where everybody goes.

Entertainment

In Central America, the larger cities are the entertainment hubs, with plays, concerts and live-music options to suit every taste. In the countryside, festivals are the main

★ Best Places to Shop for Local Souvenirs

Nim Po't, Antigua, Guatemala (p103)

Garden Shop, Granada, Nicaragua (p211)

Diconte-Axul, Ruta de las Flores, El Salvador (p170)

Karavan, Casco Viejo, Panama City (p303)

Casa de las Artesanías, Merida, Mexico (p57)

opportunity for people to let loose. Often with a cultural or religious focus, these can be fun, loud, colorful and sometimes verging on the debauched. *Fútbol* (soccer) matches tend to dominate the TV screens of rural and urban bars alike, but the real treat is to catch a game at the stadium.

From left: Bosque Nuboso Monteverde (p232); traditional weaver in Guatemala

Plan Your Trip
Month by Month

January

The dry season and tourist season are both at their peaks, with great kitesurfing and swimming available in warm Pacific waters. Quetzal-viewing season begins in Costa Rica's Monteverde (through July).

☆ Panama Jazz Festival

The weeklong jazz festival (www.panama jazzfestival.com) is one of the biggest musical events in Panama, drawing top-caliber international musicians from jazz, blues, salsa and other genres. Held mid-January around Panama City; the open-air events are usually free.

☆ Mérida Fest, Mexico

This cultural event (www.merida.gob. mx), running most of January across the city, celebrates the founding of Mérida with art exhibits, concerts, plays and book presentations.

February

It's prime time for surfing both on Pacific and Caribbean swells. Carnaval, a feature of all Central American countries, takes place in February or March.

☆ International Poetry Festival, Nicaragua

Top Spanish-language wordsmiths from around the globe gather for this festival (www.festivalpoesianicaragua.com) in Granada, celebrating the spoken word.

March

Easter celebrations may take place in March or April. Semana Santa (Holy Week) offers reenactments of the crucifixion and resurrection of Christ. On Good Friday, religious processions are held across Central America.

Above: Lent procession in Antigua

☸ Semana Santa, Guatemala

Although Semana Santa (Holy Week) is celebrated all over Central America, nowhere gets more lively – or pricey for travelers – than Antigua, Guatemala.

☸ Vernal Equinox, Mexico

On the day of the spring equinox (usually around March 20) and for about a week thereafter, thousands head to Chichén Itzá to witness the shadow formation of a serpent appear on the staircase of El Castillo pyramid.

April

The tail end of the dry season for most of Central America. In the jungle lowlands of Guatemala, March and April are scorchers; it's the best time to see whale sharks off Honduras or Belize.

☸ Día de Juan Santamaría, Costa Rica

April 11 commemorates Costa Rica's national hero, who died driving failed US

★ Top Events

Carnaval, February or March

Vernal Equinox, March

Semana Santa, March or April

Independence Day, September

Día de los Muertos, November

conqueror William Walker out of Costa Rica in 1856. The weeklong national holiday features parades, parties and other celebrations.

May

The rainy season is upon the isthmus. May begins a five- to six-month nesting season for both loggerhead and green sea turtles in the Caribbean.

Above: Día de los Muertos parade, Mérida

June

June to November is hurricane season, though big weather events are sporadic and hard to predict. Forty days after Easter, Corpus Christi features colorful celebrations throughout the region in May or June.

✗ Lobsterfest, Belize

A celebration (www.belize.com/lobster fest-in-belize) of the world's favorite crustacean, along with libations galore. Takes place on Ambergris Caye in mid-June and on Caye Caulker in early July.

July

Though it's the middle of the rainy season, the weather is relatively dry on the Caribbean side; Belize can be uncomfortably hot. It's off-peak for visitors and hotels offer better rates.

August

Breeding humpback whales can be observed in the Pacific. And though the rainy season continues, in between showers there's still plenty of sunshine to be had.

✥ Fiestas Agostinas, El Salvador

Celebrates El Salvador's patron saint. All cities have festivities, but the celebration in San Salvador is the biggest.

✥ Costa Maya Festival, Belize

This massive festival (www.international costamayafestival.com) may be held in San Pedro, Belize, but it draws participants from all over Central America. The streets come alive with music, parades, dancing and drinking. The bodybuilding contest is a bonus.

September

Though it's peak hurricane season further north, rains let up around Panama City and Costa Rica's Caribbean side is less wet than the Pacific. Flooding in Honduras is possible through February.

✥ Día de la Independencia

Costa Rica, El Salvador, Guatemala, Honduras and Nicaragua all celebrate their independence on September 15. Belize celebrates on September 21.

October

In most of the region, October 12 is Día de la Raza (Columbus Day) – a dubious legacy nonetheless celebrated by every high-school brass band. Loggerhead turtles nest on the Pacific coast from now through March.

November

Seasonal rains have tapered off in most of the region, except for Honduras' north coast, where flooding can occur through February.

✥ Día de Todos los Santos, Guatemala

In Santiago Sacatepéquez and Sumpango, just outside Antigua, celebrations marking All Saints' Day include the flying of huge kites, while in the tiny highlands town of Todos Santos Cuchumatán, November 1 is celebrated with drunken horse races through town.

✥ Día de los Muertos, Mexico

On November 1 and 2, families build altars in their homes and visit graveyards to commune with their beloved dead, taking garlands and gifts.

✥ Independencia de Panamá

In Panama, the whole country celebrates multiple independence-related holidays in November.

December

December and January are the coolest months on the Pacific coast, from Nicaragua to the jungle lowlands of Guatemala. The Christmas holidays disrupt the region's work schedule – cities empty out and beaches are full.

Plan Your Trip
Get Inspired

Read

A Mayan Life (Gaspar Pedro Gonzáles; 1995) First novel to be published by a Maya author, about rural Guatemalan life.

The Country Under My Skin (Gioconda Belli; 2003) An enthralling autobiography by a Nicaraguan poet about her role in the revolution.

Getting to Know the General (Graham Greene; 1984) Portrait of a Panamanian general by his longtime friend.

Empire of Blue Water (Stephen Talty; 2008) Intriguing pirate history and *New York Times* bestseller.

The True History of the Conquest of New Spain (Bernal Díaz de Castillo; 1568) Eyewitness account of Cortés' 1519 expedition to Mexico.

Watch

Ixcanul (2015) Multi-award-winning film about a young Kaqchiquel girl's coming of age in Guatemala.

Mosquito Coast (1986) Harrison Ford and family search for a simpler life in Central America.

Curse of the Xtabai (2012) Belizeans are quite proud of this feature-length horror film, the first to be 100% filmed and produced in Belize.

King of the Jungle (in production) The story of John McAfee, eccentric inventor of McAfee VirusScan and murder suspect in Belize, as played by Michael Keaton.

Listen

Rubén Blades The Panamanian salsa icon and ex-presidential candidate; check out his collaboration with Calle 13.

Gaby Moreno Singer-songwriter from Guatemala with a lush Latin sound.

Aurelio Martínez Albums *Garífuna Soul* and *Laru Beya* received rave reviews all over the world.

Above: Chichén Itzá (p64)

Plan Your Trip
Seven-Day Itineraries

City, Sea & Lake Sampler

Not everybody gets ample vacation time, and Central America is tough to squeeze into a week, but for those hungry for a three-in-one trip involving the region's most budget-friendly big city, verdant islands and a mountain lake, here's one way it can be done.

FROM RIGHT: GALINA SAVINA/SHUTTERSTOCK © FOTO55693/SHUTTERSTOCK ©

Bay Islands (p184) Kick back on one of these tranquil Honduran islands, swim with whale sharks and learn to dive on the cheap. ✈ 30/45 mins to San Pedro Sula, then ✈ 1 hr to Guatemala City, and 🚌 3 hrs to Panajachel

Lago Atitlán (p112) Boat to authentic villages and climb a volcano for incredible views of Central America's most picturesque lake.

Panama City (p284) Begin in Central America's most developed city, exploring the nearby rainforest and visiting the famous canal. ✈ 2 hrs to San Pedro Sula, then ✈ 30/45 mins to Utila/Roatán

Exploring the Center

Discover the highlights of Guatemala, El Salvador and Honduras – if you don't mind a couple of long, bumpy bus rides, in just a week you can take in some spectacular scenery, majestic ruins and colonial charm.

Antigua (p90) Explore the colonial city, sign up for a volcano climb and perhaps take a crash course in Spanish. 🚌 4 hrs over the El Salvador border to Tacuba

①

③ Copán (p174) Stop in the cobblestone town of Copán Ruinas, which offers river-tubing trips, horseback rides over mountains, and its namesake ruins.

②

Ruta de las Flores (p162) Take in this lovely series of villages, replete with hiking trails and food festivals. 🚌 6 hrs to Copán

①

③

FROM LEFT: LUCY BROWN - LOCA4MOTION/SHUTTERSTOCK ©, VOJTECHVLK/SHUTTERSTOCK ©

Plan Your Trip
10-Day Itinerary

Northern Jaunt

Rich in culture and coastline, this route loops through many of the region's northern highlights, including Maya ruins, reef snorkeling and jungle cruising.

Chichén Itzá (p64) Set aside a day for this Maya archaeological site, named one of the 'new seven wonders of the world.' 🚌 7 hrs to Belize City, then ⛴ 1 hr to Northern Cayes

Mérida (p42) Wander narrow streets, laze in broad plazas and browse the region's best museums in this cultural capital. 🚌 2 hrs to Chichén Itzá

Northern Cayes (p142) Splash into the Caribbean and explore the Belize Barrier Reef from either hoppin' Ambergris Caye or chilled-out Caye Caulker. ⛴ 1 hr to Belize City, then 🚌 5 hrs to Tikal

Tikal (p126) Visit the mother of all Maya sites and its towering, steep-sided temples in a lush jungle setting.

Plan Your Trip
Two-Week Itinerary

Pacific Coasting

The sinuous Pacific coastline from Nicaragua to Panama has something to suit everyone, from insatiable surfers to dedicated beach bums, while inland there are coffee farms, cloud forests and even more diverse landscapes. Get set for adventure.

Granada (p198) Land in Managua and make for this colonial gem's lovely cathedrals and nearby islets. 🚌 1 hr back to Managua, then ✈ 20 mins to Ometepe

Monteverde (p230) Relax into this cool mountain town and journey into its eponymous cloud forest reserve. 🚌🚤🚌 4 hrs the scenic way to Arenal

Manuel Antonio (p266) Spy on dangling sloths and playful monkeys in Costa Rica's smallest and most popular national park. 🚌 5 hrs to Boquete

Ometepe (p216) Outdoor adventures await on this twin-volcano island rising out of a sea-sized lake. 🚢 1 hr to the mainland, then 🚌 5 hrs to Monteverde

Arenal (p250) Behold the Arenal volcano's perfect cone, hike its flanks and soothe sore muscles in the nearby natural hot springs. 🚌 5 hrs or ✈ 30 mins to Manuel Antonio

Boquete (p332) Spend a relaxing day or two in a dreamy mountain town, beloved for its cool air and strong coffee. 🚌 8 hrs to Panama City

6

7

Panama City (p284) Finish in Central America's most developed city, peering up at skyscrapers and dining in hip restaurants.

2

5

Plan Your Trip
Family Travel

DANITA DELIMONT/ALAMY STOCK PHOTO ©

Central America is a safe and exciting destination for families with children. Beaches on two coastlines, wildlife-rich forests and endless opportunities for adventure are guaranteed to thrill kids of all ages.

For more ideas about family travel, see Lonely Planet's *Travel with Children*.

Practicalities

○ Do not expect all the amenities that are available at home, as you're unlikely to find conveniences such as high chairs in restaurants, cribs at hotels or changing tables in public toilets.

○ Formula, diapers (nappies) and other baby necessities are widely available in grocery stores.

○ Discreet public breastfeeding is common, though less so in urban areas.

○ Many car rental agencies offer child seats (for a fee), but they must be reserved in advance and quality is not guaranteed.

○ A number of tours, some low intensity, are an enjoyable way for you and your children to see Central America's lush environment. Look for agencies with tailored family outings.

Health

○ At the time of writing, pregnant women (and women who are trying to get pregnant) are advised against traveling to Central America, due to the Zika virus.

○ Be sure children are up to date on all routine immunizations. Some recommended vaccines may not be approved for children, so be careful they do not drink tap water or consume any questionable food.

○ Dengue fever and (less so) malaria are present in limited areas. Bring good insect repellent, light long-sleeved tops and long pants.

○ Child safety provisions in Central America may be less strict than what you're accustomed to. Check out things such as

CAVAN/ALAMY STOCK PHOTO ©

toddler pools, cribs, guardrails and even toys, so that you're aware of any potential hazards.

Accommodations

○ Central America has an exciting variety of different places to stay that should please most kids – anything beachside is usually a good start, and rustic *cabañas* (cabins) provide a sense of adventure (but choose one with good screens and mosquito nets).

○ Many hotels have a rambling layout and a good amount of open-air space – courtyards, pool areas, gardens – allowing for some light exploring by kids. The most family-oriented hotels, with expansive grounds and facilities such as shallow pools, playgrounds and kids clubs, tend to be found in the big resorts.

○ Family rooms are widely available, and many hotels will put an extra bed or two in a room at little or no extra cost. You can find rooms with air-conditioning nearly everywhere, and most midrange and top-end

★ **Best Kid-Friendly Adventures**

Bosque Nuboso Monteverde, Costa Rica (p232)

Hol Chan Marine Reserve, Belize (p145)

Tikal, Guatemala (p129)

Bocas del Toro (p310), Panama

Parque Nacional Volcan Arenal, Costa Rica (p252)

hotels have wi-fi access and child-friendly channels on the TV and/or DVD players for when your kids just need to flop down in front of something entertaining.

○ Make sure when reserving a room that the establishment accepts children – some are adults-only.

From left: Snorkeling in Hol Chan Marine Reserve (p145), Belize; ziplining through Bosque Nuboso Monteverde (p232)

MEXICO'S YUCATÁN & CHIAPAS

In this Chapter

Mérida's Museums 44
Mérida's Regional Cuisine 46
Uxmal Ruins 48
Cenotes 52
Sights 55
Activities 56
Tours 56
Shopping 57
Eating 58
Drinking & Nightlife 61

Mérida

Since the Spanish conquest, Mérida has been the cultural capital of the entire Yucatán Peninsula. A blend of provincial and cosmopolitan, it is a town steeped in colonial history, and a great place to explore, with narrow streets, broad plazas and top-notch museums. Long popular with European travelers looking to go beyond the hubbub of Quintana Roo's resort towns, Mérida is a tourist town, but a tourist town too big to feel like a tourist trap. And as the capital of Yucatán state, Mérida is also the cultural crossroads of the region.

Two Days in Mérida

Begin your adventures with a visit to Mérida's best museum, **Gran Museo del Mundo Maya** (p44), and indulge in a traditional Yucatecan meal at **La Chaya Maya** (p46).

On day two, fuel up on coffee at **Manifesto** (p62) and stroll the Plaza Grande, admiring its colonial charms. Dip into **Casa de las Artesanías** (p57) for handicrafts and **Hamacas El Aguacate** (p57) for hammocks, and do a fancy dinner at **Ku'uk** (p46).

Four Days in Mérida

Head to the superb ruins of **Uxmal** (p49) in the Puuc region, and have lunch at **Codornejas Restaurante** (p49). Return to Mérida for the evening and hit up **La Negrita** (p61) for mezcal and dancing.

Your final day might involve **museum hopping** (p44), a cooking class with **Los Dos** (p47) or even a day trip to one of the **cenotes** (p52). Don't leave without hunting down some *cochinita pibil* (slow-cooked pork).

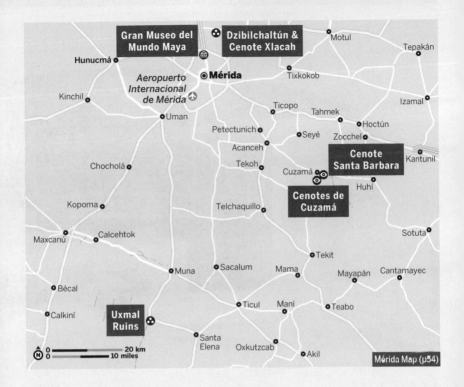

Map labels: Hunucmá, Kinchil, Chocholá, Kopoma, Maxcanú, Calcehtok, Bécal, Calkiní, **Gran Museo del Mundo Maya**, **Dzibilchaltún & Cenote Xlacah**, Motul, Tepakán, Aeropuerto Internacional de Mérida, **Mérida**, Tixkokob, Izamal, Uman, Ticopo, Tahmek, Hoctún, Petectunich, Seyé, Zocchel, Kantunil, Acanceh, Tekoh, Cuzamá, **Cenote Santa Barbara**, Huhí, Telchaquillo, **Cenotes de Cuzamá**, Sotuta, Tekit, Muna, Sacalum, Mama, Mayapán, Cantamayec, Ticul, Maní, Teabo, Santa Elena, Oxkutzcab, Akil, **Uxmal Ruins**

Mérida Map (p54)

Arriving in Mérida

Aeropuerto Internacional de Mérida
Taxis will take you downtown for M$200. Or you can catch a city cab outside the airport for M$120. A bus (M$8) stops every 15 to 30 minutes until 9pm (occasionally 11pm) outside the airport.

Terminal CAME From Mérida's main bus terminal (or any other bus terminal) you'll pay around M$30 to M$50 for a taxi to your lodgings.

Where to Stay

Although attractive options in the city's historic center are somewhat limited, you'll find ideal lodgings within restored 19th-century mansions and colonial buildings just to the north, along with some lovely B&Bs in the southwestern neighborhood of Santiago. There are some unimpressive cheapie hotels within steps of the bus stations, if you're looking to save your cash.

Gran Museo del Mundo Maya, by Grupo Arquidecture (4A Arquitectos)

FRANCISCO J RAMOS GALLEGO/SHUTTERSTOCK ©

Mérida's Museums

For those who need more than just pretty beaches, you'll be glad to know that Mérida brims with interesting museums, many of which provide fascinating background information missing from some archaeological sites.

Great For...

☑ Don't Miss

The punk-rock skull belt and reptile headdress at Gran Museo del Mundo Maya.

Gran Museo del Mundo Maya

A world-class **museum** (Map p43; ☑999-341-04-30; www.granmuseodelmundomaya.com.mx; Calle 60 Norte 299E; adult/child under 13yr M$150/75; ☺8am-5pm Wed-Mon; **P**) celebrating Maya culture, the Gran Museo houses a permanent collection of more than 1100 remarkably well-preserved artifacts, including a reclining *chacmool* sculpture from Chichén Itzá and a cool underworld figure unearthed at Ek' Balam, replete with rough-hewn accessories. If you're planning on visiting the area's ruins, drop by here first for some context.

Palacio Cantón

This massive **mansion** (Regional Anthropology Museum; Map p54; ☑999-923-05-57; Paseo de Montejo 485; adult/child under 13yr M$60/free; ☺8am-5pm Tue-Sun) was built between

Mayan hieroglyphics panel, Museo del Mundo Maya

GERALD MARELLA/SHUTTERSTOCK ©

[Map showing: Gran Museo del Mundo Maya (7km), Palacio Cantón, Calle 60, Calle 50, Calle 59, Museo Fernando García Ponce-Macay, Museo de Arte Popular de Yucatán, Museo de la Ciudad, Calle 65]

❶ Need to Know

Check the tourist publication *Yucatán Today* for events or deals going on in museums during your visit.

✕ Take a Break

After Museo del Mundo Maya, grab a delicious Yucatecan lunch and cocktail at Nectar (p47).

★ Top Tip

☑ Don't miss the free sound-and-light show at night on the wall outside Gran Museo del Mundo Maya.

1909 and 1911, though its owner, General Francisco Cantón Rosado (1833–1917), lived here for only six years before his death. The Palacio's splendor and pretension make it a fitting symbol of the grand aspirations of Mérida's elite during the last years of the Porfiriato.

Museo Fernando García Ponce-Macay

Housed in the former archbishop's palace, this attractive **museum** (Museo de Arte Contemporáneo; Map p54; ☎999-928-32-36; www.macay.org; Pasaje de la Revolución s/n btwn Calles 58 & 60; ⊙10am-5:15pm Wed-Mon) **FREE** holds permanent exhibitions of three of Yucatán's most famous painters of the Realist and Ruptura periods (Fernando Castro Pacheco, Fernando García Ponce and Gabriel Ramírez Aznar), as well as

rotating exhibitions of contemporary art from Mexico and abroad.

Museo de la Ciudad

The **Museo de la Ciudad** (City Museum; Map p54; ☎999-924-42-64; Calle 56 No 529A btwn Calles 65 & 65A; ⊙9am-6pm Tue-Fri, to 2pm Sat & Sun) **FREE** is housed in the old post office. Its exhibits trace the city's history back to preconquest days up through the belle epoque period, when *henequén* (sisal) brought riches to the region, and into the 20th century.

Museo de Arte Popular de Yucatán

In a building constructed in 1906, the **Museo de Arte Popular de Yucatán** (Yucatán Museum of Popular Art; Map p54; Calle 50A No 487; ⊙10am-5pm Tue-Sat, to 3pm Sun) **FREE** has a small rotating exhibition downstairs that features popular art from around Mexico. The permanent exhibition upstairs gives you an idea of how locals do embroidery and make ceramics.

Making tortillas in Mérida

LEON RAFAEL/SHUTTERSTOCK ©

Mérida's Regional Cuisine

Caribbean flavors and indigenous Maya recipes influence the cuisine of Mexico's Yucatán Peninsula, and Mérida is a top spot for sampling this unique regional cuisine. Even by Mexican standards it's a foodie's dream.

Great For...

☑ **Don't Miss**

A trip to Mérida wouldn't be complete without a meal at La Chaya Maya.

La Chaya Maya

Consider **La Chaya** (Map p54; ☎999-928-47-80; www.lachayamaya.com; cnr Calles 62 & 57; mains M$91-307; ☉7am-11pm) your introduction to classic Yucatecan fare (and it's a good one): *relleno negro* (black turkey stew) or *cochinita pibil*. The original branch of the popular restaurant offers tasty Yucatecan specialties, including breakfast, but is less fancy than the newer one nearby. Located in a lovely downtown colonial building, the second **restaurant** (☎999-928-22-95; www.lachayamaya.com; Calle 55 No 510; mains M$91-307; ☉7:30am-11pm) is hugely popular with locals and tourists, but doesn't serve breakfast.

Ku'uk

The stunning historic **home** (☎999-944-33-77; www.kuukrestaurant.com; Av Rómulo Rozo No 488, cnr Calle 27; mains M$290-550, tasting

this north Mérida (take a taxi) destination **restaurant** (☎999-938-08-38; www.nectarmerida.mx; Av A García Lavín 32; mains M$115-320; ☺1:30pm-midnight Tue-Sat, 2-6pm Sun; ❄). The *cebollas negras* (blackened onions; M$150) might look unappealing but the taste soon dispels any doubts. And you can't go wrong with the meat and fish mains.

Los Dos

Formerly run by the late US-educated chef David Sterling, this **cooking school** (Map p54; www.los-dos.com; Calle 68 No 517; 1-day courses & tours US$200) continues to offer courses with a focus on flavors of the Yucatán under the direction of chef Mario Canul, who worked with David for many years.

The Cochinita Quest

It seems like just about everyone in Mérida has an opinion on where you can get the best *cochinita pibil* – slow-cooked pork marinated in citrus juice and annatto spice. *Cochinita* is prepared in tacos, *tortas* (sandwiches) or as a main dish, and the best of the best is cooked in a pit, giving it a smoky flavor. Mérida has some very tasty options.

menu M$1600, with wine pairing M$2500; ☺1:30-11pm Tue-Sat, to 5pm Sun), at the end of Paseo Montejo, sets the scene for what's to come: a high-end, gourmet meal that will end up setting a very high benchmark for Mexican cuisine. You can dine in a number of elegant, if slightly bare, rooms. The cuisine gives a nod to Yucatecan cuisine with contemporary preparation and flavor twists.

Nectar

Inventive and delicious takes on traditional Yucatecan cuisine, a setting that would win design awards, and super-friendly and helpful staff make for a winning combination at

Temple, Uxmal ruins

MATTEO COLOMBO/GETTY IMAGES ©

Uxmal Ruins

Uxmal, pronounced oosh-mahl, is an impressive set of ruins, ranking among the top Maya archaeological sites. It features some well-kept structures located near the hilly Puuc region. Puuc means 'hills,' and these, rising up to about 100m, are the first relief from the flatness of the northern and western portions of the peninsula.

Great For...

☑ Don't Miss

The ruins' riotous sculptures featuring masks of rain god Chaac.

History

Uxmal was an important city in a region that encompassed the satellite towns of Sayil, Kabah, Xlapak and Labná. Although Uxmal means 'Thrice Built' in Maya, it was actually constructed five times.

That a sizable population flourished in this dry area is yet more testimony to the engineering skills of the Maya, who built a series of reservoirs and *chultunes* (cisterns) lined with lime mortar to catch and hold water during the dry season. First settled about AD 600, Uxmal was influenced by highland Mexico in its architecture, most likely through contact fostered by trade. This influence is reflected in the town's serpent imagery, phallic symbols and columns. The well-proportioned Puuc architecture, with its intricate, geometric mosaics sweeping across the upper parts

Carved wall with images of Chaac

🛈 Need to Know

Uxmal Ruins (Map p43; ☑997-976-20-64; www.inah.gob.mx/es/zonas/110-zona-arqueologica-de-uxmal; Hwy 261 Km 78; adult M$234, sound & light show M$92, parking M$30, guide M$800; ☉site 8am-5pm, sound & light show 8pm Apr-Sep & 7pm Oct-Mar; ♿)

✕ Take a Break

Try the rabbit or quail at **Codornejas Restaurante** (☑997-101-74-77; www.codornejos.com.mx; mains M$80-160; ☉12:30-6pm Wed-Sun; 🅿 🛜 ♿), en route to Uxmal.

★ Top Tip

Jump on one of the excellent tours run by Nómadas Hostel (p51) in Mérida.

of elongated facades, was strongly influenced by the slightly earlier Río Bec and Chenes styles.

The scarcity of water in the region meant that Chaac, the rain god or sky serpent, carried a lot of weight here. His image is ubiquitous at the site in the form of stucco masks protruding from facades and cornices. There is much speculation as to why Uxmal was abandoned in about AD 900; a severe drought may have forced the inhabitants to relocate.

Rediscovered by archaeologists in the 19th century, Uxmal was first excavated in 1929 by Frans Blom. Although much has been restored, there is still a good deal to discover.

Casa del Adivino

As you approach Uxmal, the **Casa del Adivino** (Pirámide del Adivino) comes into view. This 35m-high temple (the name translates as 'Magician's House') was built in an unusual oval shape. What you see is a restored version of the temple's fifth incarnation, consisting of round stones held rudely together with lots of cement. Four earlier temples were completely covered in the final rebuilding by the Maya, except for the high doorway on the west side, which remains from the fourth temple.

Decorated in elaborate Chenes style (a style that originated further south), the doorway proper forms the mouth of a gigantic Chaac mask.

Cuadrángulo de las Monjas

The 74-room, sprawling Nuns' Quadrangle is directly west of the Casa del Adivino. Archaeologists guess variously that it was a military academy, royal school or palace complex. The long-nosed face of Chaac appears everywhere on the facades of the four separate temples that form the quadrangle. The northern temple, the grandest of the four, was built first, followed by the southern, then the eastern and finally the western.

Several decorative elements on the exuberant facades show signs of Mexican, perhaps Totonac, influence. The feathered-serpent (Quetzalcóatl, or in Maya, Kukulcán) motif along the top of the west temple's facade is one of these. Note also the stylized depictions of the *na* (traditional Maya thatched hut) over some of the doorways in the northern and southern buildings.

Passing through the corbeled arch in the middle of the south building of the quadrangle and continuing down the slope takes you through the **Juego de Pelota** (Ball Court). From here you can turn left and head up the steep slope and stairs to the large terrace. If you have time, you could instead turn right to explore the western **Grupo del Cementerio** (which, though largely unrestored, holds some interesting square blocks carved with skulls in the center of its plaza), then head for the stairs and terrace.

Palacio del Gobernador

The Governor's Palace, with its magnificent facade nearly 100m long, is arguably the most impressive structure at Uxmal. The buildings have walls filled with rubble, faced with cement and then covered in a thin ve-

Palacio del Gobernador

neer of limestone squares; the lower part of the facade is plain, the upper part festooned with stylized Chaac faces and geometric designs, often lattice-like or fretted.

Other elements of Puuc style are decorated cornices, rows of half-columns (as in the Casa de las Tortugas) and round columns in doorways (as in the palace at Sayil).

Researchers recently discovered some 150 species of medicinal plants growing on the east side of the palace. Due to the high concentration of plants growing there, it's believed they were cultivated by the Maya to treat stomach infections, snake bites and many other ailments.

Gran Pirámide

The 30m-high, nine-tiered pyramid has been restored only on its northern side. Archaeologists theorize that the quadrangle at its summit was largely destroyed in order to construct another pyramid above it. That work, for reasons unknown, was never completed. At the top are some stucco carvings of Chaac, birds and flowers.

El Palomar

West of the Gran Pirámide sits a structure whose roofcomb is latticed with a pattern reminiscent of the Moorish pigeon houses built into walls in Spain and northern Africa – hence the building's name, which means the Dovecote or Pigeon House. Honeycombed triangular 'belfries' sit on top of a building that was once part of a quadrangle.

Getting There & Away

Uxmal is 80km from Mérida. Departures (around M$70, 1½ hours, four daily) on the Sur bus line leave from Mérida's **Terminal TAME** (Terminal de Segunda Clase; Map p54; ☑999-924-08-30; Calle 69 btwn Calles 68 & 70; ⊗24hr). But going back to Mérida, passing buses may be full. If you get stuck, a taxi to nearby Santa Elena costs M$150 to M$200.

Tours offered by **Nómadas Hostel** (Map p54; ☑999-924-52-23; www.nomadastravel.com; Calle 62 No 433; tours from M$665) in Mérida are always a good option, or rent a car and also visit other ruins in the area. Alternately, take a *colectivo* (shared taxi) for about M$30.

> **ⓘ Need to Know**
>
> The site is entered through the modern Unidad Uxmal building, which holds an air-conditioned restaurant, a small museum, shops selling souvenirs and crafts, a bookstore and an ATM.

CCINAR/SHUTTERSTOCK ©

> **★ Top Tip**
>
> For an additional cost, Uxmal projects a nightly sound-and-light show.

Cenote de Cuzamá

FLORIAN AUGUSTIN/SHUTTERSTOCK ©

Cenotes

The Maya considered them sacred gateways to the underworld. Once you visit your first cenote (limestone sinkhole) you'll better understand where the Maya were coming from.

Great For...

☑ **Don't Miss**

Taking a dip – a cenote swim is one of the peninsula's ultimate experiences.

Cenotes de Cuzamá

Three kilometers east of the town of Cuzamá, accessed from the small village of Chunkanan, are the **Cenotes de Cuzamá** (Map p43; 1-4 people M$400; ☉8am-4pm), a series of three amazing limestone sinkholes accessed by horse-drawn railcart in an old *henequén* hacienda. The ride will jar your fillings loose while showing you attractive scenes of agave fields.

One of the cenotes is featured in much of Yucatán's tourist literature, and all three feature rope-like roots descending along with ethereal shafts of light to the crystal-clear water. You'll likely find yourself sharing a dip with other bathers unless you get an early start.

Need to Know

The State Tourism Office gives out a map highlighting local cooperatives offering trips to cenotes.

Take a Break

Extend your trip to Dzibilchaltún with an afternoon of seafood and boozy beach time in Progreso.

★ Top Tip

To get to the cenotes, it is far easier to have your own transport.

Cenote Santa Barbara

This privately owned **cenote** (Map p43; 999-365-93-25, 999-138-78-43; www.facebook.com/santabarbarayucatan; Homún; M$150, with set lunch M$220, child 5-12yr M$75; 9:30am-6pm) is upscale and a bit officious. From the reception desk, you can take a bike or horse and cart on a 1km trip following the narrow-gauge railway-cart trail to the three cenotes. Walking is an option too.

The first (main) cenote is a cave, with lovely stalactites. The third, adjacent to a restaurant, is a bit of an overstretch – although pretty, it's more like a small pond. The complex opened in June 2016 so is still being discovered; go early to avoid crowds, as bus tours arrive in the late morning.

Dzibilchaltún & Cenote Xlacah

Lying about 17km north of central Mérida, Dzibilchaltún was the longest continuously used Maya administrative and ceremonial city, covering 15 sq km at the height of its greatness. Some 8400 structures were mapped by archaeologists in the 1960s; few of these have been excavated. Aside from the ruins, the site offers a lovely, swimmable cenote and a Maya museum.

Cenote Xlacah is more than 40m deep and a fine spot for a swim after exploring the ruins. In 1958 a National Geographic Society diving expedition recovered more than 30,000 Maya artifacts, many of ritual significance, from the cenote. The most interesting of these are now on display in the site's museum.

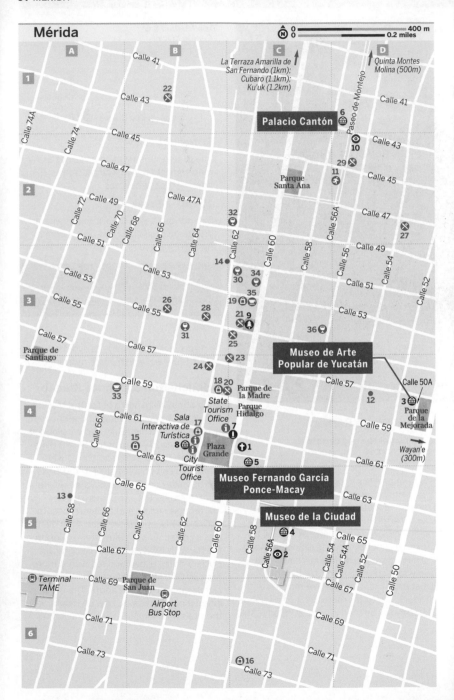

Mérida

N 0 ————————— 400 m
   0 ————————— 0.2 miles

Calle 41

La Terraza Amarilla de San Fernando (1km);
Cubaro (1.1km);
Ku'uk (1.2km)

Quinta Montes
Molina (500m)

22

Calle 43

Calle 74A

Calle 74

Calle 45

Palacio Cantón

Paseo de Montejo

Calle 41

6

Calle 43

10

29

11

Calle 45

Calle 47

Parque
Santa Ana

Calle 72

Calle 49

Calle 47A

Calle 70

Calle 68

Calle 66

Calle 64

Calle 62

32

Calle 60

Calle 56A

Calle 47

Calle 58

Calle 56

Calle 49

27

Calle 51

Calle 53

Calle 53

14

30 **34**

Calle 54

Calle 52

Calle 51

35

Calle 55

26

Calle 55

28

19

21 **9**

Calle 53

36

Calle 57

Parque de
Santiago

Calle 55

31

25

Calle 57

24

23

Museo de Arte
Popular de Yucatán

33

Calle 59

18 **20**

Parque de
la Madre

State
Tourism
Office

Parque
Hidalgo

Calle 57

Calle 50A

3

Parque
de la
Mejorada

12

Calle 66A

Calle 61

Sala
Interactiva de
Turística

17

15

8

City
Tourist
Office

Calle 63

Plaza
Grande

7

1

5

Calle 59

Wayan'e
(300m)

Calle 61

Museo Fernando García
Ponce-Macay

Calle 65

Calle 63

13

Calle 65

Museo de la Ciudad

Calle 68

Calle 66

Calle 64

Calle 62

Calle 60

Calle 58

4

Calle 56A

2

Calle 54

Calle 54A

Calle 52

Calle 65

Calle 50

Calle 67

Calle 67

Terminal
TAME

Calle 69

Parque de
San Juan

Airport
Bus Stop

Calle 69

Calle 71

Calle 71

Calle 73

16

Calle 73

⊙ SIGHTS

Quinta Montes Molina   House

(☑999-925-59-99; www.laquintamm.com; Paseo de Montejo No 469 btwn Calles 33 & 35; M$100; ☺tours in English 9am, 11am & 3pm Mon-Fri, 9am & 11am Sat) This living history house gives you a sense of the splendor and grandeur of the 'Oro Verde' (Green Gold) *henequén* era. The only original house of its kind open to the public, it is accessed via guided tour from the in-house museum, the **Casa Museo Montes Molina**, by appointment only.

Parque Santa Lucía   Park

(Map p54; cnr Calles 60 & 55) The pretty little Parque Santa Lucía has arcades on the north and west sides; this was where travelers would get on or off the stage-coaches that linked towns and villages with the provincial capital. Today it's a popular restaurant area and venue for **Serenatas Yucatecas** (Yucatecan Serenades), a free weekly concert on Thursday at 9pm.

Paseo de Montejo   Architecture

(Map p54) Paseo de Montejo, which runs parallel to Calles 56 and 58, was an attempt by Mérida's 19th-century city planners to create a wide boulevard similar to the Paseo de la Reforma in Mexico City or the Champs-Élysées in Paris. Though more modest than its predecessors, the Paseo de Montejo is still a beautiful green swath of relatively open space in an urban conglomeration of stone and concrete. There are occasional sculpture exhibits along the paseo (promenade).

Palacio de Gobierno   Public Art

(Map p54; Calle 61 s/n; ☺8am-7pm) **FREE** Built in 1892, the Palacio de Gobierno houses the state of Yucatán's executive government offices (and a tourist office). Don't miss the wonderful murals and oil paintings by local artist Fernando Castro Pacheco housed in a magnificent *sala* (hall). Completed in the late 1970s, they portray a symbolic history of the Maya and their interaction with the Spaniards, and give excellent context to any trip around the region.

Mérida

⊙ **Sights**
1 Catedral de San Ildefonso C4
2 Mercado Municipal Lucas de Gálvez C5
3 Museo de Arte Popular de Yucatán D4
4 Museo de la Ciudad C5
5 Museo Fernando García Ponce-Macay ... C4
6 Palacio Cantón D1
7 Palacio de Gobierno C4
8 Palacio Municipal B4
9 Parque Santa Lucía C3
10 Paseo de Montejo D2

🟢 **Activities, Courses & Tours**
11 Bici Mérida D2
   Historic Center Tours .... (see 8)
12 Instituto Benjamín Franklin D4
13 Los Dos A5
14 Nómadas Hostel B3

🏠 **Shopping**
15 Casa de las Artesanías B4
   Guayaberas Jack .... (see 18)
16 Hamacas El Aguacate C6
17 Librería Dante B4

18 Miniaturas Folk Art B4
19 Tejón Rojo C3

✕ **Eating**
20 Amaro B4
21 Apoala C3
22 Bistro Cultural B1
23 Cafetería Pop C4
24 La Chaya Maya B4
25 La Chaya Maya C3
26 Lo Que Hay B3
27 Oliva Enoteca D2
28 Pola B3
29 Sukra Bar de Café D2

🍷 **Drinking & Nightlife**
30 Cara Negra C3
31 Hermana Republica B3
32 La Negrita C2
33 Manifesto A4
34 Mercado 60 .... C3
35 Orgánico C3
36 PK2 .... C3

Mercado Municipal Lucas de Gálvez
Market

(Map p54; cnr Calles 56A & 67; ⊙6am-5pm) Mérida's main market is an ever-evolving mass of commerce, with stalls selling everything from *panuchos* (fried tortillas stuffed with beans and topped with meat and veggies) to *ceviche* (marinated seafood). The chaotic surrounding streets are all part of the large market district.

Catedral de San Ildefonso
Cathedral

(Map p54; Calle 60 s/n; ⊙6am-noon & 4:30-8pm) On the site of a former Maya temple is Mérida's hulking, severe cathedral, begun in 1561 and completed in 1598. Some of the stone from the Maya temple was used in its construction. The massive crucifix behind the altar is **Cristo de la Unidad** (Christ of Unity), a symbol of reconciliation between those of Spanish and Maya heritage.

🏃 ACTIVITIES

In an effort to make the city more bike-friendly, Mérida closes down stretches of Paseo de Montejo and Calle 60 to traffic on Sunday morning. For night tours, the bicycle collective **Ciclo Turixes** (www. facebook.com/ColectivoCicloTurixes) gathers at Parque Santa Ana most Wednesdays at around 8:30pm.

Bici Mérida
Cycling

(Map p54; ☎999-287-35-38; Paseo de Montejo s/n btwn Calles 45 & 47; per hour M$30; ⊙8am-10pm Mon-Fri, to 5pm Sat, to 3pm Sun) Rents out mountain bikes, tandems, bicycles for kids and other cool rides.

🧭 TOURS

Historic Center Tours
Walking

(Map p54; ☎999-942-00-00; www.merida. gob.mx/turismo; Calle 62 s/n, Plaza Grande; ⊙walking tours 9:30am Mon-Sat) FREE The city tourist office runs free 1½-hour guided walking tours of the historic center in both Spanish and English, departing daily from the **Palacio Municipal** (City Hall; Map p54; Calle 62 s/n; ⊙24hr) FREE.

Interior of Catedral de San Ildefonso

SHAKZU/GETTY IMAGES ©

Ecoturismo Yucatán
Ecotour

(☑999-920-27-72; www.ecoyuc.com.mx; Calle 3 No 235 btwn Calles 32A & 34; day tours to Chichén Itzá US$48, Uxmal & Kabah US$51; ⊗9am-6pm Mon-Fri, to 1pm Sat) The owners of reputable Ecoturismo Yucatán are passionate about both sharing and protecting the state's natural treasures. Trips focus on archaeology, birding, natural history, biking and kayaking. The price of one-day excursions to Chichén Itzá or Uxmal and Kabah include entrance fees, transportation and lunch.

🛍 SHOPPING

Librería Dante
Books

(Map p54; www.libreriadante.com.mx; cnr Calles 61 & 62, Plaza Grande; ⊗8am-10:30pm) Shelves a selection of archaeology and regional history books in English and has good Yucatecan cookbooks, too. The bookstore has other branches throughout the city.

Casa de las Artesanías
Arts & Crafts

(Map p54; ☑999-928-66-76; www.artesanias. yucatan.gob.mx; Calle 63 s/n btwn Calles 64 & 66; ⊗8:30am-9pm Mon-Sat, 10am-5pm Sun) One place to start looking for handicrafts is this government-supported market for local artisans. Prices are fixed.

Hamacas El Aguacate
Arts & Crafts

(Map p54; ☑999-947-46-51; www.hamacase laguacate.com.mx; Calle 58 No 604, cnr Calle 73; ⊗9am-7pm Mon-Fri, to 5:30pm Sat) Hamacas El Aguacate stocks quality hammocks at decent prices (M$550 to M$700), and there's absolutely no hard sell. Also has mosquito nets for M$200.

Miniaturas Folk Art
Arts & Crafts

(Map p54; ☑999-928-65-03; Calle 59 No 507A btwn Calles 60 & 62; ⊗11am-10pm Mon-Sat) Here you'll find lots of small Día de Muertos (Day of the Dead) tableaux, tinwork and figurines of every sort, from ceramics to toy soldiers. They all have two things in common: they're easy to pack and have nothing to do with Yucatán artisan traditions, originating instead from Puebla, Zacatecas or San Miguel de Allende.

 Mérida's History

Francisco de Montejo (the Younger) founded a Spanish colony at Campeche, about 160km to the southwest, in 1540. From this base he took advantage of political dissension among the Maya, conquering T'ho (now Mérida) in 1542. By decade's end Yucatán was mostly under Spanish colonial rule.

When Montejo's conquistadors entered T'ho, they found a major Maya settlement of lime-mortared stone that reminded them of the Roman architecture in Mérida, Spain. They promptly renamed the city and proceeded to build it into the regional capital, dismantling the Maya structures and using the materials to construct a cathedral and other stately buildings. Mérida took its colonial orders directly from Spain, not from Mexico City, and Yucatán has had a distinct cultural and political identity ever since.

Mérida today is the peninsula's center of commerce, a bustling city that has been growing rapidly ever since *maquiladoras* (low-paying, for-export factories) started cropping up in the 1980s and '90s, and as the tourism industry picked up during those decades as well.

Palacio Municipal
GIBAN/SHUTTERSTOCK ©

Tejón Rojo
Gifts & Souvenirs

(Map p54; www.tejonrojo.com; Calle 53 No 503; ⊗noon-9pm Mon-Sat, to 6pm Sun) Sells trendy graphic T-shirts and an assortment of

 **Yucatecan Hammocks:
the Only Way to Sleep**

Yucatecan hammocks are normally woven from strong nylon or cotton string and dyed in various colors. There are also natural, undyed cotton versions. Some sellers will try to pass these off as *henequén* (agave plant fibers) or jute, telling you it's much more durable (and valuable) than cotton, and even that it repels mosquitoes. Don't be taken in: real *henequén* hammocks are very rough and not something you'd want near your skin. Silk hammocks are no longer made, but a silk-rayon blend has a similar feel.

Hammocks come in several widths, and though much is made of the quantity of pairs of end strings they possess, a better gauge of a hammock's size and quality is its weight. The heavier the better. A *sencilla* (for one person) should be about 500g and cost around M$400 to M$450. The queen, at 1100g, runs from around M$600. *De croché* (very tightly woven) hammocks can take several weeks to produce and cost double or triple the prices given here. Nylon hammocks are usually cheaper.

Mérida and its surrounding towns have some good spots for buying a hammock.

Hammock stall in the Yucatán
ANGELA N PERRYMAN/SHUTTERSTOCK ©

Mexican pop-culture souvenirs, including coffee mugs, jewelry, handbags, caps and wrestling masks.

Guayaberas Jack Clothing
(Map p54; www.guayaberasjack.com.mx; Calle 59 No 507A; ⊗10am-8:30pm Mon-Sat, to 2:30pm Sun) The *guayabera* (embroidered dress shirt) is the classic Mérida shirt, but in buying the wrong one you run the risk of looking like a waiter. Drop into this famous shop to avoid getting asked for the bill.

✖ EATING

This is a food city, with all kinds of cuisines and all kinds of budgets. You can dine on cheap, tasty street eats or on fine china.

**La Terraza Amarilla
de San Fernando** Mexican $
(☑999-189-62-10; Av Cupules 503D; tacos & tortas M$15-24; ⊗7am-3pm) With mouthwatering cheap eats well worth detouring for, La Terraza Amarilla is a gem: you choose between four styles of mains (tacos, *tortas* etc) and one of seven different fillings, and in seconds your plastic plate arrives. Each menu item is the recipe of the chef-owner and his wife, who will lovingly detail each option for you given the chance.

Pola Ice Cream $
(Map p54; ☑999-330-34-41; www.polagelato.com; Calle 55 s/n btwn Calles 62 & 64; ice cream from M$30; ⊗noon-10pm Mon-Sat, from 11am Sun) You'd head to this place even if were you in the Arctic, it's that good. Get your tongue around full-cream, 100% natural (no additives) gelati with some of the quirkiest flavors in ice-cream land. Mondays is traditionally 'pork and beans' night in Yucatán, so you can try this flavor, too (Mondays only). 'Bleu cheese with apple' defies description...but tastes great!

Sukra Bar de Café Cafe $
(Map p54; ☑999-923-44-53; www.facebook.com/sukracafe; Paseo de Montejo 496 btwn Calles 43 & 45; mains M$70-120; ⊗9am-6pm Mon-Sat, to 2pm Sun) This easygoing spot, at the beginning of Paseo de Montejo, is framed by pretty plants and features an eclectic mix of tables and chairs, more reminiscent of a great aunt's house than

Eating at a local market

an eatery overlooking the poshest street in town. The excellent salads and sandwiches are equally as down to earth. Dig in and watch the world go by.

Wayan'e   Tacos $
(☑999-291-94-22; cnr Calles 59 & 46; tacos M$13-18, tortas M$21-34; ⏱7am-2:30pm Mon-Sat) Popular for its *castakan* (crispy pork belly), Wayan'e (meaning 'here it is' in Maya) is one of Mérida's premier breakfast spots. Vegetarians will find options here, such as the *huevo con xkatic* (egg with chili) taco and fresh juices. But if you eat meat, it's all about the greasy goodness of the *castakan torta* (sandwich, M$34). Look for the lime-green building.

Bistro Cultural   French $
(Map p54; Calle 66 No 377C btwn Calles 41 & 43; breakfast mains M$50-70, lunch mains M$65-100; ⏱8:30am-5:30pm Mon-Sat, to 4:30pm Sun) While the cuisine is French, the influence is Yucatecan, and locally grown, organic products are used where possible. The small menu varies but may include the likes of *croque chaya* (a play on a French *croque*

monsieur) and there is a daily special on top of the fixed plates.

It sells delectable French pastries too (M$12 to M$17).

Cafetería Pop   Cafe $
(Map p54; ☑999-928-61-63; www.cafeteriapop. com; Calle 57 s/n btwn Calles 60 & 62; breakfast M$20-85, lunch M$75-130; ⏱7am-11pm Mon-Sat, from 8am Sun) There's a '70s feel to this little orange-and-cream cafeteria-style restaurant, which has cheap breakfast combinations and a good variety of Mexican dishes, all served ultra-efficiently. Try the chicken in dark, rich *mole* sauce. It's the type of reliable place you'll keep returning to.

Lo Que Hay   Vegan $$
(Map p54; www.hotelmediomundo.com; Calle 55 No 533; mains M$40-120, 3-course menu M$180; ⏱7-10pm Tue-Sat; 🛜✍) Even nonvegans usually give an enthusiastic thumbs up to this dinner-only restaurant, where three-course themed vegan meals are served in a serene courtyard. The dishes range from Mexican and Lebanese cuisine to raw vegan. Lo Que Hay is in the **Hotel Medio Mundo** (☑999-

One of the world's most vibrant cuisines, Mexican food delights with its variety, its abundant use of herbs and chilies, and ingredients as diverse as fresh coastal seafood and dried beef. Yucatán is blessed with distinctive and tasty regional cuisine, and the salsas run hot, due to ample use of habanero chiles.

From left: *Enmoladas*; *cochinita pibil*; *pollo* (chicken) *pibil*

924-54-72; www.hotelmediomundo.com; Calle 55 No 533; d incl breakfast US$90; 🐕🌸🗤🏊) and it welcomes nonguests.

Apoala   Mexican $$$
(Map p54; 📞999-923-19-79; www.apoala.mx; Calle 60 No 471, Parque Santa Lucía; mains M$130-300; 🕐1pm-midnight Mon-Sat, 2-10pm Sun; 🛜) With influences from Oaxaca, which like the Yucatán is known for its extraordinary regional cuisine, Apoala reinvents popular dishes such as *enmoladas* (stuffed tortillas in a rich *mole* sauce) and *tlayudas* (a large tortilla with sliced beef, black beans and Oaxaca cheese). It's in a lovely spot on Parque Santa Lucia (p55) and rubs shoulders with some other great eateries.

Oliva Enoteca   Italian $$$
(Map p54; 📞999-923-30-81; www.olivamerida. com; cnr Calles 47 & 54; mains M$180-550; 🕐1-5pm & 7pm-midnight Mon-Sat) This contemporary restaurant with black-and-white tiled floors, Edison light bulbs, designer chairs and a viewable kitchen is a magnet for the local cool cats who descend on this smart place for excellent Italian cuisine. Those craving something other than a margarita will love the cocktail selection, as well as the wines. Desserts are to die for.

Amaro   International $$$
(Map p54; 📞999-928-24-51; www.restaurante amaro.com; Calle 59 No 507; mains M$140-400; 🕐11am-1am; 🛜📷) An old-style spot can be romantic at night, especially when there are performing *trova* acts (Latin American protest folk music; after 8:30pm). It's in the courtyard of the house where Andrés Quintana Roo – poet, statesman and drafter of Mexico's Declaration of Independence – was born in 1787. The menu includes Yu-

Learn Spanish

The nonprofit **Instituto Benjamín Franklin** (Map p54; 📞999-928-00-97; www. benjaminfranklin.com.mx; Calle 57 No 474A; per 1hr course US$18) teaches intensive Spanish-language courses.

ROBERT HOLMES/ALAMY STOCK PHOTO ©

catecan choices and a variety of vegetarian and continental dishes.

🍷 DRINKING & NIGHTLIFE

You need not look far to find a friendly neighborhood bar. These range from traditional *cantinas* to more cutting-edge wine and cocktail bars.

Mercado 60   Cocktail Bar

(Map p54; www.mercado60.com; Calle 60 btwn Calles 51 & 53; ⊙6pm-late) For a fun night of booze and cheap(ish) international eats, head to this atmospheric, lively and diverse culinary market, where the margaritas (or fine wines) will have you dancing alongside trendy locals to live salsa music. This modern concept is a cocktail bar meets beer hall, with different businesses serving up different concoctions.

The cuisine – ranging from Mexican gourmet tacos to ramen noodles – is also served from small kiosks. Dishes, while tasty, could be better but they do the 'soaking-up' trick...

La Negrita   Dancing

(Map p54; www.facebook.com/LaNegritaMerida; Calle 62 s/n, cnr Calle 49; ⊙noon-10pm; 🍸) This post modern *cantina* (think contemporary grunge) is the current hot spot in town. If the live music doesn't inspire you to get a tropical groove on, it's just a matter of time before the mojitos and mezcals have you dancing the night away. The rear garden makes a nice spot to catch a breather and chat with locals.

Musical acts go on daily from 6pm, and the clientele often includes Progresso docked cruise ship passengers.

PK2   Gay & Lesbian

(Map p54; 🕿999-154-60-12; www.facebook.com/PK2DiscoBarMerida; Calle 56 btwn Calles 53 & 55; cover from M$100; ⊙9pm-3am Wed-Sun) One of the city's top spots for gay nightlife, the PK2 has strip shows, revues, drag queens and more, set to pumping trance- and electro-themed music. Nightly specials and the variety of acts make it one of the most popular Mérida gay venues.

 Best for Coffee

Manifesto (Map p54; www.manifesto.mx; Calle 59 No 538 btwn Calles 66 & 68; coffee M$40-72; ☺8am-9pm Mon-Sat) offers coffee for focused coffee drinkers. Thanks to a trio from Calabria, Italy, you can find your cappuccinos, espressos and, yes, even flat whites, made by well-trained employees sporting the near-required barista uniform of tattoos, piercings and gauges. Steel straws are served to reduce one-time-use plastic. They roast their beans here, too.

Java junkies will also enjoy the organic coffee at **Orgánico** (Map p54; ☑999-924-77-53; Calle 53 No 502D btwn Calles 60 & 62; coffee M$25-65, mains M$70-90; ☺8am-5pm Wed-Mon; ☻), prepared with beans from the highlands of Chiapas and elsewhere. Hungry? You'll find good vegetarian pastas and sandwiches here, as well as a variety of coffee-inspired cocktails.

ICHATURON/SHUTTERSTOCK ©

Hermana Republica Bar
(Map p54; ☑999-924-89-11; Calle 64 btwn Calles 55 & 57; mains M$85-285; ☺1pm-midnight Mon-Wed, to 2am Thu & Fri, 1-6pm Sun; ☻) A sleek, fashionable spot with an industrial interior including Edison light bulbs and designer chairs. Moneyed young locals hit here for craft beers (including IPAs), while hungry folk get their teeth into everything from gourmet hamburgers to Yucatecan fare.

Cara Negra Bar
(Map p54; www.caranegra.mx; Calle 62 No 436; ☺7pm to 1am) If you've been craving a spot to sip cocktails and look at skulls, your search is over. This dark, macabre-themed place has an excellent selection of craft beers, original cocktails, and a vibe that's not so loud or pumping that you can't chat with friends or strike up a conversation with the people nearby.

Cubaro Bar
(☑999-926-03-04; cnr Paseo de Montejo & Calle 29; ☺5pm-2am) Head up the colorful spiral staircase to the terrace for a close-up view of the Fatherland monument and a cocktail. The menu is a bit more conventional, but everything is carefully prepared and the service is very crisp.

ⓘ INFORMATION

MONEY

Banks and ATMs are scattered throughout the city. There is a cluster of both along Calle 65 between Calles 60 and 62, one block south of Plaza Grande. *Casas de cambio* (money-exchange offices) have faster service and longer opening hours than banks, but often have poorer rates.

SAFE TRAVEL

Guard against pickpockets in the town's markets and when you're in any crowded area. Outright muggings are very rare. Much scarier are the buses that travel at breakneck speed along the narrow streets; sidewalks are often narrow and crowded. Hawkers can be annoying but are generally harmless.

TOURIST INFORMATION

You'll find tourist information booths at the airport. Tourist offices downtown have basic brochures, information and maps.

City Tourist Office (Map p54; ☑999-942-00-00, ext 80119; www.merida.gob.mx/turismo; Calle 62, Plaza Grande; ☺8am-8pm) Right on the main plaza, it is staffed with helpful English speakers. Here you can hook up free walking tours of the city, which depart daily at 9:30am.

Sala Interactiva (Map p54; Calle 62 btwn Calles 61 & 63, Palacio Municipal; ◷9am-8pm) On the plaza, with fancy touch screens and multimedia info displays.

State Tourist Office (Map p54; ✐999-930-31-01; www.yucatan.travel; Calle 61 s/n, Plaza Grande; ◷8am-8pm) In the entrance to the Palacio de Gobierno. There's usually an English speaker on hand.

 GETTING THERE & AWAY

AIR

Mérida's **Aeropuerto Internacional de Mérida** (Mérida International Airport; Map p43; ✐999-940-60-90; www.asur.com.mx; Hwy 180 Km 4.5; ▯R-79) is a 10km, 20-minute ride southwest of Plaza Grande off Hwy 180 (Av de los Itzáes). It has car-rental desks, several ATMs, currency-exchange services and an information desk for assisting you to find transportation into town.

BUS

Mérida is the bus transportation hub of the Yucatán Peninsula. Take care with your bags on night buses and those serving popular tourist destinations (especially 2nd-class buses): there have been reports of theft on some routes.

There are a number of bus terminals, and some lines operate from (and stop at) more than one terminal. Tickets for departure from one terminal can often be bought at another, and destinations overlap greatly among bus lines. Check out www.ado.com.mx for ticket info on some of the lines.

CAR

The most flexible way to tour the many archaeological sites around Mérida is to travel with a rental car. Assume you will pay M$1000 to M$2500 per day (tax and insurance included) for short-term rental of an economy-size vehicle. Getting around Mérida's sprawling tangle of one-way streets is better done on foot or bus.

Several agencies have branches at the airport and on Calle 60, between Calles 55 and 57. You'll get the best deal by booking online.

There is an expensive toll highway between Mérida and Cancún (M$478).

Easy Way (✐999-930-95-00; www.easyway rentacar.com; Calle 60 No 484 btwn Calles 55 & 57; car rental incl basic insurance from US$50 per day; ◷7am-11pm)

National (✐999-923-24-93; www.nationalcar. com; Calle 60 No 486F btwn Calles 55 & 57; economy car incl basic insurance from M$2500; ◷8am-1pm & 4-8pm)

ⓘ GETTING AROUND

Most parts of Mérida that you'll want to visit are within 10 blocks of Plaza Grande. Given the slow speed of city traffic, particularly in the market areas, walking is often the fastest way to get around.

BUS

City buses are cheap at M$8, but routes can be confusing. Some start in suburban neighborhoods, skirt the city center and terminate in another distant suburban neighborhood. Transpublico.com (https://merida.transpublico.com) provides detailed maps of all the routes.

To travel between Plaza Grande and the upscale neighborhoods to the north along Paseo de Montejo, catch the R-2 'Hyatt' or 'Tecnológico' line along Calle 60. To return to the city center, catch any bus heading south on Paseo de Montejo displaying the same signs and/or 'Centro.' A **bus** (Map p54) heads to/from the airport, too.

TAXI

More and more taxis in town are using meters these days. If you get one with no meter, be sure to agree on a price before getting in. M$30 to M$50 is fair for getting around downtown and to the bus terminals. Taxi stands can be found at most of the barrio parks (dispatch fees may cost extra).

Radio Taxímetro del Volante (✐999-928-30-35) For 24-hour radio taxi service.

In this Chapter
Visiting the Site 66
Valladolid 74
Sights.. 74
Activities 74
Tours 76
Eating.. 76
Drinking & Nightlife................................... 77
Entertainment 77

Chichén Itzá

The most famous and best restored of the Yucatán Maya sites, Chichén Itzá is as overcrowded as you'd expect for one of the new seven wonders of the world. Still, it's goose-bump material. Many mysteries of the Maya astronomical calendar are made clear when one understands the design of the 'time temples' here. Consider staying in Valladolid, a provincial town that makes a great hub for visits to Chichén Itzá and a number of nearby cenotes.

One Day in Chichén Itzá

You'll want to spend a full day wandering through this extraordinary Maya **complex** (p67), finding out why they named this ruin one of the 'new seven wonders of the world.' Grab dinner at one of the Mexican restaurants on the highway near Pisté and return to the ruins for the **sound-and-light show** (p73).

Two Days in Chichén Itzá

Spend your next day in the colonial town of **Valladolid** (p74), a former Maya ceremonial center with a climbable pyramid near the town square. For some respite from your Maya itinerary, drop by **Cenote X'Kekén y Samulá** (p74) on your way out of town and take a plunge into a spectacular limestone cavern pool.

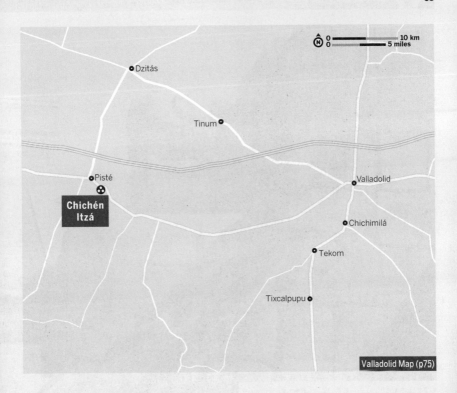

Valladolid Map (p75)

Arriving in Chichén Itzá

Buses to Pisté generally stop at the plaza at the bus station; you can make the hot walk to and from the ruins in 20 to 30 minutes. First-class buses stop at the ruins; for others, check with the driver. You can also taxi to the ruins from the west end of town for M$40 to M$50.

Where to Stay

In Valladolid, many hotels are on or near the main plaza, Parque Francisco Cantón Rosado, with one or two excellent options slightly further out of the city center. It's doable if you have your own transport. Lodgings also line the highway in Pisté.

El Castillo (p70)

Visiting the Site

Chichén Itzá has become the Yucatán's hottest bucket-list item. The massive El Castillo pyramid, Chichén Itzá's most iconic structure, will knock your socks off, especially at vernal and autumnal equinoxes, when morning and afternoon sunlight cast a shadow of a feathered serpent on the staircase.

Great For...

☑ **Don't Miss**

The nightly (except Mondays) sound-and-light show.

History

Most archaeologists agree that the first major settlement at Chichén Itzá, during the late Classic Period, was pure Maya. In about the 9th century, the city was largely abandoned for reasons unknown.

It was resettled around the late 10th century, and shortly thereafter it is believed to have been invaded by the Toltecs, who had migrated from their central highlands capital of Tula, north of Mexico City. The bellicose Toltec culture was fused with that of the Maya, incorporating the cult of Quetzalcóatl (Kukulcán, in Maya). You will see images of both Chaac, the Maya rain god, and Quetzalcóatl, the plumed serpent, throughout the city.

The substantial fusion of highland central Mexican and Puuc architectural styles

Pisté

Chichén ⊗
Itzá

❶ Need to Know

Chichén Itzá (Mouth of the Well of the Itzáes; http://chichenitza.inah.gob.mx; off Hwy 180, Pisté; adult/child under 13yr M$254/70, guided tours M$1200; ⊘8am-5pm; Ⓟ)

✖ Take a Break

The highway through Pisté is lined with dozens of eateries.

★ Top Tip

Ensure you wear comfortable walking shoes, and bring a hat, sunscreen and plenty of water for your explorations.

makes Chichén unique among the Yucatán Peninsula's ruins. The fabulous El Castillo and the Plataforma de Venus are outstanding architectural works built during the height of Toltec cultural input.

The sanguinary Toltecs contributed more than their architectural skills to the Maya: they elevated human sacrifice to a near obsession, and there are numerous carvings of the bloody ritual in Chichén demonstrating this.

After a Maya leader moved his political capital to Mayapán, while keeping Chichén as his religious capital, Chichén Itzá fell into decline. Why it was subsequently abandoned in the 14th century is a mystery, but the once-great city remained the site of Maya pilgrimages for many years.

Dredging Chichén's Sacred Cenote

Around the year 1900, Edward Thompson, a Harvard professor and US consul to Yucatán, bought the hacienda that included Chichén Itzá for M$750. No doubt intrigued by local stories of female virgins being sacrificed to the Maya deities by being thrown into the site's cenote (limestone sinkhole), Thompson resolved to have the cenote dredged.

He imported dredging equipment and set to work. Gold and jade jewelry from all parts of Mexico and as far away as Colombia was recovered, along with other artifacts and a variety of human bones. Many of the artifacts were shipped to Harvard's Peabody Museum, but some have since been returned to Mexico.

Subsequent diving expeditions in the 1920s and 1960s turned up hundreds of other valuable artifacts. It appears that all sorts of people – children and old people, the diseased and the injured, and the young

Chichén Itzá

A DAY TOUR

It doesn't take long to realize why the Maya site of Chichén Itzá is one of Mexico's most popular tourist draws. Approaching the grounds from the main entrance, the striking castle pyramid ❶ **El Castillo** jumps right out at you – and the wow factor never lets up.

It's easy to tackle Chichén Itzá in one day. Within a stone's throw of the castle, you'll find the Maya world's largest ❷ **ball court** alongside eerie carvings of skulls and heart-devouring eagles at the Temple of Jaguars and the Platform of Skulls. On the other (eastern) side are the highly adorned ❸ **Group of a Thousand Columns** and the ❹ **Temple of Warriors**. A short walk north of the castle leads to the gaping ❺ **Sacred Cenote**, an important pilgrimage site. On the other side of El Castillo, you'll find giant stone serpents watching over the High Priest's Grave, aka El Osario. Further south, marvel at the spiral-domed ❻ **Observatory**, the imposing Nunnery and Akab-Dzib, one of the oldest ruins.

Roaming the 47-hectare site, it's fun to consider that at its height Chichén Itzá was home to an estimated 90,000 inhabitants and spanned approximately 30 sq km. So essentially you're looking at just a small part of a once-great city.

El Caracol
Observatory
Today they'd probably just use a website, but back in the day priests would announce the latest rituals and celebrations from the dome of the circular observatory.

Edificio de las Monjas (Nunnery)

❻

Akab-Dzib

Entrance

Grupo de las Mil Columnas
Group of a Thousand Columns
Not unlike a hall of fame exhibit, the pillars surrounding the temple reveal carvings of gods, dignitaries and celebrated warriors.

TOP TIPS

➡ Arrive at 8am and you'll have a good three hours or so before the tour-bus madness begins. Early birds escape the merchants, too.

➡ Remember that Chichén Itzá is the name of the site; the actual town where it's located is called Pisté.

El Castillo
The Castle
Even this mighty pyramid can't bear the stress of a million visitors ascending its stairs each year. No climbing allowed, but the ground-level view doesn't disappoint.

Gran Juego de Pelota
Great Ball Court
How is it possible to hear someone talk from one end of this long, open-air court to the other? To this day, the acoustics remain a mystery.

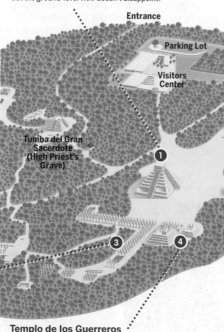

Entrance

Parking Lot

Visitors Center

Tumba del Gran Sacerdote (High Priest's Grave)

1

2

Templo de los Jaguares (Temple of Jaguars)

Plataforma de los Cráneos (Platform of Skulls)

3

4

5

Cenote Sagrado
Sacred Cenote
Diving expeditions have turned up hundreds of valuable artifacts dredged from the cenote (limestone sinkhole), not to mention human bones of sacrificial victims who were forced to jump into the eternal underworld.

Templo de los Guerreros
Temple of Warriors
The Maya associated warriors with eagles and jaguars, as depicted in the temple's friezes. The revered jaguar, in particular, was a symbol of strength and agility.

and the vigorous – were forcibly obliged to take an eternal swim in Chichén's Cenote Sagrado. (Many guides push the sacrificial angle, as tourists seem fascinated by it; other experts say this aspect is way overstressed in relationship to the real objective of the site.)

Touring the Ruins

The site's visitors center has a small **museum** (⊙9am-4pm) FREE with exhibits providing explanations in Spanish, English and French.

El Castillo

Upon entering Chichén Itzá, El Castillo (aka the Pyramid of Kukulcán) rises before you in all its grandeur. The first temple here was pre-Toltec, built around AD 800, but the present 25m-high structure, built over the old one, has the plumed serpent sculpted along the stairways and Toltec warriors represented in the doorway carvings at the top of the temple. You won't see the carvings, however, as ascending the pyramid was prohibited after a woman fell to her death in 2006.

The structure is actually a massive Maya calendar formed in stone. Each of El Castillo's nine levels is divided in two by a staircase, making 18 separate terraces that commemorate the 18 20-day months of the Maya Vague Year. The four stairways have 91 steps each; add the top platform and the total is 365, the number of days in the year. On each facade of the pyramid are 52 flat panels, which are reminders of the 52 years in the Maya calendar round.

To top it off, during the spring and autumn equinoxes, light and shadow form

Templo de los Guerreros

a series of triangles on the side of the north staircase that mimic the creep of a serpent (note the carved serpent heads flanking the bottom of the staircase).

The older pyramid inside El Castillo has a red jaguar throne with inlaid eyes and spots of jade; also lying behind the screen is a *chacmool* (Maya sacrificial stone sculpture). The entrance to **El Túnel**, the passage up to the throne, is at the base of El Castillo's north side. You can't go in, though.

ℹ Need to Know

The heat, humidity and crowds in Chichén Itzá can be fierce, as can competition between the craft sellers who line the paths. To avoid this, try to explore the site either early in the morning or late in the afternoon.

IR STONE/SHUTTERSTOCK ©

Researchers in 2015 learned that the pyramid most likely sits atop a 20m-deep cenote, which puts the structure at greater risk of collapsing.

Gran Juego de Pelota

The great ball court, the largest and most impressive in Mexico, is only one of the city's eight courts, indicative of the importance of the games held here. The court, to the left of the visitors center, is flanked by temples at either end and is bounded by towering parallel walls with stone rings cemented up high. Along the walls of the ball court are stone reliefs, including scenes of decapitations of players.

There is evidence that the ball game may have changed over the years. Some carvings show players with padding on their elbows and knees, and it is thought that they played a soccer-like game with a hard rubber ball, with the use of hands forbidden. Other carvings show players wielding bats; it appears that if a player hit the ball through one of the stone hoops, his team was declared the winner. It may be that during the Toltec period, the losing captain, and perhaps his teammates as well, was sacrificed.

The court exhibits some interesting acoustics: a conversation at one end can be heard 135m away at the other, and a clap produces multiple loud echoes.

Grupo de las Mil Columnas

This group east of El Castillo pyramid takes its name – which means 'Group of the Thousand Columns' – from the forest of pillars stretching south and east. The star attraction here is the **Templo de los Guerreros** (Temple of the Warriors), adorned with stucco and stone-carved animal deities. At the top of its steps is a classic

---

✕ Take a Break

The place to go in Pisté if you're craving decent Yucatecan fare is **Las Mestizas** (📞985-851-00 69; Calle 15 s/n; mains M$90-115; ⊘9am-10pm; ✸⧖).

reclining *chacmool* figure, but ascending to it is no longer allowed.

Templo de los Jaguares y Escudos

The Temple of the Jaguars and Shields, built atop the southeast corner of the ball court's wall, has some columns with carved rattlesnakes and tablets with etched jaguars. Inside are faded mural fragments depicting a battle.

Plataforma de los Cráneos

The Platform of Skulls (Tzompantli in Náhuatl, a Maya dialect) is between the Templo de los Jaguares y Escudos and El Castillo. You can't mistake it, because the T-shaped platform is festooned with carved skulls and eagles tearing open the chests of men to eat their hearts. In ancient days this platform was used to display the heads of sacrificial victims.

Cenote Sagrado

From the Platform of Skulls, a 400m rough stone *sacbé* (path) runs north (a five-minute walk) to the huge sunken well that gave this city its name. The Sacred Cenote is an awesome natural well, some 60m in diameter and 35m deep. The walls between the summit and the water's surface are ensnared in tangled vines and other vegetation.

El Osario

The Ossuary, otherwise known as the Bonehouse or the Tumba del Gran Sacerdote (High Priest's Grave), is a ruined pyramid to the southwest of El Castillo. As with most of the buildings in this southern section, the architecture is more Puuc than Toltec. It's notable for the beautiful serpent heads at the base of its staircases.

A square shaft at the top of the structure leads down into a cave that was used as a burial chamber; seven tombs with human remains were discovered inside.

El Caracol

Called El Caracol (the Snail) by the Spaniards for its interior spiral staircase, this observatory, to the south of the El Osario, is one of the most fascinating and important of all Chichén Itzá's buildings (but, alas, you can't enter it). Its circular design resembles some central highlands structures, although, surprisingly, not those of Toltec Tula.

In a fusion of architectural styles and religious imagery, there are Maya Chaac rain-god masks over four external doors facing the cardinal points. The windows in the observatory's dome are aligned with the appearance of certain stars at specific dates. From the dome the priests decreed the times for rituals, celebrations, corn-planting and harvests.

Detail from Plataforma de los Cráneos

The Magic of the Equinox

At the vernal and autumnal equinoxes (around March 20 and September 22), the morning and afternoon sun produces a light-and-shadow illusion of the serpent ascending or descending the side of El Castillo's staircase. The site is mobbed on these dates, however, making it difficult to see, and after the spectacle, parts of the site are sometimes closed to the public. The illusion is almost as good in the week preceding and following each equinox (and draws much smaller crowds), and is re-created nightly (except Mondays) in the **sound-and-light show** (www.nochesdekukul kan.com; Tue-Sat M$483, Sun M$240) year-round. Some find the spectacle fascinating, others think it's overrated. Either way, if you're in the area around the equinox and you have your own car, it's easy to wake up

early for the fiery sunrise at **Dzibilchaltún** (Place of Inscribed Flat Stones; Map p43; adult M$152, parking M$20; ⊘site 8am-5pm, museum 9am-5pm Tue-Sun, cenote 9am-3:30pm; P), a site north of Mérida, and then make it to Chichén Itzá by midafternoon, catching both spectacles on the same day.

✖ Take a Break

The selection of salads at **Restaurant Hacienda Xaybe'h d'Camara** (☎985-851-00-00; Calle 15A No 42; buffet lunches M$140; ⊘9am-5pm; P ❄ ☞ ⋔) make it a good option for vegetarians.

★ Top Tip

Don't hesitate to haggle for a bed near the ruins in low season (May through June and August to early December).

Valladolid

Once known as the Sultana of the East, Yucatán's third-largest city is famed for its quiet streets and sun-splashed pastel walls.

◉ SIGHTS

Casa de los Venados   Museum
(☏985-856-22-89; www.casadelosvenados.com; Calle 40 No 204 btwn Calles 41 & 43; M$100; ⊙tours 10am or by appointment) Featuring over 3000 pieces of museum-quality Mexican folk art, this private collection is interesting in that objects are presented in an actual private house, in the context that they were originally designed for, instead of being displayed in glass cases. The tour (in English or Spanish) touches on the origins of some of the more important pieces and the story of the award-winning restored colonial mansion that houses them.

Mercado Municipal   Market
(Calle 32 s/n btwn Calles 35 & 37; ⊙6am-4pm) Locals come to this good, authentic Mexican market to shop for cheap clothing, produce and what-have-you, and to eat at inexpensive *taquerías* (taco stalls). The east side is the most colorful, with flowers and stacks of fruit and vegetables on offer.

Ayuntamiento   Notable Building
(Calle 40 btwn Calles 39 & 41; ⊙8am-8pm Mon-Sat) The upstairs section, the Salón de Los Murales, has an interesting series of murals of figures that illustrate the history of the region.

Iglesia de la Candelaria   Church
The Virgin of Candelaria, the Patron of Valladolid, is celebrated at this church on February 2 (Candlemas).

Museo de San Roque   Museum
(Calle 41 s/n btwn Calles 38 & 40; ⊙8am-8pm Mon-Fri, from 9am Sat, 9am-6pm Sun) FREE Previously a 16th-century convent, San Roque has models and exhibits on the history of the city and the region. Other displays focus on various aspects of traditional Maya life.

Catedral de San Servasio   Cathedral
(San Gervasio) The original edifice was built from the main pyramid in 1545, then demolished and rebuilt in the early 1700s. This is the only church with a north-facing entrance in the Yucatán (all the others are east-facing), as a form of punishment handed down by the superiors to the local upstarts.

Templo de San Bernardino   Church
(Convento de Sisal; cnr Calles 49 & 51; Mon-Sat M$30, Sun free; ⊙9am-7pm) The Templo de San Bernardino and the adjacent Convento de Sisal are about 700m southwest of the plaza. They were constructed between 1552 and 1560 to serve the dual functions of fortress and church. The church's charming decoration includes beautiful rose-colored walls, arches, some recently uncovered 16th-century frescoes and a small image of the Virgin on the altar. These are about the only original items remaining; the grand wooden *retablo* (altarpiece) dates from the 19th century.

⚡ ACTIVITIES

Hacienda San Lorenzo Oxman   Swimming
(off Calle 54; cenote M$70, cenote & pool M$100, open bar M$50; ⊙9am-6pm) Once a *henequén* (sisal) plantation and a refuge for War of the Castes insurgents in the mid-19th century, today the hacienda's main draw is a gorgeous cenote that's far less crowded than other sinkholes in and around Valladolid, especially if you visit Monday through Thursday. If you buy the entry to both, you have a M$50 credit to use at the cafe.

Cenote X'Kekén y Samulá   Swimming
(Cenote Dzitnup & Samulá; 1/2 cenotes M$80/125; ⊙8:30am-6:30pm) One of two cenotes at Dzitnup (also known as X'Kekén Jungle Park), X'Kekén is popular with tour groups. A massive limestone formation with stalactites hangs from its ceiling. The pool is artificially lit and very swimmable. Here you can also take a dip in cenote Samulá, a lovely cavern pool with *álamo* roots stretching down many meters. You can also rent horses

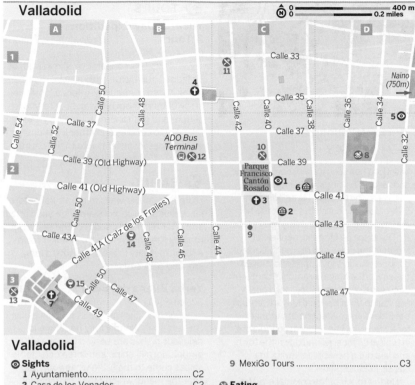

Valladolid

◉ Sights
1 Ayuntamiento..C2
2 Casa de los Venados.................................C2
3 Catedral de San Servasio.......................C2
4 Iglesia de la Candelaria..........................B1
5 Mercado Municipal...................................D2
6 Museo de San Roque...............................C2
7 Templo de San Bernardino......................A3

◈ Activities, Courses & Tours
8 Cenote Zací...D2

9 MexiGo Tours...C3

⊗ Eating
10 Hostería del Marqués...............................C2
11 La Palapita de los Tamales......................C1
12 Squimz..B2
13 Yerba Buena del Sisal..............................A3

⊖ Drinking & Nightlife
14 Cafeína Bistro Bar....................................B3
15 Taberna de los Frailes..............................A3

(M$225 per 30 minutes), ATVs (M$275 per 30 minutes) or bikes (M$100 per hour).

Cenote Suytun   Swimming
(✆cell 998-241-9957; Hwy 180, Tikuch; adult/child under 11yr M$70/50; ⊗9am-5pm) If you can get in before the bus tour groups, this cenote, run by the Tikuch community, features in many brochures and guidebooks. It is the one with the stone platform (permitted to be built after some of the roof had caved in). It's a decent cenote, if a slightly more clinical

experience than some of the others. It's 9km east of Valladolid off Hwy 180.

Cenote Zací   Swimming
(✆985-856-08-18; Calle 36 s/n btwn Calles 37 & 39; adult/child 3-11yr M$30/15; ⊗10am-5:30pm) One of few cenotes in a downtown location, this open-air swimming hole is a handy place to cool off. It's pleasant enough, but don't expect crystalline waters. You might see catfish or, overhead, a colony of bats. The park also holds small souvenir stands

 Valladolid's History

Valladolid has seen its fair share of turmoil and revolt. The city was first founded in 1543 near the Chouac-Ha lagoon some 50km from the coast, but it was too hot and there were way too many mosquitoes for Francisco de Montejo, nephew of Montejo the Elder, and his merry band of conquerors. So they upped and moved the city to the Maya ceremonial center of Zací (sah-*see*), where they faced heavy resistance from the local Maya. Eventually the Elder's son – Montejo the Younger – took the town. The Spanish conquerors, in typical fashion, ripped down the town and laid out a new city following the classic colonial plan.

During much of the colonial era, Valladolid's physical isolation from Mérida kept it relatively autonomous from royal rule, and the Maya of the area suffered brutal exploitation, which continued after Mexican independence. Barred from entering many areas of the city, the Maya made Valladolid one of their first points of attack following the 1847 outbreak of the Caste War in Tepich. After a two-month siege, the city's occupiers were finally overcome.

Today Valladolid is a prosperous seat of agricultural commerce, augmented by some light industry and a growing tourist trade.

Dancers at a fair in Valladolid
RAFAL CICHAWA/SHUTTERSTOCK ©

plus a pleasant restaurant under a large *palapa* (mains M$50 to M$150).

TOURS

Yucatán Jay Expeditions & Tours
Birdwatching, Cultural

(✆cell 999-280-5117; www.yucatanjay.com; ◐8am-8pm) This cooperative 14km south of Valladolid, run by five enthusiastic members of the Xocén community, offers a fabulous array of tours, from birdwatching to Maya culture and gastronomy tours. They can take you to cenotes and other locations, providing excellent insights into their culture.

EATING

From hole-in-the-walls to upmarket eateries, Valladolid's choices are wide and varied, and offer relief from some of the tasty, but more limited options of the smaller towns. A local specialty is the *longaniza*, a long, smoked pork sausage.

Yerba Buena del Sisal
Mexican $

(✆985-856-14-06; www.yerbabuenadelsisal.com; Calle 54A No 217; mains M$85-140; ◐8am-5pm Tue-Sun; 🛜🍴) Wonderfully healthy and delicious dishes are served in a peaceful garden. Tortilla chips and three delectable salsas come to the table while you look over the menu, which offers many great vegetarian and mostly organic dishes, such as the delightful *tacos maculum* (with handmade corn tortillas, beans, cheese and aromatic Mexican pepper leaf).

La Palapita de los Tamales
Mexican $

(✆998-106-34-72; Calle 42 s/n, cnr Calle 33; tamales M$40; ◐8-10pm Mon-Sat; 🍴) The menu changes daily, but you'll always find a welcome tamal to snack on. Sweetcorn and pork was on the menu recently, as was excellent *pozole* (a pork and hominy soup). There's casual indoor or patio seating, and takeout is popular. Great juices, breakfasts and vegan options, too.

Naino
International $$

(✆985-104-90-71; www.facebook.com/zentikproject; Calle 30 btwn Calles 27 & 29; mains M$80-150; ◐7am-10:30pm; 🅿🛜) Located on the outskirts of town, on the premises of the resort **Zenti'k** (✆985-104-91-71; www.

zentikhotel.com; Calle 30 No 192C btwn 27 & 29; cabañas M$2197; ☐P☐😊☐✳☐📶☐🐕☐), this pleasant open-air restaurant is an option for breakfast, lunch or dinner. The food is creative but a little overreaching, with chefs opting for flair over flavor. If you're craving something a bit different then this is the spot.

Squimz   Cafe $$

(☎999-856-41-56; www.squimz.com.mx; Calle 39 No 219; mains M$50-130; ☺7am-11pm; ☐P☐📶☐) A delightful, casual little cafe just a few doors east of the ADO bus terminal, Squimz offers cakes, pastries and espresso drinks, as well as heartier fare like pastas and paninis. There's even a number of cocktails to choose from. Sit at booths in front or in an open rear patio.

Hostería del Marqués   Mexican $$

(☎985-856-20-73; www.mesondelmarques.com; El Mesón del Marqués, Calle 39 No 203; mains M$120-350; ☺7am-11pm; ☐P☐✳☐📶☐) Dine in a tranquil colonial courtyard with a bubbling fountain, or the air-con salon looking on to it. The restaurant specializes in Yucatecan fare, such as *longaniza* Valladolid (Valladolid-style sausage) and *cochinita pibil* (pulled pork), and there are also international dishes such as Angus beef cuts.

🍷 DRINKING & NIGHTLIFE

Taberna de los Frailes   Cocktail Bar

(☎985-856-06-89; www.tabernadelosfrailes. com; Calle 49 s/n, cnr Calle 41A; mains M$145-280; ☺10am-10pm; 📶) Visitors mainly seem to head here as it's a pretty, romantic spot with a verdant garden. While the cuisine is good, it's even better as a spot to get a tasty cocktail at a place where you can actually have a quiet conversation.

Cafeína Bistro Bar   Bar

(☎985-858-21-26; Calle 41A s/n; mains M$90-300; ☺noon-2am; 📶) A little pub and bistro where you can catch a televised sporting event or chat over Mexican draft beer and well-made pizzas.

⭐ ENTERTAINMENT

Following a centuries-old tradition, dances are held in the main plaza from 8pm to 10pm on Sunday, with music by local groups playing *cumbia* (dance music originating from Colombia), *danzón* (dance music originating from Cuba) and other danceable styles.

ℹ️ INFORMATION

While Valladolid is generally safe, there have been reports of theft or assault on the remote biking and walking routes to/from cenotes. Be cautious if you're traveling alone.

Various banks (most with ATMs) near the town center are generally open 9am to 5pm Monday to Friday and to 1pm Saturday.

ℹ️ GETTING THERE & AWAY

Valladolid's main bus terminal is the convenient **ADO bus terminal** (☎985-856-34-48; www.ado. com.mx; cnr Calles 39 & 46; ☺24hr). The main 1st-class services are by ADO, ADO GL and OCC; Oriente and Mayab run 2nd-class buses.

Buses to Chichén Itzá/Pisté stop near the ruins during opening hours (but double-check).

ℹ️ GETTING AROUND

The old highway passes through the town center, though most signs urge motorists toward the toll road north of town. To follow the old highway eastbound, take Calle 41; westbound, take Calle 39.

Bicycles are a great way to see the town and get out to the cenotes. You can rent them at **Hostel La Candelaria** (☎985-856-22-67; www. hostelvalladolidyucatan.com; Calle 35 No 201F; dm/r incl breakfast from M$265/575; ☐😊☐@☐📶☐) or **MexiGo Tours** (☎985-856-07-77; www. mexigotours.com; Calle 43 No 204C btwn Calles 40 & 42; ☺9am-1pm & 3-7pm) for around M$20 to M$25 per hour.

It's possible to get to many of the cenotes. *Colectivos* (share taxis) depart from different points around the center; ask the locals. Note that these tend to leave in the mornings only.

In this Chapter
Visiting the Site 80
Palenque 86
Eating 86

Palenque

Swathed in morning jungle mists and echoing to a dawn chorus of howler monkeys and parrots, the mighty Maya temples of Palenque are deservedly one of the top destinations of Chiapas and one of the best examples of Maya architecture in all of Mexico. By contrast, modern Palenque town, a few kilometers to the east, is a sweaty, humdrum place without much appeal except as a jumping-off point for the ruins and a place to find internet access. Many prefer to base themselves at one of the forest hideouts along the road between the town and the ruins.

One Day in Palenque

Gather all your senses and dive head-first into the ancient Maya world at the exquisite **Palenque** (p81), where spectacular pyramids rise above emerald jungle treetops. Take your time to marvel at the abundance of reliefs, seek out the tomb of the mysterious Red Queen and wander the maze-like palace. Hit up the **Museo de Sitio** (p85) to tie it all together, then retreat to **El Huachinango Feliz** (p86) for lip-smackin' seafood.

Two Days in Palenque

Kick back for a day in **El Panchán** (p87), enjoying the dripping jungle as well as the alternative scene, complete with a meditation temple and a *temascal* (pre-Hispanic steam bath). In the evening, grab drinks and dinner at the lively **Don Mucho's** (p86), or head to town to check out a free concert in **El Parque** (p86).

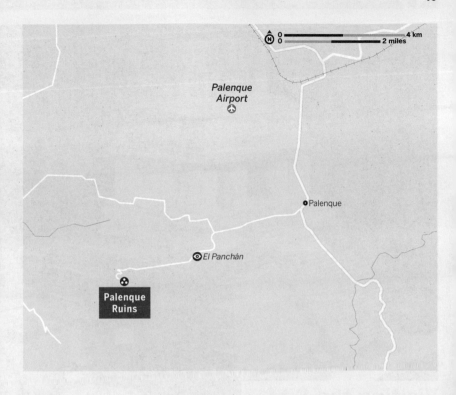

Arriving in Palenque

ADO bus terminal The main bus terminal offers deluxe and 1st-class services; you can walk from here to La Cañada in Palenque town; taxis charge M$60 to the ruins. During the day, *combis* (minibuses) run from town to the ruins (M$24 each way) about every 10 minutes.

Where to Stay

Palenque town has some good options in the leafy La Cañada neighborhood, but travelers tend to prefer the surrounding area, especially between the town and the ruins, which offers some magical spots where howler monkeys romp in the tree canopy. The compound of El Panchán is a favorite, with low-key budget cabañas (cabins) nestled in the stream-crossed jungle.

Palenque archaeological site

Visiting the Site

Ancient Palenque stands at the precise point where the first hills rise out of the Gulf coast plain, and the dense jungle covering these hills forms an evocative backdrop to Palenque's exquisite Maya architecture. Hundreds of ruined buildings are spread over 15 sq km, but only a fairly compact central area has been excavated.

Great For...

☑ Don't Miss

The Templo de las Inscripciones – perhaps the most celebrated burial monument in the Americas.

History

The name Palenque (Palisade) is Spanish and has no relation to the city's ancient name, which may have been Lakamha (Big Water). Palenque was first occupied around 100 BC, and flourished from around AD 630 to around 740. The city rose to prominence under the ruler Pakal, who reigned from AD 615 to 683. Archaeologists have determined that Pakal is represented by hieroglyphics of sun and shield, and he is also referred to as Escudo Solar (Sun Shield). He lived to the then-incredible age of 80.

During Pakal's reign, many plazas and buildings, including the superlative Templo de las Inscripciones (Pakal's own mausoleum), were constructed in Palenque. Pakal's son Kan B'alam II (r 684–702), who is represented in hieroglyphics by the jaguar and the serpent (and is also called Jaguar

Palenque

El Panchán

Palenque Ruins

ℹ Need to Know

Palenque Ruins (M$48 plus M$22 national park entry fee; ⊘8am-5pm, last entry 4:30pm)

✗ Take a Break

Retreat to Don Mucho's (p86) in the popular El Panchán for great-value meals in a verdant setting.

★ Top Tip

Opening time is a good time to visit, when it's cooler and not too crowded.

Serpent II), continued Palenque's expansion and artistic development. He presided over the construction of the Grupo de las Cruces temples.

After AD 900, Palenque was largely abandoned. In an area that receives the heaviest rainfall in Mexico, the ruins were soon overgrown, and the city remained unknown to the Western world until 1746, when Maya hunters revealed the existence of a jungle palace to a Spanish priest named Antonio de Solís. It was not until 1837, when John L Stephens, an amateur archaeology enthusiast from New York, reached Palenque with artist Frederick Catherwood, that the site was insightfully investigated. Another century passed before Alberto Ruz Lhuillier, the tireless Mexican archaeologist, uncovered Pakal's hidden crypt in 1952.

Today it continues to yield fascinating and beautiful secrets – most recently, a succession of sculptures and frescoes in the Acrópolis del Sur area, which have vastly expanded our knowledge of Palenque's history.

Digging Deeper

● **Maya Exploration Center** (www.maya exploration.org) A group of archaeologists, academics and artists who work on Maya sciences such as astronomy and math, and offer specialized tours.

● **Group of the Cross Project** (www. mesoweb.com/palenque) A Palenque archaeologists' site with detailed findings from its landmark 1997–2002 dig.

● **INAH** (www.inah.gob.mx) The Mexican national antiquities department posts news and discoveries, sometimes in English.

Palenque's Structures

As you explore the ruins, try to picture the gray stone edifices as they would have been at the peak of Palenque's power:

painted blood red, with elaborate blue and yellow stucco details.

Templo de las Inscripciones

As you walk in from the entrance, the vegetation suddenly peels away to reveal many of Palenque's most magnificent buildings in one sublime vista. A line of temples rises in front of the jungle on your right, culminating in the Templo de las Inscripciones about 100m ahead; El Palacio, with its trademark tower, stands to the left of the Templo de las Inscripciones; and the Grupo de las Cruces rises in the distance beneath a thick jungle backdrop.

The first temple on your right is Templo XII, called the **Templo de la Calavera** (Temple of the Skull) for the relief sculpture of a rabbit or deer skull at the foot of one of its pillars. Nearby **Templo XIII** contains a

tomb of a female dignitary, whose remains were found colored red (as a result of treatment with cinnabar) when unearthed in 1994. You can look into the **Tumba de la Reina Roja** (Tomb of the Red Queen) and see her sarcophagus. With the skeleton were found a malachite mask and about 1000 pieces of jade. Based on DNA tests and resemblances to Pakal's tomb next door, the theory is that the 'queen' buried here was his wife Tz'ak-b'u Ajaw. The **tomb of Alberto Ruz Lhuillier**, who discovered Pakal's tomb in 1952, lies under the trees in front of Templo XIII.

The **Templo de las Inscripciones** (Temple of the Inscriptions), perhaps the most celebrated burial monument in the Americas, is the tallest and most stately of Palenque's buildings. Constructed on eight levels, the Templo de las Inscripciones

Templo de las Inscripciones

has a central front staircase rising 25m to a series of small rooms. The tall roofcomb that once crowned it is long gone, but between the front doorways are stucco panels with reliefs of noble figures. On the interior rear wall are three panels with the long Maya inscription, recounting the history of Palenque and this building, for which Mexican archaeologist Alberto Ruz Lhuillier named the temple. From the top, interior stairs lead down into the **tomb of**

> ### ❶ Need to Know
>
> Official site guides are available by the entrance and ticket office. Two Maya guide associations offer informative two-hour tours for up to seven people, which cost M$880 in Spanish or M$1050 in English, French, German or Italian.

Pakal (now closed to visitors indefinitely, to avoid further damage to its murals from the humidity inevitably exuded by visitors). Pakal's jewel-bedecked skeleton and jade mosaic death mask were removed from the tomb to Mexico City, and the tomb was re-created in the Museo Nacional de Antropología. The priceless death mask was stolen in an elaborate heist in 1985 (though recovered a few years afterwards), but the carved stone sarcophagus lid remains in the closed tomb – you can see a replica in the site museum.

Diagonally opposite the Templo de las Inscripciones is **El Palacio** (The Palace), a large structure divided into four main courtyards, with a maze of corridors and rooms. Built and modified piecemeal over 400 years from the 5th century on, it was probably the residence of Palenque's rulers.

The northeastern courtyard, the **Patio de los Cautivos** (Patio of the Captives), contains a collection of relief sculptures that seem disproportionately large for their setting; the theory is that they represent conquered rulers and were brought from elsewhere.

Grupo de las Cruces

Pakal's son, Kan B'alam II, was a prolific builder, and soon after the death of his father started designing the temples of the Grupo de las Cruces (Group of the Crosses). All three main pyramid-shaped structures surround a plaza southeast of the Templo de las Inscripciones.

The **Templo del Sol** (Temple of the Sun), on the west side of the plaza, has the best-preserved roofcomb at Palenque. Steep steps climb to the **Templo de la Cruz** (Temple of the Cross), the largest and most elegantly proportioned in this group. On the **Templo de la Cruz Foliada** (Temple of the Foliated Cross), the corbel arches

JESS KRAFT/SHUTTERSTOCK ©

> ### ✕ Take a Break
>
> Grab a refreshing juice from Café Jade (p86) before heading to the site.

are fully exposed, revealing how Palenque's architects designed these buildings.

Acrópolis Sur

In the jungle south of the Grupo de las Cruces is the Southern Acropolis, where archaeologists have made some terrific finds in recent excavations. You may find part of the area roped off. The Acrópolis Sur appears to have been constructed as an extension of the Grupo de las Cruces, with both groups set around what was probably a single long open space.

Templo XVII, between the Cruces group and the Acrópolis Sur, contains a reproduction carved panel depicting Kan B'alam, standing with a spear, with a bound captive kneeling before him (the original is in the site museum). In 1999, in **Templo XIX**, archaeologists made the most important Palenque find for decades: an 8th-century limestone platform with stunning carvings of seated figures and lengthy hieroglyphic texts that detail Palenque's origins. Also discovered in 1999, **Templo XX** contains a red-frescoed tomb built in 540 that is currently Palenque's most active dig.

In 2002 archaeologists found in **Templo XXI** a throne with very fine carvings depicting Ahkal Mo' Nahb', his ancestor the great Pakal, and his son U Pakal.

Grupo Norte

North of El Palacio is a **Juego de Pelota** (Ball Court) and the handsome buildings of the Northern Group. Crazy Count de Waldeck lived in the so-called **Templo del Conde** (Temple of the Count), constructed in AD 647.

Northeastern Groups

East of the Grupo Norte, the main path crosses Arroyo Otolum. Some 70m beyond the stream, a right fork will take you to **Grupo C**, a set of jungle-covered buildings and plazas thought to have been lived in from about AD 750 to 800.

If you stay on the main path, you'll descend some steep steps to a group of low, elongated buildings, probably occupied residentially from around AD 770 to 850. The path goes alongside the Arroyo Otolum, which here tumbles down a series of small falls forming natural bathing pools known as the **Baño de la Reina** (Queen's Bath). Unfortunately, you can't bathe here anymore.

The path then continues to another residential quarter, the **Grupo de los Murciélagos** (Bat Group), and then crosses the **Puente de los Murciélagos**, a footbridge across Arroyo Otolum. Across the bridge and a bit further downstream, a path goes west to **Grupo I** and **Grupo II**, a short walk uphill. These ruins, only partly uncovered, are in a beautiful jungle setting. The main path continues downriver to the road, where the museum is a short distance along to the right.

Stucco glyphs, Museo de Sitio

Museo de Sitio

Palenque's site **museum** (Carretera Palenque-Ruinas Km 6.5; with ruins ticket free; ☺9am-4:30pm Tue-Sun) is worth a wander, displaying finds from the site and interpreting, in English and Spanish, Palenque's history. Highlights include a blissfully air-conditioned room displaying a copy of the lid of Pakal's sarcophagus (depicting his rebirth as the maize god, encircled by serpents, mythical monsters and glyphs recounting his reign) and finds from Templo XXI. Entry to the sarcophagus room is permitted every half-hour.

Getting There & Around

Most visitors take a *combi* or taxi to the ruins' main (upper) entrance, see the major structures and then walk downhill to the museum, visiting minor ruins along the way.

Combis to the ruins (M$24 each way) run about every 10 minutes during daylight hours. In town, look for 'Ruinas' *combis* anywhere on Av Juárez west of Allende. They will also pick you up or drop you off anywhere along the town–ruins road.

---

❶ Need to Know

Be aware that the mushrooms sold by locals along the road to the ruins from May to November are hallucinogenic.

✕ Take a Break

Celebrate a successful exploration at upmarket Restaurante Bajlum (p87).

Palenque

Highway 199 meets Palenque's main street, Av Juárez, at the **Glorieta de la Cabeza Maya** (Maya Head Statue), a roundabout with a large statue of a Maya chieftain's head, at the west end of the town. The main ADO bus station is here, and Juárez heads 1km east from this intersection to the central square, **El Parque**.

A few hundred meters south of the Maya head, the paved road to the Palenque ruins, 7.5km away, diverges west off Hwy 199. This road passes the site museum after about 6.5km, then winds on about 1km further uphill to the **main entrance to the ruins** (Upper Entrance).

EATING

Palenque is definitely not the gastronomic capital of Mexico. There's a decent variety of restaurants, though some are laughably overpriced. A number of inexpensive stands and sit-down spots can be found near the AEXA bus terminal and on the east side of El Parque in front of the church.

Café Jade — Mexican, Chiapaneco $
(📞916-688-00-15; Prolongación Hidalgo 1; breakfast M$50-100, mains M$60-120; ⏱7am-11pm; 🛜🍴) This very cool bamboo construction has indoor and outdoor seating, and is one of the most popular places in town. Its growing fame hasn't led to a reduction in quality though, and it serves good breakfasts, some Chiapan specialties and international traveler classics such as burgers. Has a reasonable number of vegetarian options and really good fresh juices too.

Don Mucho's — Mexican, International $
(📞916-112-83-38; Carretera Palenque-Ruinas Km 4.5, El Panchán; mains M$60-150; ⏱7am-1am Tue-Thu, to 2am Fri, to 3am Sat, to midnight Sun & Mon) In El Panchán, popular Don Mucho's provides great-value meals in a jungly setting, with a candlelit ambience at night. Busy waiters bring pasta, fish, meat, plenty of *antojitos* (typical Mexican snacks), and pizzas (cooked in a purpose-built Italian-designed wood-fired oven) that are some of the finest this side of Naples.

Live music – usually *andina, cumbia* or Cuban – starts around 8pm Friday through Sunday (at 9:30pm other nights), plus there's a rousing fire-dancing show most nights at 11pm.

El Huachinango Feliz — Seafood $$
(📞916-129-82-31; Hidalgo s/n; mains M$90-160; ⏱8am-11pm) A popular, atmospheric restaurant in the leafy La Cañada neighborhood. It has an attractive front patio with tables and umbrellas, and there's also an upstairs covered terrace. Seafood is the specialty here: order seafood soup, seafood cocktails, grilled fish that's beautifully crunchy on the outside and soft on the inside, or shrimp served 10 different ways. The service is *slooow* but the food is worth the wait.

Monte Verde — Italian $$
(📞916-119-17-87; mains M$100-180; ⏱2-10:30pm Sun-Tue, Thu & Fri, to 11pm Sat) There's a real Mediterranean vibe to this Italian restaurant tucked away in the forest (do a bit of bird- and monkey-watching while waiting for your lunch!), and though most people go for the delicious thin-crust pizzas, the meat and pasta dishes are worthy of your time. Try the seafood tagliatelle piled high with giant prawns and you'll leave happy.

Restaurant Las Tinajas — Mexican $$
(📞916-345-49-70; cnr Av 20 de Noviembre & Abasolo; mains M$85-130; ⏱7am-10:30pm) It doesn't take long to figure out why this place is always busy. It slings enormous portions of excellent home-style food – enough to keep you fueled up for hours. *Pollo a la veracruzana* (chicken in a tomato, olive and onion sauce) and *camarones al guajillo* (shrimp with a not-too-hot type of chili) are both delicious, as is the house salsa.

La Selva — Mexican $$
(📞916-101-70-91; Hwy 199; mains M$85-220; ⏱11:30am-10:30pm) An upscale and slightly formal (for Palenque anyway) restaurant serving up well-prepared steaks, seafood, salads and *antojitos* under an enormous *palapa* roof, with jungle-themed stained-

glass panels brightening one wall. Try the *pigua* (freshwater lobster) when it's available in the fall.

Restaurante Bajlum   Mexican $$$
(☑916-107-85-18; mains M$270-600; ⊗2-10pm)
Creative and stunningly presented Maya gastronomy fills the menu at this upmarket but very inviting restaurant. The house specials include the delicious rabbit with 'jungle herbs' and duck with orange. Much of the produce is locally produced and whatever you order the owner is sure to come over and explain the story behind each dish. Impressive cocktail list.

ⓘ INFORMATION

MONEY

Both of the following banks change dollars and euros (bring a copy of your passport).

Banco Azteca (Av Juárez, btwn Allende & Aldama)

Bancomer (Av Juárez 96; ⊗8:30am-4pm Mon-Fri) Also has an ATM.

SAFE TRAVEL

Whichever direction you come from, it's safer to travel to Palenque in daylight hours as armed hold-ups along roads leading to Palenque are not unheard of. For the moment it's best not to travel directly from Ocosingo to Palenque, and at the time of research most transportation was taking alternative, and much longer but safer, routes. There have also been recent reports of thefts on the night bus from Mérida. When taking buses along these routes, consider stowing valuables in the checked luggage compartment.

ⓘ GETTING THERE & AWAY

In 2014 Palenque's long-deserted **airport** finally opened to commercial flights. Interjet has twice-weekly service to Mexico City. Otherwise, the closest major airport is Villahermosa; ADO runs a direct airport service (M$330) in comfortable minibuses.

In a spacious location behind the Maya head statue, **ADO** (www.ado.com.mx) has the main

 Holistic Travel: El Panchán

Just off the road to the ruins, **El Panchán** (Carretera Palenque-Ruinas Km 4.5) is a legendary travelers' hangout set in a patch of dense rainforest. It's the epicenter of Palenque's alternative scene, and home to a bohemian bunch of Mexican and foreign residents and wanderers.

Once ranchland, the area has been reforested by the remarkable Morales family, some of whom are among the leading archaeological experts on Palenque. Today El Panchán has several (mostly rustic) places to stay, a couple of restaurants, a set of sinuous streams rippling their way through every part of the property, nightly entertainment (and daily drumming practice), a meditation temple, a temascal (pre-Hispanic steam bath) and a constant stream of interesting visitors from all over the world.

bus terminal, with deluxe and 1st-class services, an ATM and left-luggage facilities; it's also used by OCC (1st class). It's a good idea to buy your outward bus ticket a day in advance.

ⓘ GETTING AROUND

Taxis charge M$55 (up to M$70 at night) to El Panchán or Maya Bell, and M$60 to the ruins. *Combis* (M$25) run by **Transporte Chambalú** (☑916-345-28-49; Hidalgo) from the center ply the ruins road until dark. **Radio Taxis Santo Domingo** (☑916-345-01-26) has on-call service. There's a **taxi stand** on El Parque.

GUATEMALA

In this Chapter   90
Spanish & Salsa 92
Visiting Volcanoes 94
Splendor in the Ruins 96
Sights 98
Activities 102
Tours 102
Shopping 103
Eating 104
Drinking & Nightlife 108
Entertainment 110

Antigua

Antigua's beguiling beauty starts to seduce the moment you arrive. Once capital of Guatemala, its streetscapes of pastel facades unfold beneath the gaze of three volcanoes, and beautifully restored colonial buildings sit next to picturesque ruins in park-like surroundings. The city's World Heritage–listed status means that even fast-food chains have to hide themselves behind traditional building exteriors. Outside the city, Maya communities, coffee plantations and volcanoes offer ample opportunities for exploration.

Two Days in Antigua

Take breakfast at **Rincón Típico** (p107), then explore colonial buildings – **Catedral de Santiago** (p99), **Santo Domingo** (p98) and **La Merced** (p98). Eat a hearty traditional meal at **Tienda La Canche** (p106) before hitting up **Café No Sé** (p109) for a late-evening drink. Day two is **volcano tour** (p94) day. Afterwards enjoy dinner at **Mesón Panza Verde** (p108) and drinks at **Por Qué No?** (p110).

Four Days in Antigua

Head out of town to visit the **Centro Cultural La Azotea** (p99) at Jocotenango on day three, then eat and enjoy the views at **Earth Lodge** (p110). On day four reactivate with an out-of-town hike or mountain-bike ride with **Old Town Outfitters** (p102). In the evening, enjoy crepes and roof-deck views at **Luna de Miel** (p104) before settling in for a craft-brew session at **Antigua Brewing Company** (p109).

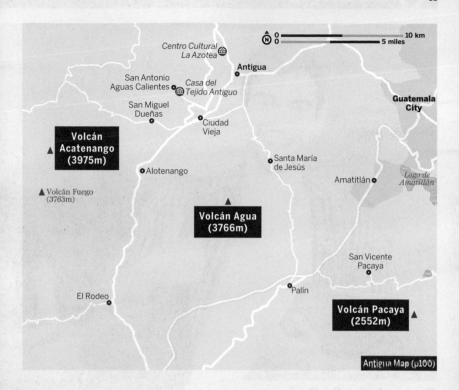

Antigua Map (p100)

Arriving in Antigua

Bus Terminal Taxis wait where the Guatemala City buses stop and on the east side of Parque Central. An in-town taxi ride costs Q25 to Q30. *Tuk-tuks* (three-wheeled motor taxis) are Q5 to Q15.

Where to Stay

With around 150 hotels, *posadas* (guesthouses) and hostels, Antigua has a wide range of accommodations, including some midrange options that allow you to wallow in colonial charm for a moderate outlay of cash. Room rates vary, and prices double during Semana Santa when demand surges – book as far ahead as you possibly can.

Spanish & Salsa

There's no better place in Latin America set up for learning Spanish, with numerous schools offering good-value one-on-one tuition. If your language acquisition skills seem to be lacking, you might want to try communicating with your feet at a salsa dancing class.

Great For...

☑ **Don't Miss**

Free salsa classes Monday and Tuesday at New Sensation Salsa Studio (www. facebook.com/salseandosevivemejor).

A spot of study here is a great way not only to learn Spanish, but also to meet locals and get an inside angle on the culture.

Guatemala's Language Schools

Guatemalan language schools are some of the cheapest in the world, but few people go away disappointed. There are so many schools to choose from that it's essential to check out a few before deciding on one.

You can start any day at most schools, and study for as long as you like. If you're coming in peak season and hoping to get into one of the more popular schools, it's a good idea to book ahead. All decent schools offer a variety of elective activities, from salsa classes to movies to volcano hikes. Many schools offer classes in Maya languages as well as Spanish.

o **Academia de Español Probigua** (Map p100; ☎7832-2998; www.probigua.org; 6a Av Norte 41B) ✐ Nonprofit Spanish school supporting mobile libraries in rural Guatemala.

Questions to Ask

o Where do the classes take place?

o What experience and qualifications do the teachers have?

o What is the atmosphere of the school? (Serious students won't fit in at a school offering all-night bar crawls, and party animals may feel out of place at schools with names like Christian Spanish Academy.)

o If the school claims to be involved in community or volunteer projects, is it a serious commitment, or a marketing ploy?

o Does the school offer further remote lessons by Skype?

o **Spanish School San José el Viejo** (Map p100; ☎7832-3028; www.sanjoseelviejo.com; 5a Av Sur 34) Spanish lessons are given in lovely park surroundings.

o **Antigüeña Spanish Academy** (Map p100; ☎5735-4638; www.spanishacademyantiguena.com; 1a Calle Poniente 10) Learn Spanish in this leafy hacienda.

o **Academia de Español Sevilla** (Map p100; ☎7832-5101; www.facebook.com/Spanish-SchoolAntigua; 1a Av Sur 17C) Mix up classes with volunteering on local community projects.

o **Proyecto Lingüístico Francisco Marroquín** (Map p100; ☎7832-1422; www.spanishschoolplfm.com; 6a Av Norte 43) ✐ Throw in some lessons on Maya languages along with Spanish classes.

Roasting marshmallows on Volcán Pacaya

MATYAS REHAK/SHUTTERSTOCK ©

Visiting Volcanoes

Sacred to the Maya and integral to the country's history, Guatemala's volcanoes dominate the skylines of the country's west, and are one of its emblematic features. You can gaze upon their domed beauty from the comfort of a cafe in Antigua or get up close and personal by climbing (at least) one.

Great For...

☑ Don't Miss

The smoking, lava-dribbling summit of Pacaya.

All three volcanoes overlooking Antigua – Agua, Acatenango and Fuego – are tempting challenges, but after Fuego's deadly 2018 eruption, hikes here are likely to be curtailed for some time. In many ways the twin-peaked Acatenango (3975m) is the most exhilarating summit. For an active-volcano experience many people take tours to Pacaya (2552m), 25km southeast of Antigua.

Volcán Acatenango

The strenuous hike up Volcán Acatenango traverses four ecosystems to reach the summit. Typical agency prices are around Q1100, including lunch and 5am transport to the trailhead in the village of La Soledad. Overnight hikes are another option, camping just below the tree line, then ascend-

Volcán Acatenango

TABACO/GETTY IMAGES ©

ⓘ Need to Know

Don't attempt Volcán Agua without a guide, as assaults on the climb have occurred.

✖ Take a Break

Visit **Restaurant Cerro San Cristóbal** (☑5941-8145; www.restcerrosancristobal. com; Calle Principal 5; mains Q50-110; ☺8:30am-7pm Mon-Thu, 8am-8pm Fri-Sun; ▣) on the way to or from a volcano hike.

★ Top Tip

Book your ascent at least a day in advance.

ing to the summit the following morning (Q1300 per person with two people).

Volcán Agua

Ascents of Volcán Agua (3766m) take off from the village of Santa María de Jesús (Q3.50 from Antigua bus terminal) on the volcano's northeast slopes. You can hire INGUAT-authorized guides (one day/ overnight Q200/250 per person, plus park entry fee of Q40) from the tourist office just off Santa María's Parque Central.

Volcán Pacaya

Most agencies run seven-hour Pacaya trips daily for Q90 (leaving Antigua at 6am and 2pm), but food and drinks are not included, nor is the Q50 admission to the Pacaya

protected area. It takes about 1½ hours to make the steep ascent to the simmering black cone. (If you're out of breath, you can rent horses on the way up.) From the summit there are stupendous views northwest to Agua and northeast to Lago de Atitlán. The descent is quicker as you slide down the powdery slope.

Volcanic Activity

Great to look at, fun to climb, scary when they erupt. Guatemala has four active volcanoes: Pacaya, Fuego, Santiaguito and Tacaná. The nastiest event to date was back in 1902 when Santa María erupted taking 6000 lives. In recent years Pacaya and Fuego have been acting up, with increased lava flow and ash. When Fuego erupted in June 2018, over 160 people were killed by the resulting ash flow. If you need to keep an eye on it, log on to the Smithsonian's volcano page (www.volcano.si.edu).

Splendor in the Ruins

Once glorious in their gilded baroque finery, Antigua's churches and monasteries have suffered indignities from both nature and humankind. A walk through town is therefore also a walk through time.

Start Cerro de la Cruz
Distance 2.3km
Duration 2½ hours

5 Continue a block west and turn right to reach the old **Convento de Santa Teresa** (4a Av Norte), which until recently served as a men's prison.

6 Head west, then south down 5a Av Norte, jam-packed with tourist-friendly locales, including a brilliant, sprawling handicrafts depot, **Nim Po't** (p103).

7 Continue to Parque Central. Ascend to the balcony of the **Palacio del Ayuntamiento** (4a Calle Poniente) for photo ops of the square and nearby **Catedral de Santiago** (p99).

Take a Break...
Hit **Café Condesa** (☎ 7832-0038; Portal del Comercio 4; cakes & pies Q20-26) for coffee and cake.

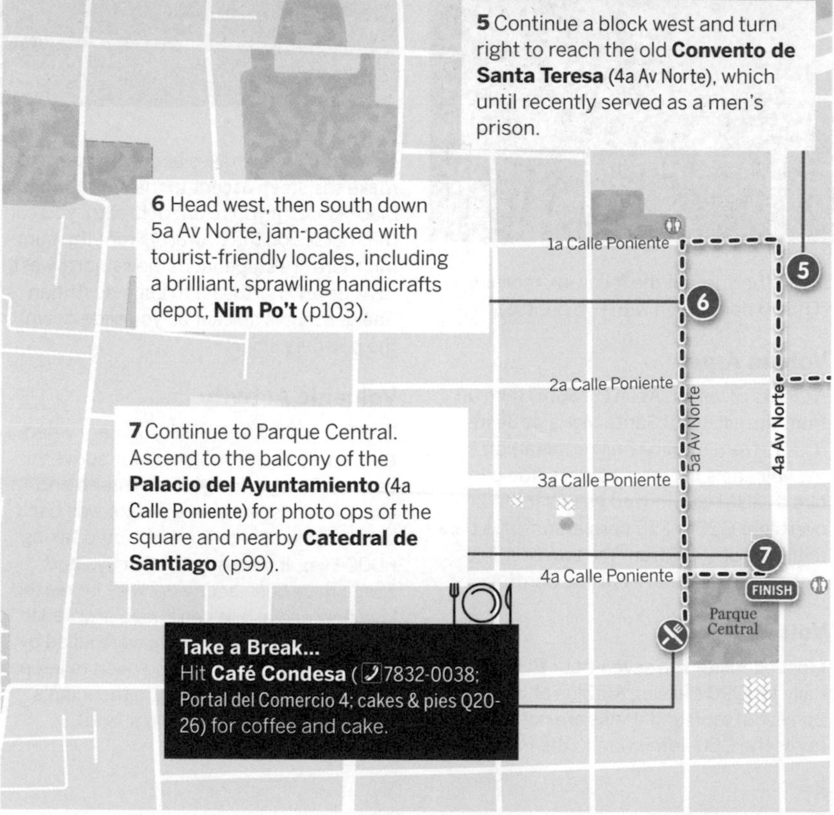

1a Calle Poniente

2a Calle Poniente

3a Calle Poniente

4a Calle Poniente

5a Av Norte

4a Av Norte

Parque Central

FINISH

Classic Photo: Cerro de la Cruz views

1 Take a taxi up **Cerro de la Cruz** for fine views looking south over town toward Volcán Agua.

2 Down the wooded slopes from the lookout point is a basketball court backed by the filigreed **Iglesia de la Candelaria** (1a Calle).

3 Twist and turn your way southwest to the ruins of the **Convento de Capuchinas** (p99), with its unique tower.

4 Go right on 2a Calle Oriente. Passing 3a Av Norte, look down to your left to see the multicolumned facade of **Iglesia El Carmen** (3a Av Norte) and an adjacent handicrafts market.

1 PIERRE MAHEUX/GETTY IMAGES © 3 LUCY BROWN - LOCA4MOTION/SHUTTERSTOCK © 5 AUTUMN SKY PHOTOGRAPHY/SHUTTERSTOCK ©

◉ SIGHTS

Echoes of Antigua's former grandeur are everywhere, rewarding a stroll in any direction. Begin exploring at **Parque Central** (Map p100; btwn 4a Calle & 5a Calle), the city's verdant heart, surrounded by superb colonial administrative buildings. Dotted around town are dozens of ecclesiastical complexes established by the myriad Catholic orders in the city's heyday, now in various states of decay. Rebuilding after earthquakes gave the churches thicker walls, lower towers and belfries, and unembellished interiors. Aside from their architectural interest, most of the complexes feature tranquil cloisters and gardens, and a few contain museums, notably the Convento de Santo Domingo.

Arco de Santa Catalina Architecture
(Map p100; 5a Av Norte) The Arco de Santa Catalina is Antigua's most iconic monument, and an early-morning or late-afternoon photo opportunity framing Volcán Agua through its arch is an essential part of any visit to the town. It was built in 1694 to enable nuns from the Santa Catalina convent to cross the street without being seen; the clock tower is a 19th-century add-on.

**Iglesia y Convento
de Santo Domingo** Monastery
(Map p100; ☎7820-1220; 3a Calle Oriente 28; Q42; ⊗9am-6pm Mon-Sat, 11:45am-6pm Sun) Founded by Dominican friars in 1542, Santo Domingo became the biggest and richest monastery in Antigua. Following three 18th-century earthquakes, the buildings were pillaged for construction material. The site was acquired as a private residence in 1970 by a North American archaeologist, who performed extensive excavations before it was taken over by the **Casa Santo Domingo Hotel** (☎7820-1220; www.casasantodomingo.com.gt; 3a Calle Oriente 28A; r from Q1400; 🅿@🛜🏊) 🎾. The archaeological zone has been innovatively restored as a 'cultural route.'

Iglesia Merced Church, Monastery
(Iglesia y Convento de Nuestra Señora de la Merced; Map p100; cnr 1a Calle Poniente & 6a Av Norte; monastery ruins Q15; ⊗church 6am-noon & 3-8pm, ruins 8:30am-5:30pm) At the northern end of 5a Av Norte is La Merced – a

From left: Arco de Santa Catalina; Catedral de Santiago; Iglesia Merced

striking yellow building trimmed with white plaster filigree. Its facade is one of the most beautiful in Guatemala The squat, thick-walled structure was built to withstand earthquakes, and three centuries after its construction it remains in good shape. Only the church is still in use; a candlelit procession, accompanied by bell ringing and firecrackers, starts and ends here on the last Thursday evening of each month.

Catedral de Santiago   Cathedral

(Map p100; cnr 4a Av Norte & 5a Calle Oriente; ruins Q8; ⊙ruins 9am-5pm, parish 6:30am-noon & 3-6:30pm Mon, Tue, Thu & Fri, 8am-noon & 3-7pm Sat, 5:30am-1pm & 3-7:30pm Sun) Antigua's cathedral was begun in 1545, wrecked by the quake of 1773, and only partially rebuilt over the next century. The present sliver of a church – the parish of San José – occupies only the entrance hall of the original edifice. Behind it are the roof-less **ruins** of the main part of the cathedral, which are entered from 5a Calle Oriente.

Convento de Capuchinas   Convent

(Iglesia y Convento de Nuestra Señora del Pilar de Zaragoza; Map p100; cnr 2a Av Norte & 2a

Calle Oriente; adult/student Q40/20; ⊙9am-5pm) Inaugurated in 1736 by nuns from Madrid, the convent of Las Capuchinas was seriously damaged by the 1773 earthquake and thereafter abandoned. Thanks to meticulous renovations in recent decades, it's possible to get a sense of the life experienced by those cloistered nuns, who ran an orphanage and women's hospital.

Palacio de los Capitanes Generales   Historic Building

(Palace of the Captains General; Map p100; ☑7832-2868; www.centroculturalrealpalacio.org.gt; 5a Calle Poniente; ⊙9am-4:30pm Wed-Sun) FREE Dating from 1549, the palace was colonial headquarters for all of Central America, from Chiapas to Costa Rica, until the capital was relocated in 1776. The stately double-arcaded facade that anchors the south side of the plaza is all that remains of the original complex. Following extensive renovations, the palace now hosts occasional art exhibits and performances.

Centro Cultural La Azotea   Museum

(Map p91; ☑7831-1120; www.azoteaestate.com; Calle del Cementerio Final; adult/child

SL PHOTOGRAPHY/SHUTTERSTOCK ©

Antigua

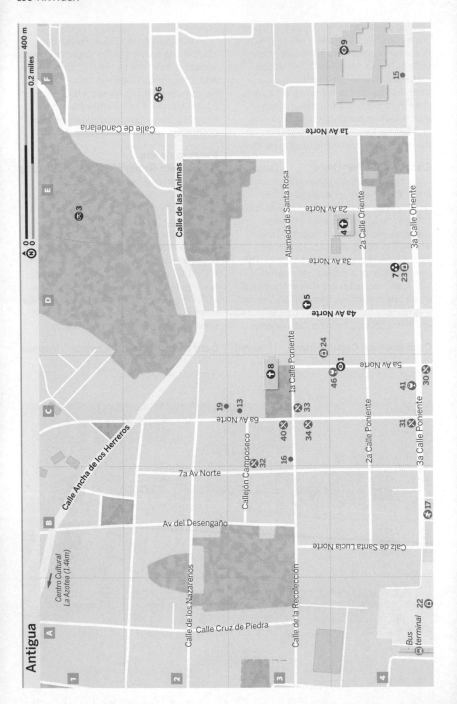

400 m
0.2 miles

Centro Cultural
La Azotea (1.4km)

Calle Ancha de los Herreros

Calle de Candelaria

Calle de las Ánimas

Alameda de Santa Rosa

1a Av Norte

2a Av Norte

3a Av Norte

4a Av Norte

5a Av Norte

6a Av Norte

7a Av Norte

2a Calle Oriente

3a Calle Oriente

1a Calle Poniente

2a Calle Poniente

3a Calle Poniente

Av del Desengaño

Callejón Camposeco

Calle de los Nazarenos

Calle Cruz de Piedra

Calle de la Recolección

Calz de Santa Lucía Norte

Bus
terminal

Callejón de la Concepción

Calle del Hermano Pedro

Calle de Belén

Calle de los Pasos

4a Calle Oriente

26

5a Calle Oriente

6a Calle Oriente

1a Av Sur

42
25
14

37

38

Parque de
La Unión

7a Calle Oriente

2a Av Sur

8a Calle Oriente

3a Av Sur

44

9a Calle Oriente

43
21

2

11

12

10

29

4a Av Sur

Portal del
Comercio

28

18
45

5a Av Sur

35

4a Calle Poniente

5a Calle Poniente

6a Av Sur

20

27

7a Calle Poniente

Calle Sucia

36
39

7a Av Sur

6a Calle Poniente

9a Calle Poniente

Calz de Santa Lucía Sur

Calle del Espíritu Santo

Carretera a Ciudad Vieja

Buses to Guatemala
City, Ciudad Vieja
& San Miguel Dueñas

Antigua

⊙ Sights
1 Arco de Santa Catalina C4
2 Catedral de Santiago................................D5
3 Cerro de la Cruz E1
4 Convento de Capuchinas..........................E4
5 Convento de Santa Teresa...................... D3
6 Iglesia de la Candelaria F2
7 Iglesia El Carmen D4
8 Iglesia Merced.. C3
9 Iglesia y Convento de Santo Domingo.....F4
10 Palacio de los Capitanes Generales.........D5
11 Palacio del Ayuntamiento.........................D5
12 Parque Central..D5

⊙ Activities, Courses & Tours
13 Academia de Español Probigua................ C3
14 Academia de Español Sevilla F6
15 Antigua Tours..F4
16 Antigüeña Spanish Academy................... C3
17 La Tortilla B4
18 Old Town Outfitters.................................. C6
19 Proyecto Lingüístico Francisco
       Marroquín C2
20 Spanish School San José el Viejo.............C7

⊙ Shopping
21 La Casa del Jade D5
22 Market A4
23 Mercado del Carmen................................ D4

24 Nim Po't...D3

⊗ Eating
25 Angie Angie..F6
26 Bistrot Cinq..E5
27 Cactus Taco Bar... C6
28 Café Condesa C5
29 Caffé Mediterráneo....................................D6
30 Casa Troccoli...C4
31 El Viejo Café C4
32 Fernando's Kaffee...................................... C3
       Fridas ....(see 24)
33 Hector's Bistro C3
34 Luna de Miel.. C3
35 Mesón Panza Verde....................................C8
36 Rainbow Café... B6
37 Restaurante Doña Luisa............................E5
38 Rincón Típico...D6
39 Samsara.. B6
40 Tienda La Canche C3

⊙ Drinking & Nightlife
41 Antigua Brewing Company.......................C4
42 Café No Sé F6
43 El Barrio D5
44 Por Qué No?...E7
45 Reilly's en la Esquina................................ C6
46 Tabacos y Vinos C4

Q50/30; ⊙8:30am-5pm Mon-Fri, 8:30am-3pm Sat) A sprawling coffee plantation outside Jocotenango, La Azotea features a complex of three museums. The **Museo del Café** covers the history and process of coffee cultivation; the **Casa K'ojom** holds a superb collection of traditional Maya musical instruments, masks, paintings and other artifacts; and the **Rincón de Sacatepéquez** displays the multicolored outfits and crafts of the Antigua valley.

 ACTIVITIES

La Tortilla   Cooking
(Map p100; ☑4181-8227; www.latortillacook ingschools.com; 3 Calle Poniente 25; lessons Q225-375) This excellent cooking school runs classes twice a day at 10:30am and 4:30pm. The personable instructors guide you through classes from a 90-minute one covering two dishes, to a three-hour lesson

with six dishes from mains and sides to dessert (and unlimited wine).

Old Town Outfitters   Adventure Sports
(Map p100; ☑5399-0440; www.adventureguate mala.com; 5a Av Sur 12C) 🚴 Mountain biking, rock climbing, kayaking and trekking are among the high-energy activities offered by this respected and highly responsible operator, which works with guides from local communities.

TOURS

INGUAT-authorized guides around Parque Central offer city walking tours, with visits to convents, ruins and museums, for around Q80 per person. Similar guided walks are offered daily by Antigua travel agencies such as **Atitrans** (http://atitrans. net). Also on offer are trips to the surrounding villages and coffee plantations.

Antigua Tours
Walking

(Map p100; ☑7832-5821; www.antiguatours.
net; 3a Calle Oriente 22; tour incl museum fees
Q190) Elizabeth Bell, historian and author of
various books on Antigua, leads excellent three-hour cultural walking tours of
the town (in English and/or Spanish) on
Tuesday, Wednesday, Friday and Saturday
mornings. Reservations can be made
through the office or inside Café Condesa
on Parque Central.

De la Gente
Tour

(☑5585-4450; www.dlgcoffee.org; tour per
person, min 2 people) Q200) ✔ This NGO,
based in San Miguel Escobar, works toward
improving the lot of local farmers and
artisans through sustainable economic
development and direct trade. Tours, led
by growers themselves (with translator if
needed), focus on coffee growing and pro-
cessing. At the end participants are guided
through traditional roasting methods and
share a cup with the family.

Other options include making your own
peanut butter in the home of a local peanut
farmer, or making *pepián* stew (indigenous

dish of chicken or pork in sesame sauce)
and tortillas in a Guatemalan kitchen. Tours
should be booked at least a day in advance.

🔒 SHOPPING
Woven and leather goods, ironwork,
paintings and jade jewelry are some of the
items to look for in Antigua's various shops
and markets. For beautiful *típico* (typical)
fabrics, first get educated at the **Casa del
Tejido Antiguo** (Map p91; ☑7832-3169; www.
casadeltejido.org; 0 Av 4-16, San Antonio Aguas
Calientes; Q15; ⊙9am-5pm Mon-Fri, to 4pm Sat),
then have a look around Nim Po't (p103) or
the big handicrafts markets near the bus
terminal and next to Iglesia El Carmen.

Nim Po't
Arts & Crafts

(Map p100; ☑7832-2681; www.nimpotexport.
com; 5a Av Norte 29; ⊙9am-9pm Sun-Thu, to
10pm Fri & Sat) This brilliant, sprawling depot
has a huge collection of Maya clothing, as
well as hundreds of masks, wood carvings,
kites, refrigerator magnets, assorted
Maximón figurines, and local coffee and
chocolate. The *huipiles* (tunics), *cortes*

Nim Po't

The most exciting time to be in Antigua is during **Semana Santa** (Holy Week; ⊙ Easter week), when hundreds of devotees garbed in deep purple robes bear revered icons from their churches in daily street processions in remembrance of Christ's crucifixion. Have Antigua room reservations well in advance of Semana Santa, or plan to stay in Guatemala City and commute to the festivities.

From left: Preparing dyed sawdust for Semana Santa; Semana Santa procession (right and far right)

(fabric) and other garments are arranged by region, so it makes for a fascinating visit whether you're buying or not.

Market
Market

(Map p100; Calz de Santa Lucía Sur; ⊙6am-6pm Mon, Thu & Sat, 7am-6pm Tue, Wed & Fri, 7am-1pm Sun) Antigua's market – chaotic, colorful and always busy – sprawls north of 4a Calle Poniente. The best days are the official market days (Monday, Thursday and especially Saturday), when villagers from the vicinity roll in and spread their wares north and west of the main market building.

La Casa del Jade
Jewelry

(Map p100; www.lacasadeljade.com; 4a Calle Oriente 10; ⊙9am-6pm) More than just a jewelry shop, the Casa has a small museum displaying dozens of pre-Hispanic jade pieces and an open workshop where you can admire the work of contemporary craftspeople. It's inside the Casa Antigua El Jaulón shopping arcade.

Mercado del Carmen
Arts & Crafts

(Map p100; cnr 3a Calle Oriente & 3a Av Norte; ⊙9am-6pm) Next to the ruins of the Iglesia

El Carmen, this excellent market is a good place to browse for textiles, pottery and jade, particularly on weekends, when activity spills out onto 3a Av Norte. The inside is a warren of individual stalls, so take your time to find the treasure you're after.

⊗ EATING

Antigua has possibly the widest range of eating options in Guatemala. All major international cuisines are represented here, as well as plenty of good local and Central American food, at all price points.

Luna de Miel
Crêpes $

(Map p100; ☎7882-4559; www.lunademie-lantigua.com; 6a Av Norte 40; crepes Q34-55; ⊙10am-9:30pm Mon & Tue, 9am-9:30pm Wed-Sun; 🛜) Loungey Luna de Miel offers dozens of savory and sweet variations on the classic crepe – try the *chapín* version stuffed with avocado, cheese and fried tomatoes – plus fabulous tropical smoothies. Eat on the roof deck, amid murals depicting Marilyn Monroe, Yoda and Maradona all

enjoying the same fare. Be prepared for long queues on weekends.

Restaurante Doña Luisa
Cafe $

(Map p100; ☏7832-2578; 4a Calle Oriente 12; sandwiches & breakfast mains Q20-45; ☺7am-9:30pm) Refreshingly local in character, this cafe is a place to enjoy the colonial patio ambience over breakfast or a light meal. It's hard to beat the selection of pastries from the attached bakery; banana bread comes hot from the oven around 2pm daily.

Tienda La Canche
Guatemalan $

(Map p100; 6a Av Norte 42; set lunch Q25; ☺7am-8pm) A hole in the wall if ever there was one, this eatery behind a 'mom and pop' store consists of two tables and a dining room behind the counter. Just a couple of traditional options are prepared daily, such as *pepián de pollo* (a hearty chicken stew), accompanied by thick tortillas. *Frescos*, home-squeezed fruit beverages, are served alongside.

Samsara
Vegetarian $

(Map p100; ☏7832-2200; 6a Calle Poniente 33; breakfast Q26-38, salads around Q40; ☺7am-10pm; ☎🖉) At this small veggie cafe – sitting just the right side of hippie-dom – fresh organic ingredients are excitingly combined in soups, salads and drinks. How about a kale, peanut butter and avocado smoothie? For breakfast there's quinoa porridge or banana and amaranth-seed pancakes, along with French-press coffee and numerous tea blends.

Fernando's Kaffee
Cafe $

(Map p100; ☏7832-6953; www.fernandoskaffee.com; cnr 7a Av Norte & Callejón Camposeco; cinnamon rolls Q10, empanadas Q40; ☺7am-7pm Mon-Sat, noon-7pm Sun; ☎) Long a draw for coffee and chocolate mavens, this friendly corner cafe also bakes an array of fine pastries, including some delightfully gooey cinnamon rolls. Beyond the counter is an inviting patio courtyard ideal for a low-key lazy breakfast. We're not sure if the house cat ever moves from the counter, but it's good at collecting tips and cuddles.

Restaurante Doña Luisa

Rincón Típico Guatemalan $$

(Map p100; 3a Av Sur 3; breakfast Q20, mains Q30; ⊙7am-8pm) This courtyard restaurant is always packed with locals who know a good thing when they see it. If you don't come for the huge Guatemalan breakfast, make it for the chicken cooked over coals with garlicky potatoes or pork *adobado* (pork marinated with paprika and pepper), served up at simple bench tables by never-stopping waitstaff.

Casa Troccoli International $$

(Map p100; ☑7832-0516; cnr 3a Calle Poniente & 5a Av Norte; mains Q90-175; ⊙11:45am-10pm) Front of house at this restaurant looks just like the early-20th-century general store it once was, but with the walls racked with a rather more impressive collection of wine bottles. Amid the period photos and bistro furniture, enjoy superior seafood and meat dishes, including good racks of lamb and local rabbit stew – all washed down with a good glass, of course.

Hector's Bistro French $$

(Map p100; ☑7832-9867; 1a Calle Poniente 9A; mains Q80-175; ⊙noon-10pm) This intimate, candlelit salon across the way from La Merced has just a few tables, with the kitchen behind the bar. Hector, who hails from Guatemala City, has garnered acclaim for his versions of *bœuf bourguignon*, grilled duck breast and so on. There's no proper menu: check the chalkboard for daily specials and the quiche of the week.

Fridas Mexican $$

(Map p100; ☑7832-1296; 5a Av Norte 29; mains Q75-140; ⊙noon-midnight) Dedicated to the eponymous artist, this brightly colored and ever-busy bar-restaurant has an enormous range of tasty Mexican fare, including some of the best soups and tacos in town. There's live music on Thursday and Friday evenings, and a lively, queer-friendly bar upstairs. The restaurant's Frida Kahlo–meets–Patti Smith poster art is inspired.

Cactus Taco Bar Mexican $$

(Map p100; ☑7832-2163; 6a Calle Poniente 21; tacos Q45-60; ⊙11am-11pm) The bright 'Andy

📖 Antigua's History

Antigua was Spain's epicenter of power in Central America, and during the 17th and 18th centuries little expense was spared on the city's architecture, despite the ominous rumbles from the ground below. Indigenous labor was marshaled to erect schools, hospitals, churches and monasteries, their grandeur only rivaled by the houses of the upper clergy and the politically connected.

At its peak, Antigua had 38 churches, as well as a university, printing presses, a newspaper, and a lively cultural and political scene. Those rumblings never stopped, though, and for a year the city was shaken by earthquakes and tremors until the devastating earthquake of July 29, 1773.

Antigua was evacuated and plundered, and orders were given for its inhabitants to relocate and for the city to be dismantled. It was never completely abandoned, though. Fueled by a coffee boom early in the next century, the town, by then known as La Antigua Guatemala (Old Guatemala), began to grow again.

Unesco designated Antigua a World Heritage site in 1979, and Spanish-language schools began popping up, pulling in foreign students and leading to a cultural renaissance. In recent years, Antigua has become a popular wedding destination, adding to its visitor numbers.

Warhol does Zapata' wall mural at Cactus gives an idea of how it mixes up traditional and new-wave Mexican food, with superb salsas served in clay bowls. The shrimp and bacon tacos are heartily recommended. It's along the nightlife corridor; start the evening with a chili-fringed margarita or a bottle of good craft beer.

El Viejo Café   Cafe $$

(Map p100; ☎7832-1576; www.elviejocafe. com; 3a Calle Poniente 12; breakfasts from Q25, mains from Q50; ⏲7am-9pm; 🛜🍽) Popular with tourists and *chapines* (Guatemalans) alike, this atmospheric cafe strewn with antique curios makes an ideal breakfast stop. Choose from an array of fresh-baked croissants and well-roasted Guatemalan coffees, and settle into a window nook to start your day.

Caffé Mediterráneo   Italian $$

(Map p100; ☎7882-7180; 6a Calle Poniente 6A; mains Q90-140; ⏲noon-3pm & 6-10pm Wed-Sat & Mon, noon-4:30pm & 7-9pm Sun) Here you'll find the finest, most authentic Italian food in Antigua, plus superb service, in a lovely candlelit setting. The chef does a tanta-lizing array of salads, homemade pasta and delicately prepared carpaccio, using seasonally available ingredients.

Mesón Panza Verde   Fusion $$$

(Map p100; ☎7832-2925; www.panzaverde.com; 5a Av Sur 19; mains Q150-200; ⏲6-10pm Mon, noon-3pm & 6-10pm Tue-Sun) The restaurant of the exclusive B&B **Mesón Panza Verde** (☎7955-8282; www.panzaverde.com; 5a Av Sur 19; r/ste from Q950/1700; 🅿@🛜🏊) dishes up divine continental cuisine in an appealing Antiguan atmosphere. The menu features an eclectic global lineup, with the French-trained chef putting an emphasis on fresh seafood and organic ingredients. Live music (jazz, Cuban) enhances the ambience Wednesday to Saturday nights, while locals turn out for the popular Sunday brunch buffet (10am to 2pm).

🔅 DRINKING & NIGHTLIFE

The bar scene jumps, especially on Friday and Saturday evenings when the hordes roll in from Guatemala City for some Antigua-style revelry. Besides the watering

From left: Traditional Maya textiles; Maya wooden masks

holes, the restaurants Fridas (p107) and **Bistrot Cinq** (Map p100; 7832-5510; www. bistrotcinq.com; 4a Calle Oriente 7; mains Q140-220; noon-10:30pm) are at least as popular for the cocktails as the cuisine. Start drinking early and save: *cuba libres* and mojitos are half price between 5pm and 8pm at many bars.

Antigua Brewing Company   Bar
(Map p100; 3a Calle Poniente 4; 11am-10pm Sun-Thu, 11am-1am Fri & Sat) Put your Gallo beer down for one moment and get to the forefront of Guatemala's craft-brewing revolution at the Antigua Brewing Company. Sup its signature Fuego IPA while looking out to Volcán Agua from the roof terrace, or try a flight of beers (Q75) ranging from Belgian blondes to rich coffee stouts.

Café No Sé   Bar
(Map p100; www.cafenose.com; 1a Av Sur 11C; 2pm-1am) Something of a local institution, this downbeat little bar is a point of reference for Antigua's budding young Burroughses and Kerouacs. It's also the core of a lively music scene, with players wailing

Purchasing Jade

Several Antigua shops specialize in jade; to discern the genuine article, look for translucency, purity, intensity of color and the absence of flaws – and ask if you can scratch the stone with a pocket knife: if it scratches, it's not true jadeite, but an inferior stone.

from a corner of the room most evenings. Be sure to try its home-brand legal Mezcal.

El Barrio   Pub
(Map p100; 5658-9028; 4a Av Norte 3; 4:30pm-1am) Just off Parque Central, this sprawling bar tavern has wall-length sofas, murals of literary and sports heroes, and board games. Upstairs is a popular and lively rooftop bar. Round up a gang for the trivia nights, but take care if you overindulge: we're never too sure about a bar that has its own tattoo parlor at the back.

Street market in Santa Maria de Jesus (p95)

LUCY BROWN · LOCAMOTION/SHUTTERSTOCK ©

Por Qué No? Pub

(Map p100; ☎4324-5407; www.porquenocafe.com; cnr 2a Av Sur & 9a Calle Oriente; ⊙6-10pm Mon-Sat) This alternative cafe is a vertically oriented space that takes up an absurdly narrow corner of an old building (grab the rope to reach the upper level). Vintage bric-a-brac hangs from the rafters and every surface is scrawled with guest-generated graffiti. The vibe is relaxed and conversational, and a crowd spills out the door each evening.

Reilly's en la Esquina Irish Pub

(Map p100; ☎7832-6251; 6a Calle Poniente 7; ⊙noon-12:30am) Holding a key corner of Antigua's nightlife corridor, Reilly's packs in both Guatemalans and gringos on weekends. The sprawling pub has several bars, but most of the action focuses on the central patio. Midweek it's mellower, with the billiards table, pub grub and Guinness on tap pulling in a faithful following. Particularly good when there's a big sporting event.

Tabacos y Vinos Wine Bar

(Map p100; 5a Av Norte 28B; ⊙10am-11pm) Tucked right next to the Santa Catalina arch is this small but perfectly formed wine bar with an extensively sourced cellar. Wine by the glass starts at Q35, but if you keep with the same bottle it gets cheaper with each refill. The bar is no smoking but it also has a wide selection of cigars, as well as local chocolates and coffee.

☻ ENTERTAINMENT

Many bars and restaurants have live music, especially at weekends.

Café No Sé (p109), **Angie Angie** (Map p100; ☎7832-3352; 1a Av Sur 11A; empanadas 2 for Q30, mains Q65-95; ⊙noon-11pm Wed-Mon), the **Rainbow Café** (Map p100; ☎7832-1919; www.rainbowcafeantigua.com; 7a Av Sur 8; mains Q40-60; ⊙8am-10pm; ☑) and Mesón Panza Verde (p108) host regular folk, rock and jazz performances.

Mesón Panza Verde (p108)

INFORMATION

The following banks around Parque Central all change US dollars and euros, and have Visa/MasterCard ATMs:

Bac Credomatic (Portal del Comercio, facing Parque Central)

Banco Agromercantil (4a Calle Poniente 8; ⊘9am-7pm Mon-Fri, to 5pm Sat & Sun)

Banco Industrial (5a Av Sur 4; ⊘9am-7pm Mon-Fri, to 1pm Sat)

Citibank (cnr 4a Calle Oriente & 4a Av Norte; ⊘9am-4:30pm Mon-Fri, 9:30am-1pm Sat)

ⓘ GETTING THERE & AWAY

Buses (Map p100; cnr 5a Calle Poniente & Calle de Recoletos) from Guatemala City arrive and depart from a street just south of the market, across from the Mercado de Artesanías. Antigua is off the major through-highways, so for most onward travel you'll need to head to the nearby junction towns of Chimaltenango or Escuintla and change there. Buses for these depart from the main **bus terminal** (Map p100; Av de la Recolección).

If you're planning to drive out of town on a reportedly hijack-prone road (such as to Panajachel via Patzún), you may request an escort from **Proatur** (☑5578-9835; operacionesproatur@inguat.gob.gt; 6a Calle Poniente Final; ⊘24hr) by emailing them at least 72 hours in advance. There's no fee other than the escort's expenses.

Antigua's many travel agencies (and every hotel and hostel) sell tickets for tourist shuttles. They cost more than buses, but are comfortable and convenient, with door-to-door pick-up and drop-off. Cross-border shuttles include those to Copán (Honduras) and Belize City.

Earth Lodge

High in the hills above Jocotenango, **Earth Lodge** (☑5664-0713; www.earthlodgeguatemala.com; dm Q65, s/d cabin Q200/280;) ✔ is an extraordinary 40-acre spread set around a working avocado farm, and its views of the Panchoy valley and volcanoes are truly mesmerizing. Developed and overseen by an affable couple, the ecofriendly retreat offers plenty to do: hiking trails, birdwatching, yoga sessions, a *chuj* (Maya sauna) or just hanging in a hammock.

TG23/SHUTTERSTOCK ©

ⓘ GETTING AROUND

To park on the street in Antigua, you must have a *marbete* (label) hanging from your rearview mirror, or risk a fine. Purchase these from traffic cops stationed on the entry roads into Antigua for Q10.

Taxis wait where the Guatemala City buses stop and on the east side of Parque Central. An in-town taxi ride costs Q25 to Q30. *Tuk-tuks* are Q5 to Q15. Note that *tuk-tuks* are not allowed in the center of town, so you'll have to hike a few blocks out to find one; they do not operate after 8pm.

In this Chapter
Lake Communities.............................. 114
Volcán San Pedro 118
Panajachel 120
Sights 120
Activities...120
Tours 121
Eating...121
Drinking & Nightlife 124

Lago de Atitlán

Nineteenth-century traveler/chronicler John L Stephens, writing in Incidents of Travel in Central America, *called Lago de Atitlán 'the most magnificent spectacle we ever saw,' and he had been around a bit. Today even seasoned travelers marvel at this incredible environment. Fishers in rustic crafts ply the lake's aquamarine surface; fertile hills dot the landscape; and over everything loom the volcanoes, permeating the entire area with a mysterious beauty. It never looks the same twice. No wonder outsiders tend to fall in love with the place and stay awhile.*

Two Days in Lago de Atitlán

Arrive in **Panajachel** (p120), shop and eat, and stop by **Casa Cakchiquel** (p120) to witness early images of Atitlán. Take off for one of the other villages around the lake – perhaps backpackers' favorite **San Pedro La Laguna** (p114) or quieter **San Juan La Laguna** (p115). Regardless of where you end up, spend at least half a day exploring 'your' village.

Four Days in Lago de Atitlán

On days three and four, hop on a boat to check out some of the quieter, more traditional Maya villages around the lake. There's **Santiago Atitlán** (p116), where the curious deity Maximón awaits, or **San Marcos La Laguna** (p116), a laid-back magnet for yoga and natural-healing types. **Santa Cruz La Laguna** (p117), meanwhile, is just plain tiny and gorgeous.

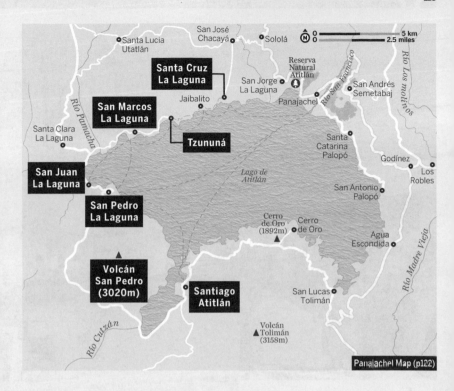

Panajachel Map (p122)

Arriving in Lago de Atitlán

Getting around the lake is easily accomplished by frequent *lancha* (motorboat) service, though some towns are linked by road as well. San Pedro, the most visited of the lakeside villages, has two docks. One serves boats going to/ from Santiago Atitlán; the other serves Panajachel. Most of the tourism activity is in the lower part of town, between and on either side of the two docks.

Where to Stay

Affordable accommodations are prevalent around the lake, with good hostels at San Pedro, Santa Cruz, Jaibalito and San Marcos. For those with deeper pockets, paradisiacal properties await along the lake banks south of Panajachel, east of Santa Cruz and at Santiago Atitlán, most of which adhere to strict ecological standards.

San Pedro La Laguna

Lake Communities

Around the volcano-fringed, blue-mirrored Lago de Atitlán, there's an eclectic array of lakeside towns and villages to stay in and visit according to your taste. Some towns are busier than others, some are all about ecofriendliness and yoga, and one's a backpacker party hub. The choice is yours.

Great For...

☑ Don't Miss

Spanish classes in San Pedro – four hours of one-on-one lessons (five days a week) are a steal at Q900.

San Pedro La Laguna

Spreading onto a peninsula at the base of the volcano of the same name, San Pedro remains among the most visited of the lakeside villages – due as much to its reasonably priced accommodations and global social scene as to its spectacular setting. It's a backpacker haven – travelers tend to dig in here for a spell, in pursuit of (in no particular order) drinking, fire-twirling, African drumming, Spanish classes, volcano hiking, hot-tub soaking, partying and hammock swinging.

While this scene unfolds around the lakefront, up the hill San Pedro follows more traditional rhythms. Clad in indigenous outfits, the predominantly Tz'utujil *pedranos* (as the locals are called) congregate around the market zone. You'll see coffee being picked on the volcano's slopes and

Weaving in San Juan La Laguna

KOBBY DAGAN/SHUTTERSTOCK ©

❶ Need to Know

Robberies sometimes occur along the lake paths. Proatur (p124) can fill you in on the current situation.

✗ Take a Break

Try dozens of cheeses or a platter of house-smoked meats at San Juan La Laguna's divine Café El Artesano (p115).

★ Top Tip

There are enough activities – from paragliding and kayaking to hiking the glorious lakeshore trails – to stay a while.

spread out to dry on wide platforms at the beginning of the dry season.

San Pedro is making a name for itself in the language game with ultra-economical rates at its various Spanish institutes. **Community Spanish School** (☏5466-7177; www.communityspanishschool.com) and **San Pedro Spanish School** (☏5715-4604; www.sanpedrospanishschool.org; 7a Av 2-20) are the top choices.

San Juan La Laguna

San Juan La Laguna is just 2km west by road from busy San Pedro, on a rise above a spectacular bay, but this neat, mellow village has escaped many of the excesses of its neighbor, and some travelers find it a more tranquil setting in which to study Spanish or experience local life. San Juan is special: the Tz'utujil inhabitants take pride

in their craft traditions – particularly painting and weaving – and have developed their own tourism infrastructure to highlight their culture to outsiders.

Perhaps part of what makes it all run so well is the communal spirit: coffee growers, fishers, organic farmers, natural dyers and widows are among the like-minded groups who've formed cooperatives here.

As you wander around the village, you'll notice various murals depicting aspects of Tz'utujil life and legend.

Take note that San Juan features one of Guatemala's most truly indulgent culinary experiences in Swiss-influenced **Café El Artesano** (☏4555-4773; Salida a Guatemala; cheese or smoked meat platter Q125, sharing platters per person Q110; ☺noon-4pm Mon-Fri), while absolutely organic meals are made at the ecolodge **Mayachik'** (☏4218-4675; www.mayachik.com; dm Q70, bungalows Q140-350; [P] [☎]) ✦.

Santiago Atitlán

Santiago Atitlán is the largest of the lake communities, with a strong indigenous identity. Many *atitecos* (as its people are known) proudly adhere to a traditional Tz'utujil Maya lifestyle. Women wear purple-striped skirts and *huipiles* embroidered with colored birds and flowers, while older men still wear lavender or maroon striped embroidered pants. The town's *cofradías* (brotherhoods) maintain the syncretic traditions and rituals of Maya Catholicism. There's a large arts and crafts scene here too. Boatbuilding is a local industry, and rows of rough-hewn *cayucos* (dugout canoes) are lined up along the shore. The liveliest days to visit are Friday and Sunday, the main market days, but any day will do.

Santiago is worth a trip to visit the home of the Maya spirit Maximón (mah-shee-mohn). He changes house every year, but he's easy enough to find by asking around (would-be guides will approach you at the dock).

San Marcos La Laguna

One of the prettiest of the lakeside villages, San Marcos La Laguna lives a double life. The mostly Maya community occupies the higher ground, while expats and visitors cover a flat jungly patch toward the shoreline with paths snaking through banana, coffee and avocado trees. The two converge under the spreading *matapalo* (strangler fig) tree of the central plaza.

San Marcos has become a magnet for global seekers, who believe the place has a spiritual energy that's conducive to learning and practicing meditation, holistic therapies, massage, Reiki and other

Boats on the shore, Santa Cruz La Laguna

spiritually oriented activities. It's an outlandish mélange of cultures – evangelical Christians, self-styled shamans, Kaqchiquel farmers and visionary artists – against a backdrop of incredible natural beauty.

Whatever you're into, it's a great spot to kick back and distance the everyday world for a spell. Lago de Atitlán is beautiful and clean here, and you can swim off the rocks.

Tzununá

Tzununá, located 2km east of San Marcos by a paved road, has seen a bit of a

> ### ✕ Take a Break
>
> Sample traditional Guatemalan dishes at **Café Sabor Cruceño** (www.amigos desantacruz.org; breakfast Q32-45, lunch Q35-50; ⊙8am-5pm Mon-Sat) in Santa Cruz La Laguna.

LUCY BROWN (LOCA4MOTION)/ALAMY STOCK PHOTO ©

gringo incursion in recent years. But this Kaqchiquel village ('Hummingbird of the Water') still retains a strong indigenous character and a lush natural beauty with year-round rivers springing from forested mountain slopes. Women in scarlet *huipiles* tread the paths between traditionally managed groves of coffee, avocados, bananas and *jocote* (tropical fruit). Whereas foreign travelers head for San Pedro to party or San Marcos to meditate, many who come here are into sustainable agriculture, which they can study at **Atitlán Organics** (☑4681-4697; www.atitlanorganics.com).

Santa Cruz La Laguna

Santa Cruz fits the typically dual nature of the Atitlán villages, comprising both a waterfront resort (home of the lake's scuba-diving outfit) and an indigenous Kaqchiquel village. The village is about 600m uphill from the dock (there are *tuktuks* – three-wheeled motor taxies – if you don't fancy the stiff walk). It's a lovely spot, with relaxing accommodations, activities on the water and a complete lack of hustle.

> ### ★ Top Tip
>
> Emanating primarily from the lakeside towns of Santiago Atitlán, San Pedro La Laguna and San Juan La Laguna, Tz'utujil oil painting has a distinctive primitivist style, with depictions of rural life, local traditions and landscapes in vibrant colors. If you've got more than a passing interest, consider taking the 'Maya Artists & Artisans' tour offered by **Posada Los Encuentros** (☑7762-1603; www.losencuentros.com; Callejón Chotzar 0-41; s/d incl breakfast from Q300/340; ☎) in Panajachel.

Lago de Atitlán and Volcán San Pedro

SIMON DANNHAUER/SHUTTERSTOCK ©

Volcán San Pedro

Looming above the eponymous village, Volcán San Pedro (3020m) almost demands to be climbed by anyone with an adventurous spirit and a reasonable level of fitness. It is the most accessible of the three volcanoes in the zone and, classified as a municipal ecological park, it's regularly patrolled by tourism police.

Great For...

☑ Don't Miss

Also tackling the hill referred to as Indian Nose – its skyline resembles the profile of a Maya dignitary.

Though volcanic explosions have been going on here for millions of years, today's landscape has its origins in the massive eruption of 85,000 years ago, termed Los Chocoyos, which blew volcanic ash as far away as Florida and Panama. The quantity of magma expelled from below the earth's crust caused the surface terrain to collapse, forming a huge, roughly circular hollow that soon filled with water – Lago de Atitlán. Smaller volcanoes rose out of the lake's southern waters thousands of years later: Volcán San Pedro (today 3020m above sea level) about 60,000 years ago, followed by Volcán Atitlán (3537m) and Volcán Tolimán (3158m). The lake today is 8km across from north to south, 18km from east to west, and averages around 300m in depth, though the water level has been on the rise since 2009.

❶ Need to Know

The ascent is through fields of maize, beans and squash, followed by primary cloud forest. It's a three- to four-hour climb and two hours back down.

✕ Take a Break

Celebrate the climb with a shot of locally grown coffee from **Café Las Cristalinas** (⊙7am-9pm; 🛜) in San Pedro.

★ Top Tip

Start the climb at dawn and be sure to carry water, snacks, a hat and sunblock.

you may observe eight volcanoes, and learn how they came to stand in a line and how Lago de Atitlán was formed. Overnight trips to Santiaguito, Fuego and Pacaya (all active volcanoes) are also offered, for around Q700 per person.

Volcano Climbing Guides

Guides are required for the volcano ascent, and will take you up from San Pedro for around Q130, including entrance fee.

Asoantur (☑4379-4545; www.facebook. com/asoantur; 4a Av A 3-60; ⊙7am-7pm) is an association of 16 INGUAT-authorized guides from the local community, some of whom speak English. The guides lead expeditions up Volcán San Pedro (or, alternatively, up Indian Nose), and they also offer cultural tours of San Pedro and nearby coffee plantations, and kayak, bicycle and motorbike rentals. The association operates from a hut just up from the Pana dock.

Geo Travel (☑3168-8625; www.geotravel guatemala.com) offers tours from geology experts, focusing on the natural environment. One popular tour ascends before dawn to Indian Nose (Q200 per person), from which

Other Atitlán Hiking Options

A less daunting day hike than the massive volcanoes in the vicinity, **Cerro de Oro** (1892m) still yields great views and features several Maya ceremonial sites. It's some 8km northeast, about halfway between Santiago and San Lucas Tolimán.

Another worthy destination is the **Mirador de Tepepul**, about 4km south of Santiago, near where the inlet ends. The hike goes through cloud forest populated with many birds, including parakeets, curassows, swifts, boat-tailed grackles and tucanets, and on to a lookout point with views all the way to the coast.

Panajachel

The busiest and most built-up lakeside town, Panajachel ('Pana') is the gateway to Lago de Atitlán for most travelers. Aside from the astounding volcano panorama, the town's excellent transportation connections, copious accommodations, varied restaurants and thumping nightlife make it a favorite destination for weekending Guatemalans.

◎ SIGHTS

Reserva Natural Atitlán   Park

(Map p113; ☎7762-2565; www.atitlanreserva.com; adult/child Q50/25; ☺8am-5pm) A former coffee plantation being reclaimed by natural vegetation, this reserve is 200m past the Hotel Atitlán on the northern outskirts of town. It makes a good outing on foot or bicycle. You can leisurely walk the main trail in an hour: it leads up over swing bridges to a waterfall, then down to a platform for viewing local spider monkeys.

La Galería   Gallery

(Map p122; ☎7762-2432; www.galeria-panajachel.com; Calle Rancho Grande; ☺9am-noon &

2-6pm Wed-Mon) FREE Overflowing with art by Guatemalan painters and sculptors, this gallery functions as both an exhibit space and cultural center, hosting lectures, films and occasional concerts. Started in 1971 by the German-K'iche' painter Nan Cuz, the gallery holds a number of the hallucinatory landscapes that garnered Cuz international acclaim.

Casa Cakchiquel   Arts Center

(Map p122; ☎7762-0969; Calle 14 de Febrero; ☺7am-8pm) Pana's cultural center started life as one of the first hotels on the lake, built by a Swedish countess in 1948. Now it holds a radio station, Japanese restaurant and a tremendous little gallery of photos and postcards of Atitlán in simpler times, when steamboats plied the lake.

✦ ACTIVITIES

RealWorld Paragliding   Gliding

(Map p122; ☎5634-5699; www.realworldparagliding.jimdo.com; Calle Santander, Centro Comercial San Rafael; tandem flights Q700) The lake has become a center for paragliding

From left: Worry dolls; handmade *huipiles* (tunics) at a market

enthusiasts and RealWorld Paragliding provides tandem flights, with passengers seated in a canvas chair attached to the flier's harness so you're free to take photos or simply gaze in amazement at the panorama below.

Pana Surf Paddleboarding

(Map p122; per hour Q100) The surf aspect of this outfit's name might be a bit out of place on such a placid lake, but it will rent you a paddleboard to explore from Pana, and donate the proceeds to local health and animal welfare charities.

TOURS

Posada Los Encuentros Tours

(Map p122; ✆7762-2093; www.losencuentros. com; Callejón Chotzar 0-41) Offers half- and full-day educational tours to lakeside villages, focusing on such topics as Maya medicine, Tz'utujil oil painting and organic coffee cultivation. Guide Richard Morgan is a scholar of Maya history and culture, and a longtime lake resident. Hiking tours and volcano climbs are also offered.

Roger's Tours Adventure Sports

(Map p122; ✆7762-6060; www.rogerstours. com; Calle Santander; bike rental per hour/day Q35/170) This outfit rents out quality mountain bikes and leads a variety of cycling tours (Q450 per person including helmet, guide and lunch). One tour travels by boat from Panajachel to Tzununá, then by bike west via dirt trail to San Marcos La Laguna and road to San Pedro La Laguna, finally returning to Pana by boat.

EATING

There are plenty of restaurants lining Calle Santander, which swells in the late afternoon and evening with taco stalls and other cheap street eats. Near the south end of Calle del Lago, there is a cluster of thatched-roof restaurants crowding the lakefront. All serve the local specialties of lake *mojarra* (perch) and black bass.

Chero's Bar Salvadoran $

(Map p122; Av Los Árboles; pupusas Q10; ⊙12:30pm-1am Tue-Sat) Usefully located in the nightlife zone, Chero's can get pretty

Bright-colored entrance sign at Reserva Natural Atitlán

Panajachel

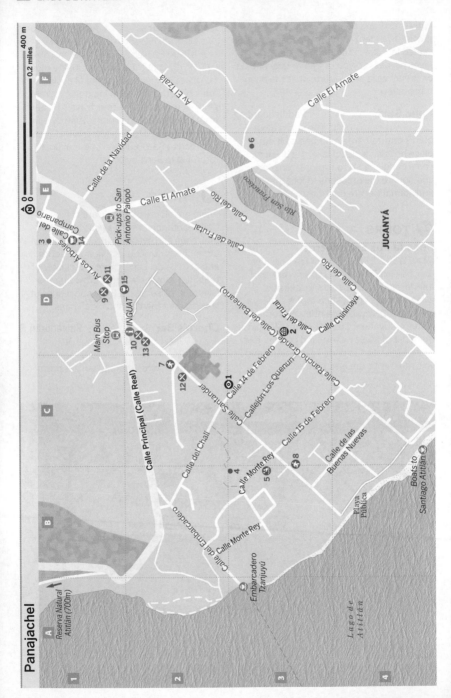

Reserva Natural Atitlán (700m)

Calle Principal (Calle Real)

Av Los Árboles

Av El Tzalá

Calle de la Navidad

Calle El Amate

Calle El Amate

Pick-ups to San Antonio Palopó

Calle del Campanario

Calle del Río

Calle del Río

Río San Francisco

Calle del Frutal

Calle del Frutal

Calle del Balneario

Calle Chinimaya

Calle del Río

Calle Rancho Grande

Calle 14 de Febrero

Calle Santander

Callejón Los Quenun

Calle 15 de Febrero

Calle de las Buenas Nuevas

Calle Monte Rey

Calle del Chalí

Calle del Embarcadero

Calle Monte Rey

Embarcadero Tzanjuyú

Playa Pública

Lago de Atitlán

Boats to Santiago Atitlán

JUCANYÁ

Main Bus Stop

INGUAT

400 m

0.2 miles

Panajachel

⊙ **Sights**
1 Casa Cakchiquel C3
2 La Galería D3

⊕ **Activities, Courses & Tours**
3 Jabel Tinamit E1
4 Jardín de América B3
5 Pana Surf B3
6 Posada Los Encuentros E3
7 RealWorld Paragliding C2
8 Roger's Tours C3

⊗ **Eating**
9 Chero's Bar D1
10 Chez Alex D2
11 Circus Bar D1
12 El Patio C2
13 Mister Jon's D2
   Restaurante Hana .... (see 1)

⊙ **Drinking & Nightlife**
14 Crossroads Café E1
15 La Palapa D2

lively, with beer-drinking patrons gathering around simple wood tables as *tuk-tuks* zip by. Salvadoran staff slap out *pupusas* (cornmeal flatbread), either straight up or filled with such items as *güicoy* (a kind of squash) or the spinach-like herb *chipilín*, and served with the customary pickled cabbage and salsa.

Circus Bar   Italian $$
(Map p122; ☑7762-2056; www.facebook.com/circusbargt; Av Los Árboles; pizzas Q30-130; ⊘noon-midnight) Behind the swinging doors, Circus Bar has a cabaret atmosphere, with live music nightly from 7:30pm to 10:30pm. There is good pizza and even better pasta, plus a respectable wine list and imported liquors. Flamenco, folk or marimbas nicely complement the cozy atmosphere.

El Patio   Guatemalan $$
(Map p122; ☑7762-2041; Plaza Los Patios, Calle Santander; mains Q30-60; ⊘7am-9:30pm) This is a locally popular joint for lunch; the front terrace makes an obvious meeting place. Try to make it for Monday lunch when everyone chows down on *caldo de res* (chunky broth), served with all the trimmings.

Restaurante Hana   Japanese $$
(Map p122; ☑4298-1415; www.restaurantehana. com; Calle 14 de Febrero; mains Q65-85; ⊘noon-9pm Tue-Sun) Serving authentic Japanese cuisine, Hana is ensconced in the serene courtyard of the Casa Cakchiquel (p120), graced by hanging plants and a gallery of photos of old Pana. Besides preparing such

classics as nigiri sushi, sashimi and tempura, Chef Mihoko does *uramaki* ('inside-out' sushi), *donburi* (rice bowls) and cold udon noodles just as they're done in her native Japan.

Mister Jon's   American $$
(Map p122; ☑4710-8697; www.mister-jon.com; Calle Santander; breakfast Q35-50; ⊘7am-10pm Tue-Sun; 🛜) All the perks of a US diner are here in abundance, including buttermilk pancakes, great omelets with hash browns or country biscuits on the side, and free

Language Courses

Jabel Tinamit (Map p122; ☑7762-6056; www.jabeltinamit.com; cnr Av de Los Árboles & Callejón Las Armonías; per week Q980, homestay per week additional Q650) is a professionally run language institute near the center of town, though it feels serene and secluded with a lovely garden and rooftop terrace for instruction, plus an extensive video library of Spanish-language documentaries.

Jardín de América (Map p122; ☑7762-2637; www.jardindeamerica.com; Calle del Chalí) is a well set-up school with tables set in shady gardens and a good atmosphere. Four hours of one-on-one study five days per week costs Q880 per week, with the option of staying with a local family (Q880) or rooming at the institute (Q440).

Panajachel Souvenirs

Calle Santander is lined with booths, stores and complexes that sell (among other things) traditional Maya clothing, colorful blankets, leather goods and wood carvings. Otherwise, head for the traditional market building in the town center, which is busiest on Sundays when every square meter of ground alongside is occupied by vendors in indigenous garb.

Handmade bags
ALEKSANDAR TODOROVIC/SHUTTERSTOCK ©

coffee refills (of Guatemala's finest). But it's no gringo ghetto – *chapines* (Guatemalans) who've been up north like it too.

Chez Alex   European $$$

(Map p122; ☑7762-0172; www.primaveraatitlan.com; Hotel Primavera, Calle Santander; mains Q95-180; ☺noon-10pm) The restaurant component of the **Hotel Primavera** (☑7762-2052; www.primaveraatitlan.com; Calle Santander; s/d/tr from Q225/300/375; ☞) serves some of Pana's finest cuisine, with a hefty dash of European influence and a wine list to back it up. After a meal of mussels in white-wine sauce or Camembert-stuffed schnitzel, kick back with a Habana cigar.

🍸 DRINKING & NIGHTLIFE

Panajachel's miniature Zona Viva (party zone) focuses on Av Los Árboles. Especially at weekends, it seems as if every other restaurant on Calle Santander has live music.

Crossroads Café   Cafe

(Map p122; ☑5292-8439; www.crossroadscafepana.com; Calle del Campanario 0-27; ☺9am-1pm & 2:30-6pm Tue-Sat) This cafe has made Panajachel a major crossroads for coffee aficionados. When he's not roasting beans, the Bay Area owner/head barista spends his time combing the highlands for small estate coffees to add to his roster, including the tangy Acatenango Eighth Wonder and smooth Huehue Organic.

La Palapa   Pub

(Map p122; Calle Principal; ☺9am-1am) As the name suggests, this party center unfolds beneath a thatched-roof shelter (actually two), with a beachy ambience. It's popular with volunteer gringos, but all sorts crowd in for the Saturday afternoon BBQ. Other diversions include weekend live music, trivia quiz nights and sports TV at all times.

ℹ️ INFORMATION

5B ATM Visa/MasterCard ATM.

Banco de América Central (Calle Santander, Centro Comercial San Rafael; ☺9am-5pm Mon-Fri, 9am-1pm Sat) Reliable ATM; Visa, American Express and MasterCard cash advances.

Banco Industrial (Calle Santander, Comercial Los Pinos; ☺9am-4pm Mon-Fri, 9am-1pm Sat) Visa/MasterCard ATM.

INGUAT (Map p122; ☑2421-2953; info-pana@inguat.gob.gt; Calle Principal 1-47; ☺9am-5pm) This tourist office is opposite the main bus stop on Calle Principal. There are lots of leaflets, and usually someone who speaks English to help with inquiries.

Proatur (Programa de Asistencia al Turista; ☑5874-9450; proatur.solola@gmail.com; Calle Rancho Grande; ☺9am-5pm) Tourist advice center.

ℹ️ GETTING THERE & AWAY

BOAT

There are two docks for passengers boats.

LUCY BROWN - LOCAAMOTION/SHUTTERSTOCK ©

Lakeside beach area, Panajachel

Boats for Santiago Atitlán (30 minutes) depart from the **Playa Pública** (Map p122) at the foot of Calle Rancho Grande. All other departures leave from the **Embarcadero Tzanjuyú** (Map p122), at the foot of Calle del Embarcadero. From here, *lanchas* go counterclockwise around the lake, with direct (Q25, 25 minutes) and local services to San Pedro La Laguna. The local services stop in Santa Cruz La Laguna (15 minutes), Jaibalito, Tzununá, San Marcos La Laguna (30 minutes), San Juan La Laguna and San Pedro La Laguna (45 minutes). The first boat to San Pedro departs at 7am; the last around 5pm.

One-way passage to San Pedro, Santiago or San Lucas costs Q25. Closer destinations like Santa Cruz shouldn't top Q10.

Lanchas are also available for private hire from the Playa Pública or Embarcadero Tzanjuyú:

expect to pay around Q400 to San Pedro La Laguna.

BUS

Panajachel's **main bus stop** (Map p122; Calle Real) is at the junction of Calles Santander and Principal, immediately west of the Centro Comercial El Dorado. There is a separate stop for minibuses to **San Antonio Palopó** (Map p122).

SHUTTLE MINIBUS

Pretty much every tourist destination you could think of is served by a shuttle minibus. You can book at a number of travel agencies on Calle Santander.

Typical one-way fares include Antigua (Q80), Chichicastenango (round trip Thursday and Sunday Q120), Guatemala City (Q160), Quetzaltenango (Q125) and San Cristóbal de Las Casas, Mexico (Q280).

In this Chapter
Visiting the Site 128
Uaxactún 134
Flores & Santa Elena 136
Sights 136
Tours 136
Eating...136
Drinking & Nightlife..........................138
El Remate 138
Activities 139
Eating...139

Tikal

The remarkably restored Maya temples that stand in this partially cleared corner of the jungle astonish for both their monumental size and architectural brilliance – as an early-morning arrival at the Gran Plaza proves. Occupied for some 16 centuries, they're an amazing testament to the cultural and artistic heights scaled by this jungle civilization. A highlight is the helicopter-like vantage from towering Templo IV on the west edge of the precinct. Equally compelling is the abundance of wildlife, which can be appreciated as you stroll ancient causeways between ceremonial centers.

Two Days in Tikal

For the full experience, you'll want to base yourself in Tikal and dedicate your entire first day to discovering its ruins, with a **guided tour** (p133) in the morning and perhaps a **canopy tour** (p133) in the afternoon. Grab a simple dinner of pasta or hamburgers from the *comedores* along the access road. On day two, bump your way up the unpaved road to **Uaxactún** (p134) with **Roxy Ortiz** (p133) or on the public bus (in which case you'll have to spend the night).

Four Days in Tikal

Return to civilization, base yourself in **Flores and Santa Elena** (p136), and take a day to explore the lakefront promenade, boat around and spot interesting waterfowl. Discuss what you've learned over a delicious meal at **Antojitos Mexicanos** (p137) in Flores or **Mon Ami** (p139) in El Remate. If you're still hungry for history, hop on a tour to **Yaxhá** (p139) on day four.

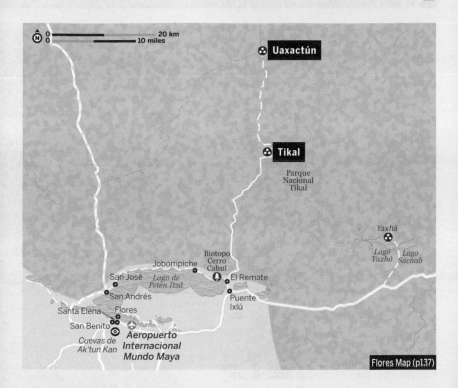

Flores Map (p137)

Arriving in Tikal

Microbuses depart Flores for Tikal between 6:30am and 3pm (Q30 to Q80, 1¼ hours). You could also take the Uaxactún-bound bus from the market of Santa Elena at 3:30pm, which is a bit slower. A daily shuttle connects Tikal and El Remate.

Where to Stay

Staying overnight at Tikal enables you to relax and savor the dawn and dusk. Other than camping, there are only three places to stay, and tour groups often have many of the rooms reserved. Alternative bases include Flores and Santa Elena and El Remate, which have plenty of economical options and a few upscale properties.

Templo II

JAVIER FERNÁNDEZ SÁNCHEZ/GETTY IMAGES ©

Visiting the Site

The dizzying pyramids of Tikal are Guatemala's most famous tourist drawcard. And what's not to love about this mighty monument to Central America's greatest civilization? But those who stop to ask what happened to the Maya are often surprised to learn that Maya culture continues to evolve today.

Tikal is set on a low hill, which becomes evident as you ascend to the Gran Plaza from the entry road. Its many plazas have been cleared of trees and vines, its temples uncovered and partially restored, but as you walk from one building to another you pass beneath a dense canopy of rainforest amid the rich, loamy aromas of earth and vegetation. Much of the delight of touring the site comes from strolling the broad causeways, originally built from packed limestone to accommodate traffic between temple complexes. By stepping softly you're more likely to spot monkeys, agoutis, foxes and ocellated turkeys.

Great For...

☑ Don't Miss

The astounding bird's-eye-view outlook from atop Templo IV.

History

Affording relief from the surrounding swampy ground, this high terrain may explain why the Maya settled here around

Enjoying the view from Templo V

ROB CRANDALL/SHUTTERSTOCK ©

⊙ Need to Know

Tikal (Map p127; ☏2367-2837; www.tikalnationalpark.org; Q150; ⊙6am-6pm)

✕ Take a Break

Choose a snack from the series of little *comedores* (eateries) along the right-hand side of the access road.

★ Top Tip

Tikal is quieter in the late afternoon and early morning, so an overnight stay is a good idea.

700 BC. Within 200 years the Maya of Tikal had begun to build stone ceremonial structures, and by 200 BC there was a complex of buildings on the site of the Acrópolis del Norte.

During the Classic period, the Gran Plaza was beginning to assume its present shape and extent by the time of Christ. By the dawn of the early Classic Period, around AD 250, Tikal had become an important religious, cultural and commercial city with a large population. In the mid-6th century, Tikal's military prowess and its association with Teotihuacán allowed it to grow until it sprawled over 30 sq km and had a population of perhaps 100,000. But in 553, Yajaw Te' K'inich II (Lord Water) came to the throne of Caracol (in southwestern Belize), and within a decade had conquered Tikal and sacrificed its king.

Then came a renaissance. A powerful king named Ha Sawa Chaan K'awil (682–734) restored not only Tikal's military strength but also its primacy in the Maya world. Tikal's greatness again waned around 900, but it was not alone in its downfall, which was part of the mysterious general collapse of lowland Maya civilization.

Rediscovery

It wasn't until 1848 that the Guatemalan government sent out an expedition to visit the site, and an account of their findings was published by the Berlin Academy of Science. Scientific exploration of Tikal began with the arrival of English archaeologist Alfred P Maudslay in 1881 and others continued his work on and off. The inscriptions at Tikal were studied and deciphered by Sylvanus G Morley.

Archaeological research and restoration was carried on by the University of Pennsylvania and the Guatemalan Instituto de Antropología e Historia until 1969. Since 1991 a joint Guatemalan–Spanish project

Tikal

SURVEYING THE CLASSIC MAYA KINGDOM

Constructed in successive waves over a period of at least 800 years, Tikal is a vast, complicated site with hundreds of temples, pyramids and stelae. There's no way you'll get to it all in a day, but by following this itinerary you'll see many of the highlights. Before setting out be sure to stop by the visitor center and examine the scale model of the site. The small ❶ **Museo Sylvanus G Morley** usually houses a wealth of artifacts, although the majority of its contents (other than Stela 31) are currently located in the CCIT research center while the museum is indefinitely under restoration. Present your ticket at the nearby ticket booth and when you reach the posted map, take a left. It's a 20-minute walk to the solitary ❷ **Templo VI**. From here it's a blissful stroll up the broad Calzada Méndez to the ❸ **Gran Plaza**, Tikal's ceremonial core, where you may examine the ancient precinct of the ❹ **North Acropolis**. Exit the plaza west, and take the first left, along a winding path, to ❺ **Templo V**. Round the rear to the right, a trail encircles the largely unexcavated South Acropolis to the ❻ **Plaza de los Siete Templos**. Immediately west stands the great pyramid of ❼ **Mundo Perdido**. From here it's a quick stroll and a rather strenuous climb to the summit of ❽ **Templo IV**, Tikal's tallest structure.

Templo IV
Arrive in the late afternoon to get magically tinted photos of Templos I, II and III poking through the jungle canopy. Sunrise tours offer mystical mists that lift as the sun finally appears.

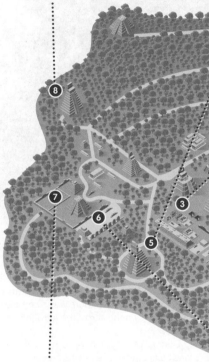

TOP TIPS

➤ Bring food and water.

➤ All tickets, including sunrise/sunset, must be purchased in advance or at the entry gate. No tickets are sold inside the park.

➤ If you enter after 3pm, your ticket is good for the next day.

➤ Stay at one of the onsite hotels to catch the sunset/sunrise.

➤ To watch the sunset/sunrise from Templo IV, you'll need to purchase an additional ticket (Q100).

➤ Bring mosquito repellent.

Mundo Perdido
This 'Lost World' features two impressive pyramids and some smaller structures, and the *talud-tablero* design hints at influences from distant Teotihuacán.

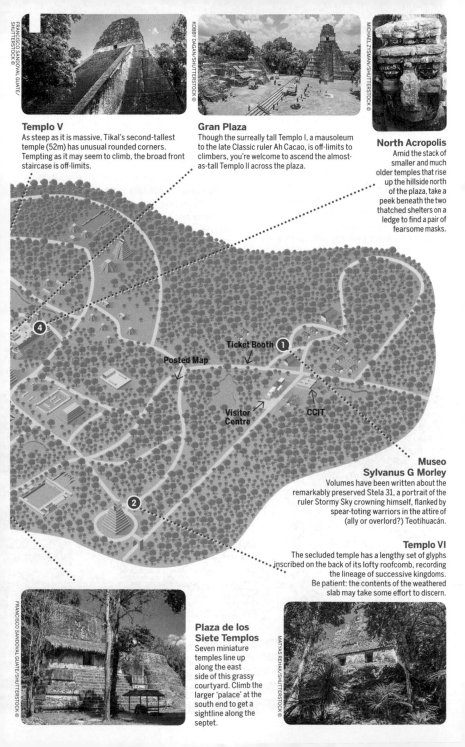

Templo V
As steep as it is massive, Tikal's second-tallest temple (52m) has unusual rounded corners. Tempting as it may seem to climb, the broad front staircase is off-limits.

Gran Plaza
Though the surreally tall Templo I, a mausoleum to the late Classic ruler Ah Cacao, is off-limits to climbers, you're welcome to ascend the almost-as-tall Templo II across the plaza.

North Acropolis
Amid the stack of smaller and much older temples that rise up the hillside north of the plaza, take a peek beneath the two thatched shelters on a ledge to find a pair of fearsome masks.

Ticket Booth ①

Posted Map

Visitor Centre

CCIT

Museo Sylvanus G Morley
Volumes have been written about the remarkably preserved Stela 31, a portrait of the ruler Stormy Sky crowning himself, flanked by spear-toting warriors in the attire of (ally or overlord?) Teotihuacán.

Templo VI
The secluded temple has a lengthy set of glyphs inscribed on the back of its lofty roofcomb, recording the lineage of successive kingdoms. Be patient: the contents of the weathered slab may take some effort to discern.

Plaza de los Siete Templos
Seven miniature temples line up along the east side of this grassy courtyard. Climb the larger 'palace' at the south end to get a sightline along the septet.

has worked on conserving and restoring Templos I and V. The Parque Nacional Tikal (Tikal National Park) was declared a Unesco World Heritage site in 1979.

This process of rediscovery is continuing, and improvements in LIDAR (Light Detection and Ranging) scanning have made it possible to map and identify ever more sections of the region's forests and swamps. This has led to spectacular discoveries and scientists are currently estimating that the Tikal complex, once estimated at 6000 structures, may exceed 10,000. Even more fascinating, newly discovered structures indicate that people may have occupied areas considered far too swampy to live in today.

Sights

The most striking feature of Tikal is its towering, steep-sided temples, rising to heights of more than 44m.

Templo I (The Temple of the Grand Jaguar) was built to honor – and bury – Ah Cacao. The king's rich burial goods included stingray spines, which were used for ritual bloodletting, 180 jade objects, pearls, and 90 pieces of bone carved with hieroglyphs.

Templo IV, at 65m, is the highest building at Tikal and the second-highest pre-Columbian building known in the Western Hemisphere, after La Danta at El Mirador. The view east is almost as good as from a helicopter – a panorama across the jungle canopy, with (from left to right) the temples of the Gran Plaza, Templo III, Templo V (just the top bit) and the great pyramid of the Mundo Perdido poking through.

Gran Plaza

Templo VI (Templo de las Inscripciones) is one of the few temples at Tikal to bear written records. On the rear of its 12m-high roofcomb is a long inscription – though it will take some effort to discern it in the bright sunlight – giving us the date AD 766.

The **Acrópolis del Norte** predates the nearby temples significantly. Archaeologists have uncovered about 100 different structures, the oldest of which dates from before the time of Christ, with evidence of occupation as far back as 600 BC.

ⓘ Need to Know

For more-complete information on the monuments at Tikal, pick up a copy of *Tikal – A Handbook of the Ancient Maya Ruins*, by William R Coe, which is available in Flores and at Tikal.

ROB CRANDALL/SHUTTERSTOCK ©

South and east of the Gran Plaza, **Acrópolis Central** is a maze of courtyards, little rooms and small temples where Tikal's nobles were thought to have lived. Others think the tiny rooms may have been used for sacred rites and ceremonies, as graffiti found within them suggest.

Museums

The larger of Tikal's two museums, **Museo Lítico** (Stone Museum; Q30, also valid for Museo Sylvanus G Morley; ◷8am-4pm), is in the visitors center and houses a number of carved stones from the ruins. The smaller museum, **Museo Sylvanus G Morley** (Museo Cerámico; Museum of Ceramics; Q30, also valid for Museo Lítico; ◷8am-4pm), exhibits superb ceramic pieces.

Tickets & Tours

Everyone must purchase an entry ticket in advance at the initial gate on the road in (or at Banrural locations such as Flores or Guatemala City). Seeing the sunrise from Templo IV at the west end of the main site is possible from about October to March, but you must purchase an additional ticket for Q100. You must also have a guide.

Family-owned **Gem Trips** (☏4051-3805, 4214-9514, USA 530-853-4329; www.gemtrips. com; Tikal sunrise US$150) offers excellent guided trips to Tikal, while archaeologist **Roxy Ortiz** (☏5197-5173; www.tikalroxy.blog spot.com) has years of experience trekking throughout the Maya world. Multilingual guides are available at the information kiosk. Before 7am a half-day tour is Q100 per person for three to six people. After that you pay for a group tour (Q600).

★ Top Tip

By the national-park entrance **Canopy Tours Tikal** (☏5615-4988; www.tikal canopy.com; tours Q240; ◷7am-5pm) offers a one-hour tour through the forest canopy, with the chance to ride a harness along a series of cables linking trees up to 300m apart and to cross several hanging bridges.

Uaxactún

Uaxactún (wah-shahk-toon), 23km north of Tikal along an unpaved road through the jungle, was Tikal's political and military rival in Late Preclassic times. It was conquered in the 4th century, and was subservient to its great sister to the south for centuries thereafter, though it experienced an apparent resurgence during the Terminal Classic, after Tikal went into decline.

Great For...

☑ Don't Miss

Stone earrings, arrowheads and gold plates in the Colección Dr Juan Antonio Valdés.

Group E

The buildings here are grouped on five low hills. From the airstrip find the sign pointing to Grupo E between the Catholic and Evangelical churches on the right side, from where it's a 10- to 15-minute walk. The most significant temple here is **Templo E-VII-Sub**, among the earliest intact temples excavated, with foundations going back perhaps to 2000 BC. The pyramid is part of a group with astronomical significance: seen from it, the sun rises behind **Templo E-I** on the longest day of the year and behind **Templo E-III** on the shortest day. The four jaguar and serpent masks affixed to the main temple's staircase were painstakingly restored in 2014 by a group of Slovak archaeologists, but then covered up again for conservation. Viewed from Templo E-VII-Sub, the sun sets behind **Templo E-II**

at the start of spring and fall. **Templo E-V** is part of a complex of unexcavated temples at Grupo E. **Templo E-X** is the tallest and possibly the oldest of a set of temples at Grupo E.

Groups B & A

About a 20-minute walk to the northwest of the airstrip are Grupo B and Grupo A, the latter featuring the more formidable structures around the city's main square. **Palacio V**, on the east side of the square, is considered a model for Tikal's North Acropolis. In 1916 the American archaeologist Sylvanus G Morley uncovered a stela dating from the 8th *baktún* at Grupo A. Thus the site was called Uaxactún, meaning 'eight

stone.' Behind Palacio V, along a path back toward the village, is the imposing **Palacio A-XVIII**, affording the most panoramic view of the site from its summit.

Stela 5, at Grupo B, displays Tikal's signature glyph, from which archaeologists deduced that Uaxactún was under that city's sway by the date inscribed, 358.

Tickets & Tours

The fee of Q50 to enter Uaxactún is collected at the gate to Tikal National Park, though there is no ticket control at the site itself.

Tours to Uaxactún can be arranged in Flores or at the hotels in El Remate and Tikal. In Uaxactún, Hector Aldana Nuñez from **Aldana's Lodge** (⊘7783-3931; posadaaldana@gmail.com) is an English-speaking guide specializing in nature-oriented tours of the region. He leads three-day treks to El Zotz and Tikal for around Q3000 per person.

Flores & Santa Elena

With its pastel houses cascading down from a central plaza to the emerald waters of Lago de Petén Itzá, the island town of Flores evokes Venice or something Mediterranean. A 500m causeway connects Flores to its humbler sister town of Santa Elena on the mainland, which then merges into the community of San Benito to the west. The three towns actually form one large settlement, often referred to simply as Flores.

⊙ SIGHTS

Flores is great for strolling, especially now that the lakefront promenade that rings the islet is complete – though rising lake levels have submerged much of the northern section. In the center, atop a rise, is the Parque Central, with its double-domed cathedral, **Nuestra Señora de los Remedios** (Map p137; Flores). Mostly the sights are just the vistas of the lake, its birdlife and the streets themselves.

Cuevas de Ak'tun Kan   Cave
(Map p127; Q35; ⊙7am-5pm) Try spelunking at the impressive limestone caverns of Ak'tun Kan, which translates from Q'eqchi' Maya as 'Cave of the Serpent.' The cave-keeper provides the authorized interpretation of the weirdly shaped stalagmite and stalactite formations, including the Frozen Falls, the Whale's Tail and the Gate of Heaven, the last within a great hall where bats flutter in the crevices.

Museo Santa Bárbara   Museum
(☑7926-2813; www.radiopeten.com.gt; Isle of Santa Bárbara; Q25; ⊙8am-5pm) On an islet to the west of Flores, this little museum holds a grab bag of Maya artifacts from nearby archaeological sites, plus some old broadcasting equipment from Radio Petén (88.5 FM), which still broadcasts from an adjacent building. Phone ahead to get picked up (Q10 per person) at the dock behind **Hotel Santana** (☑7867-5123; www.santanapeten.com.gt; Calle 30 de Junio, Flores; d/tr Q600/700; ❀❄@☎☒).

⊙ TOURS

Boats can be hired for lake tours at the *embarcaderos* (wharfs) opposite **Hotel Petenchel** (Map p137) and beside the **Hotel Santana** (Map p137) in Flores, and in the middle of the Flores–Santa Elena **causeway**. Prices are negotiable. An hour-long jaunt runs around Q150. A three-hour tour, which might include the Petencito Zoo, the isle of Santa Bárbara and its museum (p136), and the ruins of Tayazal should cost Q350, with stops and waiting time included.

Mayan Adventure   Archaeological Tour
(Map p137; ☑5830-2060; www.the-mayan-adventure.com; Calle 15 de Septiembre; ⊙bookings Mon-Fri) Coordinated by a German Mayanologist, this outfit offers 'scientific' tours to sites currently under excavation, with commentary by participating archaeologists or architects. Some of these tours are available year-round – such as to Naranjo, a huge site being restored and excavated by more than 100 scientists – others only part of the year.

Explore   Tours
(☑7926-2375; www.exploreguate.com; 2a Calle 4-68, Santa Elena; ⊙7am-6pm Mon-Fri, to noon Sat) Professionally managed agency offering custom-designed tours and its own accommodations in Santa Elena.

✪ EATING

Maple y Tocino   Cafe $
(Map p137; ☑7867-5294; www.facebook.com/mapleytocino; btwn Calle La Union & El Malecón, Flores; mains Q29-54; ⊙7am-9pm Sun-Thu, to 10pm Fri & Sat) An amazing spot for breakfasts and lunches, ranging from smoothies and frappés (some topped with a fresh doughnut) to waffles, pizza, sandwiches and wraps. Tasty coffee and espresso drinks and, to top it all, a view of the lake (and the now-submerged *malecón*).

Restaurante El Mirador   Guatemalan $
(Map p137; ☑7867-5246; Parque Central, Flores; set menu Q25; ⊙7am-10pm Mon-Sat) Refreshingly not aimed at foreign travelers, this traditional eatery does toothsome home

Flores

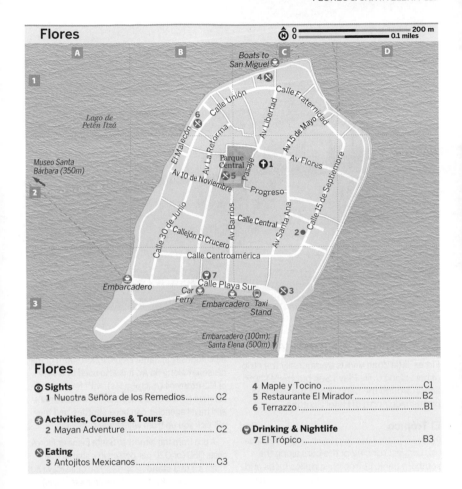

200 m
0.1 miles

Boats to San Miguel

Lago de Petén Itzá

Museo Santa Bárbara (350m)

Calle Unión
Calle Fraternidad
Av Libertad
Av 15 de Mayo
El Malecón
Calle F
Av La Reforma
Parque Central
Av Flores
Paraje
Av 10 de Noviembre
Progreso
Calle 15 de Septiembre
Av Santa Ana
Calle 30 de Junio
Callejón El Crucero
Av Barrios
Calle Central
Calle Centroamérica
Embarcadero
Car Ferry
Calle Playa Sur
Embarcadero
Taxi Stand
Embarcadero (100m);
Santa Elena (500m)

Flores

⊚ Sights
1 Nuestra Señora de los Remedios............. C2

⊕ Activities, Courses & Tours
2 Mayan Adventure C2

⊗ Eating
3 Antojitos Mexicanos.................................. C3

4 Maple y Tocino C1
5 Restaurante El Mirador B2
6 Terrazzo B1

⊕ Drinking & Nightlife
7 El Trópico B3

cookin'. You'll find such hearty options as *caldo de res* (beef stew, only on Mondays), served with all the trimmings, and *fresco* (fruit drink) in the bright lunch hall that looks over the treetops. It's next to the basketball court on the Parque Central.

Antojitos Mexicanos   Steak $$
(Don Fredy; Map p137; ☑3130-5702; Calle Playa Sur, Flores; grilled meats Q60-70; ⊗7-10:30pm; P) Every evening at the foot of the causeway these characters fire up the grill and char steak, chicken and pork ribs of exceptional quality. Their specialty is *puyazo* (sirloin) swathed with garlic sauce.

Sit outside facing the twinkly lights on the lake or, if it's raining, inside under a tin roof. Staff behave with all the formality of an elegant restaurant.

Terrazzo   Italian $$
(Map p137; ☑7867-5479; Calle Unión, Flores; pasta Q70-90; ⊗11am-10pm) Inspired by a chef from Bologna, this Italian gourmet restaurant covers a romantic rooftop terrace. The fettuccine is produced in-house, the pizzas (made of seasoned dough) are grilled rather than baked, and the fresh mint lemonade is incredible. All this, and the service is the most attentive in town.

SIMONDANNHAUER/GETTY IMAGES ©

Flores pier, Lago de Petén Itzá

🍷 DRINKING & NIGHTLIFE

Flores' little Zona Viva is traditionally the strip of bars along Calle Playa Sur, but there's also action around the bend, along the lakefront promenade north of Hotel Santana.

El Trópico   Bar

(Map p137; Calle Playa Sur, Flores; ⏰5pm-1am Mon-Sat) Longest running of the bars along the southern bank, El Trópico supplies tacos and *cerveza* (beer) to a mostly older Guatemalan clientele. It's quiet at sunset, but many *gallos* (tortilla sandwiches) later, the pulse picks up and DJs work the crowd.

ℹ️ GETTING THERE & AROUND

Aeropuerto Internacional Mundo Maya is on the eastern outskirts of Santa Elena, 2km from the causeway connecting Santa Elena and Flores. Avianca (www.avianca.com) has two flights daily between here and Guatemala City. The Belizean airline **Tropic Air** (📞7926-0348; www.tropicair. com; Aeropuerto Internacional Mundo Maya) flies once a day to/from Belize City, charging around Q1430 each way for the one-hour trip. It leaves at 8:30am daily.

Long-distance buses use the Terminal Nuevo de Autobuses in Santa Elena, 1.5km south of the causeway along 6a Av. It is also used by a slew of aka *expresos* (microbuses), with frequent services to numerous destinations. Most hotels and travel agencies can book shuttles, and they will pick you up from where you're staying.

A taxi from the airport to Santa Elena or Flores costs Q60 (or Q20 per person in a shared ride). There's a **taxi stand** (Map p137) on Calle Playa Sur in Flores. *Tuk-tuks* (three-wheeled motor taxis) will take you anywhere between or within Flores and Santa Elena for Q20; the service stops after 7pm. For lake travel, catch a **boat** (Map p137; one way Q5-20; ⏰6am-midnight) from Flores, or the **car ferry** (Map p137; car & driver Q15, per additional passenger Q2; ⏰5am-9:30pm).

El Remate

This peaceful spot at the eastern end of Lago de Petén Itzá makes a good alternative base for Tikal-bound travelers – it's more relaxed than Flores and closer to the site, and its lakeside living has a ramshackle vibe all of its own.

⊕ ACTIVITIES

Most El Remate accommodations can book two-hour boat trips for birdwatching or nocturnal crocodile spotting (each Q150 per person). Try **Hotel Mon Ami** (☎3010-0284; Jobompiche Rd; dm/s/d Q75/150/200, s/d without bathroom Q100/150; ☜), which also offers sunset lake tours with detours up the Ixlú and Ixpop Rivers (Q200 per person).

Biotopo Cerro Cahuí   Outdoors

(Map p127; Q40; ☺7am-4pm) Comprising a 7.3-sq-km swath of subtropical forest rising up from the lake over limestone terrain, this nature reserve offers mildly strenuous hiking and excellent wildlife-watching, with paths to some brilliant lookout points. As a bonus, there's an adjacent lakeside park with diving docks for a refreshing conclusion to the tour.

Project Ix-Canaan   Volunteering

(☎5804-8639; www.ixcanaan.com) This group supports the improvement of health, education and opportunities for rainforest inhabitants. Operating here since 1996, it runs a community clinic, women's center, library and research center. Volunteers work in the clinic, build and maintain infrastructure, and assist in various other ways.

⊗ EATING

Las Orquídeas   Italian $$

(☎5701-9022; Jobompiche Rd; pastas Q55-120; ☺noon-9pm Tue-Sun; ℗) Almost hidden in the forest, a 10-minute walk along the north shore from the Tikal junction, is this marvelous open-air dining hall. The genial Italian owner-chef blends *chaya*, a local herb, into his own tagliatelle and *panzarotti* (smaller version of calzones). There are tempting desserts too.

Mon Ami   French $$

(☎3010-0284, 5805-4868; Jobompiche Rd; mains Q35-85; ☺6am-10pm) On Jobompiche Rd, this peaceful palm-thatched affair is the French jungle bistro you've dreamed of. Try the lake white fish or the big *ensalada francesa* (French salad). Specials usually run Q35 to Q45, and change frequently.

Visiting Yaxhá

The Classic Maya sites of Yaxhá, Nakum and El Naranjo form a triangle that is the basis for a national park covering more than 370 sq km and bordering the Parque Nacional Tikal to the west. Yaxhá, the most visited of the trio, stands on a hill between two sizable lakes, Lago Yaxhá and Lago Sacnab. The setting, the sheer size of the site, the number of excellently restored buildings and the abundant jungle flora and fauna all make it particularly worth visiting. Not surprisingly, the foot traffic here is far less than at more popular, easy-to-reach sites.

The site is 11km north of the Puente Ixlú–Melchor de Mencos road, accessed via an unpaved road from a turnoff 32km from Puente Ixlú and 33km from Melchor de Mencos.

Agencies in Flores and El Remate offer organized trips to Yaxhá, some combined with Nakum and/or Tikal. **Horizontes Mayas** (☎5773-6193; www.horizontesmayas.com; Ruta a Tikal) in El Remate runs tours (Q125 per person, minimum three people), including guide and entrance fee, at 7am and 1pm, returning at 1pm and 6:30pm.

ⓘ GETTING THERE & AWAY

El Remate is linked to Santa Elena by frequent minibus service (Q25) from 5:30am to 6pm daily. For Tikal, a collective shuttle departs at 5:30am, starting back at 2pm (one way/round trip Q30/50). Any El Remate accommodations can make reservations. Or catch one of the **ATIM** (☎5905-0089) or other shuttles passing through from Santa Elena to Tikal from 5am to 3:30pm. For taxis, ask at **Hotel Sun Breeze** (☎5898-2665; infosunbreezehotel@gmail.com; Main Rd; s/d Q150/200, with air-con Q200/250; ℗☺❄☜). A one-way ride to Flores costs about Q250; a round-trip to Tikal costs Q350. For Melchor de Mencos on the Belizean border, get a minibus or bus from Puente Ixlú, 1km south of El Remate (Q60, 1¼ hours).

BELIZE

In this Chapter
Belize Barrier Reef 144
The Blue Hole 148
Ambergris Caye & San Pedro 150
Caye Caulker 155

Northern Cayes

What's your ultimate tropical island fantasy? With more than 100 enticing isles and two amazing atolls, chances are that one of Belize's Northern Cayes matches it. If you imagined stringing up a hammock on a deserted beach, head for an outer atoll. Pining to be pampered? You can choose from an ever-growing glut of ritzy resorts on Ambergris Caye. San Pedro is prime for dancing the night away to a reggae beat, while Caye Caulker moves at a slower pace. And the islands are only the beginning: just offshore, the Belize Barrier Reef flourishes for 190 awe-inspiring miles.

Two Days in the Northern Cayes

On your first day, relax into a hammock, indulge in a delicious **Belizean meal** (p152) and perhaps venture out to the **Belize Barrier Reef** (p144) for some snorkeling or diving. If you're staying on Ambergris Caye, day two is best spent with a sailing trip to **Caye Caulker** (p150), or a golf-cart jaunt out to **Secret Beach** (p154).

Four Days in the Northern Cayes

On day three, adventurers should set out on the long journey to Lighthouse Reef and take a dive into its awe-inspiring **Blue Hole** (p149), while less intrepid travelers can saunter around town and enjoy a spot of **shopping** (p150). The final day could involve a **food tour** (p150), some **yoga** (p150), or a **cruise** (p150) through the mangroves to find crocodiles.

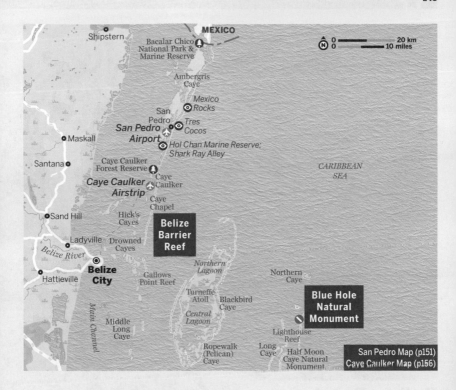

San Pedro Map (p151)
Caye Caulker Map (p156)

Arriving in the Northern Cayes

Two water-taxi companies run between San Pedro, Caye Caulker and Belize City. It's possible to walk from the dock to some accommodations; otherwise take a taxi (BZ$7 to BZ$10 on Ambergris Caye, BZ$5 to BZ$7 on Caye Caulker).

You can also walk into San Pedro from the airport terminals, located just south of the town center, in about five minutes.

Where to Stay

Accommodations in the Northern Cayes range from budget digs to beachfront boutiques to all-inclusive resorts. You'll find the greatest range in San Pedro on Ambergris Caye, and the best budget options on laid-back Caye Caulker. Far-flung Lighthouse Reef resorts cater mainly to well-heeled divers and those wanting to fish, but adventurous travelers will also appreciate them.

Tropical fish and starfish, Belize Barrier Reef

VITALYEDUSH/GETTY IMAGES ©

Belize Barrier Reef

Belize Barrier Reef is the second largest in the world, after Australia's Great Barrier Reef, and with more than 100 types of coral and some 500 species of tropical fish, it's pure paradise for scuba divers and snorkelers.

The two main centers in the northern sector of the barrier reef are Ambergris Caye and Caye Caulker, both of which are a short flight or boat ride from Belize City.

Ambergris Caye is the largest offshore island and the most developed, so it attracts most of the visiting divers. Many choose Ambergris for the variety and quality of its accommodations and nightlife, though it is pretty relaxed compared with other Caribbean destinations. Many of the accommodations along the shoreline have their own dive shops onsite.

Caye Caulker, a few miles to the south of Ambergris Caye, is smaller and more laid-back, but also a popular choice. Although prices are generally lower on Caye Caulker than Ambergris, this does not apply to snorkeling and diving, perhaps due to the

Great For...

☑ Don't Miss

Snorkeling alongside a wriggling pile of nurse sharks and stingrays in Shark Ray Alley.

❶ Need to Know

The best time to visit the reef is during the dry months between December and April. This is also high season, so expect higher prices along with the better weather.

✕ Take a Break

Have a quick lunch at Juice Dive (p152) on Ambergris Caye or Namaste Cafe (p157) on Caye Caulker.

★ Top Tip

Ambergris Caye has two hyperbaric chambers – the only ones in Belize.

choices being more limited. (There are only a handful of dive shops on Caulker.)

The barrier reef is only a few minutes by boat from either island. Diving here is quick and easy, though visibility is not always prime and the water can be somewhat surging. Some divers will put up with a longer boat ride to get better visibility and drop-off clarity. Most of the dive shops offer similar deals in terms of the sites they visit and the prices of their packages.

Snorkeling & Diving Sites

The most popular snorkeling and diving sites include the following, although you may not have too much choice about where to drop anchor, as dive masters usually choose the best sites based on weather conditions.

Hol Chan Marine Reserve

At the southern end of Ambergris Caye, **Hol Chan Marine Reserve** (Map p143; ☎226-2247; www.holchanmarinereserve.org; national park admission BZ$20) 🍢 was established more than two decades ago. The profusion of marine life is a testament to the reserve's success. A lot of Hol Chan Marine Reserve is shallow and in many cases the sites are better for snorkeling, but divers have the opportunity to explore a sunken ship at Amigos Wreck. Although the reef is fishier in the south of this section, the north holds more formations, with deep spur-and-groove cuts and interesting terrain.

Shark Ray Alley

Only snorkeling is allowed at this perennially popular **spot** (Map p143; national park admission BZ$20), which is in a shallow part of the Hol Chan Marine Reserve. Shark Ray Alley was traditionally a place for local fishers to clean fish, and the creatures attracted to the fish guts soon became a tourist attraction. As the name implies, the area is known for the big southern stingrays and mooching nurse sharks that come right up to the boat when it first arrives. Horse-eye jacks also abound.

Mexico Rocks

This snorkeling **site** (Map p143; national park admission BZ$20), 15 minutes from San Pedro and with a maximum depth of just 8ft, is a unique patch of reef toward the northern end of the island. Visitors will enjoy the shallow cluster of corals, including the *Montastrea annularis* corals, which are unique to the Northern Shelf Lagoon. Many small invertebrates inhabit the turtle grass and coral heads, while abundant fish life includes grouper, snapper, grunts, filefish

and more. Mexico Rocks was declared a marine park in 2015.

Tres Cocos

Tres Cocos (Map p143) is a bit deeper than most dive sites around San Pedro, with coral heads rising up to 50ft and a wall with spurs that spill out from 90ft to 120ft, but there's also a shallow snorkeling area nearby. The marine life here is wonderful, with a thick growth of star corals, big plating corals, red rope sponges and soft sea whips, and gorgonians on the upper reaches of the spurs. The place is renowned for shoals of schooling fish, including snapper, horse-eye jacks and spotted eagle rays.

Green sea turtle

Bacalar Chico National Park & Marine Reserve

At the northern tip of Ambergris Caye, **Bacalar Chico** (Map p143; day admission BZ$10) 🐟 is a Unesco World Heritage site made up of 41 sq miles (106 sq km) of protected land and sea, accessible only via an hour-long boat ride from San Pedro. Tour boats make snorkeling stops and motor through an ancient channel that was dug by seafaring Maya about 1500 years ago. The coral is extra colorful around the reserve, as there is significantly less damage from boats and tourists. Besides the bountiful fish, there's a chance of seeing manatees, as well as green and loggerhead turtles. If the waters are calm, some tour boats go to Rocky Point, notable as one of the only places in the world where land meets reef.

❶ Need to Know

To feed or not to feed? That has long been the question, and finally there's a fairly straightforward answer. Don't do it. There has been a strong push recently to end feeding at all sites other than Shark Ray Alley; ask the snorkel or dive operator if there will be any fish feeding taking place during your trip, and if the answer is yes, switch companies.

Responsible Diving & Snorkeling

Please consider the following tips to help preserve the ecology and beauty of reefs:

● Never use anchors on the reef, and take care not to ground boats on coral.

● If you must hold on to the reef, only touch exposed rock or dead coral.

● Be conscious of your fins. Even without contact, the surge from fin strokes near the reef can damage delicate organisms. Take care not to kick up clouds of sand, which can smother organisms.

● Practice and maintain proper buoyancy control while diving. Major damage can be done by descending too fast and colliding with the reef.

● Resist the temptation to collect or buy coral or shells, or to loot marine archaeological sites (mainly shipwrecks).

● Ensure that you take home all your rubbish and any litter you may find as well. Plastics in particular are a serious threat to marine life.

● Avoid feeding fish. Rules are in place to prevent tour operators chumming or feeding fish.

● Minimize your disturbance of marine animals. *Never* ride on the backs of turtles.

DIEGO GRANDI/SHUTTERSTOCK ©

★ Top Tip

If you want to see the reef, but don't want to get wet, jump aboard a tour with the **Reef Runner Glass Bottom Boat** (Map p151; ☎602-0858; Barrier Reef Dr; half-day tour BZ$110; ⊗9am & 2pm; 🚼).

Blue Hole

MATTEO COLOMBO/GETTY IMAGES ©

The Blue Hole

The sheer walls of the Blue Hole Natural Monument drop more than 400ft into the blue ocean. The depth creates a perfect circle of startling azure that is quite noticeable from above, but the stalactites and stalagmites inside, along with a school of reef sharks, are only visible to divers as they descend into the mysterious depths.

Great For...

☑ Don't Miss

Stopping in at the nearby island nature reserve Half Moon Caye Natural Monument.

In the 1970s, underwater pioneer Jacques Cousteau explored the sinkhole and declared the dive site one of the world's best. Since then the Blue Hole's image – a deep azure pupil with an aquamarine border surrounded by the lighter shades of the reef – has become a logo for tourist publicity and a symbol of Belize.

Diving the Blue Hole

Divers drop quickly to 130ft, from where they swim beneath an overhang, observing stalactites above and, sometimes, a few reef sharks. Although the water is clear, light levels are low, so a good dive light will enable further appreciation of the rock formations. Because of the depth, ascent begins after eight minutes; the brevity of the dive may disappoint some divers. The trip is usually combined with other dives

Scuba diving through the Blue Hole

PETE NIESEN/SHUTTERSTOCK ©

Northern
Lagoon   Northern
Cave   *CARIBBEAN*
SEA

Turneffe
Atoll   Blackbird
Central   Caye   **Blue Hole**
Lagoon   **◗ Natural Monument**
            Lighthouse
    Ropewalk   Long   Reef
    (Pelican)   Caye   Half Moon
    Caye   Caye National
            Monument

❶ Need to Know

Blue Hole Natural Monument (Map
p143; www.belizeaudubon.org; national park
admission BZ$60; ◷8am-4:30pm)

✕ Take a Break

Dive resorts on nearby islands have
restaurants for guests.

★ Top Tip

The easiest way to visit the Blue Hole
is on a day-trip from San Pedro or Caye
Caulker.

at **Lighthouse Reef**, and many divers will
tell you that those other dives are the real
highlight. But judging from its popularity –
most dive shops make twice-weekly runs
to the Blue Hole – plenty want to make the
deep descent.

On day trips the Blue Hole will be your
first dive, which can be nerve-racking if
you're unfamiliar with the dive master and
the other divers, or if you haven't been
underwater lately. It may be worth doing
some local dives with your dive masters
before the Blue Hole trip. An alternative is
to take an overnight trip to Lighthouse Reef,
where there's a dive shop offering a unique
Blue Hole experience.

Long Caye Diving Services (☏601-5181,
in USA 305-600-2585; www.itzalodge.com/
diving; Itza Lodge; per dive BZ$140) owner
Elvis Solis has been inside the Blue Hole

more than 500 times, and has mapped
out a unique course that he offers to small
groups who are either staying at **Itza
Lodge** (☏in USA 305-600-2585; www.itzalodge.
com; 3-day resort package BZ$1470-2070; 🛜) 🏊,
where the dive shop is based, or traveling
independently. The dive begins on the
northern stretch of the Blue Hole, drops
to 130ft, and at around 80ft brings divers
through a couple of small caves where
squirrel fish and nurse sharks tend to lurk.
The safety stop is a long one, around 25
minutes, and is achieved while circling
the rim of the Blue Hole, where sea fans,
sponges, turtles, barracudas and other reef
dwellers can be spotted.

Snorkeling the Blue Hole

The coral around the shallow perimeter
of the Blue Hole will appeal to snorkelers,
though the trip is expensive and you'll
probably have to tag along on a dive boat.
Diving or snorkeling, the trip involves two
hours each way by boat in possibly rough,
open waters.

Northern Cayes Yoga

Science & Soul Wellness (615-0089; www.scienceandsoulwellness.com; Mahogany Bay; yoga class from BZ$40, massage from BZ$180; 9:30am-6pm), a gorgeous and professionally run center, is a reason in itself to book a stay at Mahogany Bay, the posh new 'townlet' about 2.5 miles (4km) south of San Pedro. The yoga studio is the first in Belize to offer aerial classes, which cater to all levels of experience, and the instructors are top-notch.

Ak'bol Yoga (626-6296, 226-2073; www.akbol.com; Mile 2.25, North Island; classes BZ$30; 9am Mon-Sat, 10am Sun) offers two open, thatched-roof yoga studios (one at the end of the dock). Daily walk-in classes, in addition to the week-long yoga retreats, are scheduled throughout the year.

Yoga at Caye Caulker
ALEKSANDAR TODOROVIC/SHUTTERSTOCK ©

Ambergris Caye & San Pedro

The undisputed superstar of Belize's tourism industry, 'La Isla Bonita' strikes an impressive and perhaps even magical balance of large-scale tourism development with a fun, laid-back atmosphere. Sure it gets busy – especially in high season when an endless procession of golf carts clogs the narrow streets of the main town, San Pedro – but it's still the kind of place where it's acceptable to hold up traffic while you greet an old acquaintance.

TOURS

ACES   Wildlife Watching
(American Crocodile Education Sanctuary; Map p151; 623-7920; www.americancrocodilesanctuary.org; Esmeralda St; BZ$100; 6:45-9pm) A fantastic nighttime crocodile tour through the mangrove lagoon on the west side of the island. It's run by a local nonprofit that researches the reptiles and handles problematic ones. Tour lasts about three hours and departs from the Office restaurant.

Belize Food Tours   Food
(Map p151; 615-1321; www.belizefoodtours.com; cnr Barrier Reef Dr & Pelican St; food tours from BZ$124) For a delicious introduction to all things yummy in Belize, hop on a fabulous food tour run by one of the island's pioneering families. The lunch tour, 'Belizean Bites,' and dinner tour, 'Savor Belize,' both meander through San Pedro's mom-n-pop kitchens, sampling a wide variety of authentic dishes and drinks hailing from Belize's many cultural influences.

The company also offers a **cooking class** (BZ$150; 10:30am-1:30pm & 5:30-8:30pm Mon-Fri), and it's an absolute blast.

Seaduced by Belize   Boating
(Map p151; 226-2254; www.seaducedbybelize.com; Tarpon St, Vilma Linda Plaza; 7am-6pm;) Offers a range of sailing trips, including a sunset cruise and a full-day trip to Caye Caulker. Also runs good-value outings to spot manatees at Swallow Caye (BZ$210 plus a BZ$30 park fee), including lunch at Goff's Caye and snorkeling. Other tours include visits to Bacalar Chico and a recommended full-day trip to Robles Beach, complete with snorkel stops and beach BBQ.

SHOPPING

Belizean Arts Gallery   Art
(Map p151; www.belizeanarts.com; 18 Barrier Reef Dr; 9am-10pm Mon-Sat) This is one of the country's best shops for local art and handicrafts, selling ceramics, wood carvings, Garifuna drums and antiques alongside

San Pedro

Activities, Courses & Tours
1 ACES...A2
2 Belize Food Tours.............................C2
Belizean Kitchen Cooking Class........(see 2)
3 Reef Runner Glass Bottom Boat..............C2
4 Seaduced by Belize............................B2

Shopping
5 Belizean Arts Gallery...........................C2
6 Gallery of San Pedro, Ltd....................C2

7 Little Old Craft Shop...........................A3

Eating
8 DandE's Frozen Custard........................C2
9 Juice Dive...B2
10 Wild Mango's....................................B3

Drinking & Nightlife
11 Palapa Bar.......................................D1
12 Wahoo's Lounge................................C2

affordable and tasteful knickknacks. You'll also find a decent selection of paintings by local and national artists. Rainforest-flora beauty products, including soaps, are on sale too. It's inside Fido's.

Little Old Craft Shop — Art

(Map p151; ☎634-7075; Coconut Dr; ⊗8am-8pm) Talented and friendly local artist Ricardo Zetina crafts beautiful jewelry and figurines, as well as wonderful wood carvings. If your

purchase is too big for your suitcase he will arrange shipping for you.

Gallery of San Pedro, Ltd — Art

(Map p151; ☎226-4304; www.thegallerysp. com; Pescador Dr; ⊗9am-6pm Mon-Sat, to 3pm Sun) Maintains the largest collections of paintings by Belizean artists in the country, in addition to a wide variety of other quality arts and crafts including tapestries, hammocks and masks, all from Belize.

KEVIN CODY/SHUTTERSTOCK ©

CANNON PHOTOGRAPHY LLC/ALAMY STOCK PHOTO ©

From left: Spotted eagle ray; manatee; beach on Ambergris Caye

🍴 EATING

The island offers some of the country's freshest seafood and most innovative chefs, and the prices match the quality.

DandE's Frozen Custard Ice Cream $

(Map p151; ☑660-5966; www.dande.bz; Pescador Dr; ice cream from BZ$6; ☺2-9:30pm; 🚼) Don't be confused by 'frozen custard.' It's basically high-quality ice cream, made with eggs for extra richness, then churned as it freezes for dense creaminess. The flavors change frequently, often featuring local fruity flavors such as coconut, soursop and mango. Alternatively you can't go wrong with 'not just' vanilla. DandE's also makes sorbet, but don't forgo the frozen custard.

Truck Stop Food Hall $$

(☑226-3663; www.truckstopbz.com; North Island; mains BZ$15-27; ☺noon-9pm Wed-Sun; 🛜🚼) This absurdly cool shipping-container food park doubles as Ambergris Caye's entertainment hub, offering movie nights, live music and backyard games such as ping pong and cornhole. The colorful containers are dedicated to ice cream, Latin American food, Southeast Asian cuisine and New Haven–style pizza, and the food is all fresh and yummy, made with locally sourced ingredients.

Robin's Kitchen Jamaican $$

(☑651-3583; Sea Grape Dr; mains BZ$14-25; ☺7am-9pm Sun-Thu, to 5:30pm Fri, 6:30-9pm Sat) At this simple, small roadside restaurant south of town, Jamaican BBQ king Robin prepares the best jerk chicken and fish this side of Kingston. Dishes are spicy but with subtle flavors, and his sauces are also to die for. If you catch your own fish, Robin will prepare it for you any way you like and will only charge for sides.

Juice Dive Health Food $$

(Map p151; ☑615-7395; www.facebook.com/juicedive; Pescador Dr; juice from BZ$16, mains from BZ$21; ☺7am-8pm; 🚼) The first commercial cold-pressed juice operation in Belize also serves up all kinds of vegetarian and vegan delights: acai bowls, vegan nachos, wheatgrass shots, you name it. The salads and wraps are particularly delicious and everything here is easy on the

ALEX ROBINSON/GETTY IMAGES ©

conscience, with biodegradable packaging and utensils made of plant fiber.

Wild Mango's
International $$$

(Map p151; ☑226-2859; 42 Barrier Reef Dr; mains BZ$20-48; ⊙11:30am-9pm Mon-Sat; ☑) Exuding a carefree, casual ambience (as a beachfront restaurant should), this open-air restaurant manages to serve up some of the island's most consistent and creative cuisine. With a hint of the Caribbean and a hint of Mexico, the dishes showcase fresh seafood, Cajun spices, and local fruits and vegetables. The place is usually packed – come early or make a reservation.

Hidden Treasure
Caribbean $$$

(☑226-4111; www.hiddentreasurebelize.com; 4088 Sarstoon St; mains BZ$29-68; ⊙5-9pm Wed-Mon; ☑) Living up to its name, Hidden Treasure is a gorgeous open-air restaurant in an out-of-the-way residential neighborhood (follow the signs from Coconut Dr). Lit by candles, the beautiful bamboo and hardwood dining room is the perfect setting for a romantic dinner, which might feature almond-crusted grouper, blackened snapper with bacon-wrapped shrimp, or

pork ribs with a ginger-pineapple BBQ glaze.

Palmilla Restaurant
International $$$

(☑226-2067; www.victoria-house.com; Coconut Dr; mains BZ$48-78; ⊙7am-10pm; ❄☑) The classy, candlelit restaurant at Victoria House is the island's priciest, but also one of its best. Arrive before sunset to have a mojito on the veranda, then head into the white-tablecloth dining room to devour a cashew-crusted grouper or imported beef tenderloin. There's also a seasonal fish market, involving fresh seafood handpicked by the chef at the hotel's dock.

🍷 DRINKING & NIGHTLIFE

Stella's Sunset Wine Bar & Restaurant
Wine Bar

(☑602-5284; www.stellasmile.com; Mile 1, Tres Cocos, North Island; ⊙4-9pm Mon-Wed, Fri & Sat, 8am-1pm Sun) Stella's is a classy but unpretentious wine bar set in a lovely garden on the edge of the San Pedro Lagoon that affords fine sunset views. Sit on lounge chairs

Secret Beach

The island's worst-kept secret is a dreamy stretch of northwestern shoreline that has nonetheless retained the name Secret Beach. Getting here requires a 45-minute golf-cart ride north of San Pedro and across the North Island, past lagoons and over mangrove swamps where crocodiles lurk.

The reward for your effort is an off-the-grid paradise featuring soft white sands, clear turquoise waters, yummy seafood shacks and countless tropical cocktails. The anchoring establishment is **Wayne's World** (Secret Beach; mains BZ$20-25; ☺10am-5pm; 🛜), a restaurant and bar under the same ownership as the area's first (and only) lodgings, **Paradise on the Caye** (🗷615-2042; www.paradiseonthecaye.com; Secret Beach; r incl breakfast BZ$190; 🛜).

Other highlights include the posh **Maruba Beach Klub** (🗷610-3775; Secret Beach; ☺9am-5pm) 🏄, with its techno beats and brightly colored lounge pillows, and Blue Bayou (p154), a small, family-owned hideaway with partly submerged picnic tables and a convivial vibe.

Paddleboards, kayaks and canoes are available for rent at Wayne's World, and there's also beach volleyball, cornhole and a wandering hair-braider. For the best bites at the beach, hit up the food shack **Aurora's** and try the BBQ grouper or fish tacos.

under the trees or at a table in the *palapa* (open-air shelter with a thatched roof) and work your way through two dozen different whites and reds.

Blue Bayou · Cocktail Bar
(🗷623-8051; www.facebook.com/pg/blueba youbelize; Secret Beach; ☺10am-5pm) Tucked away from the louder bars and restaurants, this is the locals' favorite at Secret Beach, mainly for the picnic tables partially submerged in the waist-deep, turquoise cove. It's easy to spend an entire day here, throwing back Belikins and feasting on delicious *ceviche* (marinated seafood), whole jerk fish or curry venison. Cash only.

Palapa Bar · Bar
(Map p151; 🗷226-3111; www.palapabarandgrill. com; San Pedro; ☺10am-11pm) This over-the-water *palapa*, a mile south of San Pedro bridge, serves burgers and tacos, and is a fantastic place for tropical drinks any time of day. There's no law against drinking and floating, so when it's really hot you are invited to partake of a bucket of beers while relaxing in an inner tube.

❂ ENTERTAINMENT

Live music is rampant on Ambergris Caye, emanating from various bars and restaurants around the island every night of the week. **Paradise Theater** (🗷636-8123; www.facebook.com/paradisetheater; North Island; BZ$10; ☺6-11:30pm Fri-Sun) is great for a movie, **Wahoo's Lounge** (Map p151; 🗷226-2002; Barrier Reef Dr; ☺11am-midnight) continues to hold the infamous Thursday 'chicken drop,' and Truck Stop (p152) hosts super-fun events like adult spelling bees and game-show nights.

❶ GETTING THERE & AWAY

The San Pedro airstrip is just south of the town center on Coconut Dr. The Tropic Air terminal is at the north end of the strip, right on Coconut Dr, while the Maya Island Air terminal is on the west side of the strip. All flights depart between 6am and 5pm.

There are two water-taxi companies running the route between San Pedro and Belize City via Caye Caulker, both departing from docks on the reef side of the island.

❶ GETTING AROUND

Minivan taxis ply the streets looking for customers. Official rates are BZ$7 during the day and BZ$10 at night to anywhere in the town center. For hotels outside the center negotiate the rate before hopping in.

There is a small **toll bridge** over the San Pedro river. Pay a ridiculous BZ$5 for each 20m crossing on a golf cart. Bicycles cross for free.

Caye Caulker

'No Shirt, No Shoes...No Problem.' You'll see this sign everywhere in Belize, but in no place is it more apt than Caye Caulker. On this tiny island, where cars, too, are blissfully absent, dogs nap in the middle of the dirt road and suntanned cyclists pedal around them. The only traffic sign on the island instructs golf carts and bicycles to 'go slow,' and that directive is taken seriously.

❸ ACTIVITIES

RandOM Yoga   Yoga

(Map p156; ☎637-4109; www.randomyoga.com; Pasero St; ⊗9am) A couple of floors above the Namaste Cafe (p157), this excellent, long-standing yoga studio offers daily, 9am classes and occasional sunset classes on an open-air platform with a distant ocean view. The donation-based and consistently high-caliber classes are run by longtime island expat and top-notch owner/instructor Jessie Wigh. She and her husband also offer weeklong retreats.

Kitexplorer   Kitesurfing

(Map p156; ☎652-7308; www.kitexplorer.com; Front St; equipment rental per hour/half-day/full day BZ$120/200/300; ⊗8am-6pm) Offers a two-hour introductory course (BZ$360) or a six-hour basic course (BZ$980), as well as equipment rental. Also offers windsurfing classes and has stand-up

Palapa Bar

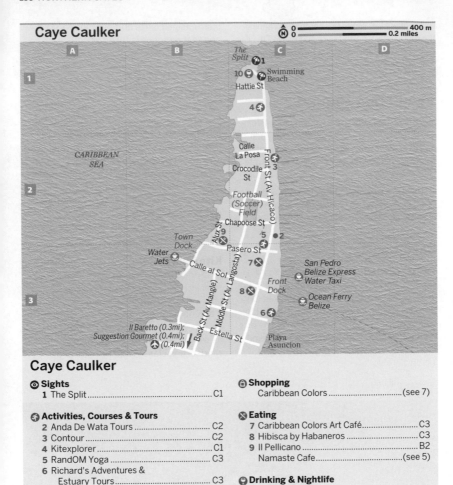

Caye Caulker

◎ **Sights**
1 The Split C1

⊕ **Activities, Courses & Tours**
2 Anda De Wata Tours C2
3 Contour C2
4 Kitexplorer C1
5 RandOM Yoga C3
6 Richard's Adventures &
   Estuary Tours C3

🛍 **Shopping**
   Caribbean Colors .... (see 7)

✖ **Eating**
7 Caribbean Colors Art Café C3
8 Hibisca by Habaneros C3
9 Il Pellicano B2
   Namaste Cafe .... (see 5)

🍸 **Drinking & Nightlife**
10 Lazy Lizard C1

paddleboards. Located at the northern end of the island near the Split.

⚡ TOURS

Anda De Wata Tours   Adventure

(Map p156; ☎226-0640, 607-9394; www.
snorkeladw.com; Front St) Does floating on
an inner tube pulled behind a slow-moving
boat sound like a dream come true? Anda
De Wata's 90-minute sunset boat-and-
float tour (BZ$70; all-you-can-drink rum

punch included) may be your own personal
paradise. The company also offers great
snorkeling tours around local reefs, including complimentary professional photos,
and flyovers to check out the Blue Hole.

Contour   Water Sports

(Map p156; ☎615-8757; www.contourbelize.
com; Front St; rentals per hour/half-day/full day
BZ$25/60/80; ☺8am-6pm) This well-run
shop brings something different to the
world of Caulker aquatic recreation: taking
visitors through mangroves or on sunset

tours on paddleboards. It also rents out its quality equipment.

Richard's Adventures & Estuary Tours
Wildlife

(Map p156; 602-0024; Playa Asuncion; snorkeling & croc tour per person BZ$70) Local guide and conservationist Richard Castillo not only excels at spotting marine life around the reefs, but he is also the only guide who can bring guests to the new crocodile reserve within **Caye Caulker Forest Reserve** (Map p143) . He is part of the team that installed the 1-mile boardwalk through the mangrove swamp, and is a virtual encyclopedia on the habitat.

EATING

Caulker is all about the creatures of the sea, with lobster season running from mid-June to mid-February, and conch season from October to June. There are plenty of street eats, too, from ad-hoc beachside grills to the island's famous 'Cake Lady,' who shows up on Front St with a cart filled with amazing homemade cakes right around dusk.

Namaste Cafe
Health Food $

(Map p156; 637-4109; Pasero St; salads & sandwiches BZ$12; 7:30am-4:30pm Mon-Sat;) From the hibiscus-lime kombucha and garlic-cilantro hummus to the chia pudding, this place absolutely oozes hippie goodness. The salads and sandwiches are fresh and healthy, and this is also a lovely spot to relax with your feet in the sand, sipping some tea, after one of the excellent, donation-based yoga (p155) classes upstairs. Ecoconscious offerings include biodegradable takeaway containers.

Caribbean Colors Art Café
Health Food $$

(Map p156; 605-9242; Front St; mains BZ$10-25; 7am-2:30pm Fri-Wed;) What began as a **gallery** (Map p156; 605-9242; Front St; 7am-2:30pm;) for owner and artist Lee Vanderwalker has morphed into a top-notch cafe. And the art's still on the walls. While you browse you can treat yourself to

👍 Caye Caulker's Best Beach Parties

For those looking to kick it on the soft white sand and in the docile sea, tropical cocktail in hand, surrounded by like-minded travelers, **Koko King** (626-8436; www.facebook.com/KokoKingCayeCaulker; 10am-midnight) reigns supreme. It's an all-in-one sort of beach party, with a fully stocked bar, a tasty Caribbean restaurant and a plethora of beach games and water toys – you can easily spend all day here.

Otherwise, head to the **Split** (Map p156), a narrow channel that divides Caye Caulker into two. The clean, deep waters are free of seaweed, making it one of the island's best swimming areas. This is particularly true following the recent construction of a seawall, a wading area with sheltered picnic tables, a spa, some restaurants, and a kayak and paddleboard rental shop.

The loud music and rowdy crowd at the adjacent bar, **Lazy Lizard** (Map p156; The Split; 10am-11pm), will either enhance or dampen your experience, depending on what you're looking for.

Lazy Lizard

a coffee or a cool smoothie, then sit down for a fresh and healthy breakfast, salad or sandwich. There are lots of veggie and vegan options too.

Suggestion Gourmet
European $$

(630-8396; Av Mulche; mains BZ$20; 7:30am-5pm & 6-8:30pm) Tucked into the jungle in the southern reaches of Caye

From left: Mojito; shrimp *ceviche*; lobster barbecue

Caulker, this delicious artsy little bistro is a local favorite thanks to head chef Frédéric Grandchamp's winning concept. Basically, he asks customers what they want, then finds a way to serve it (hence the restaurant's name). Certain menu items, such as rotisserie chicken, paella crevette and schnitzel, tend to recur.

Live Performances

On the leafy grounds of the Oasi hotel, a classy little bar and performance space dubbed **Il Baretto** (623-9401; Av Mangle; 7:30pm Sat) is an ideal venue to experience some of the talented local musicians and circus acts. Yes, the *palapa* (open-air shelter with a thatched roof) can somehow hold an acrobat dangling on a silk. Also the espresso, wines, cocktails and juices are fabulous, and there's a small Italian menu.

Hibisca by Habaneros International $$$

(Map p156; 626-4911; cnr Front St & Calle al Sol; mains BZ$32-58; 5:30-9:30pm Fri-Wed) Caulker's poshest restaurant is located in a brightly painted clapboard house in the center of town. Here chefs prepare gourmet international food, combining fresh seafood, meat and vegetables with insanely delicious sauces and flavors. Wash it down with a fine wine or a jug of sangria.

Il Pellicano Italian $$$

(Map p156; 226-0660; Pasero St; mains BZ$25-42; 5:30-9:30pm Tue-Sun) Head to the lagoon side of the island to find this wonderful garden restaurant preparing a small, but constantly changing, selection of outstanding classic Italian dishes including flavorful homemade pastas and the best pizza on the island. Accompany your meal with Italian wine served by the glass or bottle, and be sure to sample the excellent desserts.

MELLYD-100/GETTY IMAGES ©

ℹ️ GETTING THERE & AWAY

Maya Island Air (☎226-0012; www.mayaisland air.com) and **Tropic Air** (☎226-0040; www. tropicair.com) connect Caye Caulker with San Pedro and Belize City. The airline offices are at the southern end of the island.

There are two companies running boats from Caye Caulker to Belize City and San Pedro: **Ocean Ferry Belize** (Map p156; ☎226-0033; www.oceanferrybelize.com; Calle al Sol) and **San Pedro Belize Express Water Taxi** (Map p156; ☎226-0225; www.belizewatertaxi.com). The docks are beside each other on the reef side of the island. San Pedro Belize Express Water Taxi also runs a service to Chetumal, Mexico, every other day via San Pedro. **Water Jets** (Map p156; ☎206-0010; www.sanpedrowatertaxi.com; lagoon dock) runs the same service on alternate days.

ℹ️ GETTING AROUND

Caulker is so small that most people walk everywhere. A couple of golf-cart taxis hang out around Front St and charge BZ$5 to BZ$7 per short trip around town.

You can rent a golf cart at **Buddy's Golf Cart Rentals** (☎628-8508; buddysgolfcartren tals@gmail.com; Middle St; per hour/day/24hr BZ$25/100/150), but bicycle rental is far cheaper and just as fast a way to get around. You can rent bikes at grocery stores, tour operators and hotels.

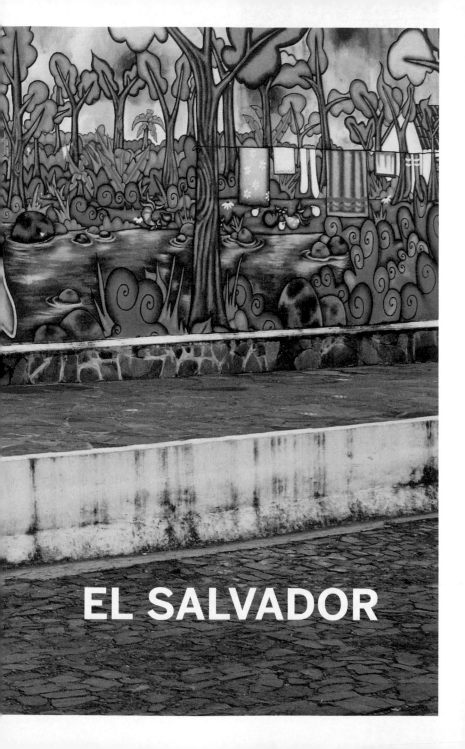

EL SALVADOR

In this Chapter
Coffee along the Flower Route...........164
Driving Tour: Ruta de las Flores 166
Juayúa 168
Apaneca...168
Ataco..170
Ahuachapán 170

Ruta de las Flores

Traveling the Ruta de las Flores, slowly and purposefully, is like a meander through the story of El Salvador. It's a beautiful series of villages, each with a mix of colonial architecture in indigenous tones. Those who like the good life can feast on local food, particularly at the weekend markets, browse the craft tiendas (stores) or undertake firsthand research into why El Salvadoran coffee is renowned across the world. If the pace is too slow, you can hit the Cordillera Apaneca, a volcanic mountain range filled with waterfalls, mountain-bike trails, and pine forest hikes where white flowers bloom in May.

Two Days in Ruta de las Flores

Take off from Sonsonate in the morning for a full day of exploring **Juayúa** (p168), ideally on a weekend to enjoy the town's *fería gastronómica*. On day one, explore the cobbled streets and grab a meal at **R&R** (p168). On day two, hike and swim around **Los Chorros de Calera** (p168), and follow the **Ruta de las Seite Cascadas** (p168) along the Río Bebedero to discover each of the seven pretty waterfalls.

Four Days in Ruta de las Flores

Head to **Apaneca** (p169) for a canopy tour or dirt buggy ride, then continue to **El Carmen Estate** (p165) for a coffee plantation tour and an overnight stay. The following day, journey to **Salto de Chacala** (p170), a 50m waterfall, or dip into **Chorros del Limo** (p170), a spring-fed pool. Finish in Ahuachapán with a jaunt to **Los Ausoles** (p171), a series of hot springs and bubbling mud pools north of town.

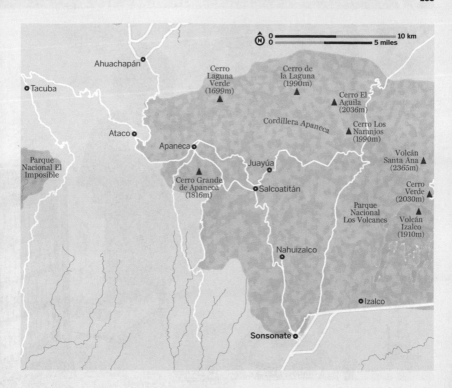

Tacuba

Ahuachapán

Cerro
Laguna
Verde
(1699m)

Cerro de
la Laguna
(1990m)

Cerro El
Aguila
(2036m)

Cordillera Apaneca

Cerro Los
Naranjos
(1990m)

Ataco

Apaneca

Juayúa

Volcán
Santa Ana
(2365m)

Parque
Nacional El
Imposible

Cerro Grande
de Apaneca
(1816m)

Salcoatitán

Cerro
Verde
(2030m)

Parque
Nacional
Los Volcanes

Volcán
Izalco
(1910m)

Nahuizalco

Izalco

Sonsonate

0   10 km
0   5 miles

Arriving in Ruta de las Flores

Sonsonate bus station Catch bus
249, which runs frequently (about every
15 minutes) between Sonsonate and
Ahuachapán, stopping in all the towns
along the way, including Juayúa, Apaneca and Ataco.

Where to Stay

Juayúa, Ataco and Apaneca have the
widest range of good-value hostels.
Some middle-end options are found in
the *fincas* (farms) lining the highway.
You can also camp at Chichicastepeque
(aka Cerro Grande), which at 1816m
affords outstanding views of the region,
although the antennae make it look a lot
less wild.

Preparing beans for brewing in Juayúa

THORNTON COHEN/ALAMY STOCK PHOTO ©

Coffee along the Flower Route

Coffee beans from El Salvador are revered across the globe. Yet with a growing international obsession with coffee, it can be surprising that until recently it was hard to find a decent latte in the country. This is changing, however, as local boutique coffee roasters try to distinguish their drink from the competition.

Great For...

☑ Don't Miss

Juayúa's sensational gastronomic fair, held each weekend with plenty of coffee included.

In the late 19th century, synthetic dyes undermined the indigo market, and coffee took the main stage. A handful of wealthy landowners expanded their properties, displacing indigenous people. Coffee became the most important cash crop and *cafetaleros* (coffee-plantation owners) earned purses full of money that was neither taxed nor redistributed as reasonable wages to the workers. By the 20th century, 95% of El Salvador's income derived from coffee exports, but only 2% of Salvadorans controlled that wealth.

Today in towns like Juayúa, Ataco, La Palma, Metapán and Alegría, the next generation of coffee-plantation owners are leading a vanguard in coffee culture. Rather than settling for the mass market, where wages are low, work is steady, and the beans are torn green from the tree,

Honey-dried coffee berries

THORNTON COHEN/ALAMY STOCK PHOTO ©

delicious coffee accompanied by pancakes or a slice of cake alongside sublime views across mist-covered mountains.

Finca Santa Leticia, Apaneca

Santa Leticia (☏2433-0357; www.hotelsantaleticia.com; Carretera de Sonsonate Km 86.5; ⊙archaeological park 9am-5pm) is a coffee farm, hotel and restaurant just south of Apaneca, also known for its small onsite archaeological park.

El Carmen Estate, Ataco

The ubiquitous Cafe Ataco brand hails from this charming **finca** (☏2243-0304; www.elcarmenestate.com; tour per person US$6; ⊙9am-4pm), which has been operating since the 1930s.

House of Coffee, Ataco

All the fuss about the dark brown liquid comes to fruition at this simple outdoor **cafe** (☏2450-5353; Av Central btwn 4a Calle Oriente & 6a Calle Poniente; ⊙11:30am-5:30pm Tue-Fri, to 9pm Sat, 8:15am-6pm Sun).

many Salvadorans are responding to an increasing demand, both here and abroad, for an authentic, nuanced blend of beans that reflects the quality of the volcanic soil, high altitude and hot climate.

Occalli Cafe, Juayúa

This pleasant **cafe** (☏2452-2783; 3a Av Sur; ⊙7:30am-6:30pm Thu-Tue) offers a fine selection of gourmet local beans brewed using a variety of methods, plus breakfasts, sandwiches and cakes.

Cafe Albania, Apaneca

Call in to **Cafe Albania** (☏7349-5124; ⊙8am-5pm Mon-Fri, to 6pm Sat & Sun; 🛜) for a cup of

Driving Tour: Ruta de las Flores

The Flower Route winds through a series of charming villages, offering a mix of thriving artisan culture, rich coffee and access to waterfalls and natural bathing pools.
Start Sonsonate
Distance 50km
Duration Two days

6 Finish in the prosperous, provincial capital of **Ahuachapán** (p170), and visit the area's steaming mud pits.

FINISH **6**

5

4

5 Head on to **Ataco** (p170) to check out some brightly colored murals, colonial buildings and a spring-fed pool.

Take a Break: Stop for a cup of joe at the delightful **El Jardin de Celeste** (p169).

4 Continue to El Salvador's second-highest town, **Apaneca** (p168), and hop on a canopy or dirty buggy tour.

$\stackrel{\circ}{N}$ 0 — 10 km
0 — 5 miles

3 Roll on to **Salcoatitán**, with its cobblestone streets and tiny art galleries.

Cordillera Apaneca

Classic Photo: Juayúa's Chorros de Calera falls

2 In **Juayúa** (p168), attend a weekend food festival and hike to waterfalls and springs. Spend the night.

Parque Nacional Los Volcanes

Nahuizalco

START **1**

1 Begin your drive or catch the chicken bus in **Sonsonate**, and head directly to Juayúa.

Juayúa

Juayúa (why-ooh-ah) is the most-visited town on Ruta de las Flores due to its attractive cobbled streets, weekend food fair, and nearby waterfalls and hot springs. The fresh mountain air led to a rich indigenous settlement here and Nahuatl roots can still be seen in the craft aesthetic.

Cristo Negro (Black Christ), an important religious statue carved by Quirio Cataño in the late 16th century and housed in the church, is significant both as a symbol of change and for its obvious beauty.

Juayúa has a tumultuous past. Indigenous uprisings in the region ignited the revolutionary movement of 1932. Backed by the coffee elite, government forces brutally quelled the ill-organized insurrection.

🗘 ACTIVITIES

A recommended place to hike and swim is **Los Chorros de Calera**, a series of falls spewing from fractured cliffs. The **Ruta de las Seite Cascadas** follows the Río Bebedero over seven scenic drops. Ask **Hotel Anáhuac** (📞2469-2401; www.hotelan ahuac.com; cnr 1a Calle Poniente & 5a Av Norte) or **Casa Mazeta** (📞English 7252-8498, Spanish 2406-3403; www.casamazeta.com; 1 Calle Poniente 22) for a guide, which is recommended due to reported robberies en route. Other guided excursions include lake visits, coffee tours and waterfall rappels.

🍴 EATING

Juayúa is famed for its weekend *fería gastronómica* (food fair). Guinea pig and frog skewers headline an ambitious menu; less risky fare includes *riguas de coco* (fried coconut and cornmeal) and the ubiquitous *elote loco* (crazy corn) slathered with parmesan cheese and mustard.

Taquería la Guadalupana Mexican $
(Calle Merceditas Caceres Poniente; mains US$3-9; ☺10:30am-9pm Tue-Sun) Gaudy and loud (the owner is a karaoke fan), Guada-

lupana serves upstanding Mexican food without much fanfare.

R&R Salvadoran $$
(📞2452-2083; Calle Merceditas Caceres Poniente; mains US$7-12; ☺11:30am-9pm Wed-Mon) R&R is still the finest restaurant in Juayúa, and possibly in the whole Ruta de las Flores. Chef Carlos puts a twist on steaks, salads and Mexican food. Even when Juayúa is quiet, the tables at this small, brightly painted corner building are filled with happy diners.

Restaurante San José Salvadoran $$
(📞2469-2349; 2a Calle Poniente; mains US$5-7.50; ☺9am-7pm) On the main square in one of Juayúa's oldest buildings, the San José serves grilled beef, chicken and seafood dishes along with a few more-exotic items such as grilled rabbit. There's a well-stocked bar and a cheery sunflower-themed decor.

ℹ️ GETTING THERE & AWAY

Bus 249 has services northwest to Apaneca (US$0.60, 20 minutes), Ataco (US$0.70, 30 minutes) and Ahuachapán (US$0.90, one hour), and also south to Sonsonate (US$0.80, 45 minutes) during daylight hours. Buses leave every 15 minutes from the park, or from four blocks west on weekends. For Santa Ana, bus 238 (US$0.75, 40 minutes) goes direct, leaving a few blocks west of Parque Central six times daily.

Apaneca

Apaneca means 'river of the wind' in Nahuatl, and there is a definite cooling in the air in El Salvador's second-highest town (1450m). One of the country's prettiest places to visit, its cobbled streets and colorful adobe houses are blissfully peaceful during the week, but come alive with increasing numbers of visitors on weekends. Apaneca's cottage craft industry is highly revered and the surrounding Sierra Apaneca Ilamatepec is a hiker's paradise.

The beautiful **Iglesia San Andres** was one of the oldest churches in the country until the 2001 earthquake reduced it to rubble, but it has been rebuilt with a similar appearance.

 ACTIVITIES

The crater lakes **Laguna de las Ninfas** and **Laguna Verde**, north and northeast of town, are within hiking distance. The former is swampy, reedy and rife with lily pads; the latter is deep and cold. For directions or a guide, stop by the tourist kiosk at the plaza (open weekends only).

 TOURS

Apaneca Canopy Tours   Adventure
(☑2433-0554; Av 15 de Abril; 1½hr tour US$35) An excellent zipline experience covering 13 cables and 2.5km of mountain forest. Tours leave daily at 9:30am, 11:30am and 3pm.

Buggy Buggy Apaneca Aventura   Adventure
(☑2612-7034; www.503apanecabuggies.wix. com/apanecaadventure; 4a Av Norte; 2hr tour for 2 people US$70) A convoy of dirt buggies in the quiet village of Apaneca jolts the senses, but it is good, honest, dirty fun to roar down to Laguna Verde with this popular outfit. Tours run at 9am, 11am, 1pm and 3pm.

 EATING

The upscale restaurants on the highway offer the inevitable *buena vista* and a relaxed atmosphere to dally in. Otherwise you'll find plenty of local food in the village, but not much after dark.

Plaza Apaneca   Market $
(1a Av Sur; mains US$2.50-6; ☺7am-8pm) In a fancy new building, this food court facing the park offers ham, eggs and beans, and *atole* (a corn-based drink), as well as chicken dishes and *pupusas* (cornmeal mass stuffed with cheese or refried beans). Look out for *piñas locas,* a cocktail of rum, pineapple and cream served in a hollowed-out pineapple.

 Religion in El Salvador

El Salvador is a very religious country. Once staunchly Catholic, like the rest of Latin America, it is experiencing an explosive growth of evangelical churches, whose fiery services seem to have brought fresh energy to the faith. Town-square services with booming speakers are becoming an all-too-typical way of spreading 'the word.' Protestant churches now account for almost 50% of believers.

Before and during the war, priests and missionaries were often outspoken critics of government repression – many, such as Archbishop Óscar Romero, were killed for their stands.

Memorial march for Archbishop Romero's death
JOSE CABEZAS/AFP/GETTY IMAGES ©

El Jardin de Celeste   International $$
(☑2433-0277; www.eljardindeceleste.com; Km 94; mains US$8-17; ☺7am-6pm;) This heavenly garden venue is one of the culinary highlights of the region and warrants stopping for a meal or, at the very least, coffee and cake. Located between Apaneca and Ataco, Celeste is best enjoyed with friends, laughing, eating and celebrating the subtropical splendor.

ⓘ **GETTING THERE & AWAY**

Buses drop off and pick up on the main street, right in front of the market. Bus 249 plies the route between Ahuachapán and Sonsonate, stopping in Apaneca every half-hour. The last bus leaves between 6pm and 7pm. Ask a local to be sure.

 Best Shopping on the Ruta de las Flores

Axul Artesanías (www.facebook.com/axulartesania; Av Central Norte; ⊘9am-6pm) This store sells a range of handicrafts made by local artists and artisans, including beautiful handwoven tablecloths, painted boxes and jewelry.

Diconte-Axul (cnr 2a Av Sur & Calle Central; ⊘8:30am-6pm) Popular for its homemade textiles, tie-dyes and hand-painted objects.

Ataco Market (2a Av Sur; ⊘7am-7pm) Ataco's sprawling market makes for a fascinating stroll.

Diconte-Axul
JOHN COLETTI/GETTY IMAGES ©

Ataco

Many people leave Ataco with a new favorite village in El Salvador. With its brightly colored murals and artisan markets, cobblestone streets and colonial-era buildings, a congenial mountain setting and excellent, cheap dining and sleeping options, this sleepy Flower Route destination even gets a little festive on Saturday nights with live music spilling into the streets. The next town along, **Salcoatitán**, was founded by the pre-Columbian Pipils and has lots of tiny art galleries down cobblestone streets.

⊕ ACTIVITIES

Ask at the tourist office for guide services to explore the countryside. Options include **Salto de Chacala**, a 50m waterfall on the Río Matala, and **Chorros del Limo**, a spring that forms a broad pool ideal for a dip.

 ## ⊗ EATING

Kafekali Salvadoran $
(Parque Concepcion de Ataco; mains US$4-7; ⊘9am-6pm) This cafe on the square is a prime spot for observing daily life in Ataco while refueling with coffee and cake. It's on the western side of the park.

Tayua International $$
(cnr 5a Calle Oriente & 2a Av Norte; mains US$6.50-13; ⊘5:30-8pm Wed & Thu, noon-10pm Fri & Sat, noon-6:30pm Sun; 🛜🖉) On weekends, Tayua is one of the most lively spots in little Ataco. Homemade pizza, salads and gourmet sandwiches use fresh herbs from the garden out back, while the decadent sweet pastries are perfect for dunking in coffee. Live music bobs up on occasion, and purchasable artwork adorns the walls.

Vocho Pizza Pizza $$
(1a Av Sur; pizzas US$5-6; ⊘noon-9pm Tue-Sun) It's a little gimmicky, sure, but a Volkswagen Beetle that's been converted into a food truck with a functioning wood-fired pizza oven is hard to pass by. Take a seat in the wood-cabin dining room while you wait for your thin-crust pizza to be baked outside.

ⓘ GETTING THERE & AWAY

Bus 249 stops on the corner of 2a Calle Oriente and 4a Av Sur. It heads north to Ahuachapán (US$0.35, 15 minutes) and south to Apaneca (US$0.25, 10 minutes), Juayúa (US$0.70, 30 minutes) and Sonsonate (US$0.80, one hour). Frequency is every 15 minutes.

Ahuachapán

Ahuachapán is either the beginning or end of the Ruta de las Flores, depending on which direction you roll. Either way, it's a prosperous, small provincial capital that supplies 15% of the country's electrical power thanks to the wonders of geothermal energy. There are some attractive colonial buildings, but for travelers it's mostly a jumping-off point for trips to Parque Nacional El Imposible or Ataco.

SIGHTS

Ahuachapán bubbles with geothermal activity, evidenced in the steaming mud pits found in the area. **Los Ausoles**, aka *los infernillos* (the little hells), is a series of hot springs 20km north of town. Ask at your hotel for guides; if you have a car, it's easy enough to explore them on your own.

Nuestra Señora de Asunción Church

(cnr 2a Av Sur & 3a Calle Oriente) This church east of Plaza Concordia has pretty *azulejo* (tile) floors and a stained-glass Virgin.

Plaza Concordia Plaza

Green gardens and palms make Plaza Concordia an agreeable spot to catch a breeze. The kiosk occasionally holds concerts and free events.

EATING

Ahuachapán has some decent places to eat offering typical local fare. Most restaurants are around Plaza Concordia.

Las Mixtas Salvadoran $

(2a Av Sur btwn Calles 3a & 1a Oriente; mains US$3-5; ⊙7am-8pm Mon-Fri, to 9pm Sat, 11am-9pm Sun) Colorful, convivial and teeming with young couples, Las Mixtas serves, you guessed it, *mixtas,* which is basically a sloppy sandwich filled with too much of everything, including pickled vegetables. Locals rave about the ice-cold *licuados* (fresh fruit drinks).

La Estancia Salvadoran $

(1a Av Sur btwn Calle Barrios & 1a Calle Oriente; mains US$3-4; ⊙7am-6pm Mon-Sat) Seats for the *típica* buffet lunch at this colonial-era building fill with business folk during the week and young families on weekends. Enjoy eating among the stuffed animals.

Típicos Kolo Kolo Salvadoran $

(cnr Av Tranceico Menéndez Sur & 1a Calle Oriente; mains US$2.50; ⊙6am-4pm) You can't miss this cheery corner place that's painted inside and out with bright murals celebrating local life. Salvadoran breakfasts, buffet lunches and *pupusas* hit the spot.

 The Arts in El Salvador

El Salvador's artisanal products can be innovative and high quality. Fernando Llort's naïve art inspired an industry of brightly painted crafts in childlike motifs in the community of La Palma. Guatajiagua in Morazán produces black pottery with a Lenca influence and Ilobasco is known for its *sorpresas,* intricate miniatures hidden in ceramic shells.

The written word is also beloved in El Salvador. Iconoclastic poet Roque Dalton was exiled for radical politics. He eventually returned home to aid the guerrilla cause, but was executed by his own side due to suspicion that he was a CIA operative. Notable works include *Taberna y otros lugares* (1969), a political vision in verse, and *Miguel Marmol* (1972). Progressive poet Claudia Lars wrote spare, bold erotic poetry and is considered one of the country's foremost writers. One of the more compelling contemporary Salvadoran novelists is Horacio Castellanos Moya. His translated *Senselessness* (2004) is a burning black comedy about government-sponsored violence.

Art tiling by Fernando Llort
DBIMAGES/ALAMY STOCK PHOTO ©

GETTING THERE & AWAY

Buses for Tacuba, Santa Ana and Sonsonate line Av Menéndez at 10a Calle Oriente, one block north of Parque Central. Buses for the Guatemalan border at Las Chinamas leave from 8a Calle Poniente, at the northwest corner of Parque Menéndez. Buses for San Salvador leave from the new terminal just past the gas station on Carretera 13, the road toward Santa Ana.

HONDURAS

In this Chapter
Visiting the Site 176
Copán Ruinas 180
Sights 180
Eating 181
Drinking & Nightlife 182

Copán

One of the most important of all Maya civilizations lived, prospered, then mysteriously crumbled around what is now the Copán archaeological ruins, a Unesco World Heritage site. During the Classic period (AD 250–900), the city at Copán Ruinas culturally dominated the region. The architecture is not as grand as that across the border in Tikal, but the city produced remarkable sculptures and hieroglyphics, and these days you'll often be virtually alone at the site, which makes it all the more haunting. Though the archaeological site is the main attraction of the Copán region, there are several museums in and around town worth visiting.

One Day in Copán

Budget your first day for the **ruins** (p176), which will give you time to take in the temples and surrounding sights. Hire a guide from Asociación de Guías Copán to get the most out of your visit or, if you fly solo, prioritize the Principal Group and Las Sepulturas. Add context with a visit to the **Museo de Escultura** (p178) and mull things over during dinner at **Cafe at La Casa de Cafe** (p181).

Two Days in Copán

Head for the forested hills around the ruins and relax into a stay at **Hacienda San Lucas** (p183), where you can explore the grounds and visit **Los Sapos** (p183), an archaeological site of stone carvings. Alternatively, keep your base in Copán Ruinas and venture north on a day-trip to **Luna Jaguar Spa Resort** (p183) for a soak in hot springs or a steam bath.

Previous page: Stepped pyramid, Copán
CALAVERAPHOTOGRAPHY/GETTY IMAGES ©

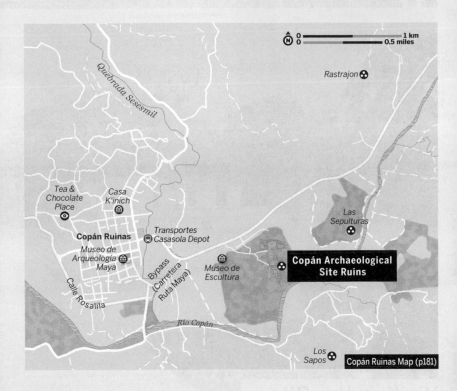

Copán Ruinas Map (p181)

Arriving in Copán

Casasola bus depot Located at the entrance to town. The Copán archaeological site is a kilometer from Copán Ruinas proper and can be walked easily enough. An alternative is to take a *mototaxi* from town (L20 per person). To get between the Archaeological Park and Sepulturas you can walk the 2km or hire a *mototaxi* (L20 per person each way).

Where to Stay

No accommodations are available at the site, so head 1km to the town of Copán Ruinas for the night. There's a great deal of choice here, from some of the best hostels in Honduras to fine boutique hotels and lots in between. There's also a lovely spot, Hacienda San Lucas, in the forested hills south of town.

Juego de Pelota (Ball Court)

JANE SWEENEY/ROBERTHARDING/GETTY IMAGES ©

Visiting the Site

At Copán, you'll gaze at extraordinary Maya stone carvings and epic ancient structures that are continuously being discovered around the site. These discoveries indicate that at the peak of civilization here, around the end of the 8th century, the valley of Copán had more than 27,500 inhabitants – a population figure not reached again until the 1980s.

So far, the remains of 3450 structures have been found in the 27 sq km surrounding the Grupo Principal, most of them within about half a kilometer of it. In a wider zone, 4509 structures have been detected in 1420 sites within 135 sq km of the ruins.

A visitors center, an excellent sculpture museum, and a cafe and gift shop are close to the main entrance, just a 1km stroll outside of Copán Ruinas.

Grupo Principal

The Principal Group of ruins is about 400m beyond the visitors center across well-kept lawns, through a gate in a fence and down shady avenues of trees. A group of resident macaws loiters around here and bird houses have been built high in the trees for their nesting. The ruins themselves have

Great For...

☑ Don't Miss

The Archaeological Park (Principal Group) – if you're short on time or money, this is the must-see section.

Stela, Gran Plaza

ℹ Need to Know

Copán Archaeological Site Ruins
(📞2651-4108; www.ihah.hn; L330;
🕒8am-6pm)

✕ Take a Break

There's a cafeteria near the entrance
that serves light meals, snacks and
drinks.

★ Top Tip

Hire a guide from the **Asociación de
Guías Copán** (📞2651-4018; guiascopan@
yahoo.com; Archaeological Park US$30,
tunnels US$15, Las Sepulturas US$18).

been numbered for easy identification and
a well-worn path circumscribes the site.

The path leads to the **Gran Plaza** (Great
Plaza; Plaza de las Estelas) and the huge,
intricately carved stelae portraying the rulers of Copán. Most of Copán's best stelae
date from AD 613 to 738. Many stelae had
vaults beneath or beside them in which
sacrifices and offerings could be placed.

South of the Gran Plaza, across what is
known as the Plaza Central, is the **Juego
de Pelota** (Ball Court; AD 731), the second
largest in Central America. Note the macaw
heads carved atop the sloping walls.

South of the Juego de Pelota is Copán's
most famous monument, the **Escalinata
de los Jeroglíficos** (Hieroglyphic Stairway;
AD 743). The flight of 63 steps bears a
history (in several thousand glyphs) of the
royal house of Copán.

The lofty flight of steps to the south of
the Hieroglyphic Stairway mounts the **Templo de las Inscripciones** (Temple of the Inscriptions). On top of the stairway, the walls
are carved with groups of hieroglyphs. On
the south side of the Temple of the Inscriptions is the **Patio Occidental** (West Court),
with the **Patio Oriental** (East Court) to its
east. This group of temples, known as the
Acrópolis, was the spiritual and political
core of the site – a place where ceremonies
were enacted and kings buried.

Las Sepulturas

Excavations at Las Sepulturas have shed
light on the daily life of the Maya in Copán
during its golden age. Once connected
to the Gran Plaza by a causeway, Las
Sepulturas may have been the residential
area where rich and powerful nobles lived.
One huge, luxurious residential compound
seems to have housed some 250 people
in 40 or 50 buildings arranged around 11
courtyards. The principal structure, called

the **Palacio de los Bacabs** (Palace of the Officials), had outer walls carved with the full-sized figures of 10 men in fancy feathered headdresses; inside was a huge hieroglyphic bench. To get to Las Sepulturas you have to go back to the main road, turn right, then right again at the sign (2km from the Gran Plaza).

Museo de Escultura

While Tikal is celebrated for its tall temple pyramids and Palenque is renowned for its limestone relief panels, Copán is unique in the Maya world for its sculpture. Some of the finest examples are on display at this impressive **museum** (Museum of Sculpture; Copán Archaeological Site; US$7; ⊘8am-6pm), which is fully signed in English. Entering the museum is an experience in itself: you go through the mouth of a serpent and wind

through the entrails of the beast before suddenly emerging into a fantastic world of sculpture and light.

Entrance Fees

Entry to the Archaeological Park (Principal Group) costs US$15 per person and includes entry to Las Sepulturas 2km away. Adding access to Tunel Rosalila and Tunel de los Jaguares – which are certainly cool but contain only a few carvings behind glass – costs another US$15 per person.

History

People have been living in the Copán Valley since at least 1200 BC; ceramic evidence has been found from around that date. Copán must have had significant commercial activity since early times, as graves showing marked Olmec influence have

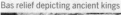
Bas relief depicting ancient kings

been dated to around 900 to 600 BC. But it was over a millennia more before Copán Ruinas began to flourish, as sculptors carved stone stelae unequaled in the Maya world, and mathematicians and astronomers calculated uncannily accurate calendars and planetary movements.

Until recently, the collapse of the civilization at Copán had been a mystery. Now archaeologists have begun to surmise that near the end of Copán's heyday the population grew at an unprecedented rate, straining agricultural resources. In the end, Copán was no longer agriculturally self-sufficient and had to import food from other areas. The urban core expanded into the fertile lowlands in the center of the valley, forcing both agricultural and residential areas to spread onto the steep slopes surrounding the valley. Wide areas were deforested, resulting in massive erosion that further decimated food production and brought flooding during rainy seasons. Skeletal remains of people who died during Copán's final years show marked evidence of malnutrition and infectious diseases, as well as decreased life spans.

New Discoveries

In addition to examining the area surrounding the Grupo Principal, archaeologists continue to make new discoveries in the Grupo Principal itself. Five separate phases of building on this site have been identified; the final phase, dating from 650 to 820, is what we see today. But buried underneath the visible ruins are layers of other ruins, which archaeologists are exploring by means of underground tunnels. This is how they found the Templo Rosalila (Rosalila Temple), a replica of which is now in the Museo de Escultura. Below Rosalila is yet another, earlier temple, Margarita, and below that, Hunal, which contains the tomb of the founder of the dynasty, Yax K'uk' Mo' (Great Sun Lord Quetzal Macaw). Two of the excavation tunnels, including Rosalila, are open to the public, though you'll need to pay a second entry fee to access them.

> ### ❶ Need to Know
> Count on 90 minutes to see the main site with a guide, or three to four hours to see the site, tunnels, Las Sepulturas and the museum.

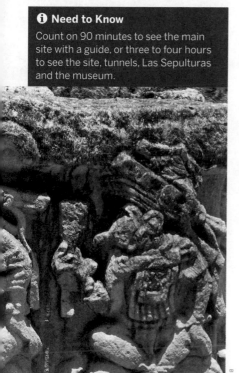

BUMIHILLS/SHUTTERSTOCK ©

★ Top Tip
Scribes, Warriors and Kings by William Fash (2001) offers a comprehensible overview of Copán.

Guided Tours

A huge number of tours can be organized from Copán Ruinas; local companies promote these widely. You can go caving, tube a river, visit a Maya village, make tortillas, manufacture ceramics, plunge into hot springs, visit a coffee plantation or head off into the wilds of Honduras.

Birdwatching tours are very popular in the area around Copán – it's said that there are more quetzals in the surrounding cloud forest than there are in the whole of Guatemala (where it's the national bird). One recommended English-speaking birdwatching guide is **Alexander Alvarado** (☑9751-1680; alexander.alvarado469@gmail.com).

Horseback riding can be arranged by any of the town's tour companies and most hotels. You can ride to the ruins or make other, lengthier excursions. Three-to five-hour rides out of **Café ViaVia** (☑2651-4652; www.viaviacafe.com/en/copan/hotel; Calle de la Plaza; r L230; 🛜) visit the hot springs, Hacienda San Lucas, Los Sapos and the small Ch'orti' village of La Pintada.

Scarlet macaw
AUTUMN SKY PHOTOGRAPHY/SHUTTERSTOCK ©

Copán Ruinas

The town of Copán Ruinas, often simply called Copán, is a beautiful place, paved with cobblestones and lined with white adobe buildings with red-tiled roofs. Many people come here just to see the famous nearby Maya ruins, but with plenty of other attractions in the town and nearby, there's reason enough to linger.

⊙ SIGHTS

Casa K'inich   Museum
(☑2651-4105; off Av Centroaméricano; L30; ⊕8am-noon & 1-5pm Tue-Sun) Casa K'inich includes an interactive re-creation of the ancient football game practiced by the Copán residents more than a millennia ago. Displays are in three languages: English, Spanish and Ch'orti'. Kids might get a kick out of the stela with a cutout hole to poke their heads through.

Tea & Chocolate Place   Agricultural Center
(☑2651-4087; ⊕4-6pm Mon-Sat) This charming place is a research center that doubles as a tea and gift shop every afternoon to support the important reforestation work carried out by its environmental charity. Enjoying a cup of tea (try the cacao and spice) on the wonderful veranda is something of a rite of passage in Copán Ruinas. Take a *mototaxi* (motorcycle taxi) to get here or walk the kilometer uphill from town.

Museo de Arqueología Maya   Museum
(☑2651-4437; Parque Central; L69; ⊕2-9pm) The Museo de Arqueología Maya is worth a visit. The exhibits include some of the best excavated ceramics, fragments from the altars and the supports of the Maya ruins, an insight into the Maya's sophisticated use of calendars and a re-creation of a female shaman's tomb. Some descriptions have English translations.

Memorias Frágiles   Gallery
(☑2651-3900; Palacio Municipal, Parque Central; ⊕8am-5pm Mon-Fri) **FREE** This fascinating photo exhibition was a gift from Boston's Peabody Museum; it features a collection of rare photos detailing the first archaeological expeditions to Copán at the turn of the 20th century. Many of these proved essential in later restoration work, as the photos showed the site decades beforehand and offered clues to how the various stone hieroglyphs had lain.

Copán Ruinas

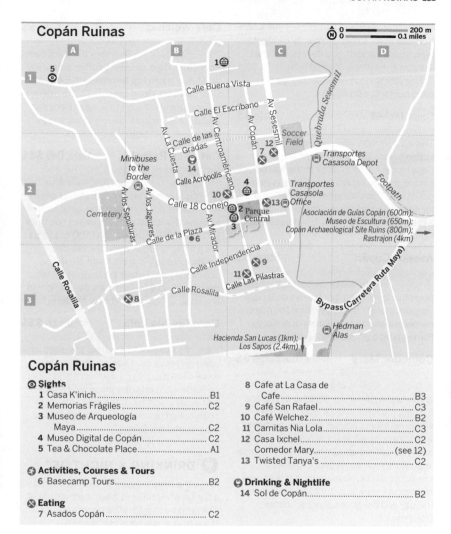

Copán Ruinas

◎ Sights
1 Casa K'inich................................B1
2 Memorias Frágiles.......................C2
3 Museo de Arqueología
   Maya.....................................C2
4 Museo Digital de Copán..............C2
5 Tea & Chocolate Place..................A1

✪ Activities, Courses & Tours
6 Basecamp Tours..........................B2

✖ Eating
7 Asados Copán.............................C2

8 Cafe at La Casa de
   Cafe.......................................B3
9 Café San Rafael..........................C3
10 Café Welchez............................B2
11 Carnitas Nia Lola.......................C3
12 Casa Ixchel...............................C2
   Comedor Mary....................(see 12)
13 Twisted Tanya's.........................C2

◉ Drinking & Nightlife
14 Sol de Copán.............................B2

Museo Digital de Copán   Museum
(Parque Central; L69; ⊙1-9pm) This museum opened in late 2015 as a gift to the people of Copán from Japan and contains some interesting old photographs. The main reason to visit, though, is to watch the excellent 12-minute video on demand that's a great primer before you visit the Copán Archaeological Site.

✖ EATING

Cafe at La Casa de Cafe   International $$
(☎2651-4620; www.casadecafecopan.com; mains L50-175; ⊙7am-8pm) With dishes inspired by trips around the world, you'll find homemade, healthy and fresh delights here from tamales to perfectly spiced curries. The pancakes, egg dishes and smoothies at breakfast are superb, as are the lunchtime

sandwiches on bread sometimes still warm from the oven. Chefs use plenty of vegetables, herbs, spreads and delicious fillings like pan-fried tilapia (cichlid fish).

Everything is served in a cozy garden patio bursting with flowers.

Casa Ixchel
Cafe $$

(Av Sesesmiles; mains L90-250; ⊙7am-6pm; 🛜) There's a friendly welcome at this serious coffee-lover's place, where locally grown Casa Ixchel Arabica coffee is the fuel of choice and the espresso machine is rarely out of use. There's a great little back patio for eating and drinking in the sunshine, and a brunchy menu for tasty breakfasts and light lunches.

Asados Copán
Steak $$

(cnr Calle Acrópolis & Av Copán; mains L120-250; ⊙8am-10pm) With one of the best settings in town, this large, open-air steakhouse is popular with tourists and locals alike. The menu's simple but effective – a variety of perfectly flame-grilled beef and chicken dishes.

Comedor Mary
Honduran $$

(Av Sesesmiles, Hotel Mary; mains L88-250; ⊙7am-9pm; 🛜) This charming space comprises a garden for alfresco dining and a dining room full of dark wood furniture where excellent *pupusas* (cornmeal stuffed with cheese or refried beans; L12 to L25 each) are served up. *Comida típica* (regional specialties) are also redefined here (try the *lomito de res a la plancha,* a grilled beef tenderloin); service is uncharacteristically friendly and the atmosphere is upscale. Don't miss it.

Twisted Tanya's
International $$

(☑2651-4182; www.twistedtanyas.com; Parque Central; daily specials from L130; ⊙2-11pm Mon-Sat; 🛜) Set upstairs, with views over Parque Central and beyond, lively Tanya's serves up some good versions of Italian, other European and Asian-influenced dishes. The Union Jack flags will draw your attention and the Moroccan-style lampshades add an artistic flourish. Happy hour runs from 5pm to 6pm. It can be loud here, so don't come for an intimate dinner.

Café Welchez
Cafe $$

(☑2651-4202; near Parque Central; mains L150-200; ⊙7am-5pm; 🛜) This very pleasant two-floor place does excellent coffee and cake and has a charming terrace with Parque Central views. Good breakfasts are available, including French toast, eggs Benedict and a 'full American.' Sandwiches, soups and salads complete the offerings.

Café San Rafael
Cafe, Deli $$$

(Av Centroaméricano; sandwiches L160-200; ⊙11am-11pm Tue-Sat, 8am-6pm Sun & Mon; 🛜) This smart cafe serves organic coffee grown at its *finca* (ranch), though it's mostly known for its delicious cheeses (platters L150 to L700). Breakfasts (L100 to L200) are a filling splurge, while the toasted sandwiches (try the excellent steak and provolone) are a great lunch option. Half the place is in a beautiful garden patio and the other is indoors and very modern.

Carnitas Nia Lola
Honduran $$$

(Av Centroaméricano; mains L180-455; ⊙7am-10pm; 🛜) Two blocks south of the plaza, this open-air restaurant has a beautiful view toward the mountains over corn and tobacco fields. It's a relaxing place with simple and economical food; the specialties are charcoal-grilled chicken and beef. Happy hour starts at 6:30pm.

🍷 DRINKING & NIGHTLIFE

Given the large traveler presence, there's a fair bit of nightlife in town, particularly at weekends – though little goes on beyond 11pm (this is still rural Honduras).

Sol de Copán
Brewery

(Av Mirador; mains L130-180; ⊙2-10pm Tue-Sat; 🛜) A terrific, German-owned microbrewery in a basement pub. The owner, Thomas, is friendly and makes sure everyone's regularly topped up with pilsner or lager. Delicious German sausages are served, and there's live music some nights too. If you're lucky, Thomas might show you his fermenting vats out the back. Sit at a big table to meet locals and other travelers.

ℹ️ INFORMATION

US dollars can be changed at most banks, though Guatemalan quetzals at present can only be changed on the black market. The following banks have ATMs that accept foreign cards.

BAC (Parque Central; ⏱9am-5pm Mon-Fri, to noon Sat) Exchanges US dollars and has a 24-hour ATM.

Banco Atlántida (cnr Calle Independencia & Av Copán) Changes US dollars and has an ATM.

Banco de Occidente (cnr Calle 18 Conejo & Av Copán) On the plaza; changes US dollars and gives cash advances on Visa and MasterCard.

ℹ️ GETTING THERE & AWAY

Casasola (📞2651-4078; Av Sesesmiles) buses arrive and depart from an open-air **bus depot** (📞2651-4078) at the entrance to town, where destinations include San Pedro Sula (L140, three hours, five daily).

Minibuses to/from the **Guatemalan border** (L25, 20 minutes, every 20 minutes) run between 6am and 5pm from near the town's cemetery at the end of Calle 18 Conejo. On the Guatemala side, buses to Esquipulas and Chiquimula leave the border regularly until about 5pm.

You can book popular shuttle buses at either **Basecamp Tours** (📞2651-4695; www.basecamphonduras.com; Calle de la Plaza) or **Hotel & Hostal Berakah** (📞9951-4288, 2651-4771; www.hotelberakahcopan.hostel.com; Av Copán; dm/d/tw L174/400/450) to Antigua (L600, six hours), Guatemala City (L600, five hours), San Salvador (L880, five hours), stopping at Santa Ana or Tunco (both L960, 4½ hours); there's one shuttle to Leon and Managua in Nicaragua (L2040, 12 hours) and also one to La Ceiba (L960, seven hours), Lago de Yojoa (L480, six hours) and to the San Pedro Sula airport (L480, four hours). Note that many shuttles only run when there are enough people.

Hedman Alas (📞2651-4037; Carretera a San Lucas Km 62) has a modern terminal just south of town, where you can get daily 1st-class buses to San Pedro Sula and the airport (L395, three hours), Tegucigalpa (L790, eight hours), Lago de Yojoa (L790, six hours), La Ceiba (L731, seven hours) and Tela (L731, six hours).

👍 Sights Around Copán

The forested hills around Copán Ruinas include a few interesting sights that are well worth visiting while you're staying in the town.

Spend a few days out here in this beautiful region basing yourself at the charming **Hacienda San Lucas** (📞2651-4495; www.haciendasanlucas.com; s/d/tr incl breakfast L2860/3300/3960; 🛜) ☕. On the grounds you'll find **Los Sapos** (Hacienda San Lucas; L30), which means 'the toads.' These are old Maya stone carvings, set along a hiking trail in the hills.

There are also some unusual remains at **Rastrajon** (L70), a site situated for defense on a mountainside, where the earth has shifted considerably due to subterranean water flow. After all the touring, soothe those muscles in the hot springs at **Luna Jaguar Spa Resort** (www.lunajaguarsparesort.com; from L250; ⏱9am-9pm).

If you're headed south to Nicaragua, stopping in at **Lago de Yojoa** is more than worthwhile. Largely undeveloped and ringed by mountains and dense tropical forest, Lago de Yojoa is an exceptionally scenic oasis, and some of the country's best coffee is grown in the surrounding mountains. Sample a cup at **El Dorao Cafe** (panini L40-60; ⏱7am-7pm; 🛜), an unbelievable find in sleepy Peña Blanca, which has fused local coffee-growing expertise with the needs of the cosmopolitan city dweller.

Lago de Yojoa
JPIKS/SHUTTERSTOCK ©

In this Chapter
Diving & Snorkeling 186
Roatán 191
Utila... 193

Bay Islands

Boasting outstanding reefs, famous wrecks and bountiful sea life, Utila and Roatán are paradise for ocean lovers, and few places are as inexpensive for learning how to dive. Unsurprisingly, the islands' economies are based mostly on tourism and fishing. Although English is the dominant spoken language, with Spanish as a second language, the islanders have a fascinating heritage, including African, Carib and European ancestry. You'll also find resident foreigners, who often work for scuba shops and other tourist-oriented businesses.

Two Days in the Bay Islands

Fly into **Roatán** (p191) and spend the first couple of days diving and snorkeling, or if you refuse to get wet, there's always the **submarine option** (p191). After long, idyllic days in the sun, retire to the West End to grab sundowners at **Blue Marlin** (p193), then indulge in a meal at **Roatán Oasis** (p192).

Four Days in the Bay Islands

Travelers sometimes prefer to spend a full four days on Roatán, but those with an interest in snorkeling with whale sharks will often zip across the sea to **Utila** (p186). The final day should be spent **free diving** (p195) or relaxing on the beach – try the white sands at **Neptune's Restaurant** (p188). In the evening enjoy a meal at **Mango Tango** (p194) and a drink at **Treetanic** (p195).

CARIBBEAN SEA

Guanaja

Barbareta

Guanaja (Bonacca)

Coxen Hole

Roatán

Carambola Botanical Gardens

Arch's Iguana Farm

West End

French Harbor

Juan Manuel Gálvez International Airport

Utila

Utila Airstrip

Utila Town

Cayos Cochinos

Bahía de Trujillo

Trujillo

La Ceiba

Sambo Creek

Nueva Armenia

Roatán Map (p190)

Arriving in the Bay Islands

Juan Manuel Gálvez International Airport Most lodging options will arrange transfers for you, but *colectivo* taxis will cost around L50 to West End and private taxis cost around L150. Same deal if you arrive by boat with Galaxy Wave or Utila Dream.

Utila Airstrip Chances are you can walk to your accommodations, but otherwise *mototaxis* will take you on short trips for L30. This is also the case if you arrive by boat with Utila Dream.

Where to Stay

Utila mainly offers budget digs, although there are a few midrange places and even some top-end choices outside Utila Town (most of which are accessible only by boat). Roatán is more midrange to top end, though there are several affordable options, particularly in and around West End.

Diving off Roatán Island

WATERFRAME/ALAMY STOCK PHOTO ©

Diving & Snorkeling

Spectacular diving and snorkeling draws visitors from around the world to Roatán and Utila – located between 25km and 50km off the north coast of Honduras. Their reefs are part of the second-largest barrier reef in the world, and teem with fish, coral, sponges, rays, sea turtles and even whale sharks.

Great For...

☑ Don't Miss

An encounter with whale sharks off Utila – this will likely be the highlight of any visit.

Diving

The Bay Islands are one of the cheapest places in the world to get a diving certification. Dive shops usually offer both introductory courses (basic instruction plus a couple of dives) and full-certification courses qualifying you to dive worldwide; PADI, NAWI and SSI courses are all available. An open-water diving certification course typically lasts three to four days and involves four open-water dives. Despite the low cost, safety and equipment standards are usually reasonable – accidents are rare, despite the high volume of divers.

There's little difference between Roatán and Utila dive prices but the sites on Utila are further from shore, so that most dives are two-tank without a stop on land in between. Rates are standardized among dive schools to prevent cut-throat discounting.

Corals off the coast of Roatán

JOHN A. ANDERSON/SHUTTERSTOCK ©

Many schools, particularly on Utila, offer free dorm beds or throw in a free dive or two – it pays to ask around. Open-water PADI certification costs around L7000 and a 10-dive package around L6000 on both islands.

When choosing a school, speak to the instructors and staff, and ask to see their equipment (is it worn and torn or shiny and new?). Some schools specialize in tech dives; all offer deep dives, wreck diving and wall- and cave-diving.

Both islands offer excellent marine life. The shallow coral in Roatán is generally in better condition than Utila's.

Dive Shops

There is a slew of dive shops throughout the region, but following are a few of the top spots.

On Roatán:

West End Divers (✆9565-4465; www.westend divers.com; dives from L830, open-water course L7150)

Grand Bleu (www.grandbleudiving.com; dives from L850, open-water courses L8350)

Native Sons (✆2445-4003; www.roatandiving nativesons.com; dives from L1300, open-water course L6675)

Roatán Divers (✆9949-3781; www.roatandiver. com; dives from L1000, open-water course L8950)

On Utila:

Alton's Dive Center (✆2425-3704; www. diveinutila.com; 2-tank dive L1600, open-water course L8400)

Parrots Diving Center (✆2425-3772; www. parrotsdivecenter.com; 2-tank dive L1440, open-water courses L6950)

Utila Dive Centre (UDC; ✆2425-3326; www.utila divecentre.com; 2-tank dive L1850, open-water course L8400).

Snorkeling

Roatán

The exquisite **coral garden** offshore at the south end of West Bay offers the best snorkeling on the island. Hotels and dive shops hire out gear.

Half Moon Bay, which forms the northern part of the West End, is a lovely sandy bay with shallow, sheltered water. Snorkeling is okay along the south shore here.

Snorkeling equipment can be rented (L120 per day) from numerous places in West End: we suggest you go to the **Marine Park office** (☎2445-4206; www.roatanmarine park.com) ⚓, as then your money will go toward helping to protect the reef.

Utila

Utila offers exceptional snorkeling, though you'll have to make a bit of an effort to access a good reef. Many dive shops rent out snorkel gear (around L150 per day), and most dive schools allow snorkelers to tag along on dive boats for a small fee (around L100).

The best place to snorkel off Utila itself is from **Neptune's Restaurant** (mains L155-210; ⊗9am-5:30pm), accessed by free boat shuttle from town. Otherwise there's some snorkeling at **Chepes Beach**, at the western end of Main St, but the water is very shallow close to shore.

Whale Shark Encounters

Imagine: you're in the open ocean, in a dive boat off the north coast of Utila, scanning the horizon. The first sign comes from the sky as seabirds plunge into the sea, picking off small baitfish from huge schools. Next up, 'boils' are created by the frenzied feeding of bonito (black-fin tuna), which also prey on baitfish. And then, with a bit of luck, there's a shout from the captain as a whale shark is spotted, gliding just below

Whale shark

the surface, hoovering up great mouthfuls of fish- and plankton-rich seawater.

It's guessed that whale sharks, the world's biggest fish, congregate around Utila because of the deep ocean currents that get pushed up to the surface here (because of the island's topography) and the plentiful food available to them. They're found in Utilan waters year-round, but most are seen March to April and between June and September, and usually only in the open ocean, not on coral reefs. Currents converge around underwater seamounts, creating an upswell of plankton and baitfish on which the whale sharks feed.

Often the shark surfaces to feed in a vertical position – an astonishing sight – its vast mouth agape sucking in tiny fish and seawater, which it filters through a gill-raker and then expels via five pairs of huge gill slits.

A code of conduct is strictly followed on Utila if you're lucky enough to snorkel with the sharks. Rules include keeping a minimum 3m to 5m distance from the creature depending on the body part, no flash photography or lights of any kind, and a professionally trained guide should scout the water first to make sure that conditions are safe for both the shark and swimmers. Boats should also keep a safe distance and drive very slowly near the animals.

Utila's **Whale Shark & Oceanic Research Center** (☑3373-1307; https://wsorc.org; Main St E; snorkeling trips L1400; ⊘9am-4pm Mon-Sat) compiles a database of sightings, gives presentations and shows videos about this marine giant. Numbers are said to be stable around Utila, though the species is classified as 'vulnerable' by the International Union for Conservation of Nature.

The sharks have a broad, flattened head, and the upperside of their body is covered in white spots and checkerboard-style markings. By photographing the intricate patterns behind the sharks' gill slits, individuals can be recognized.

Records show whale sharks can reach around 12m (40ft) in length and weigh up to 21 tons. But speak to a local fisherman over a bottle of rum and you'll hear whispers about much larger sharks – including one they call 'Old Tom,' said to be 20m or longer.

---

❶ Need to Know

The rainy season here runs roughly from October or November to February. March and August are the hottest months; at other times sea breezes temper the heat.

MAGNUSDEEPBELOW/SHUTTERSTOCK ©

✕ Take a Break

A long day of diving or snorkeling calls for a cold drink – take a boat to Roatán's Hole in the Wall (p193) or take a terrace seat at Islanders (p195) on Utila.

Roatán

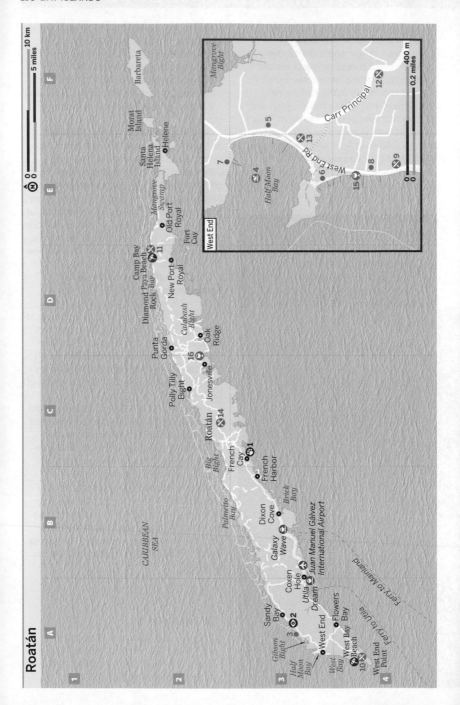

CARIBBEAN SEA

Barbareta

Morat Island

Santa Helena Island

Helene

Mangrove Swamp

Old Port Royal

Fort Cay

Camp Bay

Diamond Rock Bay

Paya Beach

New Port Royal

Calabash Bight

Punta Gorda

Oak Ridge

Polly Tilly Bight

Jonesville

Roatán

Big Bight

French Cay

French Harbor

Palmetto Bay

Dixon Cove

Brick Bay

Galaxy Wave

Coxen Hole

Juan Manuel Gálvez International Airport

Utila Dream

Sandy Bay

West End

Flowers Bay

West Bay

West Bay Beach

West End Point

Gibson Bight

Half Moon Bay

West Bay

Ferry to Mainland

Ferry to Utila

N

0   10 km
0   5 miles

West End

Mangrove Bight

Carr Principal

West End Rd

Half Moon Bay

0   400 m
0   0.2 miles

Roatán

Roatán is the largest and most developed of the Bay Islands. Long and thin, the island is a diving and snorkeling paradise – virtually its entire coastline is fringed by an astonishingly diverse coral reef teeming with tropical fish. On land, exquisite white-sand beaches, a mountainous interior of pine-forested hills and the remote wild east of the island (once a pirate hangout) beg to be explored.

⊙ SIGHTS & ACTIVITIES

Arch's Iguana Farm   Wildlife Reserve
(☑2455-7743; www.archsiguanaandmarinepark. com; L220; ☺8am-4pm) The impressive Arch's Iguana Farm in French Cay is just outside of town. Less a farm than the house of a serious iguana lover, it has iguanas pretty much everywhere you look – on the driveway, in the trees, under bushes, everywhere. In all, around 3000 of the lizards live here, some reaching lengths of 1.5m. Feeding time is at midday – the best time to visit.

**Carambola
Botanical Gardens**   Gardens
(☑2445-3117; www.carambolagardens.com; L240; ☺8am-5pm) These wonderful botanical gardens have well-maintained trails through 16 hectares of protected forest, extending up a hillside known as Carambola Mountain. It's about 1km to the summit, where you can see all the way to Utila on a clear day. Along the trail you'll encounter dozens of native species, including orchids, spice plants, medicinal plants and fruit trees.

**Roatán Institute of
Deep Sea Exploration**   Adventure
(☑3359-2887; www.stanleysubmarines.com; dives from L12,000) Karl Stanley takes passengers to depths of up to 300m, 450m or 600m in his small yellow submarine. Since light doesn't penetrate to those depths, those who dare to take the ride can witness some extraordinary marine life, including elusive six-gilled sharks.

iSoar Fun Boat   Swimming
FREE You can't miss the off-kilter silhouette of this repurposed sailboat anchored in Half Moon Bay. Swim out to swing on the rope swing or jump off one of the platforms. Local kids like to show off some crazy tricks!

⊗ EATING

The Far East of Roatán is home to two fantastic, worth-the-drive restaurants· Garifuna-inspired Temporary Cal's Cantina (p192) and **La Sirena** (☑8867-5227, 3320-6004; Camp Bay; meals L200-450; ☺11am-8pm), a lonely shack on stilts that serves up some of the island's best seafood. Ask around about the drive to La Sirena before you go to make sure the road is safe.

Head to West End for the biggest variety of eating options on the island.

Roatán

⊙ Sights
1	Arch's Iguana Farm	C3
2	Carambola Botanical Gardens	A3

⊙ Activities, Courses & Tours
3	Grand Bleu Diving	A3
4	iSoar Fun Boat	E3
5	Native Sons	F3
6	Roatán Divers	E3
7	Roatán Institute of Deep Sea Exploration	E2
8	West End Divers	E4

⊗ Eating
9	¿Por qué no?	E4
10	Java Vine	A4
11	La Sirena	D2
12	Roatán Oasis	F4
13	Tacos Raul	E3
14	Temporary Cal's Cantina	C2

⊙ Drinking & Nightlife
15	Blue Marlin	E4
16	Hole in the Wall	C2

JOHN A. ANDERSON/SHUTTERSTOCK ©

BLUE SEA.CZ/SHUTTERSTOCK ©

From left: Finger sponge; Christmas tree worm; parrot-fish and coral

Tacos Raul   Tacos $

(tacos L45; ⊘7am-midnight Sun-Thu, to 2am
Fri & Sat) This rustic outdoor stall fries up
some of the best *el pastor* (pork) tacos in
the country. Topped with *chimole* (chopped
salsa), two make a large meal. The *gringas*
(tortillas filled with melted cheese) are
filled with delicious fresh cheese imported
from the mainland. Top everything with
Raul's fiery homemade hot sauce and you
have a meal to remember.

Temporary Cal's Cantina   Fusion $$

(☑9985-8539; mains L140-325; ⊘10am-8pm
Tue-Fri) This place is packed nightly by
those willing to drive to this out-of-the-way
location between Oak Ridge and French
Harbor. Wooden tables on a beautiful garden patio overlook a panorama from jungle
to sea. Everything from the jerk chicken
to the fried conch or smoked pork chop is
delectable. For something lighter, try the
yummy fish tacos (L140).

¿Por qué no?   Mediterranean $$

(www.porquenoroatan.com; mains L240-310;
⊘8am-9pm Tue-Sat, to 3pm Sun; ⊛) This
adorable, friendly cafe with tables on the

veranda overlooking the sea does excellent
breakfasts (L190), including to-die-for
pastries, bespoke omelets and Mediterranean sets. For lunch and dinner, the salads,
wraps and Turkish-inspired mains are
deliciously healthy. After eating so well you
deserve to top off your meal with a decadent baklava, tiramisu or specialty cake.

Java Vine   Cafe $$

(www.javavine.com; sandwiches from L130;
⊘7:30am-5pm Mon-Fri, 8am-2pm & 3-5pm Sat &
Sun; ⊛) There are good sandwiches, coffee
and cake to be had at this friendly cafe and
wine bar; it's also one of the few independent and budget-oriented places to eat in
West Bay.

Roatán Oasis   International $$$

(☑9484-6659; www.roatanoasis.com; mains
L295-450; ⊘5-8:30pm Mon-Fri; ⊛) If you're
going to splurge on a meal on Roatán, go
here. The gorgeous Oasis uses seasonal
and locally sourced produce to create
delectable creations such as duck confit
risotto or scallop and shrimp ravioli. Come
Monday through Wednesday nights for the
three-course set meal (available from 5pm

to 7pm) that's amazing value from L580. Cocktails are out of this world.

🍷 DRINKING & NIGHTLIFE

The West End drag is lined with bars where live music or DJs play come dusk. Partying is limited, with most visitors getting up to dive the next day, but it's the liveliest place on the island.

Hole in the Wall   Bar

(mains L400; ☉10am-7pm) There's a party going on, way out in the mangroves at this over-the-water bar only accessible by boat (including on mangrove tours). Slip onto a stool next to fellas straight out of *Pirates of the Caribbean*, grab a beer or something stronger and try your gaming luck by tossing a ring onto a hook on the wall. There are also meals and snacks on offer.

Blue Marlin   Bar

(www.bluemarlinroatan.com; ☉noon-midnight Mon-Thu, to 2am Fri & Sat, to 10pm Sun) A highly sociable and welcoming bar-restaurant with superb sunset views from the rear

deck. Draws a good mix of locals, expats and visitors. There's popular live music on Fridays and some decent talent on karaoke Thursdays.

ℹ GETTING THERE & AWAY

Roatán's **Juan Manuel Gálvez International Airport** (RTB; ☎2445-1880) is a short distance east of Coxen Hole.

Galaxy Wave (☎2445-1775; www.roatanferry. com; one-way L900; ☉ticket office 5:30am-3:30pm) is a catamaran that connects Roatán with La Ceiba (1¼ hours). It sails from the Dixon Cove terminal at 7am and 2pm, returning from La Ceiba at 9:30am and 4:30pm.

Utila Dream (☎9440-4897; www.utilaferry. com; 1hr L700) is another comfy catamaran that goes to Utila at 2pm daily and returns at 10:15am.

Utila

Honduras' most popular backpacker haunt, little Utila is also one of the cheapest places in the world to learn how to dive. You'll meet people here daily who came to get certified, went home, sold all their stuff and came back on a one-way ticket. Utila's sublime tropical beauty and chilled-out vibe makes it hard to not also entertain that idea yourself at least once.

⊗ EATING

Utila Town has a good selection of eating options for such a small settlement, from cheapo *baleadas* (rolled tortillas) to fine dining. Several places to stay also have kitchens where you can cook. Poorly stocked supermarkets dot Main St.

Camilla's Bakery   Bakery $

(📞9969-6360; mains L71-140; ⊙6:30am-2pm & 5-9pm Sun-Tue; 📶) Our favorite breakfast stop on Utila serves fresh bread and homemade bagels with all kinds of toppings, as well as delicious egg dishes, quiche,

> ❝...little Utila is one of the cheapest places in the world to learn how to dive.❞

smoothies and croissants. There's a lot of French *savoir faire* going on and even the self-service coffee is top notch. At night it turns into Pizza Nut and churns out fantastic, cheesy pies (around L200).

Hotspot Cafe   Cafe $$

(Main St W; mains L90-150; ⊙6am-5pm Mon-Sat; 📶) With real coffee and an enormous whiteboard menu that includes breakfasts, smoothies, burgers, wraps and a popular steak sub, this cute, brightly painted shack lives up to its name – it heaves with divers and backpackers throughout the day. There are relatively few tables, but the sociable counter is a great place to meet new people.

Mango Tango   International $$$

(📞3211-9469; mains L275-390; ⊙8am-10pm; 📶) Housed in an over-the-water building that takes in views from three sides, Mango Tango has some of the best food in town. Try the Galician-style octopus, homemade shrimp and ricotta ravioli or filet mignon with chimichurri from the interesting international menu while enjoying the sea breezes. Start

Dive boat returning from Utila

with a world-class cocktail and finish with a Better Than Sex Big Tiramisu.

🍸 DRINKING & NIGHTLIFE

The party scene is strong in Utila, which at times feels like a cool college town revolving around a small diving university. There's usually a special night of the week when each bar fills up, so ask around.

Treetanic   Bar

(Cola de Mico; ⏲8pm-midnight Sat-Tue & Thu, to 1am Wed & Fri) Owned by Neil, an eccentric American artist, this psychedelic mango-treetop bar is somewhere you just have to see while visiting Utila. It always draws a cast of local characters and is one of the more fun places on the island. The 'Dark Moon' night during the new moon is one of the best parties on the island.

Islanders   Bar

(beer 12oz/tasting flight L90/160) Serving El Bosque craft beers brewed in San Pedro Sula, Islanders is a new low-key spot for quality brews and even better views from the over-the-sea terrace. Wine, cocktails and light meals like burgers and nachos are also served.

ℹ️ GETTING THERE & AWAY

Utila has an airstrip, but no terminal; buy tickets at **World Wide Travel** (🕿9891-1960; Main St E; ⏲9am-noon & 2-5pm Mon-Fri) or **Morgan's Travel** (🕿2425-3161; www.utilamorganstravel.com;

Free Dive Utila

This highly regarded **dive school** (🕿9730-3424; www.freediveutila.com; Main St E) – the first of its kind in Central America – teaches free-diving (diving without any breathing apparatus). A 2½-day course costs US$235 and features two classroom sessions and two diving sessions.

JAMES R.D. SCOTT/GETTY IMAGES ©

⏲8am-5:30pm Mon-Fri, 8am-noon Sat) in town. Planes serving Utila range from small 20-seaters to tiny five-seaters – and they all fill up fast, so book a spot as early as possible. Flights between Utila and Roatán (15 minutes) on **CM Airlines** (🕿9522-5304; www.cmairlines.com) are a good choice when the sea is rough.

The **Utila Dream** (🕿2425-3191; www.utilaferry.com) sails twice a day to/from La Ceiba (L600, 45 minutes) and once per day to/from Roatán (L700, one hour). Arrive 30 minutes before your boat's departure.

NICARAGUA

In this Chapter

Volcán Mombacho 200
Pueblos Blancos 202
Colonial Explorer Walking Tour.........206
Sights..208
Tours 209
Courses 211
Shopping 211
Eating..212
Drinking & Nightlife...........................213

Granada

Nicaragua's oldest and best-preserved town is also its most beguiling and photogenic, and has been entrancing travelers for centuries. The town boasts a meticulously restored cathedral, a well-groomed plaza and perfectly maintained mansions that shelter lush internal courtyards. Many travelers use the city as a base, spending at least a day bopping along cobblestone roads from church to church in the city center, then venturing out into the countryside for trips to nearby attractions like the evocative archipelago water world at Las Isletas, or the hiking trails and hot springs around Volcán Mombacho.

Two Days in Granada

For two days, simply wander: duck into **Convento y Museo San Francisco** (p208), have a look at **Iglesia de Xalteva** (p209) and climb the bell tower at **Iglesia La Merced** (p208) at sunset. Grab breakfast and a coffee at **Cafe del Arte** (p212) and lunch at **Bocadillos Tapas Kitchen & Bar** (p212). Relax in Parque Central, and hit **Calle La Calzada** (p213) for drinks and dinner.

Four Days in Granada

If you're lucky enough to have a couple of additional days in Granada, explore **Los Pueblos Blancos** (p202) or embark on a boat tour through the **Isletas de Granada** (p212). On your final day, hike in the cloud forest atop **Volcán Mombacho** and dip into its bubbling hot springs at **Aguas Termales de Calera** (p201).

Previous page: Street scene, Granada

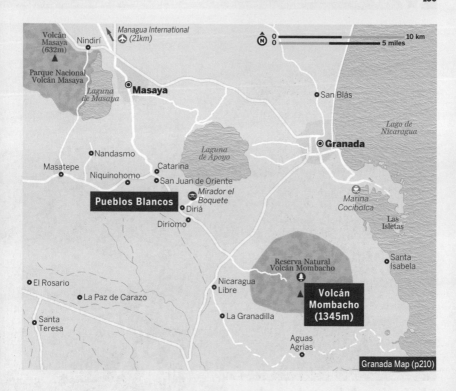

Arriving in Granada

Managua International Airport

For most travelers, daily scheduled door-to-door shuttles are the fastest and most convenient way of getting to Granada from Managua's airport. Many travelers also arrive in bus terminals scattered throughout the city. Shared taxis are plentiful, and should be less than US$1 per person. Ask the fare before getting in.

Where to Stay

There's a huge range of sleeping options in Granada, from budget-friendly hostels and guesthouses to some of the country's loveliest and most character-ful boutique and historic hotels, inside former colonial buildings. There is also a handful of beautiful, upscale ecolodges on several of the islets, privately owned by foreigners but operated by islander staff. Staying overnight is an unforgettable experience.

Walking to viewpoint, Volcán Mombacho

CNICBC/GETTY IMAGES ©

Volcán Mombacho

This looming 1345m volcano is the defining feature of the Granada skyline. It has thriving rural communities, coffee farms and cooperatives along its foothills, and the volcano's slopes, covered in ferns and cloud forest, are home to howler monkeys, dozens of bird species and many of Nicaragua's shy mammals, including the jaguarundi.

It's been a few decades since this forest-clad volcano has acted up, but it is still most certainly active and sends up the periodic puff of smoke. It's easy to get to the crown of cloud forest, steaming with fumaroles and other bubbling volcanic activity beneath the misty vines and orchids. Attractions include three hiking trails of varying difficulty, an organic coffee farm and more. Take a tour from Granada or drive yourself.

Reserva Natural Volcán Mombacho

Reserva Natural Volcán Mombacho is managed by the Fundación Cocibolca, which since 1999 has been building trails and running an eco-mobile (think refurbished military jeeps seating 25) on the 40% grade up to 1100m. Get there early to take

Great For...

☑ **Don't Miss**

The Aguas Termales de Calera hot springs.

❶ Need to Know

Reserva Natural Volcán Mombacho
(📞2552-5858; www.mombacho.org;
Empalme de Guanacaste, Carretera Granada–
Nandaime Km 50; park entrance per car/
pedestrian US$20/5, mariposario US$2;
⊗8am-5pm)

✕ Take a Break

The park's visitor center has a basic
cafeteria, and there's a popular cafe
halfway up the volcano.

★ Top Tip

It's rewarding to overnight on the volcano's misty slopes and be awakened by a
chorus of howler monkeys and birds.

the short trail through the organic coffee
farm, or check out the *mariposario* (butterfly garden) and orchid garden (free with
entrance), close to the parking lot.

There is a choice of several trails, including Sendero del Cráter, a 1.5km jaunt to the
fumaroles, with great views of Granada and
Las Isletas, and Sendero la Puma, a steeper
4km trek around the lip of the crater, with
even better views. Guides, many of whom
speak English, are available at the entrance
and cost US$12 to US$22 per group of up
to seven. Guides are required for a trek up
Sendero el Tigrillo, a heart-pumping two-
hour tromp up to two overlooks.

Time your arrival to coincide with an
eco-mobile departure, at 8:30am, 10am
or 1pm. If you have a 4WD, you can drive
up the volcano for an extra US$22 – plus
US$5 for every adult and US$3 for every
child in the car.

Aguas Termales de Calera

Tucked away on Finca Calera, inside the
reserve and right by the lake, these 45°C
(113°F) **hot springs** (📞2222-4208; Carretera
Granada–Nandaime Km 55.5, 14km E) **FREE** are
rich with sulfur, calcium and other beauti-
fying minerals. An excursion costs around
US$25 per person, including transportation.

Rural Community Tourism

○ **Aguas Agrias** (📞2552-0238; www.ucati
errayagua.org/aguas-agrias; Entrada de Monte
Verde, Carretera Granada–Nandaime, 12km E;
guided tours US$3-5; ⊗tours by reservation)
has local guides who lead hikes through a
plantation and to swimming lagoons.

○ **Nicaragua Libre** (📞2552-0238; www.ucati
errayagua.org; Entrada de Monte Verde, 500m SE;
per person guided tour US$5; ⊗tours by reser-
vation) offers guided trips through organic
coffee farms, horseback rides to San Juan
de Oriente and walks to Mombacho.

Iglesia San Juan Bautista in Masatepe (p205)

JON ARNOLD IMAGES LTD/ALAMY STOCK PHOTO ©

Pueblos Blancos

Originally built from the chalky, pale volcanic tuff upon which this pastoral scene is spread, this series of rural communities, often called the White Villages or Pueblos Blancos, once shimmered a blinding white amid the pale-green patchwork of pasture and jungle.

Today the centuries-old buildings have been painted and the shady roads are paved. Most days the roads between the villages are lined with stands selling vividly painted *artesanías* (handicrafts). Each town has its specialty: handcrafted ceramics, homemade sweets, wooden furniture or freshly cut flowers. The region is also famous for its *curanderos* (folk healers). The villages are most often visited as a day trip from Granada, but take the time to explore and the inner workings of life in rural Nicaragua may reveal themselves.

Diriomo & Diriá

Diriomo, home to a number of so-called 'witch doctors,' has long been known as the Witch Capital of the Meseta and it is here that people come if they're looking to curse an enemy, cure an ailment or bewitch a

Great For...

☑ **Don't Miss**

The exquisite pottery in San Juan de Oriente.

Pottery from San Juan de Oriente

JOHN MITCHELL/ALAMY STOCK PHOTO ©

❶ Need to Know

The popular villages – Catarina, Diriomo, Masatepe – can be reached by bus from Granada.

✕ Take a Break

There are traditional Nicaraguan restaurants, basic food kiosks and *fritangas* (grills) scattered throughout the towns.

★ Top Tip

Time your visit with one of the region's glorious festivals, such as Masatepe's Domingo de Trinidad, 40 days after Semana Santa.

paramour. Most healers work out of their homes, which are unsigned. Ask at the *alcadía* (mayor's office). Diriomo is also famous for its *cajetas* (rich, fruit-flavored sweets), *chicha bruja* (an alcoholic corn beverage) and even stiffer *calavera del gato* ('skull of the cat' – drink at your own risk).

Diriá, a twin town across the road, boasts **Mirador el Boquete** (Calle Laguna de Apoyo), the mellower, less-touristed overlook of **Laguna de Apoyo**, where the viewpoint features a few eating places that get packed with families on weekends. From the lookout, there's a steep, half-hour trail to the bottom, where a muddy little beach offers access to the bright-blue water for swimming.

San Juan de Oriente

This attractive colonial village – known to some as the sister 'bewitched village'

of Catarina – is renowned for its artisan traditions. San Juan de Oriente, indeed, has been in the pottery business since before the Spanish conquest, and 95% of the residents are artisans. While production of inexpensive and functional pottery for local consumption is still important, the recent generations of craftspeople have upped their game. A number of the local masters are international award winners who exhibit abroad, and their vases, plates, pots and other creations are exquisitely decorated and very fairly priced.

You can spend hours wandering around here, watching the masters at work and perhaps even trying your own hand at a foot-spun pottery wheel.

Pottery in San Juan de Oriente

In the 1980s there was a pottery renaissance in San Juan de Oriente, with ceramics artists adding greater flair and imagination to their designs and creating art unmatched elsewhere in Central

America. There are five distinctive styles to watch out for:

o **Utilitarian** The least expensive, these are cups and plates produced for everyday use and typically painted in traditional greens, reds and blues, depicting flowers or jungle creatures.

o **Traditional** This is the signature style for San Juan de Oriente: a terracotta background painted with flowers, monkeys, birds, frogs and plants in blues, greens and reds, with mineral oxides used for the different colors. These pieces tend to be of finer quality than the utilitarian ones.

o **Pre-Columbian** Takes its inspiration from centuries-old pieces belonging to the Chorotega culture. Several local ceramics masters specialize in recreating museum

pieces, such as jaguar jars, down to the finest detail.

o **Geometric** While geometric patterns are found in pre-Columbian design as well, done either by painting, etching or incising the vessel, contemporary San Juan de Oriente artists often incorporate nontraditional patterns, such as MC Escher designs.

o **Contemporary** These tend to be unique pieces that are nontraditional in shape and/or design: unusually shaped vessels, a blend of several decoration techniques, and global influences at play.

Some ceramic artists blend two or more of the above styles, and all of the styles can incorporate incised designs, when a pattern is cut into the clay, or relief designs – a bas relief effect created by pecking away at the outer clay layer. While 95% of the villagers

Pottery shop, San Juan de Oriente

work in the ceramics trade, a number of ceramics masters truly stand out due to the outstanding quality of their work, and if you're looking to buy a one-of-a-kind piece, it's best to go straight to their workshop.

Catarina

At the crossroads of Los Pueblos Blancos, Catarina is known for its spectacular *mirador* (viewpoint) over Lago de Nicaragua and Laguna de Apoyo, and for its *viveros* (nurseries) that supply ornamental plants for households across Nicaragua.

★ Top Tip

Transporting ceramics can be tricky and most of San Juan de Oriente's ceramics masters don't offer shipping. It's best to come with your own packing material and FedEx your treasure home.

PHILIP SCALIA/ALAMY STOCK PHOTO ©

Niquinohomo

This quiet, 16th-century Spanish-colonial village is the birthplace of General Augusto César Sandino, the Nicaraguan revolutionary who fought against US military occupation of Nicaragua between 1927 and 1933, and who did indeed appreciate the fact that its name is Náhuatl for 'Valley of the Warriors.' Sandino's childhood home, located just steps away from the quiet Parque Central, has been turned into a basic museum. Anyone in town can point you toward the building. Nearby, the town's church, **Parroquia Santa Ana**, is over 320 years old and allegedly Nicaragua's oldest.

Masatepe

This photogenic colonial town has well-kept plazas and churches, and is renowned for two things: the exuberant horse parade in June that's part of its *fiestas patronales* (saints' days), and its carpenters, who make Nicaragua's finest furniture, showcased at Masatepe's old train station, which has been reincarnated as one of the better **artisan markets** (Carretera Masatepe-Masaya; ⊗9am-6pm) in the country.

Towering over Masatepe's attractive central plaza, **Iglesia San Juan Bautista** is home to El Cristo Negro de La Santísima Trinidad, whose feast days mean a month of parties between mid-May and mid-June. The sweeping adobe makes a fine colonial centerpiece, but it's the views from its gates, of fuming Volcán Masaya, that will add depth to your prayers.

✗ Take a Break

Masatepe is well known for its *mondongo* (tripe soup marinated with bitter oranges and fresh herbs) – sample the stew at **Mondongo Veracruz** (Parque de Veracruz, 2c E; dishes US$3-6; ⊗10am-8pm).

Colonial Explorer Walking Tour

Wander the fine Parque Central and nearby streets, taking in the best of Granada's colonial architecture and enjoying the pleasantly shaded park's mango and malinche trees.
Start Parque Central
Distance 1.5km
Duration Two hours

Take a Break: Grab a street-food snack in **Parque Central**.

Calle 14 de Septiembre

Av Barricada

Parque Xalteva

Calle Real Xalteva

6

7
FINISH

7 The old indigenous neighborhood is marked by **Iglesia de Xalteva** (p209), a 19th-century church housing La Virgen de la Asunción.

6 Head back to Parque Central, then four blocks west to **Iglesia La Merced** (p208), considered the most beautiful of Granada's churches.

4 Proceed to the **Fundación Casa de los Tres Mundos**, which hosts art exhibitions, poetry readings and other cultural events.

3 Head north to **Plaza de la Independencia**. The obelisk is dedicated to the heroes of the 1821 struggle for independence.

Av Guzmán

Calle Cervantes

Calle El Arsenal

Calle del Beso

Calle La Libertad

Calle Atravesada

Parque Central

START ①

Calle El Caimito

Classic Photo: Convento y Museo San Francisco

5 Check out the awesome facade of **Convento y Museo San Francisco** (p208), best captured on film close to sunset.

Av Vega

Av Guzmán

2 On the park's southeastern corner, the beautifully restored **Hotel Gran Francia** (Av Guzmán) was formerly the home of American mercenary William Walker.

Mercado Municipal

1 The **Catedral de Granada**, on the eastern side of the Parque Central, was originally built in 1583.

◎ SIGHTS

Convento y Museo
San Francisco   Church

(☎2552-5535; Plaza de los Leones 1c N, 1c E; US$5; ⊙8am-4pm Mon-Fri, 9am-4pm Sat & Sun) One of the oldest churches in Central America, Convento San Francisco boasts a striking birthday-cake facade and houses both an important convent and one of the best museums in the region. The highlight is the museum that focuses on Nicaragua's pre-Columbian people. Don't miss the Zapatera statuary, two solemn regiments of black-basalt statues, carved between AD 800 and 1200, then left behind on the ritual island of Zapatera.

Museo de Chocolate   Museum

(☎2552-4678; www.chocomuseo.com; Calle Atravesada, frente Bancentro; chocolate workshop adult/child US$21/12; ⊙7am-6:30pm; ⌨) **FREE** Granada's new chocolate museum is excellent if you're traveling with children: the 'beans to bar' chocolate workshop, where participants learn to roast and grind cacao beans, and mold their very own Nicaraguan chocolate bar, is hands-on fun for all ages. Cigar-making workshops are also held here. The museum is at the **Mansión de Chocolate hotel** (☎2552-4678; www.mansiondechocolate.com; Calle Atravesada, frente Bancentro; r/tr from US$77/101; ❄🛜🏊), which also has a chocolate-oriented spa and a popular buffet breakfast (US$7), plus a great swimming pool you can use for an extra US$6.

Iglesia La Merced   Church

(cnr Calle Real Xalteva & Av 14 de Septiembre; bell tower US$1; ⊙11am-6pm) Perhaps the most beautiful church in the city, this landmark was built in 1534. Most come here for the spectacular views from the **bell tower** – especially picturesque at sunset. Originally completed in 1539, it was razed by pirates in 1655 and rebuilt with its current baroque facade between 1781 and 1783. Damaged by William Walker's forces in 1854, it was restored with the current elaborate interior in 1862. Today Catholics come here to see the Virgen de Fatima.

Mi Museo   Museum

(☎2552-7614; Calle Atravesada, Cine Karawala, ½c N; US$5; ⊙8am-5pm) This museum

From left: Convent y Museo San Francisco; Convent Museum; Mi Museo; Iglesia La Merced

displays a private collection of ceramics dating from at least 2000 BC to the present. Hundreds of beautifully crafted pieces were chosen with as much an eye for their artistic merit as their archaeological significance.

Iglesia de Xalteva   Church

(frente Parque Xalteva; ☉hours vary) The dilapidated but attractive colonial church that houses La Virgen de la Asunción was almost completely rebuilt in the 1890s after suffering serious earthquake damage.

TOURS

Adventour Nicaragua   Outdoors

(☑5760-6733; www.adventournicaragua.com; Calle La Calzada, el catedral, ½c E; ☉8am-9pm) Ramiro and his passionate, professional team run highly recommended tours of Las Isletas, Isla Zapatero, Volcán Mombacho (from US$25) and Granada itself, with small groups accompanied by bilingual guides. Shuttles available to destinations across the country too.

 The Best Coffee in Nicaragua

Self-respecting coffee connoisseurs should make the journey back to Managua for **DeLaFinca Cafe** (☑2252-8974; www.delafincanicaragua.com; Parque El Dorado, costado Sureste; ☉7am-8pm Mon-Fri, 8am-7pm Sat & Sun; ☎), an altar to the coffee bean. The owner comes from generations of coffee farmers and has perfected *viñedo* – a novel coffee-bean fermentation method. Come here to buy beans and to sample the best of Nicaragua's single-origin coffees, each prepared using the optimum method according to its type.

Livit Water   Water Sports

(☑8580-7014; www.livitwater.com; Marina Cocibolca; SUP tours per person from US$40) Scott and Gea run professional stand-up paddleboarding (SUP) tours on the water, both here and in Laguna Apoyo, with pick-up from Granada. Combine your SUP

STEFANO PATERNA/ALAMY STOCK PHOTO ©

ELIZABETH WINTERBOURNE/SHUTTERSTOCK ©

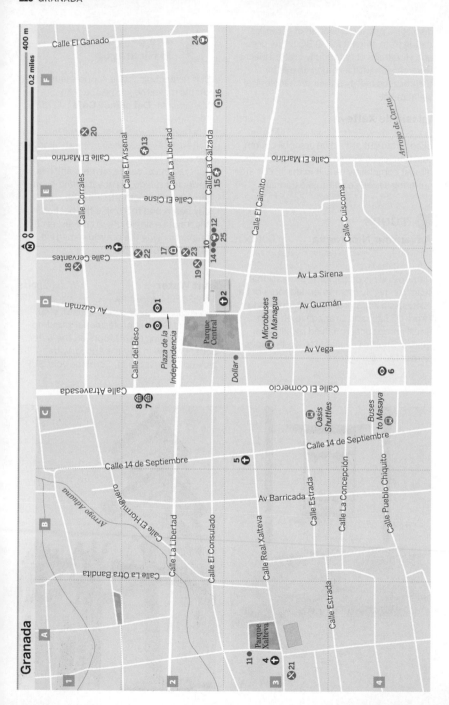

Granada

Calle El Ganado

Calle Corrales

Calle El Martirio

Calle El Arsenal

Calle La Libertad

Calle El Cisne

Calle La Calzada

Calle El Caimito

Calle El Martirio

Calle Cuiscoma

Calle Cervantes

Av La Sirena

Av Guzmán

Av Vega

Av Guzmán

Calle del Beso

Plaza de la Independencia

Parque Central

Calle Atravesada

Dollar

Calle El Comercio

Microbuses to Managua

Oasis Shuttles

Calle 14 de Septiembre

Buses to Masaya

Calle 14 de Septiembre

Calle El Hormiguero

Calle La Libertad

Calle El Consulado

Av Barricada

Calle Estrada

Calle La Concepción

Calle Pueblo Chiquito

Arroyo Aduana

Calle La Otra Bandita

Calle Real Xalteva

Calle Estrada

Parque Xalteva

Arroyo de Curita

400 m
0.2 miles

Granada

⊙ **Sights**
1 Casa de los Leones & Fundación
  Casa de los Tres Mundos D2
2 Catedral de Granada D2
3 Convento y Museo San Francisco D1
4 Iglesia de Xalteva A3
5 Iglesia La Merced C3
6 Mercado Municipal C4
7 Mi Museo C2
8 Museo de Chocolate C2
9 Plaza de la Independencia D2

◉ **Activities, Courses & Tours**
10 Adventour Nicaragua E2
11 Casa Xalteva A3
12 Erick Tours E2
13 La Tortilla Cooking School E2
14 Leo Tours Comunitarios D2

15 Massiel Torres E2

⊙ **Shopping**
16 Soy Nica F2
17 The Garden Shop D2

✴ **Eating**
18 Bocadillos Tapas Kitchen & Bar D1
19 Cafe del Arte D2
20 El Garaje F1
21 Espressonista A3
22 Miss Dell's Kitchen D2
23 Pita Pita D2

◉ **Drinking & Nightlife**
24 Hog's Breath Saloon F2
25 Nectar E2

experience with yoga or half-day tours up Volcán Mombacho.

Leo Tours Comunitarios   Tours

(☑8422-7905; www.facebook.com/leotourscomunitarios; Calla La Calzada, Parque Central, 1½c E; ☺8am-9pm) Enthusiastic locally owned business that offers all the usual options – Las Isletas boat tours (US$15), Mombacho (US$30) and a full-day trip to Masaya (US$40) – as well as some interesting visits to local communities.

⊛ COURSES

La Tortilla Cooking School   Cooking

(☑5503-2805; Calle El Martirio 305, entre Calle La Libertad y El Arsenal; basic class US$45 per person; ☺cooking classes 10:30am & 4:30pm) A really fun, hands-on experience that teaches you all about the origins and methods of Nicaraguan cuisine. Spend two or three hours learning to make five typical dishes and throw in a market tour (US$15) to learn about the ingredients.

Massiel Torres   Pottery Class

(☑8672-7465; Calle La Calzada, el catedral, 1½c E; pottery classes from US$15; ☺noon-9pm) Near Wok & Roll, this ceramics artist from San Juan de Oriente offers pottery-making classes to visitors.

Casa Xalteva   Language

(☑2552-2993; www.casaxalteva.org; Calle Real Xalteva, Iglesia Xalteva, 25m N; 1-week language course from US$160; ☺8am-5pm Mon-Fri) ✐ Next to the church of the same name, Casa Xalteva also runs a program providing breakfast and education for street kids, as well as language classes and homestays.

⊕ SHOPPING

There are several excellent shops where you can buy high-quality crafts handmade in Nicaragua, as well as gourmet coffee. Granada is also the best place in Nicaragua to find English-language books (including Lonely Planet guidebooks).

Garden Shop   Arts & Crafts

(www.gardencafegranada.com; Calle La Libertad, Parque Central, 1c E; ☺9am-6pm; ☜) ✐ A fantastic addition to the popular Garden Café, this sustainably minded boutique offers crafts, jewelry, clothing and artwork produced through NGOs and fair-trade organizations throughout Nicaragua. Artisans from Chinandega, Diriamba, Granada, Masatepe, Managua and Masaya are all represented here; you can also buy coffee beans and postcards, and there's a good-sized book exchange at the entrance.

Isletas de Granada

With an islet for every day of the year (there are 365 in total), this spectacular archipelago, within easy reach of Granada, was created during a spectacular eruption by Volcán Mombacho some 20,000 years ago. Several hundred fishing folk make the islets their home; if you're out on the water after daybreak, you can see them casting their nets among the herons and other birdlife.

Most tour companies run trips to Las Isletas, or do it yourself with Inuit Kayaks, about 1km from the Centro Turístico entrance, an outfitter that runs several guided kayak tours. Half-day trips from Granada (around US$20 per person) typically involve a boat ride, though morning tours get to the lake too late to catch the early-morning birdlife. Most tours also pass Isla de los Monos (Monkey Island).

Soy Nica
Fashion & Accessories

(📞2552-0234; www.facebook.com/soynica.dk; Calle La Calzada, Iglesia de Guadelupe, 100m O; ☺9am-6pm Mon-Thu, to 8pm Fri & Sat, to 2pm Sun) Come here for stylish purses, shoulder bags, belts and other accessories made of Nicaraguan leather. You can see them being made at the workshop next to the store.

EATING

Granada caters to international tastes with a wide variety of cuisines, and new options are opening all the time. The city has excellent street food too. Look for it around Parque Central and **Mercado Municipal** (Calle Atravesada; ☺7am-5pm Mon-Sat) in the morning, and just before sunset, at *fritangas* (grills) set up around town.

Bocadillos Tapas Kitchen & Bar
International $$

(📞2552-5089; www.bocadillosgranada.com; frente Convento San Francisco; dishes US$4-8;

☺noon-9pm; 🛜) The interior leafy courtyard of this stylish yet casual restaurant is an ideal setting for a cocktail (including some original ones!), a local craft beer or two or three, and imaginative tapas that span the globe, from spicy samosas and pulled pork sliders to Thai noodle salad and roasted garlic hummus. There's a handful of substantial dishes too.

Cafe del Arte
Nicaraguan $$

(📞2552-6461; Calle Cervantes, el catedral, 1c E, ½c N; mains US$4-7; ☺7:30am-9pm) Sit in the courtyard, filled with greenery and paintings by local artists, and savor an excellent coffee and an ample Nica breakfast.

El Garaje
Vegetarian $$

(📞8651-7412; Calle Corrales, Convento San Francisco, 2c E; mains US$5-8; ☺11:30am-3:30pm Mon-Fri; 🖋) Hands down the best place for vegetarians in Granada, El Garaje serves imaginative fare such as curry chickpea pita, vegan 'pulled pork,' sloppy joes and salads, all in a bright setting, surrounded by contemporary art. Outstanding lime cheesecake, too.

Miss Dell's Kitchen
Fusion $$$

(📞2552-2815; cnr Calle Cervantes & Calle El Arsenal; mains US$10-14; ☺5:30pm-midnight) Mellow jazz plays in the background at this candlelit spot, with a mural of a rooster, Mr Beautiful, gracing the back wall. The rooster belonged to Miss Dell, a Haitian cook, whose recipes have been adapted by the chef for the short and sweet menu. The *piri piri pescado* (fish in a chili sauce) is one of the best things we've ever tried, anywhere.

Espressonista
Fusion $$$

(📞2552-4325; www.facebook.com/espressonistacoffee; Calle Real Xalteva, frente Iglesia de Xalteva; mains US$10-18; ☺noon-8pm Wed-Sun; 🛜) Tall ceilings, hand-carved furniture and gilded mirrors give this place a certain old-world grandeur, but the succinct menu is as contemporary as it gets, with French influences. Feast on the likes of mackerel and passion-fruit *ceviche* (marinated seafood), rabbit confit and ox cheek à la bourguignonne, along with some of Granada's best gourmet coffee.

Pita Pita
Middle Eastern **$$$**

(📞2552-4117; www.facebook.com/ThePitaPita; Calle La Libertad, Parque Central, 1c E; mains US$10-12; ⏰noon-10pm; 📶🖨) A longtime favorite Italian trattoria has expanded and morphed into a Middle Eastern restaurant, though the wood-fired thin-crust pizza remains the best in town. Roasted, garlicky eggplant with yogurt hits the spot, as does the Palestinian kebab and the Israeli shakshuka.

🍷 DRINKING & NIGHTLIFE

Granada hops most nights, but Thursday to Saturday is when the real action takes place. Most people start or end the night at one of the numerous bars along or just off Calle La Calzada, known for outdoor drinking and prime people-watching.

Hog's Breath Saloon
Lounge

(📞8337-6225; www.hogsbreathgranada.com; Calle La Calzada, frente Iglesia de Guadelupe; ⏰noon-11pm) Modeled on the original Hog's Breath Saloon in Florida and run by a friendly Minnesotan couple, this safari-themed lounge bar is the antithesis of the backpacker haunts up the street – a place to sip a whiskey, gin or a cocktail and munch on some delicious tapas while checking out the stuffed animal heads and guitars that deck the walls.

Nectar
Bar

(www.facebook.com/NectarNicaragua; Calle La Calzada, Parque Central, 1½c E; dishes US$5-8; ⏰11am-11pm) This place wears many hats and we like all of them. It's a small lounge-bar with a good list of cocktails and local craft beers (come for happy hour). In high season it often gets visiting DJs and live rock bands to liven the place up. Internationally inspired light dishes and snacks make up the creative menu.

 Political Unrest in Nicaragua

The antigovernment protests that erupted in mid-April 2018 did not spare Granada. There were violent clashes between government-funded Sandinista mobs and protesters, and some looting of businesses also occurred.

While the use of deadly force by the paramilitaries and the police against antigovernment protesters is at a minimum, the situation on the ground is still unpredictable. The general population is living with the consequences of the failed protests, with the police rounding up those suspected of having taken part in demonstrations.

Notwithstanding all this, events on the ground do not pose a direct threat to visitors, as foreigners are not deliberately targeted by the violence. If you're unlucky, however, you could get caught up in it, so make sure you get the latest information before traveling to or around Nicaragua. At time of writing, the US, UK and Canadian governments had issued recent alerts to reconsider travel or exercise a high degree of caution.

ℹ️ GETTING THERE & AWAY

BOAT

Marina Cocibolca (📞2552-2269; desvio a Posintepe), about 2km southeast of town, has boats for Las Isletas and Parque Nacional Archipiélago Zapatera.

BUS

Microbuses to Managua (US$1, one hour, every 20 minutes, from 5am to 7pm), arriving at UCA in Managua, leave from the convenient lot just south of the Parque Central on Calle Vega; change at UCA for microbuses and chicken buses to León.

Buses to Masaya (US$0.50, 30 minutes, every 20 to 30 minutes, from 4:30am to 4:30pm) leave from Calle 14 de Septiembre two blocks west of the Mercado Municipal, around the corner from Palí.

SHUTTLE

Shuttles are a fast and convenient way of getting to Managua Airport and San Jorge (for Isla Ometepe). Top choices include **Oasis Shuttles** (☑2552-8005; Calle Estrada 109, Oasis Hostel), **Adelante Express** (☑2568-2083; www.adelante-express.com) or **Erick Tours** (☑8974-5575; www.ericktoursnicaragua.com; Parque Central, 3c E).

❶ GETTING AROUND

BICYCLE

While cycling in town might require nerves of steel, there are several mellow rides around town; many tour operators and some hostels rent bikes for around US$7 to $10 per day.

CAR & MOTORCYCLE

Nicaragua is (relatively) traffic-free, and decent roads around Granada make motorbiking an enjoyable way of getting around, particularly if you're planning a day trip to Pueblos Blancos. Ask at tour operators around town. Several accommodations rent scooters for around US$20 per day.

It's generally cheaper to rent cars in Managua, where your rental is probably parked right now – so be sure to allow a couple of hours for it to arrive. This region has good roads, and many attractions. Parking in Granada's narrow streets can be a nightmare. There's a **Budget** (☑2552-2323; www.budget.com.ni; Calle Inmaculada, Plaza Inmaculada) at the Shell station and a **Dollar** (☑2552-8515; www.dollar.com.ni; Calle Vega) at Hotel Plaza Colón.

TAXI

Taxis are plentiful. Always agree on a fare before getting into the taxi, which should be less than US$1 per person if you're getting into a shared taxi anywhere in the city.

San Juan de Oriente, one of the Los Pueblos Blancos, is famous for its pottery, which borrows from pre-Columbian themes. Ceramic handicrafts are sold in the shops along the main road.

From left: Pottery on sale in handicraft shops in San Juan de Oriente (p203)

In this Chapter
Outdoor Activities 218
Moyogalpa 223
Playa Santo Domingo
& Santa Cruz 225
Around Volcán Maderas 226

Isla de Ometepe

Ometepe never fails to impress. Its twin volcanic peaks rising up out of Lago de Nicaragua have captured the imagination of everyone from precolonial Aztecs (who thought they'd found the promised land) to Mark Twain (who waxed lyrical about it in his book Travels with Mr Brown) *– not to mention the relatively few travelers who make it out here. The island's fertile volcanic soil, clean waters, wide beaches, wildlife population, off-the-beaten-track farmstays, archaeological sites and dramatic profile are quickly propelling it up traveler must-see lists. More than 1700 petroglyphs have been found on Ometepe, making this a DIY archaeologists' fantasy island.*

Two Days in Isla de Ometepe

For your first days on otherworldly Isla de Ometepe, touch down in Moyogalpa and arrange a climb up **Volcán Concepción** (p218) for the following day. Then, in the meantime, feast on a gourmet sandwich at **Cornerhouse** (p223), and go **horseback riding** (p227) or rent a motorbike and cruise down south to **Museos El Ceibo** (p226).

Four Days in Isla de Ometepe

Switch up your base, ideally landing at a cool **farmstay** (p227) on the wilder side of the island, near Balgüe. If you skipped Volcán Concepción, hike **Volcán Maderas** (p219). Otherwise, visit **Cascada San Ramón** (p226) and enjoy a delicious meal at **Café Campestre** (p227). On day four head down to **Playa Santo Domingo** (p225) for some beach time and kayaking on Río Istiam.

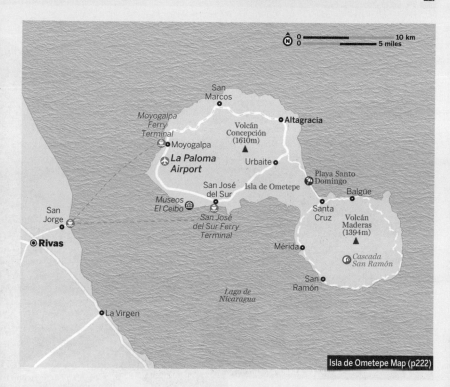

0 / 0 10 km / 5 miles

San Marcos

Moyogalpa Ferry Terminal

Moyogalpa

La Paloma Airport

Volcán Concepción (1610m)

Urbaite

San José del Sur

Museos El Ceibo

San José del Sur Ferry Terminal

San Jorge

Rivas

Isla de Ometepe

Altagracia

Playa Santo Domingo

Balgüe

Santa Cruz

Volcán Maderas (1394m)

Mérida

Cascada San Ramón

San Ramón

Lago de Nicaragua

La Virgen

Isla de Ometepe Map (p222)

Arriving in Isla de Ometepe

Up to 15 boats and ferries ply the 17km route daily between San Jorge on the mainland and the Moyogalpa ferry terminal, Ometepe's main port.

La Costeña Airlines flies 12-seater aircraft from Managua to La Paloma Airport (around US$80, 20 minutes, twice weekly) – an airstrip some 2km south of Moyogalpa.

Where to Stay

Around the island, sleeping options range from basic hostels and terrific, remote ecofarmstays to high-end hotels with swimming pools and first-rate restaurants. Moyogalpa offers the island's most atmospheric stays, while around Volcán Maderas there's an ever-increasing number of ecofarms, good hostels, and guesthouses, many with a sustainable ethic.

Volcán Maderas

Outdoor Activities

Looking for the ultimate rush? Ometepe's fascinating geography and anything-goes attitude are perfect for exhilarating outdoor adventures. Even in the 'land of lakes and volcanoes,' Ometepe stands out for its natural thrills. At many key attractions, there are no signs and few crowds, so get ready to check off lots of new experiences from your list.

Great For...

☑ Don't Miss

Taking on Volcán Concepción or Volcán Maderas, be it on foot, on horseback or by bike.

Hiking

The island's two volcanoes can be ascended from Moyogalpa or Altagracia for Volcán Concepción, and Fincas Magdelena, El Porvenir and Hacienda Mérida for Volcán Maderas.

Volcán Concepción

This massive (and active) volcano is an Ometepe landmark. The seven- to 10-hour hike up loose volcanic stone to the summit of this looming peak can be tough, so be in good physical condition and bring water, snacks and real hiking shoes.

There are three main trails to the top: La Concha and La Flor (the most popular trail), both close to Moyogalpa, and La Sabana, a short distance from Altagracia. It's almost always cloudy at the top, which means your chances of seeing the fuming

White-throated blue magpie jay

MILOSZ MASLANKA/SHUTTERSTOCK ©

❶ Need to Know

Moyogalpa is an access point to most major attractions and activities on the island.

✕ Take a Break

Fill up before you head out with a fabulous breakfast from Cornerhouse (p223).

★ Top Tip

Remember that there's no shade above the tree line, and these volcanoes are steeper than they look.

Prices depend on where you start, whether you need transportation and how many are in your group: you'll pay anywhere between US$15 and US$30 per person. Your lodgings can help you arrange the excursion.

If climbing is not your thing, consider horseback riding or cycling around the circumference of Maderas (35km) on the rough dirt road; you'll be passing through one of the remotest parts of Nicaragua. Both can be arranged through local accommodations.

Other Hikes

The uphill slog to Cascada San Ramón (p226), more a walk than a hike, makes for an excellent half-day trip. Other less challenging hikes abound, including to the halfway point up Maderas on the Finca Magdalena trail, and **El Floral**, a five- to seven-hour round trip to a viewpoint about 1000m up Concepción (around US$30 per person).

Hiking Gear Checklist

Trekking for leisure is not popular among Nicaraguans and quality gear is hard to find on the ground. If you plan on getting off the beaten track, bring the following:

● **Comfortable footwear** Consider both leather hiking boots for long days in the

craters and awesome views over the lake and across Central America's volcanic spine are slim, even during dry season.

Guided treks up the volcano cost around US$25 to US$40 per person and can be organized by most outfitters on the island.

Volcán Maderas

Climbing this 1394m volcano is challenging but worthwhile. Guides are required for the seven- to eight-hour round-trip trek (with four to five hours of climbing); at the top, you'll reach cloud forest ending with a steep crater descent to a chilly jade-green lake. There are three trails to the top: the most popular at Finca Magdelena and two slightly longer trails beginning at Hacienda Mérida and Finca El Porvenir. The Finca Magdalena trail offers the money shot of Volcán Concepción.

mountains and comfortable, sturdy sports sandals for treks involving river crossings.

○ **Water purification tablets**

○ **Lightweight sleeping bag** It gets cold in mountainous regions of Nicaragua.

○ **Hammock** Indispensable for long boat rides or taking a break in the jungle high above the creepy crawlies.

○ **Tent** If you find one in Nicaragua, it's likely to be bulky and barely waterproof; bring a lightweight hiking model from home.

Swimming

Swimming off Ometepe's beaches is excellent. Keep in mind that Lago de Nicaragua rises dramatically in the rainy season (and, if the rains are particularly heavy, the couple of months afterwards), shrinking the beaches to thin strands. By the end of the dry season in April, however, some 20m of gray volcanic sand may stretch out to the water.

The most popular beaches are **Playa Santo Domingo**, **Playa Balcón** and the other beaches around **Charco Verde** and **Punta Jesús María**. If you're just looking for a dip, the mineral-rich rock pools at Ojo de Agua (p225) make a fine day trip.

Kayaking

Being relatively sheltered, the southwest area of the island is perfect for kayaking. An obvious destination is Isla del Congo, now called **Isla de los Monos** (Monkey Island), home to the descendants of four spider monkeys. Spider monkeys aren't present anywhere else on the island (howler and white-faced monkeys are), so these

Kayaking on Isla de Ometepe

creatures are pretty much alone. Don't get too close – these little guys bite. **Hacienda Mérida** (☎8868-8973; www.hmerida.com; campsites or hammock per person US$5, dm US$8, r with/without lake view US$35/25; P 📶) is the closest place to the island that rents kayaks.

The other classic kayaking trip is to the Río Istiam (p225), a swampy inlet that's home to turtles, caimans, the occasional howler monkey and an array of birdlife. **Caballito's Mar** (☎8842-6120; www.caballitosmar.com; dm/r/cabins US$8/25/35) is the closest kayak-rental place to the entrance of the river and it has guides who know where all the wild things are.

ℹ Need to Know

After various tourists got lost and died climbing volcanoes solo, it's now illegal to climb the volcanoes without a guide. Guides are available at or near the major trailheads in Altagracia, Moyogalpa, Balgüe and Mérida.

JOHN & LISA MERRILL/GETTY IMAGES ©

Horseback Riding

Horseback riding is another popular local transportation choice here. Any tour operator or hotel can set you up with a ride. Prices are generally US$5 to US$7 per hour, with guides US$10 to US$20 per group. Hari's Horses (p227) offers the most challenging day rides.

Cycling

Cycling is a fun way to get around, and mountain bikes can be rented in Moyogalpa, Altagracia, Playa Santo Domingo and at many lodgings.

Kitesurfing

When the wind whips up the waves along Playa Santo Domingo, it's easy to see why the location is so popular with kitesurfers. Sun Kite School (p226) on Playa Santa Cruz offers instruction.

Volunteering

Volunteering options abound – check around at the hostels. A growing number of farms on the island have signed up to the **Fincas Verdes agro-tourism program** (ask around locally if www.fincasverdes.com is still down), offering farmstays, horseback-riding expeditions and tours of farm facilities explaining traditional, often organic, farming techniques.

★ Top Tip

See www.ometepenicaragua.com for more information about local activities.

Isla de Ometepe

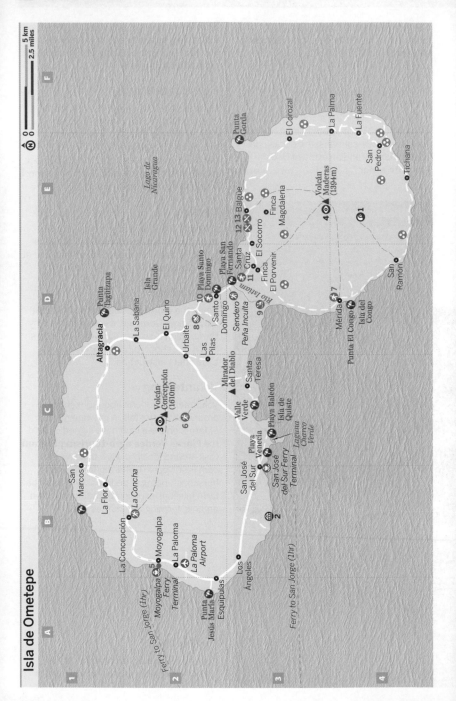

0 5 km
0 2.5 miles

Moyogalpa

Moyogalpa is home to the ferry terminal for hourly boats from the mainland, and, as such is the nerve center for Ometepe's nascent tourist industry. There are numerous guesthouses, budget hotels and restaurants here, and many of the island's tour companies; it's also base camp for the climb up Volcán Concepción. However, it's not exactly an island paradise you'll want to linger in.

ACTIVITIES

Cultu Natural   Outdoors
(📞8364-7211; NIC-64, al lado de supermercado; Volcán Concepción ascents US$30, waterfall hike US$15; ⊙9am-5pm) Friendly Danilo and his team get great feedback from travelers for their combination of local knowledge and bilingual tours to Ometepe's biggest attractions. Ascents of Volcán Concepción, kayaking at dawn, the waterfall hike, horseback riding and more can be organized here.

Green Expeditions Ometepe   Outdoors
(📞8421-1439; www.facebook.com/greenometepe; Frente a Hospedaje Central; Volcán Concepción trek per person US$25; ⊙9am-5pm) This highly regarded operator runs trekking tours up Volcán Concepción with bilingual guides and transport included. The motorbikes for rent are in excellent condition.

Fundación Entre Volcánes   Volunteering
(📞2569-4118; www.fundacionentrevolcanes.org; Frente a BanPro) ✈ A locally founded grassroots NGO involved in education, health, nutrition and environmental projects on the island. It accepts volunteers with an intermediate level of Spanish and a minimum two-month commitment.

⊗ EATING

Moyogalpa has a few good places to eat, particularly along the street leading up from the ferry dock, or immediately off it. In terms of nightlife, there's a bit of a scene at the laid-back bars near the ferry dock, though nothing too crazy (this is a small town on a remote island, after all).

Viky's BBQ   Nicaraguan $
(El muelle, 3½c E; mains US$3-5; ⊙6-9pm Wed-Mon) Viky cooks up nightly portions of chicken, pork and beef on the grill, accompanied by generous helpings of fried plantains, *gallo pinto* (rice and beans) and cabbage salad. Look for the unmarked red place next to the grocery store.

Cornerhouse   Cafe $$
(📞2569-4177; www.thecornerhouseometepe.com; El muelle, 1c E; mains US$4-7; ⊙7am-5pm Mon-Fri, to 3pm Sat; 🛜🖊) Easily the most stylish eating venue on this corner of the island. All-day breakfast is served at this rustic-chic cafe just uphill from the port; the menu features eggs Benedict with roasted

Isla de Ometepe

⊙ Sights
1 Cascada San Ramón	E4
2 Museos El Ceibo	B3
3 Volcán Concepción	C2
4 Volcán Maderas	E3

⊕ Activities, Courses & Tours
5 Cultu Natural	B2
6 El Floral	C2
Fundación Entre Volcánes	(see 5)
Green Expeditions Ometepe	(see 5)
7 Hari's Horses	D4
8 Ojo de Agua	D2

9 Río Istiam	D3
10 Sendero Peña Inculta	D2
11 Sun Kite School	D3

⊗ Eating
Bamboo	(see 13)
12 Café Campestre	E3
Café Comedor Isabel	(see 12)
13 Cafe de las Artistas	E3
Cornerhouse	(see 5)
Pizzeria Buon Appetito	(see 5)
Viky's BBQ	(see 5)

tomatoes and fresh basil. There are also gourmet sandwiches and salads (including a great one with papaya and toasted almonds) and wi-fi. It's part of the **Corner-house B&B** (s/d/tr US$25/35/45; 🛜).

Pizzeria Buon Appetito Pizza $$

(📞2569-4205; El muelle, 100m E; mains US$6-12; ⏱11am-10pm; 🍴) Moyogalpa's favorite pizzeria, right on the main drag, offers a wide menu of pies, pastas and seafood dishes.

ⓘ INFORMATION

Banco Lafise (El muelle, 200m E)

BanPro Credit (El muelle, 3c E) Accepts Visa. Not always operational.

Police Station (📞2569-4231; El muelle, 3c E, 1c S)

ⓘ GETTING THERE & AWAY

AIR

On Thursdays and Sundays at noon, La Costeña Airlines flies 12-seater aircraft from Managua to La Paloma Airport (around US$80, 20 minutes) – an airstrip some 2km south of Moyogalpa. From Ometepe, the flights continue to San Carlos and San Juan del Norte.

BOAT

Up to 15 boats and ferries ply the 17km route daily between San Jorge on the mainland and the **Moyogalpa ferry terminal** (El muelle; Calle Santa Ana), Ometepe's main port. Departures are between 7am and 5:45pm (US$1.50 to US$3, one hour); some are more reliable than others. There are departures from San Jorge to the **San José del Sur ferry terminal** (El muelle) at 9:30am, 2pm and 5pm. Between November and February, winds can make the sea rough, particularly in the afternoon; consider taking a car ferry instead of a smaller boat. The Ferry Schedules page on www.ometepenicaragua.com has up-to-date departure information.

Most boats can transport bikes and other equipment without a problem. If you're loading your car onto the ferry, you might have to wait, depending on availability; otherwise, no reservations are required. Passengers pay on the boat.

Boating off the coast of Isla de Ometepe, Volcán Concepción in the background

MATTHEW MICAH WRIGHT/GETTY IMAGES ©

❶ GETTING AROUND

Moyogalpa has the greatest choice of motorbike, ATV and scooter hire places on the island. It typically costs US$15 per day for a scooter, US$25 per day for a motorbike and US$60 per day for an ATV. Vehicle condition varies, so shop around before you commit to renting.

Playa Santo Domingo & Santa Cruz

Windswept sandy beaches and several good hotels lie southeast of Altagracia, on the long and lovely lava isthmus that cradles Playas Santo Domingo, San Fernando and Santa Cruz, which flow seamlessly from north to south.

Heading south to Santa Cruz along the island's main road, the beach gets progressively less crowded and the waves are popular with kiteboarders.

❸ ACTIVITIES

The main attraction is the **beach**, a 30m to 70m (depending on lake levels) expanse of gray volcanic sand that retreats almost to the sea wall during the rainy season.

Río Istiam   Kayaking

On the south side of the isthmus, this river shimmers as it snakes through the island's lava valley. The best way to explore the river (which is really a swamp) is by kayak – you're pretty much guaranteed to see turtles, caimans and howler monkeys. Inquire at nearby hotels, like Caballito's Mar (p221), which offers the trip for US$25 per person.

Ojo de Agua   Swimming

(btwn El Quino & Santo Domingo; US$5; ☯7am-6pm) Take a pleasant stroll through banana plantations to the well-signed, shady swimming hole about 1.5km north of Playa Santo Domingo. The mineral-infused water in the pool here bubbles up from 35 small underground springs; with an average temperature of 22°C to 28°C (71°F to 82°F), it makes for a refreshing dip.

 Navigating the Island

Isla de Ometepe's 78km main road runs in a rough barbell shape, circling each volcano and running along the northern shore of the isthmus between them. The Concepción side of the island is more developed, and the major towns of Moyogalpa and Altagracia are connected by a paved road.

Moyogalpa is the island's largest and busiest town: you'll find the majority of services for tourists here. Altagracia is the only other real population center and is a smaller, much more laid-back and less-touristed place. That said, there's not much reason to come here, except to check out the ancient monoliths beside the church and the local museum.

Playa Santo Domingo is the most popular lodging spot on the isthmus; the road splits upon arriving on the less-developed Volcán Maderas side of the island, going right to Mérida and the San Ramón waterfall, and left to Balgüe, a backpacker hot spot where new accommodations keep popping up.

The island is bigger than it looks and very few destinations are really walkable. The lack of traffic makes hitchhiking a problem (although any passing pickup will almost certainly give you a ride) – but you'll also be happy if you have your own wheels.

Isla de Ometepe beach and Volcán Concepción
DAVORLOVINCIC/GETTY IMAGES ©

Museos El Ceibo

The island's best museums are the two neighboring structures collectively referred to as **Museos El Ceibo** (📞8874-8706; www.museoselceibo.com; Camino Moyogalpa a Altagracia; 1/2 museums US$5/8; ⊗8am-5pm). One building houses the excellent **Museo Numismástico** (Money Museum), which documents the troubled history of the Nicaraguan economy through its coins and banknotes. Across the road, **Museo Precolombino** (Pre-Columbian Museum) displays an excellent collection of more than 1500 pieces of ceramics, metates, funeral urns and jewelry, spanning the different civilizations from all around the island, and some over 5000 years old. The museums are located 2km down a shady lane off the main road, about halfway between Esquipulas and San José del Sur.

Sendero Peña Inculta
Wildlife Watching
(US$2.50; ⊗8am-5pm) A 1.5km interpretative trail meandering through the forest on the outskirts of Playa Santo Domingo. The trail starts just north of the village and ends opposite Villa Paraíso. At least 63 species of birds, as well as numerous monkeys, inhabit these parts, so walk quietly. And make sure you wear good shoes – the loose volcanic-rock path can get very spiky!

Sun Kite School
Kitesurfing
(📞8287-5023; www.kiteboardingnicaragua.com; Santa Cruz, 700m del Norte; 3hr advanced course US$150, intermediate refresher US$260) Toward the south end of Playa Santa Cruz, Ometepe's only kitesurfing operator offers instruction for all abilities. If you want to ride Lago Nicaragua's waves, choose from the half-day introduction or three-hour advanced course that teaches you to land jumps, the two-day beginner package or intermediate refresher.

🛈 GETTING AROUND

You can hire bikes (US$10 per day) and motor-bikes (US$25 per day) along this stretch of road.

Around Volcán Maderas

This is the lusher, wilder side of the island. It's even less developed than Concepción's side, and petroglyphs are much more common. The star attraction, of course, is the towering, dormant Volcán Maderas (p219), covered with coffee plantations at the bottom and cloud forest at the top, and with a lake in its crater.

The northern side of Volcán Maderas has become one of the island's hot spots: apart from being an excellent base for volcano ascents, spread-out little Balgüe has an organic chocolate farm for you to explore, an increasing number of excellent budget accommodations and a burgeoning dining scene.

Things get progressively wilder and more untamed the further south you travel. Here, lush *fincas* (farms) dot the foothills of Volcán Maderas and, if you travel past San Ramón, beyond the reach of public transportation, you'll find yourself in one of the remotest parts of Nicaragua, amid indigenous villages where visitors are seldom encountered.

⊙ SIGHTS & ACTIVITIES

Cascada San Ramón
Waterfall
(US$5; ⊗8am-5:30pm) This stunning 40m waterfall is one of the jewels of the island. The 3.7km trail begins at the Estación Biológica de Ometepe. You can drive 2.2km up to the parking area, from where it's a 30- to 40-minute hike up to the waterfall, with a steep scramble near the end. At the top, the cascade tumbles down a sheer, mossy rock face into a cold pool that's fabulous for a dip on a hot day.

Hari's Horses
Horseback Riding
(📞8383-8499; www.harishorsesnicaragua.com; Finca Montania Sagrada, Mérida) Located at the Finca Montania Sagrada, this reliable operator offers several different horseback

riding outings in the vicinity of Volcán Maderas. These include rides to the San Ramón waterfall (US$50), trail rides with swimming in the lake (US$25) and, for expert riders only, a five to six-hour endurance gallop all the way around the volcano (US$100).

✖ EATING

Some of the best dining options on the island are found in and around Balgüe, offering increasingly sophisticated cuisine. There's also a cluster of casual, locally run cafes near the main road, just to the north of town.

Cafe de las Artistas   Cafe $

(☑8691-7445; Lazy Crab Hostel, 150m SE; mains US$3-5; ☺7am-9pm) Decorated with colorful murals, this arty cafe serves excellent fruit juices and abundant helpings of Nica standards, with a few international options thrown in.

Café Comedor Isabel   Nicaraguan $

(Hospedaje Así Es Mi Tierra, 50m O; mains US$4-6; ☺8am-9pm) Run by a friendly woman, this no-frills cafe is the place to come for hearty portions of traditional Nicaraguan food.

Café Campestre   International $$

(☑8571-5930; www.campestreometepe.com; Hospedaje Así es Mi Tierra, 50m O; mains US$5-10; ☺11:30am-9pm; 🛜🚲) 🌱 This popular cafe using local ingredients from the adjacent organic farm has something for everyone: excellent coffee, freshly baked breads, huge salads and international dishes from hummus platters to Thai curries. They do wonderful things with eggplant and you can buy local coffee and honey here.

Island Farmstay

Travelers looking for ecofriendly accommodations in the midst of lush jungle hit the mother lode with **Finca Mystica** (☑8751-9653; www.fincamystica.com; Punta El Congo, 500m S, 300m E; dm/d/f US$15/42/46; 🌐🛜). A labor of love by US expats Ryan and Angela, this ecofarm receives its guests in round cob (soil, rice straw, sand and horse manure) cabins, with a chorus of howler monkeys at dawn and nights filled with fireflies. There's an exceptional restaurant, too. Horseback riding, waterfall hikes and kayaking in the mangroves can all be arranged.

Horseback riding on Isla de Ometepe
FOTO5593/SHUTTERSTOCK ©

Bamboo   International $$

(☑8716-7640; Lazy Crab Hostel, 30m S; mains US$7-12; ☺noon-10pm; 🚲) Che and friends cook up delicious homemade pasta, whole grilled fish from the lake with *gallo pinto* and fried plantain, and more, at this Argentinian-run place. Eat it under the giant palapa-style thatched roof and then swing in a hammock with a beer.

COSTA RICA

In this Chapter

Bosque Nuboso Monteverde 232
Coffee Tours 236
Canopy Tours 238
Monteverde & Santa Elena 241
Sights 241
Activities 242
Courses 242
Tours 243
Eating 244
Drinking & Nightlife 246

Monteverde

Spread out on the slopes of the Cordillera de Tilarán, this area is a sprawling chain of villages, farms and nature reserves. The Reserva Biológica Bosque Nuboso Monteverde (Monteverde Cloud Forest Reserve) is the most famous, but there are properties of all shapes and sizes – from tiny family farms to the vast Bosque Eterno de los Niños (Children's Eternal Rainforest) – that blanket the area in luscious green. As a result, there are trails to hike, birds to spot, waterfalls to swim and adventures to be had at every turn.

Two Days in Monteverde

For your first day, register in advance for a guided tour at the **Bosque Nuboso Monteverde** (p232), taking time afterwards to explore independently. Your second day is devoted to getting your adventure on, either flying through the treetops on a **canopy tour** (p238) or climbing trees and canyoning down waterfalls at **Finca Modelo Ecologica** (p243). Don't miss dinner in a fig tree at **Tree House Restaurant** (p245).

Four Days in Monteverde

On your third day, visit a local farm for an enlightening (and energizing) **coffee tour**. When the sun sets, check out the area nightlife on a night tour at **Bosque Eterno de los Niños** (p241). Use your final day to learn about bugs at the **Butterfly Garden** (p241), followed by lunch at **Orchid Coffee** (p244).

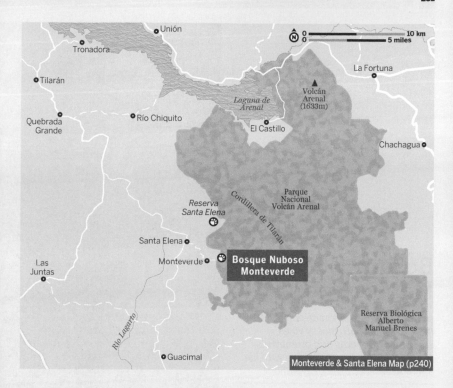

Union

Tronadora

Tilarán

Quebrada
Grande

Río Chiquito

Laguna de
Arenal

Volcán
Arenal
(1633m)

La Fortuna

El Castillo

Chachagua

Parque
Nacional
Volcán Arenal

Reserva
Santa Elena

Cordillera de Tilarán

Santa Elena

Monteverde

Las
Juntas

**Bosque Nuboso
Monteverde**

Reserva Biológica
Alberto
Manuel Brenes

Río Lagarto

Guacimal

Monteverde & Santa Elena Map (p240)

Arriving in Monteverde

Bus terminal Most buses stop at the bus terminal in downtown Santa Elena and do not continue into Monteverde. To get into town you'll have to walk or take a taxi.

Where to Stay

Many lodgings are clustered in the villages of Santa Elena and Monteverde, but many more dot the landscape in the hills above Santa Elena and beyond. Before booking, consider carefully how remote you want to be (and whether or not you'll have your own vehicle). This area has a huge variety of accommodations at all price levels.

Hiking through the cloud forest

Bosque Nuboso Monteverde

Here is a virginal forest dripping with mist, dangling with mossy vines, sprouting with ferns and bromeliads, gushing with creeks, blooming with life and nurturing rivulets of evolution.

Great For...

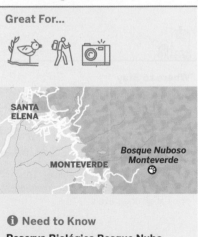

ℹ️ Need to Know

Reserva Biológica Bosque Nuboso Monteverde (Monteverde Cloud Forest Wildlife Biological Reserve; Map p231; ☏2645-5122; www.reservamonteverde.com; adult/student/child under 6yr US$20/10/ free; ⏱7am-4pm)

★ **Top Tip**

The reserve's walking trails are almost always muddy, even during the dry season. Bring your boots!

History

This beautiful reserve came into being in 1972, when the Quaker community, spurred on by the threat of encroaching squatters, joined forces with environmental and wildlife organizations to purchase and protect an extra 328 hectares (811 acres) of land. This fragile environment relies almost entirely on public donations to survive. Today, the reserve totals 10,500 hectares.

Plan Ahead

Due to its fragile environment, the reserve allows a maximum of 160 people at any given time, which is usually reached by 10am in the dry season. Make a reservation for a spot on a tour, or arrive before the gates open.

Hiking

There are 13km of marked and maintained trails – a free map is provided with your entrance fee. The three most popular trails, suitable for day hikes, make a rough triangle, El Triángulo, to the east of the reserve entrance. The triangle sides are made up of the popular **Sendero Bosque Nuboso**, a 1.9km interpretive walk through the cloud forest that begins at the ranger station, paralleled by the more open, 2km **El Camino**, a favorite of birdwatchers. **Sendero Pantanoso** forms the far side of El Triángulo, traversing swamps, pine forests and the continental divide. Sendero Río follows the Quebrada Cuecha past a few photogenic waterfalls.

Bisecting the triangle, the gorgeous **Chomogo Trail** (1.8km) lifts hikers to 1680m, the highest point within the triangle. Other little trails crisscross the region, including the worthwhile **Sendero Brillante** (300m), with bird's-eye views of a miniature forest. The trail to the **Mirador La Ventana** (elevation 1550m) is moderately steep and leads further afield to a wooden deck overlooking the continental divide.

Agouti

Wildlife-Watching

Monteverde is a birdwatching paradise, with the list of recorded species topping out at more than 400. The resplendent quetzal is most often spotted during the March and April nesting season, though you may get lucky any time of year. Keep your ears open for the three-wattled bellbird, a kind of cotinga that is famous for its distinctive call. If you're keen on birds, a bird tour is highly recommended.

For those interested in spotting mammals, the cloud forest's limited visibility and abundance of higher primates (human beings) can make wildlife-watching quite difficult. That said, there are some commonly sighted species (especially in the backcountry), including coatis, howler monkeys, capuchins, sloths, agoutis and squirrels (as in 'real' squirrel, not the squirrel monkey). Most animals avoid the main trails, so get off the beaten track.

Tours

Although you can (and should) hike around the reserve on your own, a guide provides an informative overview and enhances your experience. Make reservations at least a day in advance for park-run tours. The English-speaking guides are trained naturalists; proceeds benefit environmental education programs in local schools. The reserve can also recommend excellent guides for private tours.

Birdwatching (☑2645-5122; per person incl entry fee US$64; ⊙tours depart 6am) These early-morning walks usually last four to five hours (for three to six people), checking off as many as 40 species of birds (out of a possible 500).

Natural History (☑2645-5122, reservations 2645-5112; adult/student excl entry fee US$37/27, 2-person minimum; ⊙tours depart 7:30am, 11am & 1:30pm) Take a 2½- to three-hour guided walk in the woods. You'll learn all about the characteristics of a cloud forest and identify some of its unique flora. Your ticket is valid for the entire day, so you can continue to explore on your own when the tour is over.

Night Tours (☑2645-5122; www.reserva monteverde.com; with/without transportation US$25/20; ⊙tours depart 5:45pm) Observe the 70% of regional wildlife that has nocturnal habits. Frogs, bats and other night critters are increasingly active as the sun sets. Tours are by flashlight (bring your own for the best visibility).

> ☑ **Don't Miss**
>
> The magical, misty view from the Continental Divide.

MILAN ZYGMUNT/SHUTTERSTOCK ©

> ✗ **Take a Break**
>
> Stop at **Cafe Colibrí** (Map p240; ☑2645-7768; sandwiches US$5-6; ⊙7am-4pm) for a post-hike snack and to snap some hummingbird photos.

Brewing coffee in Monteverde

Coffee Tours

If you're curious about the magical brew that for many makes life worth living, tour one of the coffee plantations and learn all about how Costa Rica's golden bean goes from plant to cup.

Great For...

☑ **Don't Miss**

Taking a ride in a traditional ox cart.

Café de Monteverde

Stop by this **shop** (Map p240; ☎2645-7550; www.cafedemonteverde.com; Monteverde; tour adult/child US$32/15; ☺coffee tasting 7:30am-4:30pm, tours 8am & 1:30pm) ✐ in Monteverde to take a crash course in coffee and sample the delicious blends. Or sign on for the three-hour tour on sustainable agriculture, which visits organic *fincas* implementing techniques like composting and solar energy. Learn how coffee growing has helped to shape this community and how it can improve the local environment. Kind of makes you want to pour yourself another cup!

El Trapiche

Visit this picturesque family **finca** (Map p240; ☎2645-7650; www.eltrapichetour.com; Santa Elena; adult/child US$33/12; ☺tours

Coffee berries

XENIA_PHOTOGRAPHY/SHUTTERSTOCK ©

drink Coopeldós blends back home – this fair-trade-certified organization sells to Starbucks, among other clients.

Don Juan Coffee Tour

Three-in-one tours by **Don Juan** (Map p240; ☑2645-7100; www.donjuancr.com; Santa Elena; adult/child US$35/15, night tour US$40/20; ⊙7am-4:30pm, tours 8am, 10am, 1pm & 6pm) cover all your favorite vices (OK, maybe not all your favorites, but three of the good ones). It's a pretty cursory overview of how sugarcane is harvested and processed; how cacao beans are transformed into dark, decadent chocolate; and how coffee happens, from plant to bean to cup.

Chocolate, Too!

And if you're not a coffee drinker, try the **Caburé Chocolate Tour** (Map p240; ☑2645-5020; www.cabure.net; Monteverde; per person US$15; ⊙tours 1pm & 4pm Mon-Sat). Bob, the owner of the Caburé chocolate shop in Monteverde, shares his secrets about the magical cacao pod and how to transform it into the food of the gods. There are plenty of opportunities for taste-testing along the way, and you'll try your hand at making truffles.

10am & 3pm Mon-Sat, 3pm Sun) in Santa Elena, where they grow not only coffee but also sugarcane, bananas and plantains. See the coffee process firsthand, take a ride in a traditional ox cart, and try your hand at making sugar. Bonus: lots of samples along the way, including sugarcane liquor, sugarcane toffee and – of course – delicious coffee. Kids love this one.

Coopeldós RL

Coopeldós (☑2693-8441; https://coopeldos. com/cms) ☞ is a cooperative of 450 small- and medium-sized organic coffee growers from the area. You can visit this co-op store and buy their coffee in the village of El Dós de Tilarán, about halfway between Tilarán and Monteverde. Or you might even

Ziplining through the canopy

WOLLERTZ/SHUTTERSTOCK ©

Canopy Tours

The wild-eyed faces and whoop-de-whoop soundtrack are all the proof you need: clipping into a high-speed cable and soaring across the treetops is pure joy.

Santa Elena is the site of Costa Rica's first ziplines, today eclipsed in adrenaline by the many imitators who have followed. If you came to Costa Rica to fly, this is the absolute best place to do it.

Original Canopy Tour

The storied zipline **tour** (Map p240; ☑2645-5243; www.theoriginalcanopy.com; adult/student/child US$45/35/25; ☉tours 7:30am, 10:30am & 2:30pm) that started the trend. With 15 cables, a Tarzan swing and a rappel through the center of an old fig tree, it's a lot more fun than most history museums. Your adrenaline rush may not be as big as at some of the other canopy tours, but you'll enjoy smaller groups and more emphasis on the natural surroundings.

Great For...

☑ **Don't Miss**

Howling like Tarzan as you sail through the jungle on the aptly named swing.

SkyTrek

This seriously fast canopy tour consists of 11 platforms attached to steel towers that are spread out along a road and zoom over swatches of primary forest. We're talking serious speeds of up to 64km/h, which is probably why **SkyTrek** (☑2479-4100, toll free USA 1-804-GOTOSKY; www.skyadventures. travel; Santa Elena; adult/student/child SkyWalk US$39/32/27, SkyTrek US$81/67/56; ☑7:30am-5pm) was the first canopy tour with a real brake system. The SkyWalk is a 2km guided tour over five suspended bridges; a night tour is also available.

100% Aventura

Aventura (☑2645-6388; www.aventuracanopy tour.com; Rte 619, Santa Elena; canopy tour adult/child US$50/40, bridges US$35/30; ☑tours 8am, 11am, 1pm & 3pm) boasts the longest zipline in Latin America (which is nearly 1600m in case you were wondering). The 19 platforms are spiced up with a Tarzan swing, a 15m rappel and a Superman zipline that makes you feel as if you really are flying. They also have a network of suspension bridges, laced through secondary forest. Reservations required.

Original Canopy is located way uphill near the Cloud Forest Lodge, 2km off the main Santa Elena–Monteverde Rd.

Selvatura

One of the bigger games in town, **Selvatura** (☑2645-5929; www.selvatura.com; canopy tour US$50, walkways US$30, each exhibit US$5-15; ☑7:30am-4pm) has 3km of cables, 18 platforms and one Tarzan swing over a stretch of incredibly beautiful primary cloud forest. In addition to the cables, it has 3km of 'Treetops Walkways,' as well as a hummingbird garden, a butterfly garden and an amphibian and reptile exhibition.

Selvatura is 6km north of Santa Elena, near the reserve. There's a booking office in town near the church.

Monteverde & Santa Elena

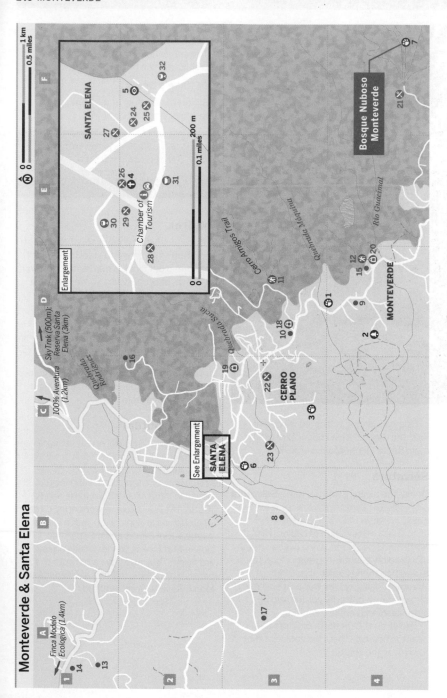

Monteverde & Santa Elena

Strung between two lovingly preserved cloud forests, this slim corridor of civilization consists of the Tico village of Santa Elena and the Quaker settlement of Monteverde, each with an eponymous cloud forest reserve.

⊚ SIGHTS

Butterfly Garden   Zoo
(Jardín de Mariposas; Map p240; ☑2645-5512; www.monteverdebutterflygarden.com; Cerro Plano; adult/student/child US$15/12/5; ☺8:30am-4pm) Head here for everything you ever wanted to know about butterflies. There are four gardens representing different habitats; they're home to more than 40 species. Up-close observation cases allow you to witness the butterflies as they emerge from the chrysalis (if your timing is right). Other exhibits feature the industrious leafcutter ant, the ruthless tarantula hawk (actually a wasp that eats tarantulas) and lots of scorpions. Kids love this place, and knowledgeable naturalist guides truly enhance the experience.

Bosque Eterno de los Niños   Nature Reserve
(Children's Eternal Rainforest, BEN; Map p240; ☑2645-5305; www.acmcr.org; ⊞) ✔ What became of the 1980s efforts of a group of Swedish schoolchildren to save the rainforest? Only this enormous 220-sq-km reserve – the largest private reserve in the country. It's mostly inaccessible to tourists, with the exception of the well-marked 3.5km **Sendero Bajo del Tigre** (Map p240; ☑2645-5200; www.acmcr.org/contenido/estaciones-y-senderos/reserva-bajo-del-tigre; adult/student/child US$13/11/8, night hike adult/student/child/transportation US$23/20/18.50/4; ☺8am-5pm, night hike 5:30pm; ⊞), which is actually a series of shorter trails. Make reservations in advance for the popular two-hour night hikes.

At the entrance there's an education center for children and a fabulous vista over the reserve.

Ranario   Zoo
(Monteverde Frog Pond; Map p240; ☑2645-6320; Santa Elena; per attraction US$14, package ticket US$23, night tour US$40; ☺mariposario 9am-3pm, frog pond to 8.30pm) Returning to its

Monteverde & Santa Elena

⊚ **Sights**
1 Bat Jungle.. D4
2 Bosque Eterno de los Niños.................... D4
3 Butterfly Garden...................................... C3
4 Iglesia... E2
5 Jardín de Orquídeas................................ F2
6 Ranario... C3
7 Reserva Biológica Bosque Nuboso
    Monteverde.. F4

⊕ **Activities, Courses & Tours**
8 Caballeriza El Rodeo................................ B3
    Caburé Chocolate Tour.......................(see 1)
9 Café de Monteverde................................ D4
10 Centro Panamericano de Idiomas............ D3
11 Cerro Amigos... D3
12 Curi-Cancha Reserve............................... D4
13 Don Juan Coffee Tour.............................. A1
14 El Trapiche... A1
15 Monteverde Institute............................... D4
16 Original Canopy Tour............................... C2
    Reserva Bajo del Tigre........................(see 2)

17 Sabine's Smiling Horses.......................... A3

⊛ **Shopping**
18 Luna Azul... D3
19 Monteverde Art House............................ C3
20 Monteverde Cheese Factory................... D4

⊗ **Eating**
21 Cafe Colibrí... F4
22 d'Sofia... C3
23 El Jardín.. C3
24 Morpho's Restaurant.............................. F2
25 Orchid Coffee.. F2
26 Raulito's Pollo Asado.............................. E2
27 Taco Taco.. F1
28 Toro Tinto.. D2
29 Tree House Restaurant & Café............... E2

⊙ **Drinking & Nightlife**
30 Bar Amigos.. E1
31 Beso Cafe.. E2
32 Monteverde Beer House.......................... F2

Reserva Santa Elena

The exquisitely misty 310-hectare **Reserva Santa Elena** (Reserva Bosque Nuboso Santa Elena; Map p231; ☑2645-7107, 2645-5390; www.reservasantaelena.org; entrance adult/student US$16/9, guided hike US$17; ☺7am-4pm) offers a completely different cloud forest experience from Monteverde. Cutting through the veiled forest, the reserve's 12km of dewy trails see much less traffic, retaining a magic that is sometimes missing at Monteverde. Open since 1992, Santa Elena was one of the first community-managed conservation projects in the country.

The reserve itself is about 6km northeast of the village of Santa Elena; the reserve office is in town. The reserve has a simple restaurant, coffee shop and gift store. Note that all proceeds go toward managing the reserve, as well as to environmental education programs in local schools.

former glory as the Ranario, or Frog Pond (it's changed names a few times), this place has added an insect house and a butterfly garden. The frogs are still the highlight – about 25 species reside in transparent enclosures lining the winding indoor jungle paths. Sharp-eyed guides point out frogs, eggs and tadpoles with flashlights. Your ticket entitles you to two visits, so come back in the evening to see the nocturnal species.

Bat Jungle   Zoo
(Map p240; ☑2645-7701; www.batjungle.com; Monteverde; adult/child US$13/11; ☺9am-7pm) The Bat Jungle in Monteverde is a small but informative exhibit, with good bilingual educational displays and a habitat housing almost 100 free-flying bats. Make a reservation for your 45-minute tour to learn about echolocation, bat wing aerodynamics and other amazing flying mammal facts.

The bats are on a reversed day/night schedule so they are most active from 9am to 5pm.

🏃 ACTIVITIES
Cerro Amigos   Hiking
(Map p240) Take a hike up to the highest peak in the area (1842m) for good views of the surrounding rainforest and, on a clear day, Volcán Arenal, 20km away to the northeast. Behind **Hotel Belmar** (☑2645-5201; www.hotelbelmar.net; Cerro Plano; peninsula r US$225-255, deluxe chalets US$288-405, ste US$450-554; 🅿@🛜🏊) ✈ in Cerro Plano, take the dirt road going downhill, then the next left. The trail ascends roughly 300m in 3km.

Note that this trail does not connect to the trails in the Monteverde reserve.

Curi-Cancha Reserve   Hiking, Birdwatching
(Map p240; ☑2645-6915, 8356-1431; www.curi-cancha.com; US$15, night tour US$20, natural history tour US$35, bird tour US$85; ☺7am-3pm, guided hike 7:30am & 1:30pm) Bordering Monteverde but without the crowds, this lovely private reserve on the banks of the Río Cuecha is popular among birders. There is about 10km of well-marked trails, a hummingbird garden and a view of the continental divide. Make reservations for the guided hikes, including the early-morning bird walks and specialized three-hour natural history walks.

🎓 COURSES
Monteverde Institute   Language
(Map p240; ☑2645-5053; www.monteverde-institute.org; Monteverde; week-long courses US$390, homestay per day incl meals US$25.50) This nonprofit educational institute in Monteverde offers interdisciplinary courses in Spanish, as well as more specialized programs in tropical ecology, conservation and ecotourism, among other topics. Courses are occasionally open to the public, as are

volunteer opportunities in education and reforestation.

Centro Panamericano de Idiomas
Language

(CPI; Map p240; ☑2265-6306; www.cpi-edu.com; Cerro Plano; weeklong classes from US$460; ⊙8am-5pm) Specializes in Spanish-language education, with courses geared toward families, teenagers, medical professionals and retirees. For fun: optional dance and cooking classes are included in tuition fees.

🕒 Tours

Finca Modelo Ecologica
Adventure

(☑2645-5581; www.familiabrenestours.com; La Cruz; treetop/canyoning/combo US$45/79/113; ⊙treetop 8am-4pm, canyoning 8am, 11am & 2pm) The Brenes family *finca* offers a number of unique and thrilling diversions. Their masterpiece is the two-hour canyoning tour, which descends six glorious waterfalls, the highest of which is 40m. No experience necessary, just an adventurous spirit. The treetop tour involves climbing a

40m ficus tree, using ropes and rappels to go up and down.

Sabine's Smiling Horses
Horseback Riding

(Map p240; ☑2645-6894, 8385-2424; www.horseback-riding-tour.com; 2hr/3hr/all-day ride per person US$45/65/105; ⊙tours 9am, 1pm & 3pm) Conversant in four languages (in addition to equine), Sabine will make sure you're comfortable on your horse, whether you're a novice rider or an experienced cowboy. Her long-standing operation offers a variety of treks including a popular waterfall tour (three hours) and a magical full-moon tour (monthly). And yes, the horses really do smile.

Caballeriza El Rodeo
Horseback Riding

(Map p240; ☑2645-5764, 2645-6306; elrodeo02@gmail.com; Santa Elena; US$40-55) Based at a local *finca*, this outfit offers tours on private trails through rainforest, coffee plantations and grasslands, with plenty of pauses to spot wildlife and admire the fantastic landscapes. The specialty is a

Clouds of mist in the forest

KEVIN WELLS PHOTOGRAPHY/SHUTTERSTOCK ©

From left: Violet sabrewing; resplendent quetzal; keel-billed toucan

sunset tour to a spot overlooking the Golfo de Nicoya. *¡Que hermoso!*

✕ EATING

The kitchens of Santa Elena and Monteverde offer high quality but poor value. You'll be delighted by the organic ingredients, local flavors and international zest, but not by the high price tags. Even the local *sodas* (places serving counter lunches) and bakeries are more expensive than they ought to be. Santa Elena has the most budget options.

Orchid Coffee   Cafe $

(Map p240; ☑2645-6850; www.orchidcoffeecr. com; Santa Elena; mains US$8-12; ☺7am-7pm; ☜☑) Feeling peckish? Go straight to this lovely Santa Elena cafe, filled with art and light. Grab a seat on the front porch and take a bite of heaven. It calls itself a coffee shop, but there's a full menu of traditional and nontraditional breakfast items, sweet and savory crepes, interesting and unusual salads and thoroughly satisfying sandwiches.

Taco Taco   Mexican $

(Map p240; ☑2645-7900; www.tacotaco.net; Santa Elena; mains US$5-8; ☺11am-10pm; ☜) Quick and convenient, this *taquería* (taco stall) offers tasty Tex-Mex tacos, and burritos and quesadillas filled with shredded chicken. There's also slow-roasted short rib, roasted veggies and battered mahi-mahi. The only difficulty is deciding what to eat (though you really can't go wrong).

Choose from two locations: this, the original deck location in front of **Pensión Santa Elena** (☑2645-5051; www.pensionsanta elena.com; Santa Elena; incl breakfast d US$32-38, d without bathroom US$28, ste US$45-60; ℗@☜), is perfect for people-watching, but the newer two-toned terrace restaurant next to SuperCompro is a step up in comfort.

d'Sofia   Fusion $$

(Map p240; ☑2645-7017; Cerro Plano; mains US$12-16; ☺11:30am-9:30pm; ☜) With its Nuevo Latino cuisine – a modern fusion of traditional Latin American cooking styles – d'Sofia has established itself as one of the best places in town. Think plantain-crusted

ONDREJ PROSICKY/SHUTTERSTOCK ©

sea bass, seafood chimichanga or beef tenderloin with roasted red pepper and cashew sauce. The ambience is enhanced by groovy music, picture windows, romantic candle lighting and potent cocktails.

Toro Tinto
Steak $$

(Map p240; ☎2645-6252; www.facebook.com/torotinto.cr; Santa Elena; mains $9-14; ◎noon-10pm) This Argentinean steakhouse lures in customers with soft lighting and a cozy brick-and-wood interior. It keeps them sated with steaks that are perfectly cut and grilled to order, plus unexpected specials and delicious desserts. The wine selection is good – mostly Chilean and Argentine – but pricey. This place will warm your cloud-soaked soul.

Tree House Restaurant & Café
Cafe $$$

(Map p240; ☎2645-5751; www.treehouse.cr; Santa Elena; mains US$15-22; ◎11am-10pm; ☎) It's a fine line between hokey and happy. But this restaurant – built around a half-century-old *higuerón* (fig) tree – definitely raises a smile. There's a menu of well-prepared if overpriced standards,

from *ceviche* (marinated seafood) to *sopa Azteca* (Mexican tortilla soup) to burgers. The service is spot-on. It's a lively space to have a bite, linger over wine and occasionally catch live music.

Cold? Try the Chocolate Tree House, a devilish dash of coffee and chocolate-flavored liqueurs.

El Jardín
International $$$

(Map p240; ☎2645-5057; www.monteverde lodge.com; Monteverde Lodge, Santa Elena; lunch US$12-15, dinner US$19-28; ◎7am-10pm; ☎) Arguably the 'finest' dining in the area. The menu is wide ranging, always highlighting the local flavors. But these are not your usual *tipica* (traditional plates) – beef tenderloin served on a sugarcane kebab, and pan-fried trout topped with orange sauce. The setting – with windows to the trees – is lovely and the service is superb. Romantics can opt for a private table in the garden. Worth the drive in off the main road.

Morpho's Restaurant
International $$$

(Map p240; ☎2645-7373; Santa Elena; mains US$8-20; ◎11am-9pm; ☎) Dine among

Best
for Shopping

Luna Azul (Map p240; ☏2645-6638; www.facebook.com/lunaazulmonteverde; Cerro Plano; ☺9am-6pm Mon-Sat, from 10:30am Sun) This super-cute gallery and gift shop is packed to the gills with jewelry, clothing, soaps, sculpture and macramé, among other things. Owner Stephanie's jewelry in particular is stylish and stunning, crafted from silver, shell, crystals and turquoise.

Monteverde Art House (Casa de Arte; Map p240; ☏2645-5275; www.facebook. com/monteverde.arthouse; Cerro Plano; ☺9am-6pm) You'll find several rooms stuffed with colorful Costa Rican artistry here. The goods include jewelry, ceramic work, Boruca textiles and traditional handicrafts. There's a big variety of offerings, including some paintings and more contemporary work, but it's mostly at the crafts end of the arty-crafty spectrum. Great for souvenirs.

Monteverde Cheese Factory (La Lechería; Map p240; ☏2645-7090; Monteverde; ☺9am-5pm) The Monteverde Cheese Factory was started in 1953 by Monteverde's original Quaker settlers. The factory produces everything from a creamy Gouda to a very nice sharp white cheddar, as well as other dairy products such as yogurt and, most importantly, ice cream. Don't miss the chance to sample Monte Rico, a Monteverde original. Sadly, they no longer offer tours.

Monteverde Art House
IAN BOTTLE/ALAMY STOCK PHOTO ©

gushing waterfalls and fluttering butterflies at this downtown restaurant. Some call it 'romantic,' others call it 'kitschy' – but nobody can dispute the varied menu, which combines local ingredients with gourmet flair. Veggies, a word of caution: the 'veggie burger' is really just an egg sandwich; there are other vegetarian options such as salads, soups and pastas.

Your receipt earns a discount to the adjoining **orchid garden** (Map p240; ☏2645-5308; www.monteverdeorchidgarden.net; Santa Elena; adult/child over 6yr/under 6yr US$12/6/free; ☺8am-5pm).

 DRINKING & NIGHTLIFE

Nightlife in these parts generally involves a guided hike and nocturnal critters, but since these misty green mountains draw artists and dreamers, there's a smattering of regular cultural offerings. When there's anything going on, you'll see it heavily advertised around town. You'll see some action at the bars in Santa Elena, especially during the dry season.

Bar Amigos   Bar
(Map p240; ☏2645-5071; www.baramigos.com; Santa Elena; ☺noon-3am) With picture windows overlooking the mountainside, this Santa Elena mainstay evokes the atmosphere of a ski lodge. But, no, there are DJs, karaoke and pool tables plus sports on the screens. This is the one consistent place in the area to let loose, so there's usually a good, rowdy mix of Ticos and tourists.

Beso Cafe   Cafe
(Map p240; ☏2645-6874; Santa Elena; ☺9am-7pm) We overheard someone saying, 'This is the best cup of coffee I've had in Costa Rica.' Hard to quantify in the Monteverde region, but espressos, lattes and cappuccinos are about all they do here (plus a couple of sandwiches on offer), and they do it very well indeed.

Orchid at Monteverde Orchid Garden

Monteverde Beer House
Beer Garden

(Map p240; ☑8659-2054; www.facebook.com/monteverdebeerhouse; Santa Elena; ☺10am-10pm; ☎) It's not a brewery – contrary to the sign – but it does offer a selection of local craft beers. There's a shady deck out back and smiling servers on hand; it's a perfect atmosphere for kicking back after a day of adventures.

ℹ INFORMATION

Banks and ATMs are clustered in the downtown quadrant of Santa Elena.

Banco de Costa Rica (Cerro Plano; ☺9am-4pm Mon-Fri)

Banco Nacional (Santa Elena; ☺8:30am-3:45pm Mon-Fri, 9am-1pm Sat)

Banco Popular (☑2542-3390; Centro Comercial Plaza Monteverde, Santa Elena; ☺8:45am-4:30pm Mon-Fri)

Monteverde Info (www.monteverdeinfo.com) This comprehensive website is chock full of information, with listings for hotels, tours, restaurants, transportation and more.

Monteverde Tours (Desafío Adventure Company; ☑2645-5874; www.monteverdetours.com; Santa Elena; ☺7am-7pm Mon-Fri, 10am-6pm Sat & Sun) This travel agency and vacation planner can help you find the activity you're looking for. It can make arrangements for guided hikes, horseback riding, canopy tours, coffee tours and more, plus transportation such as the taxi-boat-taxi to Arenal. It's a good resource if you're unsure how you want to spend your time.

Police (☑2645-6248; Santa Elena)

ℹ GETTING THERE & AWAY

BUS

Most buses stop at the bus terminal across from the Centro Comercial mini-mall on the hill above downtown Santa Elena, and do not continue to Monteverde; you'll have to walk or take a taxi if

Paving the Way

A 1983 feature article in *National Geographic* billed the Monteverde and Santa Elena area as the place to view one of Central America's most famous birds – the resplendent quetzal. Suddenly, hordes of tourists armed with tripods and telephoto lenses started braving Monteverde's notoriously awful access roads, which came as a huge shock to its Quaker community. In an effort to stem the tourist flow, local communities lobbied to stop developers from paving the roads. It worked for a while, but eventually the lobby to spur development bested the lobby to limit development. With the paving of the main access road – tentative first steps began in 2017 – this precious experiment in sustainable ecotourism will undergo a new set of trials. At the time of research, delays of up to 30 minutes could be expected approaching from Guacimal (Route 606), and it was recommended to take Route 145 if possible.

Resplendent quetzal
MICHAEL FISCHER/GETTY IMAGES ©

that's where you plan to stay. On the trip in, keep all bags at your feet and not in the overhead bin.

CAR

While most Costa Rican communities regularly request paved roads in their region, preservationists in Monteverde have done the opposite. All roads around here are shockingly rough. Even if you arrive on a newly paved road via Guacimal, you'll still want a 4WD to get to the more remote lodges and reserves.

There are three roads from the Interamericana. Coming from the south, the first well-signed turnoff is at Rancho Grande (18km north of the Puntarenas exit). The first stretch of this route (from Sardinal to Guacimal) was paved in 2011. The remaining 17km (from Guacimal to Santa Elena) was scheduled to be paved in 2016. That hasn't happened yet; at the time of research, it took about three hours to drive to San José, but that time will be reduced with the road improvements.

A second, shorter road goes via Juntas, but it's not paved except for the first few kilometers.

Finally, if coming from the north, drivers can take the paved road from Cañas via Tilarán and then take the rough road from Tilarán to Santa Elena.

If you're coming from Arenal, consider taking the lakeside route through Tronadora and Río Chiquito, instead of going through Tilarán. The roads are rougher, but the panoramas of the lake, volcano and surrounding countryside are magnificent.

There are two gas stations open for business in the area, one of which is in Cerro Plano.

TAXI

Taxis (Map p240; Santa Elena) wait in front of the Chamber of Tourism next to the Catholic Church and chicken stand in Santa Elena to take travelers to the reserves (about US$10) or other out-of-town destinations.

TAXI-BOAT-TAXI

The fastest route between Monteverde–Santa Elena and La Fortuna is via a taxi-boat-taxi combo (US$25 to US$30, four hours, departs 8am and 2pm), which can be arranged through almost any hotel or tour operator – including Monteverde Tours (p247) – in either town. A 4WD minivan can pick you up at your hotel and take you to Río Chiquito, meeting a boat that crosses Laguna de Arenal, where a van on the other side continues to La Fortuna. This is increasingly becoming the primary transportation between La Fortuna and Monteverde as it's incredibly scenic, reasonably priced and saves half a day of rough travel.

Cloud forests occur in tropical or subtropical areas where the humidity causes fairly consistent cloud cover. The resulting moist environment is ideal for epiphytes (parasitic plants), which make up almost 30% of the forest's species of flora.

Top: Heliconia plant; bottom left: tree fungi; bottom right: wild ginger

In this Chapter

Parque Nacional Volcán Arenal 252
Hot Springs 256
La Fortuna 258
Sights... 258
Activities... 258
Tours 258
Shopping 260
Eating 261
Drinking & Nightlife.......................... 263
El Castillo 264

Volcán Arenal

You know about the region's main attraction: that volcano, surrounded by old lava fields, bubbling hot springs and a stunning lake. Even though the regular eruptions have ceased, plenty of adventure still awaits. There are trails to hike, waterfalls to rappel down and sloths to spot. No matter your preferred method of exploring – hiking, biking, horseback riding, ziplining – you can do it here. And when your body's had enough, you can ease into a volcano-heated pool to soak away your aches and pains.

Two Days in Volcán Arenal

On your first day, set out on the well-marked trail system within **Parque Nacional Volcán Arenal** (p252), venturing to waterfalls, lava flows or crater lakes. Afterwards, head to the **hot springs** (p256) for a well-deserved soak. On your second day, take a detour to El Castillo to visit the **Arenal EcoZoo** (p264) and have lunch at **La Ventanita** (p265).

Four Days in Volcán Arenal

If you have the luxury of a third day, return to the park to hike along old lava flows and spy on sloths. Travel on **horseback** (p255) or by mountain bike if you prefer. Your fourth day is free for a hike and swim at **Catarata Río Fortuna** (p260) or a **canopy tour** (p259) with a stunning view of the volcano.

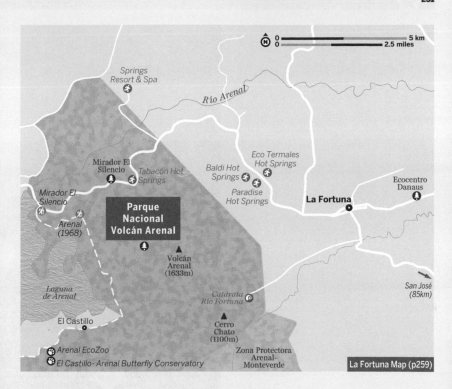

Parque Nacional Volcán Arenal

La Fortuna Map (p259)

Arriving in Volcán Arenal

The roads in the region are mostly in fine condition, with good highways branching out from La Fortuna: heading west, past the park entrance and around the lake; heading south through Chachagua and beyond; or heading east toward Muelle and Ciudad Quesada (San Carlos). Buses ply all of these routes. Tour operators and shuttle buses supplement the public transportation, making it one of the easiest regions to navigate without your own vehicle.

Where to Stay

While there are some decent lodgings in La Fortuna itself (especially budget options), you might want to base yourself uphill – nearer to the hiking, hanging bridges and hot springs – or a bit south of town where you'll hardly hear a peep at night. Even the lakefront properties around El Castillo and the Laguna de Arenal are close enough to use as a base for exploring the region.

Hiking the Arenal 1968 trail

Parque Nacional Volcán Arenal

Volcán Arenal no longer lights up the night sky with molten lava, but it still provides a rugged terrain for hiking and a rich habitat for wildlife – hikers routinely spot sloths, coatis, howler monkeys, white-faced capuchins and even anteaters.

Great For...

ⓘ Need to Know

Parque Nacional Volcán Arenal (Map p251; ☎2461-8499; adult/child US$15/5; ⊙8am-4pm, last entrance 2:30pm)

★ **Top Tip**
The ranger station has trail maps available.

For most of modern history, Volcán Arenal was just another dormant volcano surrounded by fertile farmland. But for about 42 years – from its destructive explosion in 1968 until its sudden subsiding in 2010 – the volcano was an awe-striking natural wonder, producing menacing ash columns, massive explosions and streams of glowing molten rock almost daily.

The fiery views are gone for now, but Arenal is still a worthy destination, thanks to the dense forest covering its lower slopes and foothills, and its picture-perfect conical shape up top (often shrouded in clouds, but still). The Parque Nacional Volcán Arenal is part of the Area de Conservación Arenal, which protects most of the Cordillera de Tilarán. This area is rugged and varied, rich with wildlife and laced with trails.

Hiking

Although it's no longer erupting (or perhaps because it is not), Volcán Arenal is the big hiking draw here. There is a well-marked trail system within the park, and several private reserves on its outskirts. Waterfalls, lava flows and crater lakes are all worthy destinations, which you can reach without a guide.

From the ranger station, you can hike the **Sendero Los Heliconias**, a 1km circular track that passes by the site of the 1968 lava flow. A 1.5km-long path branches off this trail and leads to an overlook. The **Sendero Las Coladas** also branches off the Heliconias trail and wraps around the volcano for 2km past the 1993 lava flow before connecting with the **Sendero Los Tucanes**, which extends for another 3km through the tropical rainforest at the base

Hiking the 1968 lava flow trail

of the volcano. To return to the parking area, you'll have to turn back – you'll get good views of the summit on the way.

From the park headquarters (not the ranger station) is the 1.3km **Sendero Los Miradores**, which leads down to the shores of the volcanic lake and provides a good angle for volcano viewing. Also from park headquarters, the **Old Lava Flow Trail** is an interesting and strenuous lower-elevation trail following the flow of the massive 1992 eruption. The 4km round trip takes two hours to complete. If you want to keep hiking, combine it with the **Sendero El Ceibo**,

a scenic 1.8km trail through secondary forest.

In 2017 a new 'sector peninsula' set of trails opened, comprising 1.2km of trails, an observation tower and scenic lake overlook. Although the last entrance to the national park is at 2:30pm, you may be allowed to enter and stay later at the new sector.

There are also trails departing from Arenal Observatory Lodge (www.arenal observatorylodge.com) and on a nearby private reserve, Arenal 1968. This network of trails along the original 1968 lava flow is right next to the park entrance. There's a *mirador* (lookout) that on a clear day offers a picture-perfect volcano view. It's located 1.2km from the highway turnoff to the park, just before the ranger station.

Tours

In addition to hiking, it's also possible to explore the park and surrounding areas on horseback, mountain bike or ATV.

○ **Arenal Wilberth Stables** (☏2479-7522; www.arenalwilberthstable.com; 1/2hr US$40/65; ⏱7:30am, 11am & 2:30pm) Two-hour horseback-riding tours depart from these stables at the foot of Arenal. The ride takes in forest and farmland, as well as lake and volcano views. The stables are opposite the entrance to the national park, but there's an office in La Fortuna, next to Arenal Hostel Resort.

○ **Desafío Adventure Company** (Map p259; ☏2479-0020; www.desafiocostarica.com; Calle 2; tours from US$65; ⏱6:30am-9pm) A tour agency with the widest range of tours in Fortuna, including horseback-riding treks and mountain-bike expeditions to Volcán Arenal.

☑ **Don't Miss**

Picture-perfect views of the cone of the volcano (although you'll have to wait for the clouds to momentarily clear).

✕ **Take a Break**

There are no restaurants near the park, so pack a picnic from Rainforest Café (p261).

IAN BOTTLE/ALAMY STOCK PHOTO ©

Hot Springs

Beneath La Fortuna the lava is still curdling and heating countless bubbling springs. The pools range from free, natural hot springs that any local can point you toward to more comfortable resort-style experiences with prices to match.

Great For...

☑ Don't Miss

Sitting in a hot tub with a cool cocktail and a marvelous volcano view.

Eco Termales Hot Springs

Everything from the natural circulation systems in the pools to the soft lighting is understated, luxurious and romantic at this gated, reservations-only **complex** (Map p251; ☎2479-8787; www.ecotermalesfortuna.cr; Via 142; with/without meal US$62/40; ◷10am, 1pm & 5pm; 🚼) ✆ about 4.5km northwest of town. Lush greenery surrounds the walking paths that cut through these gorgeous grounds. Only 150 visitors are admitted at a time, to maintain the ambience of serenity and seclusion.

Paradise Hot Springs

This low-key **place** (Map p251; www.paradise hotspringscr.com; Via 142; adult/child US$28/16, with meal $45/27; ◷11am-9pm) has one lovely, large pool with a waterfall and several smaller, secluded pools, surrounded by

part to reveal a 40°C waterfall pouring over a fake cliff, concealing constructed caves complete with camouflaged cup holders. Lounged across each well-placed stonelike substance are overheated tourists of various shapes and sizes, relaxing.

Springs Resort & Spa

If you're looking for a luxurious hot-spring experience, **Springs** (Map p251; ☑2401-3313, in USA 954-727-8333; www.thespringscostarica. com; 2-day admission US$65; ☺8am-10pm; ♨) features 28 free-form pools with varying temperatures, volcano views, landscaped gardens, waterfalls and swim-up bars, including a jungle bar with a waterslide. The whole scene is human-made, yet lovely.

Baldi Hot Springs

Big enough so that there's something for everyone, **Baldi** (Map p251; ☑2479-9917; www. baldihotsprings.cr; with/without buffet US$57/35; ☺9am-10pm; ♨), about 4.5km northwest of town, has 25 thermal pools ranging in temperature from 32°C to a scalding 67°C. There are waterfalls and soaking pools for chill-seekers and 'Xtreme' slides for thrill-seekers, plus a good-size children's play area. At night, the thumping music and swim-up bars attract a young party crowd.

lush vegetation and tropical blooms. The pools vary in temperature (up to 40°C), some with hydromassage. Paradise is much simpler than the other larger spring settings, but there are fewer people, and your experience is bound to be more relaxing and romantic.

Tabacón Hot Springs

Some say it's cheesy and some say it's fun. (We say it's both.) At **Tabacón Hot Springs** (Map p251; ☑2519-1999; www.tabacon.com; day pass incl lunch & dinner adult/child US$115/40; ☺10am-10pm) ♨, broad-leaf palms, rare orchids and other florid tropical blooms

Caffeine Pitstop

On the road up to La Fortuna Waterfall, **Down to Earth** (☏2479-8568; www.godowntoearth.org; Diagonal 301; tour US$27; ☺8am-8pm, tours 8am, 10:30am, 1pm & 3pm) is all about the coffee, which is brewed from single-origin beans from the owner's farm in the Dota Tarrazu Valley. There's no food here, just coffee – smooth, strong and revitalizing. Matias explains the 'biology of good taste' for coffee cognoscenti and novice alike.

THORNTON COHEN/ALAMY STOCK PHOTO ©

La Fortuna

At eye level, you see plenty of tourists and tour-selling touts, postcards and pizza: evidence of a somnolent mountain town whose innocence has been shattered. But look up: whether the majestic volcano is cloud-shrouded or sunshine-soaked, it's always something to behold.

◎ SIGHTS

Ecocentro Danaus   Nature Reserve
(Map p251; ☏2479-7019; www.ecocentrodanaus.com; with/without guide US$18/12, guided night tour US$35; ☺7:30am-5pm, night tour 5:30pm; 👪) ✿ This center, 4km east of town, has a well-developed trail system that's good for birding, as well as for spotting mammals such as sloths, coatis and howler monkeys. The admission fee also includes a visit to a butterfly garden, a ranarium featuring poison-dart frogs, and a small lake containing caiman and turtles. Reserve in advance for the excellent night tour.

Mirador El Silencio   Nature Reserve
(Map p251; ☏2479-9900; www.miradorelsilencio.com; US$6) ✿ Set on 22 hectares, this private reserve about 11km west of La Fortuna is a mix of primary and secondary forest, filled with life, from vibrant blue morpho butterflies to three species of monkeys, plus a wide variety of plant life. Four trails are marked with informative signs, not to mention a couple of fabulous lookouts.

✪ ACTIVITIES

La Fortuna is not a river-running hub like you'll find in other parts of the country, but there are a few companies offering canoeing and kayaking in the area. If you wish to go white-water rafting, tour companies do take groups from La Fortuna to run the Sarapiquí and other distant rivers. Some offer the option to get dropped afterwards in San José or on the Caribbean coast – a good way to have some fun on a travel day.

◉ TOURS

Don Olivo Chocolate Tour   Tours
(☏6110-3556, 2469-1371; http://chocolatedonolivo.wixsite.com/chocolatedonolivo; Via 142; tour US$25; ☺8am, 10am, 1pm & 3pm; 👪) Let Don Olivo or his son show you around their family *finca* (farm), showing off their sugarcane, oranges and – of course – cacao plants. The process of turning this funny fruit into the decadent treat that we all know and love is truly fascinating. Bonus: lots of taste-testing along the way.

Arenal Oasis   Birdwatching
(☏2479-9526; www.arenaloasis.com; night/bird walks US$40/65, child under 12yr half price; ☺bird walk 6am, night tour 5:45pm) The Rojas Bonilla family has created this wild frog sanctuary, home to some 35 species of croaking critters. The frogs are just the beginning of this night walk, which continues into the rainforest to see what other nocturnal animals await. If you're more of a

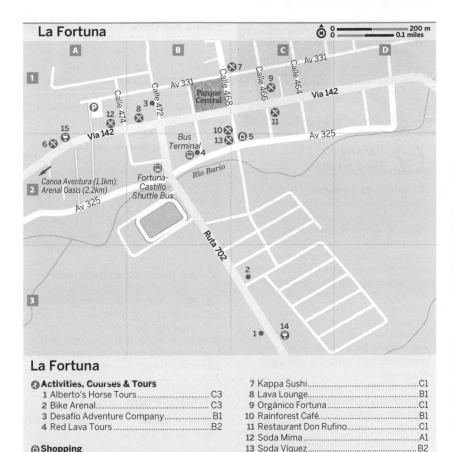

La Fortuna

Activities, Courses & Tours
1 Alberto's Horse Tours	C3
2 Bike Arenal	C3
3 Desafío Adventure Company	B1
4 Red Lava Tours	B2

Shopping
5 Hecho A Mano	C2

Eating
6 Anch'io Ristorante & Pizzeria	A2
7 Kappa Sushi	C1
8 Lava Lounge	B1
9 Orgánico Fortuna	C1
10 Rainforest Café	B1
11 Restaurant Don Rufino	C1
12 Soda Mima	A1
13 Soda Víquez	B2

Drinking & Nightlife
14 El Establo	C3
15 La Fortuna Pub	A2

morning person, it also does a birdwatching tour. Reservations recommended. Located 3km from La Fortuna's center; hotel pick-up costs US$10.

Arenal Paraíso Canopy Tours
Canopy Tour

(☎2479-1100; www.arenalparaiso.com; Via 142; tours US$50; ☺8am-5pm; 🔊) A dozen cables zip across the canyon of the Río Arenal, giving a unique perspective on two waterfalls, as well as the rainforest canopy. Also includes admission to the resort's

swimming pool and 13 thermal pools, which are hidden among the rocks and greenery on the hillside.

Alberto's Horse Tours
Horseback Riding

(Map p259; ☎2479-9043, 2479-7711; www. facebook.com/albertoshorses; Ruta 702; US$85; ☺8:30am-1:30pm) Alberto and his son lead popular horseback-riding trips to the Catarata de la Fortuna. It's a three- or four-hour trip, but you'll spend about an hour off your horse, when you hike down to the falls for

 **Catarata
Río Fortuna**

At this majestic **waterfall** (Map p251;
www.catarataleriofortuna.com; Diagonal 301;
US$15; ☉8am-5pm; P), you can glimpse a
sparkling 70m ribbon of clear water that
pours through a sheer canyon of dark
volcanic rock arrayed in bromeliads and
ferns with minimal effort, but it's worth
the climb down and out to see it from
the jungle floor. Though it's dangerous
to dive beneath the thundering falls, a
series of perfect swimming holes with
spectacular views tile the canyon in
aquamarine. Early arrival means you
might beat the crowds: the parking lot
fills quickly.

The waterfall is located at the end of
the main road (301) going uphill from La
Fortuna.

PAVEL TVRDY/SHUTTERSTOCK ©

a swim or a photo op. Beautiful setting,
beautiful horses. Cash only. You'll find Alberto on Ruta 702, about 2km south of town.

Bike Arenal   Cycling
(Map p259; ☑2479-7150, 2479-9020; www.
bikearenal.com; cnr Ruta 702 & Av 319A; rental
per day/week US$25/150, half-/full-day tour
US$75/110; ☉7am-6pm) This outfit offers a
variety of bike tours for all levels of rider, including a popular ride around the lake and
a half-day ride to El Castillo. You can also do
versions of these rides on your own. Make
advance arrangements for rental and an
English-speaking bike mechanic will bring
the bicycle to you.

On the road south out of town (702).

Canoa Aventura   Canoeing
(☑2479-8200; www.canoa-aventura.com; Via
142; canoe or kayak trip US$57; ☉6:30am-
9:30pm) ✐ This long-standing family-run
company specializes in canoe and float
trips (leisurely trips aimed at observation
and relaxation) led by bilingual naturalist
guides. Most are geared toward wildlife-
and birdwatching. Canoa is the sister
company of the **Maquenque Lodge**
(☑2479-7785; www.maquenqueecolodge.com;
s/d/tr incl breakfast from US$105/130/155;
P☎❄) ✐ in Boca Tapada and can arrange
an overnight stay there.

PureTrek Canyoning   Canyoning
(☑2479-1313, USA toll free 1-866-569-5723;
www.puretrekcanyoning.com; 4hr incl transportation & lunch US$101; ☉7am-10pm; ⛟) ✐ The
reputable PureTrek leads guided rappels
down three waterfalls, one of which is 50m
high. Also included: rock climbing and a
'monkey drop,' which is actually a zipline
with a rappel at the end of it. High marks for
attention to safety and high-quality gear.
It gets some big groups, but it does a good
job keeping things moving.

🛍 **SHOPPING**

Hecho A Mano   Arts & Crafts
(Handmade Art Shop; Map p259; ☑8611-0018;
www.facebook.com/handmadeartshop; Calle
468; ☉9am-9pm Mon-Fri, from 10am Sat &
Sun) There's no shortage of souvenirs for
sale in La Fortuna, but this unique shop is
something special, carrying an excellent
selection of arts and crafts by local and
national artists. You'll find representative
pieces from Costa Rica's many subcultures,
including Boruca masks, rasta handicrafts,
lots of macrame and some lovely handmade jewelry.

**Neptune's House
of Hammocks**   Homewares
(☑2479-8269; Diagonal 301; hammocks US$40-
50; ☉8am-6pm) On the road to La Catarata
de la Fortuna, Daniel has been watching the
tourist traffic come and go for over a dec-

ade while he weaves his magic hammocks. Take a breather and test one out.

EATING

Unless you're eating exclusively at *sodas* (cheap lunch counters), you'll find the restaurants in La Fortuna to be more expensive than in other parts of the country. But there are some excellent, innovative kitchens, including a few that are part of the farm-to-table movement. The restaurants are mostly clustered in town, but there are also places to eat on the road heading west.

Soda Mima
Soda $

(Map p259; off Via 142; ☉6am-8pm Mon-Sat, to noon Sun) Nothing fancy from afar, the love radiates outward from Don Alvaro's kitchen to warm your belly and your heart. Cheap, delicious *casados* (set meals) and *gallo pintos* (rice and beans) are standard fare, but add some marinated peppers from the big jar if you dare. Customer artwork in various languages adorns the walls, the most fitting of which reads: 'Don Alvaro Rocks.'

In the parking lot behind Cafeto Chill Out and the big chicken restaurant.

Rainforest Café
Cafe $

(Map p259; ☑2479-7239; Calle 468; mains US$7-10; ☉7am-10pm; ☎🖋) We know it's bad form to start with dessert, but the irresistible sweets at this popular spot are beautiful to behold and delicious to devour. The savory menu features tasty burritos, *casados*, sandwiches etc. There's also a full menu of coffees, including some tempting specialty drinks (such as Mono Loco: coffee, banana, milk, chocolate and cinnamon).

There's a dash of urban-coffeehouse atmosphere here, and it's popular with cool Costa Rican kids with plastic to-go cups.

Soda Víquez
Soda $

(Map p259; ☑2479-8772; cnr Calle 468 & Av 325; mains US$5-10; ☉8am-10pm; 🖋) Travelers adore the 'local flavor' that's served up at Soda Víquez (in all senses of the expression). It's a super-friendly spot, offering tasty *típico* (traditional dishes), especially *casados*, rice dishes and fresh fruit *batidos*

Horseback riding along the Arenal River

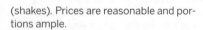
From left: Sendero Las Coladas trail (p254); ziplining near La Fortuna (p252); tour guide at Parque Nacional Volcán Arenal

(shakes). Prices are reasonable and portions ample.

Kappa Sushi   Sushi $
(Map p259; Calle 468 btwn Av 331 & Av 333; sushi & rolls US$6-12; ☺noon-10pm; 🚗) When you're surrounded by mountains and cattle farms, who's thinking of sushi? Well, you should. The fish is fresh (you're not *that* far from the ocean) and the preparations innovative. The dragon roll (shrimp tempura, avocado and eel sauce) is a favorite. Enjoy the view of Arenal (or is it Fuji?) while you feast on raw fish – or go for the veg options.

Anch'io Ristorante
& Pizzeria   Italian $$
(Map p259; 🗐2479-7024; Via 142; mains US$10-18; ☺noon-10pm; P🛜🍴) If you have a hankering for pizza, you can't do better than Anch'io, where the crust is crispy thin, the toppings are plentiful and the pie is cooked in a wood-fired oven. Start yourself off with a traditional antipasto. Accompany it with cold beer or a bottle of red. Add super service and pleasant patio seating, and you've got yourself a winner.

Lava Lounge   International $$
(Map p259; 🗐2479-7365; www.facebook.com/lava loungecostarica; Via 142; mains US$8-15, specials US$22-24; ☺7am-10:30pm; P🛜🚗) This hip, open-air restaurant is a relief when you just can't abide another *casado*. There is pizza and pasta, wraps and salads, and loads of vegetarian options. Service can be variable during peak hours, but the picnic tables and *palapa* (thatched) roof create a cool, rustic vibe. With colorful cocktails and occasional live music, the place is pretty irresistible.

Orgánico Fortuna   Vegetarian $$
(Map p259; 🗐8572-2115; www.organicofortuna. com; Calle 466; mains US$10-15; ☺9am-7pm Mon-Sat) A lovely little family operation that preaches better living through better eating, and the proof is in the pudding (or maybe the falafel). Delicious locally sourced ingredients are prepared with care. Smoothies, coffee with almond milk, and even some gluten-free bread and other options. If you're there long enough, you may even overhear a violin lesson in the back room.

Restaurant
Don Rufino International $$$

(Map p259; ☏2479-9997; www.donrufino.
com; cnr Vía 142 & Calle 466; mains US$16-40;
⊙11:30am-9:30pm) The vibe is trendy at this
indoor-outdoor grill. The highlight is the
perfectly prepared grilled meats: the New
York Steak with mushrooms is to die for.
If you're cutting back, go for Grandma's
BBQ chicken (with chocolate, wrapped in
a banana leaf) or the chef's special tuna
(seasoned with ginger oil, served with rice
noodles, tamarind sauce and cashew nuts).

DRINKING & NIGHTLIFE

Despite the tourist influx, or maybe be-
cause of it, La Fortuna remains a cultural
wasteland. Take advantage of occasional
live music at Lava Lounge (p262) and **La
Fortuna Pub** (Map p259; www.facebook.com/
lafortunapub; Vía 142; ⊙2pm-midnight Sun-Thu,
to 1am Fri-Sat). Or just drink *cerveza* (beer)
and hang out with the *sabaneros* (cowboys)
at **El Establo** (Map p259; ☏2479-7675; Ruta
702; ⊙5pm-2am Wed-Sat).

ⓘ GETTING THERE & AWAY

BUS

The **bus terminal** (Map p259; Av 325) is on the
river road. Keep an eye on your bags, as this is a
busy transit center.

A great and friendly source of bus information
for the entire country is **Red Lava Tours** (Map
p259; ☏2479-8004; www.redlavatouristser-
vicecenter.com; Volcano Valley Hike/2-Volcano
Extreme Hike US$70/75), located right next to
the terminal. Manager Sonia is known to locals
as the Google of La Fortuna.

TAXI-BOAT-TAXI

The fastest route between Monteverde–Santa
Elena and La Fortuna is the taxi-boat-taxi
combo (formerly known as jeep-boat-jeep,
which sounds sexy but it was the same thing).
It is actually a minivan with the requisite yellow
'turismo' tattoo, which takes you to Laguna de
Arenal, meeting a boat that crosses the lake,
where a 4WD van on the other side continues to
Monteverde. It's a terrific transportation option
that can be arranged through almost any hotel
or tour operator in La Fortuna or Monteverde
(US$25, four hours).

BOB HILSCHER/SHUTTERSTOCK ©

Sky Tram

❶ GETTING AROUND

BICYCLE

Cycling is a reasonable option to get around town and reach some of the top tourist attractions. The challenging 7km ride from town to La Catarata is a classic. Make advance arrangement to rent a bike from Bike Arenal (p260) and they'll drop it off at your hotel.

CAR

La Fortuna is easy to access by public transportation, but nearby attractions such as the hot springs, Parque Nacional Volcán Arenal and Laguna de Arenal demand internal combustion (or a tour operator). If you're thinking of doing a day trip to Río Celeste, Caño Negro or Venada Caves, you might also consider renting a car for the day.

Adobe Rent a Car (☑2479-7202; www.adobecar. com; Av 325; ⏱8am-5pm)

Alamo (☑2479-9090; www.alamocostarica.com; cnr Via 142 & Calle 472; ⏱7:30am-5:30pm)

El Castillo

Just an hour around the bend from La Fortuna, the tiny mountain village of El Castillo is a beautiful, bucolic and bumpy alternative, if you don't mind the somewhat treacherous roads. This picturesque locale, created as a relocation zone after the great eruption of 1968, has easy access to Parque Nacional Volcán Arenal and amazing, up-close views of the looming mountain – with little of the tourist madness of its bigger neighbor.

There is a tight-knit expat community here, some of whom have opened appealing lodges and top-notch restaurants. There are hiking trails and swimming holes. There are even a few worthy attractions – a **butterfly house** (Map p251; ☑2479-1149; www.butterflyconservatory.org; El Castillo–La Fortuna road; adult/student US$15/11; ⏱8am-4pm) and the **Arenal EcoZoo** (El Serpentario; Map p251; ☑2479-1059; www.arenalecozoo.com; La Fortuna–El Castillo road; adult/child US$15/12, with guide US$23/16; ⊗8am-7pm). The only thing El Castillo doesn't have is a sidewalk. And maybe that's a good thing.

TOURS

Sky Adventures   Canopy Tour
(✆2479-4100; www.skyadventures.travel; adult/child Sky Walk US$39/27, Sky Tram US$46/32, Sky River Drift US$72/57, Sky Limit US$81/56, Sky Trek US$81/56; ⊗7:30am-4pm) El Castillo's entry in the canopy-tour category has ziplines (Sky Trek), a floating gondola (Sky Tram) and a series of hanging bridges (Sky Walk). It's safe and well run, and visitors tend to leave smiling. A unique combo, Sky River Drift combines a zipline with tree-climbing and river tubing, while Sky Limit combines ziplining with rappel and other high-altitude challenges.

EATING

La Ventanita   Cafe **$**
(✆2479-1735; El Castillo–La Fortuna road; mains US$3-5; ⊗11am-9pm; 🖉) *La Ventanita* is the 'little window' where you place your order. Soon enough, you'll be devouring the best *chifrijo* (rice and pinto beans with fried pork, capped with fresh tomato salsa and corn chips) that you've ever had, along with a nutritious and delicious *batido*. It's typical food with a twist – pulled pork and bacon burritos, for example.

California expat Kelly is a wealth of information about the area, so ask away. It's on the main El Castillo–La Fortuna road.

GETTING THERE & AWAY

El Castillo is located 8km past the entrance to Parque Nacional Volcán Arenal. It's a rough gravel road, and it gets a bit worse once you get to the village.

Costa Rica Cooking

Scott's Alan's 3½-hour **cooking classes** (✆2479-1569; www.costaricacooking.com; per person US$125) focus on Costa Rican food with a modern twist, starting with a Tico mojito. Recipes include *ceviche* (marinated seafood), *patacones* (fried green plantains) and other Costa Rican staples sourced from local and sometimes organic ingredients. Menus vary but always involve three courses, and you can enjoy a great view while you cook.

Located inside **Gecko's Waterfall Grill** (✆2479-1569; www.facebook.com/geckogourmet; mains US$6-7; ⊗11am-5pm), just before the La Fortuna waterfall.

Patacones
EQROY/SHUTTERSTOCK ©

There is no public transportation, but a private **shuttle bus** (Map p259; ✆8887-9141; Calle 472) runs from the Super Christian in La Fortuna (one hour, US$9) at 7:30am, 12:30pm and 5:30pm. The bus departs **Rancho Margot** (✆8302-7318; www.ranchomargot.org; cnr El Castillo-La Fortuna road & Rancho Margot road; incl meals dm per person US$80, bungalow s/d US$175/250; 🅿 🛜 ☳) 🝁 at 6am, 10am and 4pm, returning from La Fortuna at 6am, 10am and 4pm. Contact the father and son drivers Arturo and Luis at 8887-9141, whose van will be either white, grey or green. This bus will also drop you at the entrance to the national park for US$4.

In this Chapter
Parque Nacional Manuel Antonio 268
Wildlife-Watching 272
Quepos 274
Manuel Antonio 278
Sights 278
Activities 279
Eating 279
Drinking & Nightlife 280

Manuel Antonio

For visitors arriving at this small outcrop of land jutting into the Pacific, the air is heavy with humidity, scented with thick vegetation and alive with the calls of birds and monkeys, making it apparent that this is the tropics. The reason to come here is Parque Nacional Manuel Antonio, one of the most picturesque bits of tropical shoreline in Costa Rica. If you get bored of cooing at the baby monkeys scurrying in the canopy and scanning for birds and sloths, the turquoise waves and perfect sand provide endless entertainment. Despite the area's overdevelopment, the rainforested hills and blissful beaches make the park a stunning destination worthy of the tourist hype.

One Day in Manuel Antonio

Spend your first day at the **Parque Nacional Manuel Antonio** (p268), hiking the well-trodden trails and lounging on the picture-perfect beaches. Keep a lookout for monkeys, sloths and other **wildlife**. At the end of the day, head to **Ronny's Place** (p280) for cocktails and splendid sunset views.

Two Days in Manuel Antonio

Spend your second day taking an adventure tour, whether a paddleboarding outing with **Paddle 9** (p274), a guided coastal hike with **Unique Tours** (p274) or a canopy tour with **Amigos del Río** (p279). In the evening, head to Quepos for a scrumptious seafood dinner at **Z Gastro Bar** (p276).

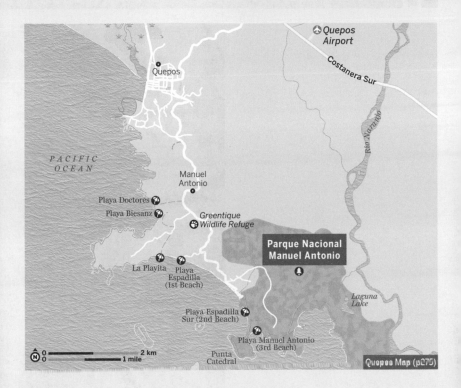

Arriving in Manuel Antonio

Bus stop Manuel Antonio's main bus stop is at the end of the road into the village that runs along the beach. The area is served by frequent buses and flights, and the roads are good (though the one leading from Quepos to Parque Nacional Manuel Antonio is winding, steep and narrow).

Where to Stay

The village of Manuel Antonio is the closest base for exploring the national park, though the selection of sleeping options is more varied in Quepos or on the Quepos–Manuel Antonio stretch of road. The Quepos–Manuel Antonio road is skewed toward ultra-top-end hotels, but plenty of noteworthy midrange and budget options are hidden along the way and staying in Quepos offers another cheaper alternative.

Three-toed sloth

Parque Nacional Manuel Antonio

A place of swaying palms and playful monkeys, sparkling blue water and a riot of tropical birds, Parque Nacional Manuel Antonio is the country's smallest (19.83 sq km) and most popular national park.

Great For...

❶ Need to Know

Parque Nacional Manuel Antonio (Map p267; ☎2777-8551; park entrance US$16; ⏲7am-3:30pm Tue-Sun)

★ **Top Tip**

Get here early (7am) and head for the park's furthest reaches to avoid the crowds.

Parque Nacional Manuel Antonio is a truly lovely place; the clearly marked trail system winds through rainforest-backed white-sand beaches and rocky headlands, the wildlife (iguanas, sloths, monkeys) is plentiful, and the views across the bay to the pristine outer islands are gorgeous.

The downside? The crowds. Visitors are confined to around 6.8 sq km of the park (the rest is set aside for ranger patrols battling poaching) and the place gets packed when midmorning tour buses roll in.

Beaches

There are five beautiful beaches – three within the park and two just outside the entrance. The beaches are often numbered – most people call Playa Espadilla (outside the park) '1st beach,' Playa Espadilla Sur '2nd beach,' Playa Manuel Antonio '3rd beach,' Playa Puerto Escondido '4th beach' and Playa Playitas (outside the park) '5th beach.' Some people begin counting at Espadilla Sur, which is the first beach in the park, so it can be a bit confusing trying to figure out which beach people may be talking about. Regardless, they're all equally pristine, and provide sunbathing opportunities; check conditions with the rangers to see which ones are safe for swimming.

Playa Espadilla Sur

The exposed Playa Espadilla Sur is to the north of Punta Catedral and swimming here can be dangerous. The beach is a half-hour hike from the park entrance.

Punta Catedral

Geography fun fact: this isthmus, which is the centerpiece of the park, is called a

Playa Espadilla

tombolo and was formed by the accumulation of sand between the mainland and the peninsula beyond, which was once an island. At its end, the isthmus widens into a rocky peninsula, with thick forest in the middle, encircled by Sendero Punta Catedral. There are good views of the Pacific Ocean and various rocky islets – nesting sites for brown boobies and pelicans.

Playa Manuel Antonio

With its turquoise waters, this lovely beach fronts a deep bay, sheltered by the Punta Catedral on the west side and a promontory on the east. This is the best beach for swimming, but it also gets the most crowded with picnicking families, so get here early.

Hiking

Parque Manuel Antonio has an official road, Sendero El Perezoso, which is paved and wheelchair-accessible and connects the entrance to the network of short trails. None of them are strenuous, and all are well marked and heavily traversed, though there are some quiet corners near the ends of the trails. Off-trail hiking is not permitted. A new boardwalk stretching from the ranger station to Playa Espadilla Sur was nearly completed at the time of research.

Sendero Principal

The longest trail in the park, the 2.2km Sendero Principal fringes Playa Espadilla Sur in the Manuel Antonio village.

Sendero Punta Catedral

This 1.4km loop takes in the whole of Punta Catedral, passing through dense vegetation and with glorious views of the Pacific and the offshore islands. The blink-and-you'll-miss-it 200m **Sendero La Tampa** cuts across part of the loop.

Sendero El Mirador

Heading inland and into the forest from the east side of Playa Manuel Antonio, this 1.3km trail climbs to a lookout on a bluff overlooking Puerto Escondido and Punta Serrucho beyond – a stunning vista. Rangers limit the number of hikers on this trail to 45.

Kayaking

Sea kayaking around the park's mangroves is a good way to glimpse the wildlife that this habitat supports. Long-standing operator **Iguana Tours** (Map p275; ☎2777-2052; ⏰6:30am-9pm) runs responsible kayaking trips.

> ☑ **Don't Miss**
>
> The pre-Columbian turtle trap, built out of rocks, at the western end of Playa Manuel Antonio.

SIMON DANNHAUER/SHUTTERSTOCK ©

> ✕ **Take a Break**
>
> Discuss animal sightings over fancy coffee drinks at Café Milagro (p279).

Green iguana

TANGUY DE SAINT-CYR/SHUTTERSTOCK ©

Wildlife-Watching

In this tiny park that's packed with life, capuchin monkeys scurry across idyllic beaches, brown pelicans dive-bomb clear waters and sloths spy on hikers on the trail.

Great For...

☑ **Don't Miss**

Howlers crossing the 'monkey bridges' along the road between Quepos and Manuel Antonio.

Mammals

White-faced capuchins are very used to people, and normally troops feed and interact within a short distance of visitors; they can be encountered anywhere along the main access road and around Playa Manuel Antonio. The capuchins are the worst for snatching bags, so watch your stuff.

You'll probably also hear mantled howler monkeys soon after sunrise. Like capuchins, they can be seen anywhere inside the park and even along the road to Quepos – watch for them crossing the monkey bridges that were erected by local conservation groups.

Coatis can be seen darting across various paths and can get aggressive on the beach if you're eating. Three-toed and two-toed sloths are also common in the park. Guides are extremely helpful in

Coati

TANGUY DE SAINT-CYR/SHUTTERSTOCK ©

spotting sloths, as they tend not to move around much.

The movements of the park's star and Central America's rarest primate, the Central American squirrel monkey, are far less predictable. These adorable monkeys are more retiring than capuchins, and though they are occasionally seen near the park entrance in the early morning, they usually melt into the forest well before opening time. With luck, however, a troop could be encountered during a morning's walk, and they often reappear in beachside trees and on the fringes of Manuel Antonio village in the early evening.

Marine Animals

Offshore, keep your eyes peeled for pantropical spotted and bottlenose dolphins, as well as humpback whales passing by on their regular migration routes. Other possibilities include orcas (killer whales), false killers and rough-toothed dolphins.

Reptiles

Big lizards are also a feature at Manuel Antonio – it's hard to miss the large ctenosaurs and green iguanas that bask along the beach at Playa Manuel Antonio and in vegetation behind Playa Espadilla Sur. To spot the well-camouflaged basilisk, listen for the rustle of leaves along the edges of trails, especially near the lagoon.

Birds

Manuel Antonio is not usually on the serious birdwatchers' trail of Costa Rica, though the list of birds here is respectable, and includes the blue-gray and palm tanagers, great-tailed grackles, bananaquits, blue dacnises and at least 15 species of hummingbird. Regional endemics to look out for include the fiery-billed aracaris, black-hooded antshrikes, Baird's trogons, black-bellied whistling ducks, yellow-crowned night herons, brown pelicans, magnificent frigate birds, brown boobies, spotted sandpipers, green herons and ringed kingfishers.

Quepos

Located just 7km from the entrance to Manuel Antonio, the small, busy town of Quepos serves as the gateway to the national park, as well as a convenient port of call for travelers in need of goods and services. Although the Manuel Antonio area was rapidly and irreversibly transformed following the ecotourism boom, Quepos has largely retained an authentic Tico feel.

TOURS

Paddle 9   Adventure
(Map p275; ☎2777-7436; www.paddle9sup.com; tours US$65-165) These newer kids on the block are a passionate, safety-conscious team who've introduced stand-up paddleboarding (SUP) to Quepos and who delight in showing visitors around the Pacific coast. Apart from the two-hour mangrove or ocean paddleboarding tours, the most popular outing is a eight-hour journey involving paddleboarding, lunch at a tilapia fish farm and swimming in various waterfalls.

You can add $30 to any tour to make it private.

Unique Tours   Adventure
(☎8844-0900, 2777-1119; www.costaricaunique tours.com) This established local operator organizes entertaining rafting tours of the Río Savegre, ocean and mangrove kayaking outings and more. But what makes it unique is that it's the only operator to offer a trip to a hidden, remote hot spring, as well as coastal hikes to Parque Nacional Manuel Antonio. Prices vary depending on group size.

H2O Adventures   Adventure
(Ríos Tropicales; Map p275; ☎2777-4092; www. h2ocr.com) The venerable Costa Rican rafting company Ríos Tropicales has a hugely popular franchise in Quepos called H2O Adventures, which organizes rafting outings on the Naranjo, El Chorro and Savegre Rivers, as well as kayaking and tubing outings. Rates start at US$75 for Class II through IV rapids.

EATING

One benefit of staying in Quepos proper is the accessibility of a wide range of dining opportunities, and there are also a couple of good markets.

Marisquería Jiuberths   Seafood $
(☎2777-1292; mains from US$7; ⊙11am-10pm) Run by a hardworking fisherman's family, this institution with brightly tiled floors serves the best seafood in town, yet is practically unknown to visitors because it's tucked away. Whether you have the catch of the day or the satisfying fish soup, the portions are generous and the service attentive. Follow unpaved Calle 2 out of town. Cash only.

Brooklyn Bakery   Bakery $
(Map p275; www.facebook.com/TheBrooklyn-BakeryCR; Av 3; bagels US$1.50, mains US$5-8; ⊙6am-3pm Mon-Sat; 🗢🗷) Real New York–style bagels and lox (a real rarity in Costa Rica)! Rye bread! Iced coffee! This adorable little bakery bakes its fresh wares every morning, as well as serving light bites and amazing salads throughout the day and specials at lunchtime, such as delicious Italian meatball sandwiches.

L'Angolo   Deli $
(Restorante L'Angolo Gastronomia Italian Deli; Map p275; ☎2777-7865, 8887-9538; Calle 2;

Fishing Expeditions

Sportfishing is big here, and offshore ventures are best from December to April, when sailfish are being hooked. By and large this is a high-dollar activity and you can expect to pay upwards of US$900 to hire a boat for the day. If you want to shop around a bit, visit the office of **Marina Pez Vela** (Map p275; ☎2774-9000; www.marinapezvela.com), 500m south of the town center.

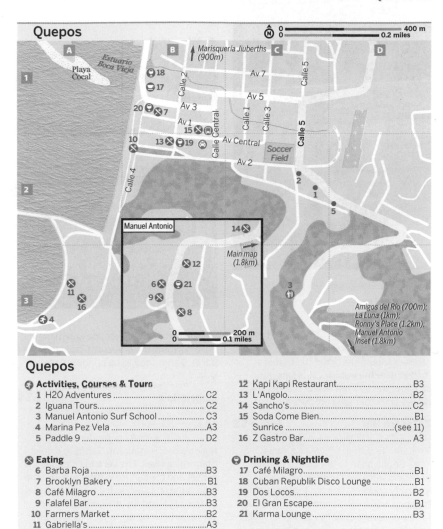

Quepos

⊕ Activities, Courses & Tours
1	H2O Adventures	C2
2	Iguana Tours	C2
3	Manuel Antonio Surf School	C3
4	Marina Pez Vela	A3
5	Paddle 9	D2

⊗ Eating
6	Barba Roja	B3
7	Brooklyn Bakery	B1
8	Café Milagro	B3
9	Falafel Bar	B3
10	Farmers Market	B2
11	Gabriella's	A3

12	Kapi Kapi Restaurant	B3
13	L'Angolo	B2
14	Sancho's	C2
15	Soda Come Bien	B1
	Sunrice	(see 11)
16	Z Gastro Bar	A3

⊕ Drinking & Nightlife
17	Café Milagro	B1
18	Cuban Republik Disco Lounge	B1
19	Dos Locos	B2
20	El Gran Escape	B1
21	Karma Lounge	B3

sandwiches US$5-7; ⊙11am-10pm Mon-Sat)
This deli makes excellent sandwiches with
imported Italian meats and cheeses, served
with a side of ill grace from the grumpy
waiter, but perfect for toting on excursions
to Manuel Antonio.

Soda Come Bien　　　　Cafeteria **$**
(Map p275; ☑2777-2550; Av 1, Mercado Central;
mains US$3.50-8; ⊙6am-5pm Mon-Sat, to 11am

Sun) The daily rotation of delicious cafeteria
options might include fish in tomato sauce,
olla de carne (beef soup with rice) or
chicken soup, but everything is fresh, the
women behind the counter are friendly and
the burly portions are a dream come true
for hungry shoestringers. Or pick up a fresh
empanada before or after a long bus ride.

From left: El Avión (p280); Z Gastro Bar; Marina Pez Vela (p274)

Farmers Market   Market $

(Map p275; Calle 4; ⊘4pm Fri-noon Sat) Self-caterers should check out the farmers market near the waterfront, where you can buy directly from farmers, fisherfolk, bakers and other food producers.

Z Gastro Bar   Fusion $$

(Map p275; ☎2777-6948; www.zgastrobar.com; Marina Pez Vela; mains US$15-25; ⊘7am-10pm; P ☎) Bright, open to the breeze from all sides and with colorful cushions strewn on its comfy couches, this is a terrific spot for lingering with a coffee and dessert, or over a meal of dorado *ceviche* in coconut milk, an octopus burger or delicious homemade pasta with mussels. The arty presentation matches the terrific flavors and the service is excellent.

Sunrice   Sushi $$

(Map p275; ☎2519-9955; www.sunriceres taurant.com; sushi rolls US$9-12, mains US$9; ⊘noon-9pm Tue-Sun) A relative newcomer to the Marina Pez Vela, this Latin-influenced sushi and sake bar fills its rolls with fresh tropical produce and local seafood bits. The spicy tuna over crispy rice cakes is a big hit,

along with the tuna, avocado and mango poke bowl and the *omusubi* (Japanese rice balls). Dishes tend to be on the smaller side.

Gabriella's   Seafood $$$

(Map p275; ☎2519-9300; www.gabriellassteak house.com; Marina Pez Vela; mains US$25-35; ⊘4-10pm; P ❄ ☎) A contender for the region's best restaurant, Gabriella's does many things well. The veranda catches the sunset and the service is attentive, but the food is the real star, with a great emphasis on fresh fish and mouthwatering steak. We're particularly big fans of the seared tuna with chipotle sauce and the spicy sausage and shrimp pasta. In a word: terrific.

🍷 DRINKING & NIGHTLIFE

Café Milagro   Cafe

(Map p275; ☎2777-1707; http://elpatiodecafemi lagro.com; Calle 4; ⊘7am-9pm Mon-Sat) Café Milagro sources its coffee beans from all over Costa Rica and produces a variety of estate, single-origin and blended roasts to suit any coffee fiend's palate, with 1% of its

JAMES HACKLAND/ALAMY STOCK PHOTO ©

profits going to environmental causes via international nonprofit 1% for the Planet.

Live music nightly; plenty of vegan and veggie options on the dinner menu.

Cuban Republik Disco Lounge   Club

(Map p275; ☑8345-9922; www.facebook.com/ cubanrepublik.quepos; cover charge Fri & Sat US$2-4; ☺10pm-2:30am Thu-Sat) Cuban Republik hosts the most reliable party in central Quepos, and it has various drinks specials. The DJs get loud late into the night and women get in free before midnight on Friday night. It's a nice, mixed Tico and gringo scene.

El Gran Escape   Bar

(Map p275; ☑2777-7850; http://elgran escapequepos.com; Av 3; ☺11am-11pm; 🛜) This long-standing pub is famous for all the fishing hats draped from the ceiling. It offers excellent fresh seafood, sports on the big screen and delicious (though pricey) burgers. Prompt bar staff too.

Dos Locos   Bar

(Map p275; ☑2777-1526; Av Central; ☺10am-10pm Mon-Sat, 11am-7pm Sun) This popular pseudo-Mexican restaurant is the regular watering hole for the local expat community, and serves as a venue for live music on Wednesdays and Saturdays. Opening onto the central cross streets of town, its fun for people-watching (and cheap Imperials). There's an English-language trivia night every Thursday. Added bonus: breakfast is served all day.

🛈 GETTING THERE & AWAY

Sansa (www.sansa.com) services Quepos. Prices vary according to season and availability, though you can pay a little less than US$75 for a flight from San José or Liberia. Flights are packed in the high season, so book (and pay) for your ticket well ahead of time and reconfirm often. The airport is 5km out of town, and taxis make the trip for US$8.

There's also a US$3 entry/exit fee at the airport.

Scheduled private shuttles, operated by Gray Line, Easy Ride and Monkey Ride, run between Quepos/Manuel Antonio and popular destinations such as Jacó (US$35), Monteverde

LGBT
Manuel Antonio

For jet-setting gay and lesbian travelers the world over, Manuel Antonio has a reputation as something of a dream destination. Homosexuality has been decriminalized in Costa Rica since the 1970s – a rarity in all-too-often machismo-fueled, conservative Central America – and a well-established gay scene blossomed in Manuel Antonio soon after. It's not hard to understand why.

Not only is the area stunningly beautiful but it has also long attracted liberal-minded individuals, creating a burgeoning artist community and a sophisticated restaurant scene. Check out www.gaymanuelantonio.com for a full list of gay and gay-friendly accommodations, events, restaurants and bars. A few venues occasionally host gay-oriented events, and **Karma Lounge** (Map p275; ☑2777-7230; www.face book.com/karmaloungema; ⊗7pm-2:30am Tue-Sun) is a very friendly spot with an excellent happy hour.

During daylight hours, the epicenter of gay Manuel Antonio is the famous **La Playita**, a beach with a long history of nude sunbathing for gay men. Alas, the days when you could sun in the buff are gone, but the end of La Playita is still widely regarded as a playful pickup scene for gay men.

(US$59), Puerto Jiménez (US$79), San José (US$50) and Uvita (US$35).

All buses arrive at and depart from the busy, chaotic main **terminal** (Map p275) in the center of town. If you're coming and going in the high season, buy tickets for San José in advance at the **Tracopa ticket office** (☑2777-0263; ⊗6am-6pm) at the bus terminal; *colectivo* (shared taxi) fares to San José are slightly cheaper and take two hours longer.

 GETTING AROUND

A number of international car-rental companies, such as **Budget** (☑2774-0140; www.budget. co.cr; Quepos Airport; ⊗8am-5pm Mon-Sat, to 4pm Sun), operate in Quepos; reserve ahead and reconfirm to guarantee availability.

Colectivo taxis run between Quepos and Manuel Antonio (US$1 for a short hop). A private taxi will cost a few thousand colones. Catch one at the **taxi stand** (Map p275; Av Central) south of the market. The trip between Quepos and the park should cost about US$15.

Manuel Antonio

As you travel the road between Quepos and Parque Nacional Manuel Antonio, the din from roaring buses, packs of tourists and locals hunting foreign dollars becomes increasingly loud, reaching its somewhat chaotic climax at Manuel Antonio village. Hordes descend on this tiny oceanside village at the entrance to the country's most visited national park.

 SIGHTS

Greentique
Wildlife Refuge   Wildlife Reserve

(Map p267; ☑2777-0850; www.greentique hotels.com/nature-reserves/#wlr; guided tours US$15-39; ⊗8am-4pm; 🎋) Resident biologist Jimmy Mata leads magical two-hour sojourns through the Butterfly Atrium, Reptile & Amphibian Water Gardens and Crocodile Lagoon, as well as a night tour, in this 5-hectare haven of second-growth Pacific Coast wet forest. Sloths, monkeys, armadillos and coatis are among the mammals you might see as your eye wanders from the forest floor to the dripping canopy.

This refuge was formerly known as the Manuel Antonio Nature Park and Preserve. It's across from the Si Como No Resort and tours are operated by the hotel.

ACTIVITIES

Amigos del Río — Adventure

(☑2777-0082; www.adradventurepark.com; tours US$130) Pack all of your canopy-tour jungle fantasies into one day on Amigos del Río's '10-in-One Adventure,' featuring ziplining, a Tarzan swing, rappelling down a waterfall and more. The seven-hour adventure tour includes a free transfer from the Quepos and Manuel Antonio area as well as breakfast and lunch.

Amigos del Río is also a reliable outfit for white-water rafting trips.

Manuel Antonio Surf School — Surfing

(MASS; Map p275; ☑2777-1955, 2777-4842; www.manuelantoniosurfschool.com; group lesson US$70-85) MASS offers friendly, safe and fun small-group lessons daily, lasting for three hours and with a three-to-one student-instructor ratio. Find its stand about 500m up the Manuel Antonio road south of Quepos.

Cala Spa — Spa

(☑2777-0777, ext 220; www.cicomono.com/wellness; Hotel Sí Como No; treatments US$70-140; ⊙10am-7pm) If you're sunburned and sore from exploring Manuel Antonio – even better if you're not – the Cala Spa offers aloe body wraps, citrus salt scrubs and various types of massage to restore body and spirit. Open daily by appointment only.

EATING

The road to Manuel Antonio plays host to some of the best restaurants in the area, and many hotels along this road also have good restaurants open to the public. As with sleeping venues, eating and drinking establishments along this stretch are skewed toward the upmarket. Reservations are recommended on weekends and holidays and during the busy dry season.

Falafel Bar — Mediterranean $

(Map p275; ☑2777-4135; mains US$5-9; ⊙noon-8pm Tue-Sun; ☜☝) Adding to the diversity of cuisine to be found along the road, this

falafel spot dishes up authentic Israeli favorites. You'll also find plenty of vegetarian options, including couscous, fresh salads, stuffed grape leaves, fab fruit smoothies and even french fries for the picky little ones.

Sancho's — Mexican $

(Map p275; ☑2777-0340; tacos from US$3; ⊙11:30am-10pm; ☜) A great view from the open-air terrace, potent house margaritas, excellent fish tacos and humongous *chile verde* (green chili) burritos are just some of the draws at this friendly expat-run joint. A place to knock back a few beers with friends in a convivial, chilled-out atmosphere, rather than woo your date.

Café Milagro — Fusion $$

(Map p275; ☑2777-2272; www.cafemilagro.com; mains from US$7; ⊙7am-9pm) This is a fine stop for fancy coffee drinks, and even better for decadent breakfasts (banana pancakes with macadamia nuts), sandwiches (mango mahi-mahi wrap) and sophisticated interpretations of Tico fare for dinner (Creole pork tenderloin). The patio itself is a lovely setting surrounded by tropical gardens; you can also order your sandwich packed for a picnic in the park.

Agua Azul — International $$

(☑2777-5280; www.cafeaguaazul.com; meals US$10-25; ⊙11am-10pm Thu-Tue; ☜) Perched on the 2nd floor with uninterrupted ocean views, Agua Azul is a killer lunch spot on this stretch of road – perfect for early-morning park visitors who are heading back to their hotel. The breezy, unpretentious open-air restaurant, renowned for its 'big-ass burger,' also serves up the likes of fajitas, *panko*-crusted tuna and a tasty fish salad.

Barba Roja — Seafood $$

(Map p275; ☑2777-0331; www.barbarojarestaurant.com; meals US$9-22; ⊙11:30am-9pm Tue-Sun) A Manuel Antonio–area institution, the Barba Roja is both a lively bar and a seafood-and-steak spot with a respectable sushi menu and weekly specials (Friday is smoked-rib and blues night). The terrace affords fantastic ocean views, best enjoyed with a local Libertas y La Segua craft brew (pints are US$6) or Mexican-style *michelada* (a spicy beer drink).

La Luna International $$

(☎2777-9797; www.gaiahr.com; Gaia Hotel; mains US$8-24; ⊗6am-11pm; 🛜🍴) Unpretentious and friendly, La Luna makes a lovely spot for a special-occasion dinner, with a spectacular backdrop of jungle and ocean. An international menu offers everything from spicy tuna and mango tacos to mahi-mahi *ceviche* to lobster tails, with a Tico-style twist – such as grouper baked *en papillote* (in paper), with plantain puree and coconut milk. Separate vegetarian and vegan menu available.

Kapi Kapi Restaurant Fusion $$$

(Map p275; ☎2777-5049; meals US$16-40; ⊗3-10pm; ❄🛜🍴) While there is some stiff competition for the title of best restaurant in the area, this Californian creation certainly raises the bar. The menu at Kapi Kapi (a traditional greeting of the indigenous Maleku) spans the globe from America to Asia. Pan-Asian-style seafood features prominently; macadamia-nut-crusted mahi-mahi, lobster ravioli and sugar-cane-skewered prawns are all standouts.

> *The road to Manuel Antonio plays host to some of the best restaurants in the area*

🍷 DRINKING & NIGHTLIFE

Bars in several accommodations aside, there's no nightlife in Manuel Antonio village to speak of, though there are several clubs and bars along the road to Quepos.

El Avión Bar

(☎2777-3378; http://elavion.net; ⊗noon-11pm; 🛜) Constructed around a 1954 Fairchild C-123 plane, allegedly purchased by the US government in the '80s for the Nicaraguan Contras but never used, this striking bar-restaurant is a great spot for a beer and stellar sunset-watching. Skip the food, though, and double-check the check, as complaints have been made about inaccuracies.

In 2000 the enterprising owners of El Avión purchased the plane for the surprisingly reasonable sum of US$3000 (it never made it out of its hangar in San José because of the Iran-Contra scandal that embroiled Oliver North and his cohorts), and proceeded to cart it piece by piece to Manuel Antonio. It now sits on the side of the main road, where it looks as if it had crash-landed into the side of the hill.

Ronny's Place Bar

(☎2777-5120; www.ronnysplace.com; ⊗noon-9pm) The insane views of two pristine bays and jungle on all sides at Ronny's Place make it worth a detour for a drink and a tasty meal. While plenty of places along this stretch of road boast similar views, the off-the-beaten-path location makes it feel like a secret find. Look for the well-marked dirt road off the main drag.

ⓘ GETTING THERE & AWAY

Driving the winding 7km road between Quepos and Manuel Antonio village on any day but Monday means spending time in traffic jams and paying potentially exorbitant parking fees.

Parque Nacional Manuel Antonio may not be big (it's the smallest national park in Costa Rica), but it is home to more than 100 species of mammals and around 180 species of birds.

Top: Red-eyed leaf frog; bottom left: scarlet macaws; bottom right: blue morpho butterfly

In this Chapter
Casco Viejo.................................286
Panama Canal.............................288
Panama Rainforest
Discovery Center........................292
Isla Taboga.................................294
Panamá Viejo Walking Tour.........296
Sights..299
Activities...................................301
Tours...301
Shopping...................................303
Eating.......................................304
Drinking & Nightlife....................307
Entertainment...........................308

Panama City

The most cosmopolitan capital in Central America, Panama City is both vibrant metropolis and gateway to tropical escapes. Many worlds coexist here. Welcoming both east and west, Panama is a regional hub of trade and immigration. The resulting cultural cocktail mix leads to a refreshing 'anything goes' attitude, more dynamic and fluid than that of its neighbors. The sultry skyline shimmers with glass and steel towers reminiscent of Miami, and in contrast the colonial peninsula of Casco Viejo has become a hip neighborhood where cobblestones link boutique hotels with rooftop bars and crumbled ruins with pirate lore.

Two Days in Panama City

Spend your first day exploring Panama City's great rooftop bars and museums and, of course, the historic ambience of **Casco Viejo** (p286). Take meals at **Mercado de Mariscos** (p304) and **Lo Que Hay** (p305). On day two, stroll through **Panamá Viejo** (p300), the ruins of the original Panama City, then feast at **Donde José** (p306), sample craft beer at **La Rana Dorada** (p307) and catch a performance at **Teatro Nacional** (p308).

Four Days in Panama City

Time for some day trips! Mosey over to the **Miraflores Visitors Center** (p290) and lay your peepers on the awe-inspiring Panama Canal. Return to the city, grab some street *empanadas* and venture out to the city's hottest club, **Casa Jaguar** (p308). On your final day, either boat over to **Isla Taboga** (p295) for snorkeling and whale-watching or hop over to **Panama Rainforest Discovery** (p292) for some wildlife stalking.

Previous page: Aerial view of Panama City

Panama City Map (p302)
Casco Viejo Map (p298)

Arriving in Panama City

Tocumen International Airport Most international flights arrive here. Hire taxis (from around US$30) at the transport desk near baggage claim. It's a 40-minute ride to downtown. In daylight hours local buses (US$1.25) depart every 15 minutes for Albrook Bus Terminal, near Albrook regional airport (one hour), and some other destinations.

Where to Stay

Panama City offers every kind of accommodations. A glut of options means that many charge bargain rates for their category. For those who prefer the quiet life, outlying neighborhoods in the Canal Zone have excellent B&B options. Central neighborhoods are a bit noisier, while the old-world charmer Casco Viejo remains thoroughly desirable.

Street in Casco Viejo

HELOVI/GETTY IMAGES ©

Casco Viejo

Casco Viejo is Panama City's most historical living neighborhood, home to crumbling convents and 18th-century cathedrals alongside hip plaza restaurants, chic rooftop bars and up-and-coming galleries. The colonial architecture may hark back to Havana, but this is not a spot where time stands still. It's as much about today's urban mix as the eclectic, easygoing vibe.

Great For...

☑ Don't Miss

Seeing the Casco on film – the streets feature prominently in scenes from the James Bond film *Quantum of Solace*.

History

Following the destruction of the old city by Captain Henry Morgan in 1671, the Spanish moved their city 8km southwest to a rocky peninsula at the foot of Cerro Ancón. The new location was easier to defend, as the reefs prevented ships from approaching the city except at high tide. The new city was also easy to defend, as a massive wall surrounded it, which is how Casco Viejo (Old Compound) got its name.

In 1904, when construction began on the Panama Canal, all of Panama City existed where Casco Viejo stands today. However, as population growth and urban expansion pushed the boundaries of Panama City further east, the city's elite abandoned Casco Viejo and the neighborhood rapidly deteriorated into a slum.

❶ Need to Know

Casco Viejo (www.cascoviejo.org) offers information on the neighborhood.

✗ Take a Break

A walk in Casco Viejo is not complete until you've hit up Granclement (p304) for ice cream.

★ Top Tip

Shop here. There's a wide selection of high-quality handicrafts and traditional artwork.

Casco Viejo Today

Casco Viejo's crumbling facades have been mostly replaced by immaculate renovations. Declared a Unesco World Heritage site in 2003, the area is getting international recognition. The newly restored architecture gives a sense of how magnificent the neighborhood must have looked in past years. Some developers, committed to mitigating the effects of gentrification here, are creating one affordable unit for each high-end one constructed, and working on interesting local cultural initiatives. Yet the consensus is that, unfortunately, most of the neighborhood's former occupants have already been relegated to the periphery.

The Jazz Solution

Once a down-and-out section of the city, Casco Viejo is coming into a new chapter.

Joining this push toward revitalization is the Panamanian music community.

Jazz great and native Panamanian Danilo Perez returned here to the musical conservatory where he learned his first notes to establish **Fundación Danilo Perez** (Map p298; ☎211-0272; www.facebook.com/FundacionDaniloPerez; 1069 Av A, Casco Viejo), a musical foundation that has generated over US$1 million in youth scholarships. It also houses a library and music museum, and sponsors the wildly popular **Panama Jazz Festival** (☎317-1466; www.panamajazzfestival.com; ⊙mid-Jan).

Perez believes the discipline of music helps to create leaders and good citizens who can address the problems of society. Young people are chosen from inner-city Panama and all parts of the country. Some grants take students as far as the Berklee College of Music and the New England Conservatory, and many come back to the music conservatory to teach others and complete the cycle of community participation.

Panama Canal

One of the world's greatest marvels, the Panama Canal stretches 80km from Panama City on the Pacific side to Colón on the Atlantic side. Around 14,500 vessels pass through each year, and ships worldwide have traditionally been built with the dimensions of the canal's original locks in mind.

Great For...

ℹ Need to Know

The Panama Canal can be reached by taxi (US$15 to US$20) from Panama City, or by tour, private transport or public bus.

★ **Top Tip**
The easiest way to visit the Panama Canal is to head to the Miraflores Visitors Center, just outside Panama City.

EVENFH/SHUTTERSTOCK ©

Just as stunning as the hulking steel container ships passing through the locks are the legions of creatures watching from the jungle fringes. Two visitor centers offer viewing platforms and museums that lay bare the construction and its expansion. There are also worthwhile boat and kayak trips on the waterway, or you can book a partial transit and squeeze through the locks yourself.

The Locks

The canal has three sets of double locks: Miraflores and Pedro Miguel on the Pacific side and Gatún on the Atlantic. A 10-year expansion completed in 2016 added two three-chambered locks, allowing the passage of super-sized 'neoPanamax' ships: Cocoli on the Pacific and Agua Clara on the Atlantic. Between the locks, ships pass through a huge artificial lake, Lago Gatún, created by the Gatún Dam across the Río Chagres, and the Culebra Cut, a 12.7km trough through the mountains. With each ship's passage, a staggering 197 million liters of fresh water are released into the ocean.

Visiting the Canal

Of the three sets of locks on the Pacific side, only Miraflores can be viewed up close at its superb **visitors center** (Map p285; ☏276-8617; http://visitcanaldepanama.com/en/centro-de-visitantes-de-miraflores; adult/child US$15/10; ☺8am-6pm). The center features a four-floor interactive museum that looks at the canal's history, operations, expansion and ecology; it also has an instructive 15-minute film and several viewing platforms. The other two locks have no

Miraflores locks

infrastructure for tourism, but visitors can glimpse them on the road to Gamboa.

On the Caribbean side, **Agua Clara Visitors Center** (Map p285; ☎276-8325; http://visitcanaldepanama.com/en/centro-de-visitantes-de-agua-clara; adult/child US$15/10; ◷8am-4pm) is open to the public and helps explain the recent canal expansion. The Gatún Locks' viewing platforms have now closed, but the locks can be viewed from outside.

Canal Tours

Visitors can do either partial canal-transit tours (the most popular option), which run through two of the six locks, or

---

☑ **Don't Miss**

The partial canal-transit tours that run through two of the six locks and take about a half-day.

DIEGO LEZAMA/GETTY IMAGES ©

---

less-frequent full transits. Boats depart from Muelle (Pier) 19 in Balboa, a western suburb of Panama City. They travel through the Miraflores Locks to Lago Miraflores and back, and then cruise out into the bay for scenic views of the city. These tours last a half-day. Make reservations in advance.

Yala Tours

This small Swiss-run **operation** (☎232-0215, 6641-6676; www.yalatourspanama.com) provides specialized trips throughout Panama, including day trips to Gamboa and the Canal Zone. A highlight is kayaking Río Chagres and Lago Gatún (US$160) while watching canal ships mow through. Also offers a canal-boat tour in Lago Gatún, wildlife-watching and hiking in Parque Nacional Soberanía (US$70), and cultural visits to an Emberá village.

Manakin Adventures Panama

This highly recommended **agency** (☎6384-4466, 908-9621; www.manakinadventures.com; canal/islands tour per person from US$60/70) knows the Panama Canal better than most and leads half-day tours to the Miraflores Visitors Center and Canal Zone. Nature lovers will want to join the boating trip on Lago Gatún to watch container ships in transit, stopping off at one of the lake's islands to meet and feed a colony of Geoffroy's tamarin monkeys. This trip is usually combined with a visit to one of the Emberá or Wounaan villages on the Río Chagres.

EcoCircuitos

This reputable, sustainable **operator** (Map p302; ☎315-1488; www.ecocircuitos.com; Albrook Plaza, 2nd fl, No 31, Ancón) ☙ offers conventional tours to the Panama Canal and canal transits, tours of Parque Nacional Soberanía, birdwatching on Pipeline Rd (p293) and fun kayaking trips on Lago Gatún.

✕ **Take a Break**

In addition to its buffet restaurant, Miraflores Visitors Center has a cafe/snack bar.

Tourists at Rainforest Discovery Center

ROB CRANDALL/SHUTTERSTOCK ©

Panama Rainforest Discovery Center

With a 32m observation tower, a sustainably built visitors center and a new sloth sanctuary, the Panama Rainforest Discovery Center is geared toward ecotourism and environmental education.

Great For...

☑ Don't Miss

The wildlife! It's worth making an effort to roll out of bed early – 6am to 8am is the best time to visit.

Visiting the Discovery Center

A 32m-high observation tower (172 steps) made of recycled material from the canal is great for spotting blue cotinga and toucans; during premium hours, just 25 visitors are admitted at one time to minimize the impact on wildlife. The sustainably built visitors center provides information and has 15 species of hummingbirds (of Panama's 57) feeding nearby. A new sloth-rescue center offers sanctuary to these shy creatures and prepares them for reintroduction into the wild.

Guides at the visitors center and tower can point out wildlife. Currently, a 1.2km circuit of two forest trails offers options that range from easy to difficult. Lakeside you can view aquatic birds such as wattled jacanas, least grebes, herons and snail kites.

Violet-bellied hummingbird

❶ Need to Know

Panama Rainforest Discovery Center
(Map p285; ☎314-9386, 6588-0697; www.
pipelineroad.org; adult/child US$30/5, night
walk US$30; ⊙6am-4pm) ✎

✕ Take a Break

There are no restaurants here – bring
snacks and water.

★ Top Tip

With advance reservations, groups can
set up special night tours.

Other animals around include monkeys,
crocodiles, coatis, butterflies and two- and
three-toed sloths.

Bird Migration Counts

Contact the center if you'd like to partic-
ipate in bird migration counts. These are
run by the **Fundación Avifauna Eugene
Eisenmann** (☎306-3133; www.avifauna.
org.pa), a nonprofit organization with the
mission to protect Panama's bird fauna and
rainforest habitat. Within the center, scientific research includes studies of migratory
birds, green macaws and raptors as well as
investigations into carbon capture.

Getting There

There's no bus access to the park. It's
best to book a taxi, rent a car or go with an
organized tour. The center is located 2km
from the entrance to Pipeline Rd. Pass the
town of Gamboa, at the end of Gaillard Rd,
and follow the signs.

What's Nearby?

Pipeline Road

Pipeline Rd is considered to be one of
the world's premier birdwatching sites.
Unsurprisingly, it is intensely popular with
birders, especially in the early morning.
More than 400 different species of birds
have been spotted on the trail, and it's fairly
likely you will spot everything from toucans
to trogons.

Also known as the Camino del Oleo-
ducto, the 17km-long dirt track was built
to service an oil pipeline constructed (and
never used) by the USA during WWII.

San Pedro village

MAREK POPLAWSKI/SHUTTERSTOCK ©

Isla Taboga

A tropical island with just one road and no traffic, Isla Taboga is a pleasant escape from the rush of Panama City, and only 20km offshore. While there are better beaches elsewhere, this quick, almost Caribbean getaway is a salve for city living.

Named the 'Island of Flowers,' Isla Taboga is covered with sweet-smelling blossoms much of the year. First settled by the Spanish in 1515, the quaint village is also home to the Western Hemisphere's second-oldest church. And with the addition of some decent restaurants and boutique lodgings in the town of San Pedro, along with plenty of activities, it's growing as a destination.

Great For...

☑ Don't Miss

The grand views from the island's highest point.

Sights

Fine sand beaches lie in either direction from the ferry dock. Walk north (right) from the pier to **Playa Restinga** and south (left) along the island's narrow main road to San Pedro and the more urban **Playa Honda**. After a fork, a high road leads to the church and a simple square. Further down the road, a pretty 307m-tall public garden displays the statue of the island's patron,

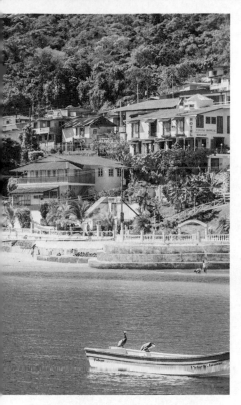

⊙ Need to Know

At the Taboga pier, local taxis wait to take passengers to their hotels.

✕ Take a Break

London's Pier Bar & Grill (☑6456-0484; www.facebook.com/londonPBG; mains US$7-16; ⊗8am-5pm Mon-Fri, to 9pm Sat & Sun) is the best place for *ceviche* and cocktails on the seafront.

★ Top Tip

There are no ATMS on the island, so bring sufficient cash with you.

Isla El Morro, which doesn't have coral but attracts some large fish.

Diving

The Pacific-style diving here has rocky formations, schools of fish and a wide variety of marine life. On a good dive you can see jacks, snapper, jewfish, eels, rays, lobsters and octopuses. With a little luck, you may also come across old bottles, spent WWII-era shells and artifacts from pirate days (remember: look but don't take). Dive outfitters in Panama City occasionally make the trip; check with the Taboga Tour Center.

Whale-Watching

Keep an eye out for whales while on the ferry over to the island. In August and September migrating humpback and sei whales can be seen leaping from the water near Taboga in spectacular displays.

the Virgen del Carmen; nearby is the supposed home of 16th-century conquistador Francisco Pizarro, who led the expedition that conquered the Inca Empire. The road meanders a total of 5.2km, ending at the old US military installation and bunker atop the island's highest point, **Cerro Vigía**.

Activities

The wonderful people at **Taboga Tour Center** (☑6704-4028; www.tabogatourcenter. com; 1½hr tours US$25-35; ⊗9am-4pm) can arrange pretty much anything.

Snorkeling

On weekends, fishers at the pier take visitors around the island to good snorkeling spots and caves on the western side, which are rumored to hold pirate treasure. During the week you can snorkel around

Panamá Viejo Walking Tour

This historic stroll takes you through the ruins of the first European settlement along the Pacific, founded on August 15, 1519 by Spanish conquistador Pedro Arias de Ávila.

Start Puente del Matadero
Distance 3.5km
Duration 1½ to two hours

2 Continue two blocks east along Av Cincuentenario to the ruins of **Iglesia y Convento de La Merced** (Av Cincnuentenario s/n).

1 Enter the sector over a modern bridge parallel to **Puente del Matadero**, an old stone bridge named after a slaughterhouse.

3 Also bordering the avenue are the remains of **Iglesia y Convento de San Francisco**, erected by the Franciscans.

Take a Break: Indulge post-walk at nearby **Maito** (p306).

Corredor Sur

Bahía de Panamá

7 Puente del Rey (p300), possibly the oldest standing bridge in the Americas, is visible from Av Cincuentenario.

Classic photo: Catedral de Nuestra Señora de la Asunción

5 Catedral de Nuestra Señora de la Asunción (p300), built between 1619 and 1626, is the best-preserved building of the ruins.

⑦

Calle del Obispo

Av Cincuentenario

③

Av 6 Sur (Av Cincuentenario)

Calle de la Empredada

Av Cincuentenario

④

⑥

⑤

Plaza Mayor

4 The Jesuits built **Iglesia y Convento de la Compañía de Jesús**, whose stone ruins are visible today.

6 Just north lies the **Iglesia y Convento de Santo Domingo**. The convent dates from the 1570s, though the church was built 20 or more years later.

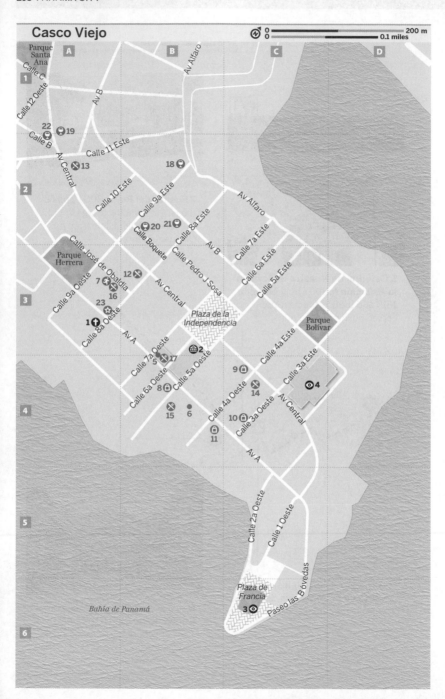

Casco Viejo

Parque Santa Ana

Calle C

A

B

Av Alfaro

C

D

0 200 m
0 0.1 miles

Calle 12 Oeste

1

Av B

Calle B

22 19

Av Central

Calle 11 Este

13

Calle 10 Este

18

Calle 9a Este

2

Av Alfaro

Calle Boquete

20 21

Calle 8a Este

Av B

Calle 7a Este

Calle 6a Este

Calle 5a Este

Calle José de Obaldía

Parque Herrera

Calle Pedro J Sosa

Calle 9a Oeste

7

12

16

Av Central

3

23

Plaza de la Independencia

Calle 4a Este

Parque Bolívar

1

Av A

Calle 8a Oeste

2

9

4

Calle 7a Oeste

5 17

Calle 4a Oeste

14

Calle 3a Este

Av Central

Calle 6a Oeste

8

Calle 5a Oeste

15 6

10

11

Calle 3a Oeste

Av A

4

Calle 2a Oeste

Calle 1 Oeste

5

Bahía de Panamá

Paseo las Bóvedas

Plaza de Francia

3

6

⊙ SIGHTS

◎ Casco Viejo

Plaza de Francia   Plaza

(Map p298) At the tip of the southern point of Casco Viejo, this beautiful plaza pays homage to the French role in the construction of the canal. Its large stone tablets and statues are dedicated to the memory of the 22,000 workers who died trying to create the canal.

Museo del Canal Interoceánico   Museum

(Panama Canal Museum; Map p298; ☑211-1649; www.museodelcanal.com; Calle 6a Oeste, Casco Viejo; adult/child US$10/5; ◎9am-5pm Tue-Sun) This impressive museum is housed in a beautifully restored building that once served as the headquarters for the original French canal company. The Panama Canal Museum (as it's more commonly known) presents excellent exhibits on the famous waterway, framed in their historical and political context. Signs are in Spanish, but English-speaking guides and audio guides (US$5) are available.

Teatro Nacional   Theater

(Map p298; ☑501-4107; www.inac.gob.pa/teatros/73-teatro-nacional; Av B) Built in 1907, the interior of this ornate Casco Viejo theater has been completely restored. It boasts red and gold decorations, a once-magnificent ceiling mural by Roberto Lewis (one of Panama's finest painters) and an impressive crystal chandelier. Performances are still held here. For information visit the office at the side of the building.

Iglesia de San José   Church

(Map p298; Av A, Casco Viejo) This Casco Viejo church protects the famous Altar de Oro (Golden Altar), the sole relic salvaged after privateer Henry Morgan sacked Panamá Viejo.

◎ Parque Natural Metropolitano

On a hill north of downtown, the 265-hectare **Parque Natural Metropolitano** (Map p302; ☑info 232-5516; www.parquemetropolitano.org; Av Juan Pablo II; US$5; ◎8am-5pm Mon-Fri, to 1pm Sat) protects vast expanses of tropical semideciduous forest within the city limits. It serves as an incredible wilderness escape from the trappings of the capital.

Pick up a pamphlet for a self-guided tour in Spanish and English at the **visitors center** (Map p302; ◎8am-4:30pm Mon-Fri, to 1pm Sat), 40m north of the park entrance.

Casco Viejo

◎ Sights	
1 Iglesia de San José	A3
2 Museo del Canal	
Interoceánico	B3
3 Plaza de Francia	C6
4 Teatro Nacional	C4

✪ Activities, Courses & Tours	
5 Barefoot Panama	B3
6 Casco Antiguo Spanish	
School	B4
7 Casco Yoga	A3

⊕ Shopping	
8 Casa Latina	B4
9 El Palacio del Sombrero	C4
10 Karavan	C4
11 No Me Olvides	B4

✪ Eating	
12 Barrio Pizza	B3
13 Donde José	A2
14 Granclement	C4
15 Lo Que Hay	B4
16 Ochoymedio	A3
17 Super Gourmet	B4

⊜ Drinking & Nightlife	
18 Bar Relic	B2
19 Casa Jaguar	A1
20 La Rana Dorada	B2
21 Tántalo Bar	B2
22 The Stranger's Club	A2

✪ Entertainment	
23 Fundación Danilo Perez	A3
Teatro Nacional	(see 4)

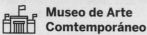
Museo de Arte Comtemporáneo

This wonderful privately owned **museum** (MAC; Map p302; ☑262-8012; www.macpanama.org; Av de los Mártires, Ancón; admission by donation US$3-5; ⊗10am-5pm Tue-Sun, to 8pm Thu) features the best collection of Panamanian art anywhere, an excellent collection of works on paper by Latin American artists, and the occasional temporary exhibition by a foreign or national artist.

GABRIEL GUANDIQUE ©

Mariposario Metropolitano   Nature Center

(Butterfly Garden; Map p302; https://mariposario metropolitano.com; Parque Metropolitano; adult/child US$5/1.25; ⊗9:30am-4:30pm Tue-Sun) With 1600 species, Panama City's butterfly garden is a worthy stop for nature lovers. Fifteen-minute guided tours explain the life cycle of butterflies and point out their favorite plants. Panama itself is home to 30 native butterfly species. Note that the butterflies themselves are most active on hot and sunny days.

◎ Panamá Viejo

Founded on August 15, 1519, by Spanish conquistador Pedro Arias de Ávila, the city of Panamá was the first European settlement along the Pacific. For 150 years it flourished as Spain exported Peruvian gold and silver to Europe via Panamá. In 1671 Captain Henry Morgan sacked the city and it was relocated to the present-day Casco Viejo. Today much of Panamá Viejo lies buried under a poor residential neighborhood, though the **ruins** (☑226-8915; www.panamaviejo.org; Vía Cincuentenario s/n; adult/child US$15/5; ⊗9am-5pm Tue-Sun) are a must-see.

Puente del Rey   Bridge

(Bridge of the King; Map p302;) Built in 1617, this Panamá Viejo landmark may be the oldest standing bridge in the Americas.

Catedral de Nuestra Señora de la Asunción   Cathedral

(Cathedral of Our Lady of Asunción; Map p302; ⊗9am-5pm Tue-Sun) Built between 1619 and 1626, this cathedral is the best-preserved building of the Panamá Viejo ruins. In traditional fashion, it was designed so that its two side chapels gave the cathedral a cross-like shape when viewed from the heavens. The bell tower at the back of the church may have served double duty as a watchtower for the **Casas Reales** (Royal Houses; Map p302; ⊗9am-5pm Tue-Sun). The main facade, which faced the Plaza Mayor, is gone; only the walls remain.

◎ The Causeway

At the Pacific entrance to the Panama Canal, a 2km palm tree–lined *calzada* (causeway) connects the four small islands of Naos, Culebra, Perico and Flamenco to the mainland. The Causeway is popular in the early morning and late afternoon, when residents walk, jog, skate and cycle its narrow length.

If you don't have your own vehicle, it's most convenient to take a taxi to the Causeway (US$4 to US$8). Any of the restaurants or bars can call one for you.

BioMuseo   Museum

(Museum of Biodiversity; Map p302; www.biomuseopanama.org; adult/child US$18/11; ⊗10am-4pm Tue-Fri, to 5pm Sat & Sun) Celebrating Panama as the land bridge that has permitted astonishing biodiversity in the region, this world-class museum is a visual feast. Exhibits tell the story of Panama's rich biodiversity through engaging, oversized visuals, examining human presence throughout time, how the Atlantic and Pacific evolved differently, and the interconnectedness of all species. A more abstract than literal approach creates a fresh view. World-renowned architect Frank Gehry, who created the Guggenheim Museum in Bilbao (Spain), designed this landmark museum of crumpled multicolor forms.

🟢 ACTIVITIES

Panama Audubon Society   Outdoors
(Map p302; ☑232-5977; www.audubonpanama. org; Parque Natural Metropolitano visitors center) Organizes birding walks and monthly meetings with interesting speakers at the Parque Natural Metropolitano visitors center (p299). It's a good opportunity to get to know some Panamanian birdwatchers and to learn more about tropical bird species. Both English and Spanish are spoken.

Scubapanama   Diving
(Map p302; ☑261-3841; www.scubapanama. com; Calle 52c Oeste, Vista Hermosa; ⊙8am-6pm Mon-Fri, to 4pm Sat) Panama's oldest dive op-

erator, offering a variety of trips throughout the country.

Bicicletas Moses   Cycling
(Map p302; ☑211-2718; Amador Causeway; per hour from US$4; ⊙9am-7pm) This bike tent has mountain bikes as well as reclining bikes, tandems, bicycle carts and options for kids. See the Facebook page for more details.

Casco Yoga   Yoga
(Map p298; ☑6265-5588; www.cascoyogapan ama.com; Calle José de Obaldía s/n, Casco Viejo) Offers a variety of quality yoga classes in a 2nd-floor studio, with English-speaking instruction. Check the website for special events and schedules.

🟢 TOURS

Ancon Expeditions   Tours
(Map p302; ☑269-9415; www.anconexpeditions. com; Edificio Dorado, 2nd fl, Calle 49a Este, El Cangrejo; ⊙9am-5pm Mon-Fri, to 1pm Sat) A pioneer in Panamanian tour operations, Ancon Expeditions offers city and nationwide

BioMuseo

AUTUMN SKY PHOTOGRAPHY/SHUTTERSTOCK ©

Panama City

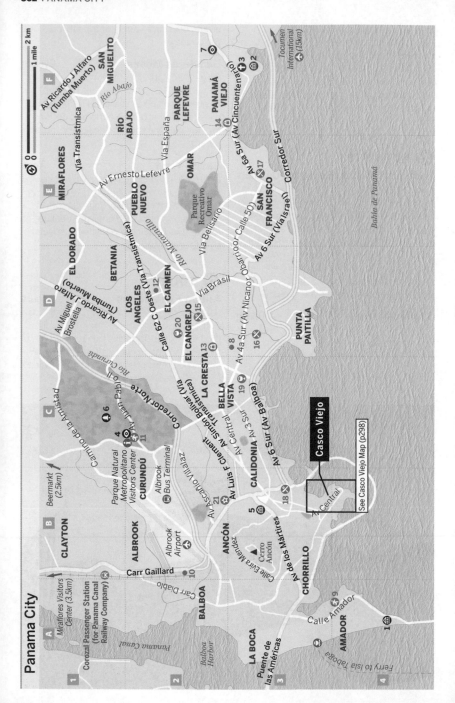

Panama City

⦿ **Sights**
1 BioMuseo A4
2 Casas Reales F3
3 Catedral de Nuestra Señora de la
   Asunción F3
4 Mariposario Metropolitano..................C2
5 Museo de Arte Contemporáneo..............B3
6 Parque Natural Metropolitano............C1
7 Puente del Rey F2

🎯 **Activities, Courses & Tours**
8 Ancon Expeditions D3
9 Bicicletas Moses A4
10 EcoCircuitos B2
11 Panama Audubon Society..................C2
12 Scubapanama D2

🛍 **Shopping**
13 Joyería La Huaca..........................D2
14 Mercado Nacional de Artesanías.............F2

🍴 **Eating**
15 Avatar D2
16 Hikaru D3
17 Maito E3
18 Mercado de Mariscos B3

🍷 **Drinking & Nightlife**
19 El Apartamento C3
20 La Rana Dorada D2

🎭 **Entertainment**
21 Ancon Guild Theater......................B2

tours as well as regularly scheduled canal transits. Try to book in advance, as this is one of the company's most popular offerings.

Barefoot Panama
Tours

(Map p298; ☎211-3700; www.barefootpanama. com; cnr Av A & Calle 7; city tour per person US$90; ◷9:30am-6:30pm) Prompt and professional, this American-run agency based in Casco Viejo does a great tour of Panama City that takes in everything from the history to the flora and fauna. They offer 14 different tours, including day trips to San Lorenzo and Gamboa, with visits to a Wounaan indigenous village, and trips throughout the country.

Panama Road Trips
Tours

(☎6800-7727; www.panamaroadtrips.com; tours from US$25) This small enterprise runs affordable day trips to Portobelo or an Emberá village in addition to popular canal and city tours. Also works with interesting rural tourism options throughout Panama.

🅐 SHOPPING

Karavan
Art

(Map p298; ☎228-7177; www.karavan-gallery. com; Calle 3a Oeste, Casco Viejo; ◷10am-6pm Mon-Sat, 11am-3:30pm Sun) 🍃 An excellent place to find original Guna embroidery

with modern designs and Congo art from Portobelo, Karavan commissions local artists, works closely to develop new talent, and recovers endangered culture and arts through nonprofit Fundación Mua Mua. Artisans work onsite.

Beermarkt
Alcohol

(https://beermarkt.com.pa; Calle Hospital, Clayton Mall; ◷10am-8pm Mon-Sat; 🚇Zona Azul) German owned and run, Beermarkt is the go-to place for beer lovers in Panama. Located in the expat area of Clayton, it offers a great range of brews ($2 to $8), from traditional European to more innovative variations, including organic.

El Palacio del Sombrero
Hats

(Map p298; ☎389-8544; Calle 4, Casco Viejo; ◷9am-9:30pm) For a panama hat with a twist, head to this shop with a small selection of traditional hats dwarfed by other bright, bold designs. Choose from a rainbow of colors or make a statement with checks and stripes.

No Me Olvides
Clothing

(Map p298; ☎211-1209; cnr Calle 4a Oeste & Av A, Casco Viejo; ◷10am-6pm Mon-Fri, 9am-5pm Sat) Featuring the classic Panamanian-made *guayaberas* (tropical dress shirts) made popular in the 1950s, in all colors and patterns, with a few selections for women as well.

Selling *molas* (handmade textiles) in an open-air market

Joyería La Huaca — Jewelry
(Map p302; ☎269-7254; www.facebook.com/
joyerialahuaca; cnr Calle Ricardo Arias & Vía
España, Campo Alegre; ⏰10am-6pm Mon-Fri, to
1pm Sat) A reputable jewelry store in front of
Hotel Continental.

Casa Latina — Arts & Crafts
(Map p298; ☎228-9828; cnr Av A & Calle 5, Casco
Viejo; ⏰10am-7pm) Colorful Casa Latina has
a large selection of beautiful handicrafts,
ranging from the affordable to a panama
hat on sale for US$2500! Some of the
items on collectors' lists include the detailed animal masks made by the Embera
people and the handmade baskets created
by women of the Wounaan communities.

Mercado Nacional de Artesanías — Market
(National Artisans Market; Map p302; Panamá
Viejo; ⏰9am-4pm Mon-Sat, to 1pm Sun) A great
place to shop for memorable souvenirs.

 EATING

Boasting the most innovative contemporary cuisine of Central America, Panama
City is a fun place to dine out. There are
literally hundreds of places to eat and –
thanks to a big immigrant population –
cuisine from every corner of the globe.

Granclement — Gelato $
(Map p298; www.granclement.com; Av Central,
Casco Viejo; gelato US$3.50-5; ⏰12:30pm-9pm
Mon-Fri, to 10pm Sat, 10am-8pm Sun) Pure pleas-
ure defines these intense tropical-fruit gelati
and rich, creamy flavors such as coffee,
orange-chocolate and ginger. A few scoops
of these fussy French creations will sweeten
a leisurely stroll through the Casco.

Mercado de Mariscos — Market $
(Map p302; ☎506-5741; Av Balboa, Casco Viejo;
mains US$3-14; ⏰6am-5pm) Get your seafood
fix above a bustling fish market. Come
early, as service at peak time is painfully
slow. Gems include whole fried fish and
cavernous bowls of 'Get Up Lazarus' soup
(a sure hangover cure). Outside, stands
ladle out delicious US$3 plastic cups of
ceviche (marinated seafood), including
classic concoctions, Mediterranean style
(with olives) and curry.

Super Gourmet — Deli $

(Map p298; ☑212-3487; www.supergourmet
cascoviejo.com; Av A, Casco Viejo; mains US$3-9;
⊗8am-5pm Mon-Sat, 10am-4pm Sun; 🍴) With
the cheeriest staff around, Super Gourmet
is a favorite of both locals and travelers.
Stop by the air-conditioned cafe for traditional soups, fresh tropical juices or a ba-
guette deli sandwich done American style.
For breakfast, eggs on English muffins with
cheese, bacon or vegetables or *arepas*
(savory corn cakes) with an espresso drink
hit the spot.

Barrio Pizza — Pizza $

(Map p298; ☑393-4444; www.barriopizza.com;
Av Central s/n, Casco Viejo; mains US$8-13;
⊗11am-11pm; ❄🍴) Happiness is blistering
wood-fired pizza cooked to order and
topped with truffle oil, roasted eggplant
or meatballs. The simple menu also has
Caesar salads, wine and beer. Come early
for a seat.

Lo Que Hay — Panamanian $$

(Map p298; Calle 5 Oeste s/n, Casco Viejo; mains
US$12-20; ⊗noon-3pm & 6:30-10pm Thu-Sat,
11am-4:30pm Sun) Neighborhood *fondas*
(cheap restaurants) serve cheap Panamanian classics, but this one – by Panama's
top chef – delivers a massive twist. Sexy
rice *(concolón)* has a crust of crisp per-
fection, served with smoked tomatoes or
fragrant clams. There's also tender whole
fish, yucca *tostadas* with carpaccio, and
mango kimchee served as a streetside *en-
curtido*. It's overpacked, not air-conditioned
and good fun. End with a massive *raspado*
(shaved ice flavored with fruit).

Hikaru — Japanese $$

(Map p302; ☑203-5087; www.hikaru.restaurant;
Calle 50 Este Alley, Marbella; mains US$10-16;
⊗noon-2:30pm & 6-11pm Mon-Sat) For authentic Japanese food prepared by a Tokyo chef,
this unassuming alleyside restaurant is pay
dirt. While Hikaru serves good sushi and
sashimi, you would be amiss not to sample
the ramen noodles, prepared in a complex,
buttery broth, or *takoyaki* (melt-in-your-

👍 Eating by Neighborhood

Casco Viejo is home to a number of
boutique eateries and European-
inspired cafes. Bella Vista has a good
concentration of satisfying restaurants.
San Francisco and Marbella also have
some good options.

With so many salaried earners on
their lunch break, the banking district
of El Cangrejo is home to a number of
pricey eateries. These tend to be slightly
more conservative and less trendy.

Owing to the wealth of city denizens and the popularity of dining out,
reservations are a good idea. Although
you can probably get a table most days
of the week, don't even think about just
showing up on Friday or Saturday night
without calling ahead.

Seafood meal at Mercado de Mariscos
MATYAS REHAK/SHUTTERSTOCK ©

mouth octopus fritters). Start with a cold
Sapporo beer and some edamame in rock
salt. Reservations recommended for dinner.

Avatar — Indian $$

(Map p302; ☑393-9006; www.avatarindian
cuisine.com; cnr Vías Argentina & España, El
Cangrejo; mains US$9-16; ⊗11am-11pm) Serving
rich kormas, fragrant rice and complex
curries in a swanky piano bar, Canadian-run
Avatar is sheer delight for spice enthusiasts. Southern Indian cuisine is the house
specialty, though if you want it really hot
you will have to insist. On weekdays, lunch
is 25% off.

From left: Mercado de Mariscos; seafood vendor, Mercado de Mariscos; garlic lobsters

Donde José · Panamanian $$$

(Map p298; 262-1682; www.dondejose.com; Av Central s/n, Casco Viejo; 8-course meal US$80, chef bar US$90; ⏱7pm & 9:30pm seatings Tue-Sat) Elevating humble Panamanian staples to haute cuisine, this 16-seat eatery is Panama's hottest reservation. Chef Jose prepares *ñandu* beans (native black beans), crisp, tender pork and *ñame* (an indigenous tuber) in playful, revelatory fashion. Servers have an intimate, casual rapport through

 Casco Antiguo Spanish School

This recommended Spanish **school** (Map p298; 228-3258; www.cascospanish.com; Av A s/n; 1-week 20hr intensive US$250; ⏱7am-7pm Mon-Fri, 8am-noon Sat) sits in the heart of Casco Viejo. Group lessons have only four students and private classes are available with excellent instructors. Also offers accommodations and activities.

a cascade of eight courses. Reservations are best made months in advance. Drinks are extra.

Maito · Panamanian $$$

(Map p302; 391-4657; www.maitopanama. com; Av 3m Sur, San Francisco; mains US$16-25; ⏱noon-10:30pm Mon-Sat) 🖋 With both style and pedigree, Maito toys with the classics, folding in everyday Caribbean, Latin and Chinese influences. While results can be mixed, it's still worthwhile. Start with a watermelon Waldorf salad. Ribs glazed in passion fruit are tender but lack the crispness of the duck chow mein. Seafood risotto in squid ink proves divine. There's garden seating and impeccable service.

Ochoymedio · Fusion $$$

(Map p298; 209-4185; www.ochoymediopanama.com; Calle José de Obaldía btwn Calles 8 & 9, Casco Viejo; ⏱7-11pm Mon-Sun) Under hanging vines and fairy lights, this gastronomical garden by Michelin-starred chef Andres Madrigal is romance incarnate. Start with a tropical-style lychee *ceviche*. Keep it fresh and light with an arugula salad or spicy lan-

PAVEL TVRDY/SHUTTERSTOCK ©

gostino yakitori. Opt for a table in the inner courtyard and kick-start your evening with an excellent cocktail named for a Beatles song. Service is great.

🍸 DRINKING & NIGHTLIFE

Bars and clubs open and close with alarming frequency in Panama City, though generally speaking nightlife is stylish, sophisticated and fairly pricey. The well-to-do denizens of the capital love a good scene, so it's worth scrubbing up and donning some nice threads. Remember to bring ID. Most clubs have a cover charge of US$10 to US$25.

La Rana Dorada Microbrewery

(Map p298; ☑392-0660; www.laranadorada.com; cnr Calle 9 & Calle Boquete, Casco Viejo; ⊙noon-12:30am Sun-Wed, to 3am Thu-Sat) Replete with brass fixtures and polished wood bars, this gorgeous low-lit brewpub serves its own award-winning small craft beers, alongside tasty thin-crust pizzas or bratwursts (mains US$3 to US$9). After-work happy hour is just catching on, but it goes gang-

busters here in indoor and outdoor spaces. A second location is on **Vía Argentina** (Map p302; ☑269-2989; www.laranadorada.com; Vía Argentina 20, El Cangrejo; ⊙noon-2am).

Stranger's Club Cocktail Bar

(Map p298; ☑282-0064; www.facebook.com/strangersclubpanama; Av Central s/n, Casco Viejo; ⊙6pm-2am Mon-Wed, to 4am Thu-Sat, noon-4pm & 6pm-midnight Sun) For a buzzy scene of 20- to 40-somethings, duck into this dimly lit cocktail bar. The Consuelo, a revelation of muddled cucumber, gin and elderflower liqueur, is worth the trip in itself.

Bar Relic Bar

(Map p298; www.relicbar.com; Calle 9a Este, Casco Viejo; ⊙9pm-2am Tue-Sat) Wildly popular with travelers and hip young Panamanians, this cavernous hostel bar is a hit. Service is friendly and patrons easily mingle in the ample courtyard with shared picnic tables. Not only are you partying outside (a rarity in Panama City) but you're also next to the historical wall of the city.

Upstairs in the hostel there's a calmer, more grown-up option for cocktails.

Tántalo Bar — Cocktail Bar

(Map p298; http://tantalohotel.com/roofbar; cnr Calle 8a Este & Av B, Casco Viejo; cover US$5-10; ⊙rooftop deck 5pm-2am) Though it serves casual lunches, this ultra-hip cafe-bar is best known for sunset happy hours on its rooftop deck. Pair your cocktail with fusion-style tapas. Cover is charged after 10pm, but to get a spot on the tiny roof deck, show up around 7pm. Wednesday is salsa night.

Casa Jaguar — Club

(Map p298; ☎6866-8483; http://casajaguarpanama.com; Av Central s/n; ⊙8pm-2am Tue-Thu, to 4am Fri & Sat) Don your stilettos and glitter for a night out at the Casco's hottest club, located on the 2nd floor next to Teatro Amador. There's no hurry, though, as things don't heat up until late at night, with dedicated reggaetón and electronica rooms in addition to smaller nooks and crannies. Check the website for theme nights.

El Apartamento — Bar

(The Apartment; Map p302; ☎6617-3038; www.facebook.com/elapartamentopanama; Av Federico Boyd; ⊙7pm-4am Tue-Sat) At any given time there's three floors of mischief going on at the Apartment, a yellow villa with a *discoteca,* live music floor and great bar with bottle service.

⊛ ENTERTAINMENT

If you're not looking to get blotto, there are numerous ways to spend a moonlit (or rainy) evening in the city. A good place to start is the arts section in the Sunday edition of *La Prensa* or the back pages of the *Panama News*.

Teatro Nacional — Theater

(Map p298; ☎262-3525; Av B, Casco Viejo) Casco Viejo's lovely 19th-century playhouse stages ballet, concerts and plays.

Ancon Guild Theater — Theater

(Map p302; http://anconguild.com; Av Gaillard, Ancon; ⊙6:30-11pm Mon-Sun) Broadway it is not, but this character-filled wooden building houses a charming 166-seat theater. Founded in 1950 by a group of Panamanian and American artists, it now serves as Pan-

Teatro Nacional (p299), Casco Viejo

AGE FOTOSTOCK/ALAMY STOCK PHOTO ©

ama's longest-running theater and stages a range of good English-language performances from improvisational comedy to classic dramas such as *Clue*. During the interval a makeshift bar is erected on the veranda, and beers and spirits are served.

 INFORMATION

ATMs are abundant throughout the city. The Banco Nacional de Panamá counter at Tocumen International Airport is one of the few places in Panama City that exchanges foreign currency.

Panacambios (☏223-1800; ground fl, Plaza Regency Bldg, Vía España, El Cangrejo; ◷8am-5pm Mon-Fri) Buys and sells international currencies.

 GETTING THERE & AWAY

International flights arrive at and depart from **Tocumen International Airport** (Map p285; ☏238-2700; www.tocumenpanama.aero; Av Domingo Díaz, Panama City; ◷24hr), **35km** northeast of the city center. It's in the process of undergoing a major expansion that should expand offerings considerably. Domestic flights and a few international flights depart from **Albrook Airport** (Aeropuerto Marcos A Gelabert; Map p285; ☏501-9272; Av Canfield, Albrook) in the former Albrook Air Force Station near the canal.

There are regular ferries to Islas Taboga and Contadora, leaving from Panama City's Causeway and the Balboa Yacht Club.

Albrook Bus Terminal (Gran Terminal; Map p302; ☏303-3030; www.grantnt.com; Albrook; ◷24hr), near Albrook Airport, is a convenient and modern one-stop location for most buses leaving Panama City.

Rental rates start at US$22 per day for the most economical cars, including unlimited kilometers. Insurance is considerably extra.

The **Panama Canal Railway Company** (PCRC; ☏317-6070; www.panarail.com; Carretera Gaillard, Corozal; one way adult/child US$25/15) operates a glass-domed train that takes passen-

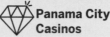 **Panama City Casinos**

None of the casinos in Panama City are competition for Las Vegas, but there are three attractive and popular houses of chance in the capital. Most casinos in the city are located inside top hotels including the Sheraton, Miramar Inter-Continental and Hotel Continental. By Panamanian law casinos do not serve alcohol.

PICTURES COLOUR LIBRARY/ALAMY STOCK PHOTO ©

gers on a lovely ride from Panama City to Colón on weekdays.

 GETTING AROUND

You can rent bicycles in some hostels and at the Causeway. Bicicletas Moses (p301) operates a booth with mountain bikes, tandems, bicycle carts and kids' bikes for rent.

Panama City has almost finished phasing out its *diablos rojos* (red devils) for modern, safe, air-conditioned Metrobus buses.

Panama City's mostly underground transportation system is known as **El Metro** (☏504-7200; www.elmetrodepanama.com; fare US$0.35-1.35; ◷5am-11pm Mon-Fri, to 10pm Sat, 7am-10pm Sun).

Taxis are plentiful but problematic. Some drivers do not know the city, and there is no meter.

Companies like Uber and Cabify offer an alternative solution to taking a taxi. They are cheaper and more convenient in off-peak hours.

In this Chapter

Surfing 312
Isla Colón & Bocas Town 314
Isla Bastimentos 320
Isla San Cristóbal 322
Isla Carenero 322

Bocas del Toro

With its Caribbean islands dotting a shock of blue waters, Bocas del Toro is all that's tropical. This is Panama's principal tourist draw and it will provide some of your most memorable experiences. The archipelago consists of six densely forested islands, scores of uninhabited islets and Panama's oldest marine park. Most visitors come for a hefty dose of sun and surf, and few are disappointed with the Bocas cocktail of water, fun and thatched luxury, but there's a lot more to what might be Panama's most beautiful corner.

Two Days in Bocas del Toro

On your first day of Caribbean sun and fun, grab a surfboard and head for **Playa Bluff** (p314) – or admit you aren't worthy and take a **lesson** (p313). Fuel up on seafood then party till late at **Selina Bar** (p319). Spend day two hydrating and exploring Isla Colón by **bicycle** (p317), then slow down with a relaxed dinner at **El Último Refugio** (p319).

Four Days in Bocas del Toro

Boat out to the thatched resorts at **Isla Bastimentos** (p320), where you can bask on the **beach** (p321), go **scuba diving** (p321) or learn about **permaculture** (p321). On day four, take a **chocolate farm tour** (p321) on Isla San Cristóbal or visit indigenous groups on other islands with a community-tourism initiative. Stop in on Isla Carenero for a tasty **vegetarian meal** (p322).

Map labels:
Punta Norte
Punta Cauro
Punta Rocosa
Boca del Drago
Playa Bluff
Isla Colón
Punta Rancho
CARIBBEAN SEA
Punta Bluff
Playa Punch
Conch Point
Big Creek
Punta Puss Head
Wizard Beach
Playa Segunda
Playa Polo
Finca Los Monos Botanical Garden
Isla Careñero
Old Bank
Playa El Istmito
Isla Colon International Airport
Bocas del Toro
Red Frog Beach
Playa Larga
Bahía de Almirante
Isla Solarte
Nivida Bat Cave
Isla Bastimentos
Ferry to Almirante
Parque Nacional Marino Isla Bastimentos
Quebrada Sal (Salt Creek)
Isla San Cristóbal
Green Acres Chocolate Farm (6.5km)

Archipiélago de Bocas del Toro Map (p316)

0   5 km
0   2.5 miles

Arriving in Bocas del Toro

The main transport hub in the archipelago is Bocas town, which is reached by ferry from Almirante on the mainland. To get from island to island you must hire water taxis. An international airport at Bocas town links the archipelago with Panama City, David and Changuinola, as well as San José in Costa Rica.

Where to Stay

Archipiélago Bocas del Toro offers perhaps the widest choice of accommodations outside Panama City, from very basic hostels to five-star boutique hotels. You'll find plenty of cheap stays but also some lovely hotels in Bocas town, and a mix of luxury seaside resorts and rustic B&Bs over on Isla Bastimentos.

Surfing at Bocas del Toro

JOHN SEATON CALLAHAN/GETTY IMAGES ©

Surfing

Although the joy of Panama is riding some of the lesser-known surf breaks – or even discovering your own – the country has a couple of well-known world-class spots, and one of those is Archipiélago de Bocas del Toro.

Great For...

☑ Don't Miss

The infamous Playa Bluff – the tubes are dangerously incredible.

Isla Colón

Beginner surfers looking for a bit of reef experience should check out **Playa Punch**, which offers a good mix of lefts and rights. Although it can get heavy when big, Punch generally offers some of the kindest waves around.

Just past Punch en route to Playa Bluff is a popular reef break known as **Dumpers**. This left break can get up to 3m and should only be ridden by experienced surfers; wiping out on the reef here is dangerous. There is also an inner break known as **Inner Dumps**, which also breaks left but is more forgiving than its outer mate.

The island's most infamous surf spot is **Playa Bluff** (p314), which throws out powerful barreling waves that break in shallow water along the beach and have a reputation for snapping boards.

❶ Need to Know

Rent boards from **Tropix** (☑757-9727; http://tropixsurf.tripod.com; Calle 3; ☺9am-7pm Mon-Sat) in Bocas town or **Red Frog Bungalows** (☑6539-5151; www.redfrog bungalows.com; Red Frog Beach; s/d incl 2 meals & transport from US$190/320; @⌖) on Isla Bastimentos.

✘ Take a Break

Grab a bite at Playa Bluff's **Paki Point** (☑6948-6562; mains US$7-15; ☺11am-6pm).

★ Top Tip

The biggest swells for surfers to ride are from December to March.

Isla Bastimentos

If you're looking for a solid beach break, both **Wizard Beach** (Playa Primera) and **Red Frog Beach** (p321) offer fairly constant sets of lefts and rights, perfect for beginners and intermediates. When the swells are in, however, Wizard occasionally throws out some huge barrels, though they tend to close up pretty quickly.

Isla Carenero

Very experienced surfers may want to tackle **Silverbacks**, an enormous barreling right between Isla Bastimentos and Isla Carenero that breaks over a reef and can reach heights of more than 5m during winter months. Silverbacks breaks off the coast, so you're going to need to hire a water taxi (from US$3) to get out there.

Two places suitable for beginners are **Old Man's**, which has an A-frame that breaks in the middle of a channel, and **Black Rock**, with a right suitable for beginners that also breaks in the middle of the channel with a sandy reef bottom.

Top Three Surf Schools

○ **Bocas Surf School** (☑757-9057, 6852-5291; www.bocassurfschool.com; cnr Av H & Calle 5, Bocas Town; half-/full-day courses US$59/89)

○ **Escuela de Mar Surf School** (☑6981-2749, 757-7008; www.surfschoolpanama.com; Isla Carenero; ☺9am-6pm)

○ **Mono Loco Surf School** (☑760-9877; http://monolocosurfschool.com; Calle 2, Bocas Town; 3hr lessons US$50; ☺9am-6pm)

Isla Colón & Bocas Town

The archipelago's most developed island is home to the provincial capital of Bocas del Toro. From the mid-1990s, foreign investors flooded the island, creating hotels, restaurants and condos while infrastructure for water, trash and sewage lagged far behind. Today the island, which runs on diesel, struggles to find a balance between satisfying development and serving community needs.

Note that the town, the archipelago and the province all share the name Bocas del Toro. To avoid confusion, we refer to the provincial capital as Bocas town or simply Bocas.

◎ SIGHTS

Finca Los Monos Botanical Garden
Gardens

(☎757-9461, 6729-9443; www.bocasdeltoro botanicalgarden.com; garden/birdwatching tours US$15/25; ⊗garden tours 1pm Mon & 8:30am Fri, birdwatching tours 6:30am & 5pm on request) One

of the joys of visiting Bocas is touring the 'Monkey Farm' botanical garden a couple of kilometers northwest of the center. Painstakingly carved out of 10 hectares of secondary rainforest over almost two decades, it contains hundreds of species of local and imported trees and ornamental plants, and is teeming with wildlife.

Playa Bluff
Beach

This lovely beach is pounded by intense waves. Though you wouldn't want to get into the water here without a board, the soft, yellow sand and palm-fringed shores are pristine. The beach is 8km from Bocas town, alongside the road after you round Punta Bluff. It serves as a nesting area for sea turtles from May to September.

Boca del Drago
Beach

(Dragon's Mouth) Boca del Drago, in the northwest of Isla Colón, is one of the best beaches on the island, though the surf can be rough at times. Just offshore from the beach is a patchy coral-and-sand sea bottom that offers good snorkeling when the sea is calm and the water clear.

From left: Surf shop, Bocas town; Isla Bastimentos; eco resort on Bastimentos; surfing at Wizard Beach (p313)

🟢 ACTIVITIES

Flying Pirates   Adventure Sports
(📱6689-5050; www.flyingpiratesbocas.com; cnr Calle 3 & Av C; half-/full day US$110/140; ☺9am-7pm) One of the best ways to explore Isla Colón is by ATV/quad bike, and the people at Flying Pirates, based on their own 600-hecatre *finca* (farm) on the way to Playa Bluff, can oblige. They rent out more than 30 of the fat-tired vehicles for use on or off-road, including 15km of trails on private land. The beach is off-limits.

Lil' Spa Shop   Spa
(📱6591-3814; www.spashopbythesea.com; cnr Av H & Calle 7; ☺10am-6pm) Should you need a bit of pampering after a hard day on the waves, head for this lovely ocean-front spa run by a gregarious New Yorker offering massage, reflexology and beauty treatments.

Bocas Yoga   Yoga
(www.bocasyoga.com; Calle 4; classes US$6) Geared to both locals and travelers, this hatha yoga studio run by the effervescent Laura makes a good break from the party scene. Offers daily classes in English.

DIVING
A two-tank dive will cost around US$85; there are also dive certification courses.

La Buga   Diving
(📱757-9534, 6781-0755; www.labugapanama.com; Calle 3; ☺8am-8pm) A very well regarded dive shop with a new approach boat, La Buga leads two to three dive trips a day. Highlights include night dives and visits to the caves off Bastimentos (US$100). It also offers surfboard rentals and surf lessons, stand-up paddles (US$15 per hour) and kayak rentals. While you explore your options, grab a bite at the cute cafe attached.

Panama Dive School   Diving
(📱6984-4745; Av H; ☺8am-6:30pm) Guests give this PADI dive shop high marks. It offers two-tank dives (US$75), open-water certification (US$280) and snorkeling (US$20 for a half-day). If you are new to scuba diving, you can try it out on a discovery dive (US$100). It is also insured.

Archipiélago de Bocas del Toro

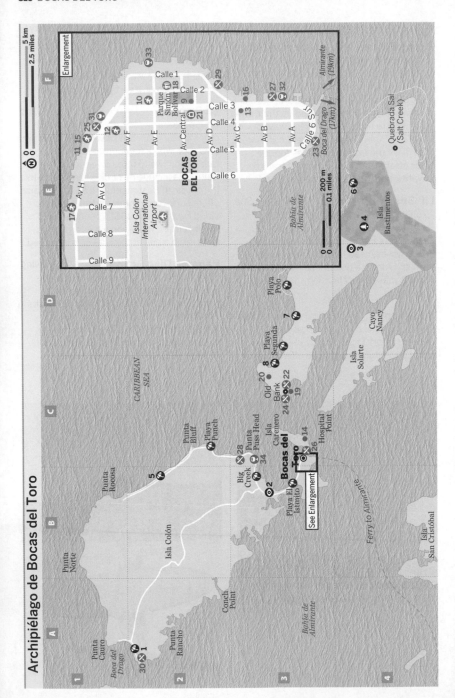

Archipiélago de Bocas del Toro

◉ Sights
1 Boca del Drago..A2
2 Finca Los Monos Botanical Garden..........B3
3 Nivida Bat Cave...D4
4 Parque Nacional Marino Isla
   Bastimentos..E4
5 Playa Bluff..B2
6 Playa Larga...E4
7 Red Frog Beach...D3
8 Wizard Beach..C3

◎ Activities, Courses & Tours
9 Anaboca..F2
10 Bocas Bicis..F2
11 Bocas Surf School.....................................E1
12 Bocas Yoga..F1
13 Dragon Tours...F3
14 Escuela de Mar Surf School.....................C3
   Flying Pirates.................................(see 16)
15 Ixa's Bike World..E1
16 La Buga..F3
17 Lil' Spa Shop..E1
18 Mono Loco Surf School.............................F2
   Panama Dive School.......................(see 11)

19 Scuba 6 Ecodiving.....................................C3
20 Up in the Hill...C3

◎ Shopping
21 Tropix Surfboards......................................F2

✕ Eating
   Bibi's on the Beach.........................(see 14)
22 Chavela..C3
23 El Último Refugio.......................................E3
24 Firefly Restaurant.....................................C3
25 La Casbah..F1
26 Leaf Eaters Cafe..C3
27 Om Café...F3
28 Paki Point..C3
29 Raw...F2
   Sea Monkey....................................(see 22)
30 Yarisnori Restaurant.................................A2

◎ Drinking & Nightlife
31 Bookstore Bar..F1
32 La Iguana Surf Bar.....................................F3
33 Selina Bar...F2
34 Skully's...C3

CYCLING

Bikes are available from some hostels as well as from **Ixa's Bike World** (Av H; bikes per hr US$3, fat bikes per 24hr US$15; ☺8am-6pm Mon-Sat) and **Bocas Bicis** (Av E; per hr/day US$3/12; ☺9am-7pm) in Boca town. Flying Pirates (p315) rents out ATVs/quad bikes.

TOURS

The most popular tours in the area are all-day snorkeling trips, which are perfect for nondivers who want a taste of the area's rich marine life. A typical tour costs US$25 per person, and goes to Dolphin Bay, Cayo Crawl, Red Frog Beach (p321) and Hospital Point.

Dragon Tours   Boating

(☏6879-5506, 757-7010; www.facebook.com/Jadedragon9; Calle 3; per person incl lunch US$45; ☺9am-5pm) This perennially popular charter company sails its purpose-built 19m catamaran complete with waterslide to various islands on day trips. It usually rents to groups of 45 people, but if there's

space individuals can get on a trip. Snorkeling and coolers filled with ice included.

Anaboca   Tours

(La Asociación Natural Bocas Carey; ☏6843-7244; www.anaboca.bocasdeltoro.org; Calle 3era; per person US$20) ✔ This nonprofit run by the local community addresses marine-turtle conservation. In season (April to August), certified guides offer nighttime tours to groups of eight or fewer to view turtle hatching on Playa Bluff. You can also arrange overnight community stays, a good idea if you are there to watch hatching in the wee hours.

✕ EATING

You'll find a large assortment of eateries in Bocas town, and beachfront restaurants at Playa Bluff and even far-flung Boca del Drago.

Om Café   Indian $$

(☏6127-0671; http://omcafebocas.com; Calle 3; mains US$9-19; ☺4-10pm Mon-Fri year-round, plus Sat Dec-Apr; 🖋) When you smell gorgeous aromas spilling out onto the

From left:Strawberry poison-dart frog; palm forest, Cayos Zapatillas (p320); dive shop on Bocas del Toro

sidewalk, you're at this welcoming Indian cafe serving classic curries, korma and thalis. Service can be slow, so pass the wait with an original cocktail, such as the Tipsy Turban (US$6), a dizzy mix of passion fruit or lime juice, rum and sugar. Good selection of vegetarian dishes.

La Casbah   Mediterranean $$
(☏6477-4727; Av H; menu US$14, mains US$13-16; ☻6-10pm Tue-Sat) Locals and travelers love this Mediterranean restaurant serving up gazpacho, goat's cheese salad, and seafood and meat dishes such as tabbouleh couscous salad with chicken. The fish of the day comes in cream or white-wine

Filthy Fridays

Filthy Fridays (www.filthyfridaybocas.com) is a wildly popular three-island party crawl. Your ticket (US$35) includes boat rides, shots and temporary tattoos, but you're on your own with the hangover.

sauce, and there's a nice veggie plate for noncarnivores.

Raw   Asian $$
(☏6938-8473; www.facebook.com/RawFusion-Bocas; Calle 1 s/n; mains US$12-15; ☻3-10pm Tue-Sun) It's just a little plank restaurant on the water, but the Asian-fusion offerings are spot on. Sake accompanies fresh tofu spring rolls and amazing tuna tapas. The salads are wonderful, and service is friendly and attentive. At night candles are lit and the full bar, specializing in original martinis (from US$7) and cocktails, starts humming.

Yarisnori Restaurant Panamanian $$
(☏6615-5580; www.yarisnori.com; Boca del Drago; mains US$8-25; ☻9am-6pm Wed-Mon) Overlooking the water and with hammocks strung between the palms on the beach, this open-air restaurant is a local favorite, due in large part to the warm hospitality of owners Juany and Willy. Grab a table on the sand and feast on the catch of the day, served with beans and coconut rice. Breakfast is good, too.

El Último Refugio Caribbean $$$

(☎6726-9851; www.ultimorefugio.com; Calle 6 Sur; mains US$14-20; ☺6-10pm Mon-Sat) A favorite splurge of Bocas locals, this mellow North American–run place on the edge of the sea does date night right. Caribbean and seafood dishes include red curry calamari and miso-crusted grouper on the chalkboard. Service is friendly and the tranquil location makes it a great spot for a quiet, romantic dinner. Reserve ahead.

❷ DRINKING & NIGHTLIFE

For its size, Bocas offers a surprisingly varied and lively nightlife, with bars and clubs along the waterfront or just a short water-taxi ride away on Isla Carenero.

Selina Bar Club

(☎202-7966; www.selinahostels.com; Calle 1; ☺7pm-midnight Sun-Thu, to 2am Fri & Sat) The bar at this landmark hostel is open daily, with happy hour between 7pm and 8pm, but most people make it here between 10pm and 2am on a Friday, when all the stops are pulled out and it's party time.

Bookstore Bar Bar

(☎6452-5905; Calle 2; ☺noon-1am Mon-Sat, 5pm-12:30am Sun) Just what its name suggests: this cavernous spot sells both books and drinks, though most seem more interested in the latter. It's the best spot for live music in Bocas, with rock, salsa and punk on Tuesday and Saturday. Run by a couple of affable North Americans, it's a mecca for gringos at the start (and sometimes at the end) of an evening.

La Iguana Surf Bar Club

(Calle 3; ☺9:30pm-3am Sun-Wed, to 4am Thu-Sat) Kick off your crazy Bocas night at this popular surfer and skate bar on the waterfront. Start with a US$2 beer-tequila combo. You probably won't be in the mood for the dancing pole yet, though.

Skully's Pub

(☎6689-5050; Playa Punch; mains US$7-15; ☺4-10pm) A waterfront tiki bar with good pub grub, this is a nice place to gather for sunsets and cocktails, and the burgers ain't bad either. It's a US$2 taxi ride from Bocas town.

Isla Bastimentos

Although it's just a 10-minute boat ride from the town of Bocas del Toro, Isla Bastimentos is like a different world. Some travelers say this is their favorite island in their favorite part of Panama. The northwest coast of the island is home to palm-fringed beaches that serve as nesting grounds for sea turtles, while most of the northern and southern coasts consists of mangrove islands and coral reefs that lie within the boundaries of the Parque Nacional Marino Isla Bastimentos.

The main settlement on Bastimentos is Old Bank. It has a prominent West Indian population whose origins are in the banana industry. The island is also home to the Ngöbe-Buglé village of Quebrada Sal (Salt Creek).

> " ... Isla Bastimentos is like a different world "

◉ SIGHTS & ACTIVITIES

Parque Nacional Marino Isla Bastimentos   Park

Established in 1988, this 132-sq-km marine park was Panama's first. Protecting 130 islands of the Bocas del Toro archipelago, including the coral-fringed Cayos Zapatillas, and the wetlands in the center of Isla Bastimentos, the marine park is an important nature reserve for mangroves, monkeys, sloths, caimans, crocodiles and 28 species of amphibians and reptiles.

Playa Larga   Beach

(Long Beach) This 6km-long beach on the southeast side of the island falls under the protection of the marine park. Hawksbill, leatherback and green sea turtles nest here from March to September. It's also good for surfing. To get here, you can follow the path past Red Frog Beach, but the best access is the one-hour walk with a guide from Salt Creek.

Cayos Zapatillas

DAMSEA/SHUTTERSTOCK ©

Red Frog Beach   Beach

(US$5) Small but perfectly formed, Red Frog Beach is named after the *rana rojo* (strawberry poison-dart frog), an amphibian you're most unlikely to encounter here due to development, local kids trapping them to impress tourists, and a tidal wave of day-trippers in season. From Bocas town, water taxis (US$7) head to the public dock next to a small marina on the south side of the island, from where the beach is an easy 15-minute walk.

Nivida Bat Cave   Cave

(Bahía Honda; US$5) One of Bastimentos' most fascinating natural wonders, Nivida is a massive cavern with swarms of nectar bats and a subterranean lake. The cave lies within the borders of the Parque Nacional Marino Isla Bastimentos and half the fun is getting here. But it's next to impossible to do it on your own. An organized tour from Old Bank costs US$45 per person.

Scuba 6 Ecodiving   Diving

(✆6722-5245; www.scuba6ecodiving.com; Old Bank; 2-tank dive $95; ☻8am-8pm) ◢ A PADI five-star resort, this recommended scuba-diving agency makes it a priority to educate about the marine environment and operates with a Leave No Trace ethic. Instructors speak English, Spanish and French, and have Blue and Green Fin certifications. The office is located in **Tío Tom's Guesthouse** (✆6951-6615; www.tiotomsguesthouse.com; Old Bank; dm US$25-30, 2-person bungalow US$35; ☏).

⊕ TOURS

Up in the Hill   Tours

(✆6570-8277, 6607-8962; www.upinthehill.com; Old Bank; 2hr tour & tasting US$25) It's worth the hot 20-minute haul up to this organic farm at the highest point on Isla Bastimentos to see a wonderful permaculture project with chocolate groves and many exotic fruits. Linger at the wonderful cafe

 Green Acres Chocolate Farm

Facing Isla San Cristóbal's Dolphin Bay, but actually on the mainland's Cerro Bruja peninsula, this **chocolate farm** (✆6716-4422; www.greenacreschocolatefarm.com; Cerro Bruja Peninsula; adult/child US$15/free; ☻10am & 2pm Thu-Tue) sitting within 12 hectares of forested slopes is one of the largest in the archipelago that's open to the public. A two-hour tour led by North American owner Robert will take you seamlessly from cocoa pod to candy bar and leave no question unanswered.

serving all-day breakfast, chocolate with coconut milk and delectable baked goods. There's also coffee from Boquete, golden milk with fresh turmeric, and homemade hibiscus tea.

✖ EATING

There are a handful of interesting spots in Old Bank worth checking out. Elsewhere you'll most likely be taking your meals at your hotel.

Chavela   Seafood $

(✆6246-5193; www.facebook.com/bar restaurantechavela; Old Bank; mains US$4-12; ☻6-10pm) In an attractive little lime-green shack at the bottom of the landmark Hostel Bastimentos, a Panamanian-American couple serve cheap-as-chips burgers but emphasize seafood in all its guises, from *ceviche de pulpo* (octopus cured in lime juice) and fish tacos to barracuda steak. Locals say it's the best eats in town.

Firefly Restaurant   Fusion $$

(✆6524-4809; www.thefireflybocasdeltoro.com; Old Bank; mains US$8-15; ☻5-9pm Wed-Mon; ☏) A clutch of open-air tables facing rough surf, this reservation-only restaurant is the perfect sunset date. An American chef cooks up local and organic ingredients in Thai and Caribbean preparations. Think sweet chili calamari, coconut gnocchi and fresh seafood curries. The tapas menu allows you to sample a range of flavors.

Sea Monkey   Fusion $$

(☑6693-9168; Old Bank; mains US$13-16; ⊗8am-11am & 5-10pm Mon-Sat) In a simple over-the-water clapboard house, this breezy little restaurant churns out wonderful plates of Asian beer fish and local *patuk* greens with handmade cocktails (from US$5). Perfect for a sundowner. Moreover, the end-of-the-pier location provides a bit of peace and quiet in raucous Old Bank.

Isla San Cristóbal

A half-hour away from Bocas town and you're in another world among the Ngöbe-Buglé indigenous community on Isla San Cristóbal. These subsistence farmers and fishers have a strong sense of their cultural identity, though they live mostly in difficult circumstances. There are some community tourism initiatives in their communities. To the south, Dolphin Bay is famous for sightings of dolphin pods. Beyond there is a lodging on another nearby island and a mainland restaurant accessed by boat.

Isla Carenero

Slightly larger than a postage stamp, this tiny isle ringed by sand feels a notch more relaxed than the main island. It lies a few hundred meters southeast from Isla Colón and its close location makes it a go-to for

a leisurely waterfront lunch or happy-hour action. Often overlooked, it takes its name from 'careening,' which in nautical talk means to lean a ship on one side for cleaning or repairing. In October 1502 Columbus' ships were careened and cleaned on this cay while the admiral recovered from a bellyache.

 EATING

From seafood on the beach to gourmet vegetarian, this pint-sized island has a lot to offer food-wise.

Leaf Eaters Cafe   Vegetarian $

(☑6675-1354; www.facebook.com/bocasleaf eaters; dishes US$8-12; ⊗11am-5pm Mon-Sat; ☑) For excellent pescatarian, vegetarian and vegan lunches, head to this over-the-water restaurant on Isla Carenero. Start with a cool cucumber-mint-coconut-watermelon shake. Quirky and flavorful offerings include 'hippie bowls' (brown rice with vegetables and dressing), grilled fish sandwiches with caramelized onions, blackened fish tacos and scrumptious shiitake burgers. Cheery decor and friendly atmosphere.

Bibi's on the Beach   Seafood $$

(☑757-9137, 6981-2749; http://bocasbuccaneer resort.com/surfside-restaurant-and-bar; mains US$7-15; ⊗9am-9pm) With great atmosphere, this over-the-water restaurant and surf outfitter makes tasty soups, killer *ceviche* (citrus-cured seafood), whole lobsters (US$27) and lightly fried fish. The service couldn't be friendlier and the sea views (and cocktails) will keep you lingering. Happy hour coincides with sundown: 4pm to 7pm.

Bocas del Toro is a prime surfing destination, and strikes a good balance of development and natural beauty. Handicrafts include hand-woven hammocks, and there are also some great food options to be found.

Top: Colorful buildings, Isla Colón (p314); bottom left: handwovern hammocks; seaside restaurant meal

In this Chapter
Parque Nacional Volcán Barú............ 326
Chiriquí Coffee Farms...................... 330
Boquete... 332
Sights & Activities........................... 332
Tours... 333
Courses... 335
Eating.. 335

Chiriquí Province

Panama's tallest mountains, longest rivers and most fertile valleys can all be found here, in this land of immense beauty. On the coast, the pristine Golfo de Chiriquí boasts long sandy beaches and a rich diversity of marine life. The mist-covered mountains near the town of Boquete, a favorite of North American and European retirees, is a good base for adventures such as white-water rafting and hiking the flanks of Panama's highest point, Volcán Barú (3474m). Boquete is also the center of Panama's coffee industry, which means that a potent cup of shade-grown arabica is never more than a cafe away.

Two Days in Chiriquí Province

Base yourself in the highland retreat of Boquete, and on day one wander around the gorgeous town, **smell the flowers** (p333) and take a **coffee tour** (p330). On day two, set out on an adventure, be it **rafting** (p333), **ATV touring** (p333) or flying through the **canopy** (p333). Indulge in a delicious farm-to-table dinner at **Colibri** (p336).

Four Days in Chiriquí Province

On day three, head up to Volcán and drop your things in a charming rain-forest cabin before a hike up **Sendero Los Quetzales** (p327), a stunning trail through wildlife-rich cloud forest. Return to Boquete on day four and relax in the park awhile, then celebrate the previous day's athletic achievements with **pizza** (p335) and **craft brews** (p336).

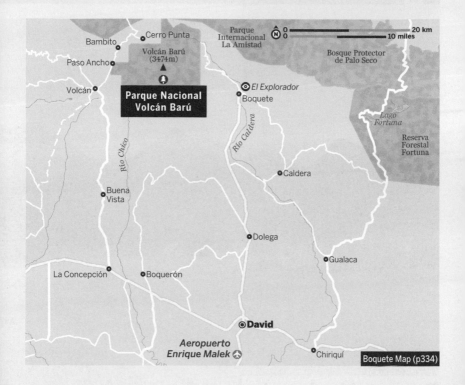

Parque
Internacional
La Amistad

Cerro Punta

Bambito

Volcán Barú
(3474m)

Paso Ancho

Bosque Protector
de Palo Seco

20 km
10 miles

Volcán

El Explorador
Boquete

**Parque Nacional
Volcán Barú**

Lago
Fortuna

Reserva
Forestal
Fortuna

Río Caldera

Río Chico

Caldera

Buena
Vista

Dolega

Gualaca

La Concepción

Boquerón

David

Aeropuerto
Enrique Malek

Chiriquí

Boquete Map (p334)

Arriving in Chiriquí Province

Aeropuerto Enrique Malek David's
airport frequently handles flights to and
from San José (Costa Rica). It's about
5km from town; take a taxi (US$5).

Chiriquí's cities and towns are easily
accessible from Panama City and neighboring provinces, and the Interamericana Hwy runs the length of the province.

Where to Stay

The selection of places to stay is epic
in places such as Boquete, including historic hotels, inns, cottages and B&Bs. In
Parque Nacional Volcán Barú, camping
is the only option, but there are also
some real gems along the road over the
cordillera, and plenty of decent stays in
David and along the Pacific coast.

Volcán Barú landscape

Parque Nacional Volcán Barú

This 143-sq-km national park is home to Volcán Barú, Panama's only volcano and the dominant geographical feature of Chiriquí Province. Volcán Barú is no longer active, but it does have seven craters, and its summit, the highest point in Panama, affords views of both the Pacific and Caribbean coasts when clear.

Great For...

☑ Don't Miss

Sendero Los Quetzales – one of Panama's most beautiful trails.

The park provides ample opportunities for hiking, mountain climbing and camping, and it's home to abundant wildlife, including pumas and the resplendent quetzal.

Hiking Volcán Barú

Climbing **Volcán Barú** is a goal of many visitors seeking views from the summit of both the Pacific and the Caribbean coasts. It might not be worth it in poor weather, as the going is strenuous and rough, and there is little to see in cloud cover. You can enter the national park on the eastern (Boquete) and western (Volcán) sides of the volcano.

The eastern summit access from Boquete is the easier, but it involves a strenuous uphill hike along a 13.5km road that goes from the park entrance – about 8km northwest of the center of town – to the summit. The road is paved to the ranger

Cerro Punta • Sendero *Los Quetzales* • Parque Internacional La Amistad

Bambito •

Volcán Barú (3474m) ▲

Paso Ancho •

Río Caldera

• Volcán

⊙ Parque Nacional Volcán Barú

Boquete •

❶ Need to Know

Overnight temperatures in the park can drop below freezing, and it may be windy and cold during the day, particularly in the morning. Dress accordingly and bring a flashlight (torch).

✕ Take a Break

Pick up lunch before the hike at one of the supermarkets in Volcán or Boquete.

★ Top Tip

The best time to visit is during the dry season (February to May), especially early in the morning when wildlife is most active.

station and several kilometers beyond. If you drive or taxi as far up as possible and then walk the rest of the way, it takes about five or six hours to reach the summit from the park gate; walking from town would take another two or three hours each way.

We recommended you hike at night, starting at 11pm or midnight and arriving at dawn to see the sunrise. But for this you'll need to hire a guide and be prepared for the cold. Another option is to spend the night. Camping will also allow you to be at the top during the morning, when the views are best.

The western access is just outside the town of Volcán, on the road to Cerro Punta. From this side, the views of the volcano are far more dynamic. The rugged 16.5km-long road into the park (requiring a 4WD vehicle) goes only a short way off the main

road to the foot of the volcano. The view of the summit and the nearby peaks from this entrance are impressive, and there's a lovely loop trail that winds through secondary and virgin forest. The ascent takes 10 to 12 hours.

Sendero Los Quetzales

The national park is also home to the **Sendero Los Quetzales** (trail fee US$3), one of the most scenic treks in the entire country. As its name implies, the trail is one of the best places in Central America to spot the rare quetzal, especially during the dry season. However, even if the Maya bird of paradise fails to show, the park is home to more than 250 bird species as well as pumas, tapirs and the agouti paca, a large spotted rodent also called *conejo pintado* (painted rabbit).

The trail runs between Cerro Punta and Boquete, crisscrossing Río Caldera. You can hike from either direction, but west to east offers more downhill: the town of Cerro Punta is almost 1000m higher than Boquete. The 8km route takes between four and six hours. Getting to and from the trailhead takes another couple of hours either side. A guide is recommended.

A 4WD taxi can take you to the trailhead on the Cerro Punta side for about US$35 per person; a *colectivo* (shared taxi) will cost US$6. Taxi drivers know the area as Respingo. Road conditions may be very poor due to landslides. The trail is approximately 10km from Cerro Punta, first by paved road (6km) and later dirt (3.5km). When you exit the trail, it's another 8km along the road to Boquete, though you may be able to catch a taxi along the road.

In total, the hike is about 23km, so plan accordingly if you intend to walk the length of the trail.

Buses run from David to Cerro Punta (US$3.50, 2¼ hours); last departure is 6pm. Consider leaving your luggage at one of the hotels in David to save yourself the hassle of backtracking. Take only the bare essentials with you on the walk, and a little cash for a good meal and/or lodging when you arrive in Boquete.

Be aware that conditions can change any time, especially after heavy rain. There's talk that hiking the trail with a guide may become a requirement – in recent times many travelers have gotten lost on this stretch and resources for rescue are practically nonexistent.

Sleeping in the Park

Camping (campsites US$5) is possible in the park and on the trail to the summit from the Boquete side, along the Sendero Los Quetzales at a picnic spot called Mirador La Roca or at the ranger station at the entrance to the Sendero Los Quetzales on the Cerro Punta side.

❶ Need to Know

The fertile soil and the temperate climate of Volcán Barú's mid-altitude slopes support some of Panama's most productive agriculture, especially in the areas around Boquete and Cerro Punta, which is effectively Panama's vegetable garden. Large trees dominate the volcano's lower slopes, giving way on the upper slopes to smaller plants, bushes, scrub and alpine wildflowers.

MARKS2/SHUTTERSTOCK ©

Birdwatching: The Resplendent Quetzal

The lore of the resplendent quetzal originated during the era of the Maya and the Aztecs, who worshipped a deity known as Quetzalcoatl (Plumed Serpent). This mythical figure was often depicted wearing a crown of male quetzal tail feathers and was believed to be responsible for bestowing corn upon humans.

A popular legend regarding the scarlet-red breast of the quetzal originated during the colonial period. In 1524 in the highlands of Guatemala, the Spanish conquistador Pedro de Alvarado defeated Tecun Uman, the last ruler of the Quiché people. As Uman lay dying, his spiritual guide, the quetzal, stained its breast with Uman's blood and then died of remorse. From that day on, all male quetzals bore a scarlet breast, and their song hasn't been heard since.

Today quetzals are regarded in Central America as a symbol of freedom, and it's commonly believed that they cannot survive if held in captivity. Birdwatchers from far and wide continue to brave the clements in Panama for the chance to see the most famous bird in Central America.

The best time to spot a quetzal is in April and May when they nest in the highlands and wait for their young to hatch. Look for their nests in rotted tree trunks that they carve out with their beaks.

✗ Take a Break

If you're in town on a Friday, Volcán's **Friday Market** (⊙9-11am Fri) has plenty of hike-fueling offerings. Or stop by for the corn tamales alone.

Finca Lérida

JORGE TUTOR/ALAMY STOCK PHOTO ©

Chiriquí Coffee Farms

During the 19th century, farmers discovered that the cool climate and rich volcanic soil of Chiriquí were perfectly suited for the cultivation of coffee. Since dried beans are relatively nonperishable and thus easy to ship, coffee surpassed other crops and became an important source of revenue.

Great For...

☑ Don't Miss

Indulging in a cup of (expensive, fruity, delicious) geisha coffee.

Café Ruiz Coffee Tour

Café Ruíz (☎730-9575, 6672-3786; www. caferuiz-boquete.com; tours US$30; ⊙9am & 1pm Mon-Sat) is Panama's most famous coffee-grower, and produces the award-winning geisha varietal. The three-hour tour includes transportation, a presentation on the history of coffee in Boquete, a tour of a roasting facility and a tasting session. Reservations required.

Cafes de la Luna Coffee Tour

If you are looking to learn about small-scale organic coffee production, check out this **tour** (☎6677-7748; www.boquetecoffeetour. com; El Salto; tours US$30; ⊙tours 9am & 2pm) of Finca Dos Jefes in the highlands. In addition to guiding the tour, Californian coffee aficionado Richard Lipner is the brains behind the beans. The tour is 2½ hours.

DANITA DELIMONT/ALAMY STOCK PHOTO ©

Finca Lérida

This coffee **farm** (📞720-1111; www.fincalerida.com; 2hr tours US$45; ⊙9:30am & 1:30pm) with its adjoining forest makes for an excellent hike, and the entrance fee includes a trail map and water. At 5000ft, it's a significant jump in altitude above Boquete, so dress for cooler weather. You can also do a guided hike (US$55 for two to three hours).

The Geisha Coffee Bean

Although less well known than the Costa Rican competition, Panamanian coffee is praised for its high caffeine content and acidic, multidimensional flavor. There are reasons for this.

In the early 1990s the collapse in the world quota cartel system dealt the coffee industry a severe blow. Growers could no longer rely on a stable price for their harvest. In turn, a few growers switched tactics, planting quality varieties in smaller amounts, aiming at the gourmet market instead of the usual high-yield crops.

Selectivity paid off. The biggest coup was the emergence of geisha coffee on the world scene. After winning first place in multiple international competitions, geisha became a rock-star bean. Originally from Ethiopia, geisha is coveted for its light body, citrus and honey notes, and jasmine-like aroma.

Geisha has been auctioned for up to US$260 per kg and sold at Starbucks for US$7 a cup. While Boquete's Finca Esmeralda was the first to make good on geisha, it's now found at Café Ruiz, Finca Lérida and a growing number of local estates.

Boquete

Boquete is known for its cool, fresh climate and pristine natural surroundings. Flowers, coffee, vegetables and citrus fruits flourish in its rich soil, and the friendliness of the locals seems to rub off on everyone who passes through. Boquete gained a deluge of expats after the American Association for Retired Persons (AARP) named it a top retirement spot. Until you see the gated communities and sprawling estates dotting the hillsides up close, though, you'd be hard-pressed to see what the fuss is about.

The surrounds, however, are another matter. Boquete is one of the country's top destinations for outdoor lovers. It's a hub for hiking, climbing, rafting, visiting coffee farms, soaking in hot springs, studying Spanish or canopy touring. And, of course, there's nothing quite like a cup of locally grown coffee.

> *Boquete is one of the country's top destinations for outdoor lovers.*

Caldera River outside Boquete

⊙ SIGHTS & ACTIVITIES

With its flower-lined streets and forested hillsides, Boquete is ideal for taking picturesque strolls. Visit **Parque José Domingo Médica** (Map p334) in the central plaza for flowers, a fountain and a children's playground. Nearby is an old railway and an exhibition wagon left over from the days when a train linked Boquete with the coast.

Adventure-hub Boquete has the lion's share of outfitters in the region, so it's not a stretch to book coastal trips such as sea kayaking or sportfishing here. Hostels and various agencies rent bicycles, scooters and ATVs (quad bikes), which are a good way to explore the charms of the surrounding hillsides.

La Piedra Pintada
de Caldera   Archaeological Site

(Painted Rock Archaeological Park) FREE Some of the best examples of petroglyphs found in Panama can be seen in this park at Caldera, about 23km southeast of Boquete. It's located 400m down a marked trail about 1km past the police station on the right.

MILOSK50/SHUTTERSTOCK ©

El Explorador
Gardens

(Map p325; 720-1989; www.facebook.com/ ElExploradorBQT; Calle Jaramillo Alto; adult/child US$5/2; 10am-6pm) Great for families, this private garden is located in a hilly area 3km northeast of the town center. You can walk to it in about 45 minutes. The 2 hectares of gardens are designed to look like something out of *Alice in Wonderland*, with no shortage of quirky eye-catching displays, including fanciful suspension bridges, koi ponds and playful sculptures.

TOURS

Boquete Outdoor Adventures
Adventure

(Map p334; 6630-1453, 720-2284; www. boqueteoutdooradventures.com; Plaza Los Establos, Av Central; 8am-7:30pm) This highly recommended outfitter run by veteran outdoorsman Jim Omer offers quality rafting trips (US$65 to US$75) and tailored vacations that are ideal for families. Also offers cloud-forest hiking (US$35) and snorkeling by the coastal islands (US$75). Guides are bilingual and the company uses local service providers. Excellent source of information.

Coffee Adventures Tours
Birdwatching

(720-3852, 6634-4698; www.coffeeadventures.net; half-day tours per 2 people US$65) Dutch naturalist guides Terry and Hans are locally renowned as great birding and nature guides. They also offer hiking in the cloud forest, including Sendero Los Quetzales (US$175 per person) and visits to indigenous communities. They have lodgings in three lovely cottages in dense forest 3km southwest of the town center.

Finca Lérida Birdwatching Tour
Birdwatching

(720-1111, 720-2816; www.fincalerida.com; tours US$75; 7:30am) Finca Lérida, located 9km northwest of Boquete, is a stunning coffee farm dating back to 1924. It's also considered one of the premier birdwatching spots in Panama, with hundreds of species spotted regularly. A birdwatching

 Rafting

Adventure seekers shouldn't miss the excellent white-water rafting that's within a 1½-hour drive of Boquete. Ríos Chiriquí and Chiriquí Viejo both flow from the fertile hills of Volcán Barú, and are flanked by forest for much of their lengths. In some places, waterfalls can be seen at the edges of the rivers, and both rivers pass through narrow canyons with awesome, sheer rock walls.

The Río Chiriquí is most often run from May to December, while the Chiriquí Viejo is run the rest of the year. Rapids are III and III-plus, and tours last four to five hours.

When booking a trip, inquire if the outfitter uses a safety kayak for descents and if guides are certified in swift-water rescue. These should be minimum requirements for a safe trip.

trip includes a knowledgeable guide, lunch and transportation.

Boquete Tree Trek
Adventure

(Map p334; 720-1635; www.boquetetreetrek. com; Plaza Los Establos, Av Central; canopy tours US$65; tours 8am, 10:30am & 1pm) Travelers love this four-hour canopy tour with 12 ziplines, 12 platforms and a rappel in secondary forest. The lines pick up some serious speed, so you might want to consider going heavy on the handbrake. Its newest feature is a hanging bridge walk (US$30) crossing six bridges. Includes transportation from the center.

ATV Adventures Boquete
Adventure

(Map p334; 6678-5666; www.facebook.com/ atv4x4boquete; Av Central; guided 2hr tour per person $90, minimum 2 people; 9am-7pm) Offers tours of Boquete and surrounds on 4WD ATVs (quad bikes) and side-by-side UTVs, including a 1½-hour Scenic Tour. Longer trips include the 3½-hour Coffee Tour and a five-hour Hot Springs Tour ($160 for two guests).

Boquete

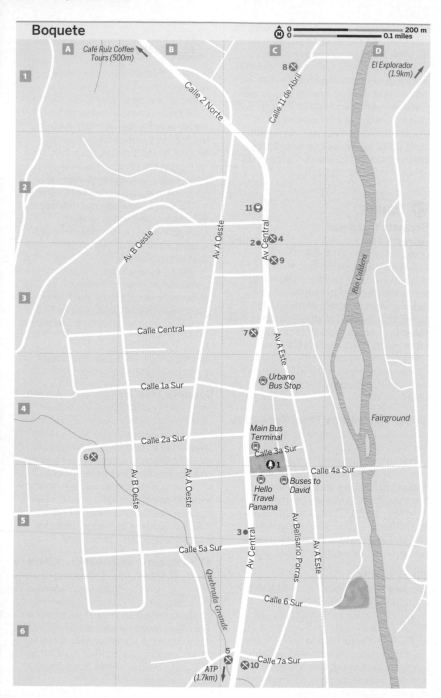

N 0 ____ 200 m
0 ____ 0.1 miles

Café Ruiz Coffee
Tours (500m)

El Explorador
(1.9km)

Calle 2 Norte

Calle 11 de Abril

8

11

Av B Oeste

Av A Oeste

Av Central

2 4

9

Río Caldera

Calle Central

7

Av A Este

Calle 1a Sur

Urbano
Bus Stop

Fairground

Calle 2a Sur

Main Bus
Terminal

6

Calle 3a Sur

1

Calle 4a Sur

Av B Oeste

Av A Oeste

Hello
Travel
Panama

Buses to
David

Av Central

Av Belisario Porras

Av A Este

3

Calle 5a Sur

Quebrada Grande

Calle 6 Sur

5

Calle 7a Sur

10

ATP
(1.7km)

Boquete

⊙ **Sights**
1 Parque José Domingo Médica C4

⊕ **Activities, Courses & Tours**
2 ATV Adventures Boquete C2
3 Boquete Outdoor Adventures C5
Boquete Tree Trek .... (see 3)
Habla Ya Language Center .... (see 3)

⊗ **Eating**
4 APizza C2

5 Boquete Fish House C6
6 Colibri A4
7 Gelateria La Ghiotta C3
8 Hotel Panamonte Restaurant C1
9 Retrogusto C3
10 Sugar & Spice C6

⊖ **Drinking & Nightlife**
11 Boquete Brewing Company C2

🎓 COURSES

Spanish by the River   Language

(☎720-3456; www.spanishatlocations.com; Entrada a Palmira) The sister school to the popular Spanish school in Bocas del Toro is located 5km south of Boquete near the turnoff to Palmira. Standard/intensive lessons cost US$225/300 for a one-week course. Discounts come with comprehensive packages and longer stays. Also offers homestays (US$22), simple dorms (US$14) and private rooms (US$24).

Habla Ya Language Center   Language

(Map p334; ☎730-8344; www.hablayapanama.com; Plaza Los Establos, Av Central; ⊗8am-6pm Mon-Fri, 9am-noon Sun) Habla Ya offers both group and private Spanish lessons. A week of group lessons (20 hours) starts at US$275. The language school is also well connected to local businesses, so students can take advantage of discounts on everything from accommodations to tours and participate in volunteer projects.

🍴 EATING

APizza   Pizza $

(Map p334; ☎720-2358; www.apizzapanama.com; Av Central s/n; mains US$6-10; ⊗3-10pm Tue-Fri, from noon Sat & Sun) Crisp, thin-crust Neapolitan pies are the simple stars of this casual eatery. They're made from local mozzarella, San Marzano tomatoes and flour imported from the home country. Local Italians say it's the best in town, and who are we to argue? Also has soups and gluten-free options.

Gelateria La Ghiotta   Ice Cream $

(Map p334; ☎6107-1465; cnr Av Central & Calle Central; cones US$2-4; ⊗11am-8pm Thu-Tue) Great selection of Italian ice cream at this central and very friendly little *gelateria*. Choose from 10 flavors, including *guanabana* (soursop), pineapple and coffee.

Sugar & Spice   Bakery, Deli $

(Map p334; ☎730-9376; cnr Av Central & Calle 7a Sur; breakfast & sandwiches US$4-7.50; ⊗8am-6pm Thu-Sat, Mon & Tue, to 4pm Sun) Throngs gather at this artisan bakery, a modest storefront with a couple of patio tables, for US-style sandwiches, organic salads and oh-so-good brownies. You can also take away fresh bread, including whole-grain and ciabatta, and cinnamon buns.

Boquete Fish House   Seafood $$

(Map p334; ☎6918-7111, 6521-2120; www.facebook.com/BoqueteFishHouseRestaurant; Av Central; mains from US$16; ⊗noon-8pm Mon-Sat; 🖉) One of our favorite places in Boquete for great seafood is this fish house along the Quebrada Grande. It offers sea bass prepared in eight different ways – from the delightful version that's steamed and wrapped in lettuce leaves to good ol' fish and chips. There are wonderful veggie sides as well as meat and vegetarian choices.

Boquete Brewing Company

With craft-beer bars all the rage in Panama these days, the **Boquete Brewing Company** (Map p334; ☑6494-4992; www.boquetebrewingcompany.com; Av Central; ☺3-10pm Tue, Wed & Sun, to midnight Thu-Sat) is more than hipster-friendly, with an outdoor patio with a food truck serving great pub grub. There are eight beers and two hard ciders on tap at any given time, and they range from the sublime (hard lemonade) to the ridiculous (watermelon ale). Cheers!

Retrogusto   Italian $$

(Map p334; ☑720-2933; www.ilretrogusto.com; Av Central s/n; mains US$7-19; ☺5:30-10pm Tue-Sat, 11:30am-3pm & 5:30-9:30pm Sun) At this new Italian farm-to-table restaurant, it's a struggle not to order everything on the menu – it all looks and smells so good. But you can't go astray starting with stuffed mushrooms or an exuberant salad. Hormone-free beef, homemade pastas and bubbly artisanal pizzas with sourdough crust are all hits. Watch the action in the open kitchen. Service is attentive.

Colibri   International $$$

(Map p334; ☑6379-1300; Calle 2a Sur; mains US$12-28; ☺noon-9pm Tue-Sat, 11am-1pm Sun) Run by a warm Italian couple from Padua, this farm-to-table restaurant serves up fresh and delicious meals. The menu items are a real fusion between local and international, with gorgeous beef salad with passion-fruit dressing, lobster from Boca Chica and local goat's cheese ice cream. There's also a good wine list and *limoncello* liqueur to cap the night.

Hotel Panamonte Restaurant   International $$$

(Map p334; ☑720-1327; www.panamonte.com; Calle 11 de Abril; mains US$18-28; ☺noon-10pm) This sophisticated restaurant has a long-standing reputation. Chef Charlie Collins takes a modern approach, exquisitely preparing everything from smoked pork chops with a rum glaze to fresh salad in blackberry vinaigrette and sublime lemon pie. While the powder-blue dining room is romantic, you may prefer a tiny table near the cracking hearth in the bar-lounge. Also ideal for cocktails and wine. Reserve ahead.

INFORMATION

Banco Nacional de Panama (☑720-1328; Av Central; ☺8am-3pm Mon-Fri, 9am-noon Sat) and **Global Bank** (☑720-2329; Av Central; ☺8am-3pm Mon-Fri, 9am-noon Sat) both have an ATM.

GETTING THERE & AWAY

The **main bus terminal** (Map p334) is on the main road near the main plaza. Buses to David (US$1.75, one hour) depart from the south side of Boquete's main plaza every 30 minutes from 5am to 6:30pm. From David they run from 6am to 9:30pm. Hourly buses run to the town of Caldera (US$2, 45 minutes).

Hello Travel Panama (Map p334; www.hellotravelpanama.com; Mamallena Hostel) has shuttle vans linking Boquete with Bocas del Toro (US$30 including boat, four hours), stopping at the **Lost & Found Hostel** (☑6432-8182; www.thelostandfoundhostel.com; Valle de la Mina; dm/d/tr without bathroom US$15/35/50; @☏), and Santa Catalina (US$35, five hours).

GETTING AROUND

Boquete's small size lends itself to easy exploration. The *urbano* (local) buses that wind through the hills cost US$0.50. They depart on the **main road one block north of the plaza** (Map p334). Taxis charge US$3 to US$6 for most places around town.

For scooter or bike rentals, check out local travel agencies and hostels. Cars can be rented at **Dollar** (☑721-1103; Plaza Los Establos, Av Central; ☺8:30am-5pm), and are a great option to explore more of the local area.

KIKE CALVO/ALAMY STOCK PHOTO ©

LEFT: IAM-PHOTOGRAPHY/GETTY IMAGES © RIGHT: WHITE GOLD PHOTOS/SHUTTERSTOCK ©

Chiriquí Province is a great place to spot the elusive resplendent quetzal, and makes a great base for hiking. But it's also known for its coffee production and tours of coffee planations, many of which are still family owned.

Top: Coffee tasting at Finca Lérida; bottom left: drying coffee berries; bottom right: drum-type coffee roaster

Maya elders preparing for a festival

In Focus

Central America Today   340
Power struggles, US relations and poverty feature in this snapshot of contemporary Central American life.

History   342
Since pre-Columbian times, the isthmus has seen everything from conquistadors to colonialism, civil wars to coups.

People & Society   350
What began as a Mesoamerican melting pot also drew influence from European colonizers and African immigrants.

Arts & Culture   353
Art and culture are the lifeblood of Central America, and you'll find them in the strangest places.

Outdoor Activities   356
Swim it, surf it, hike it, climb it, ride it! Central America's awe-inspiring outdoors await.

Weaving in Panajachel (p120)

VICTOR HUGO GUIDEL MOSCOSO/500PX/GETTY IMAGES ©

Central America Today

The outlook for Central America depends on where one is standing. In the region's southern stretches, the future looks bright, with mostly stable politics and expanding economic opportunities in tourism and transportation. Things look bleaker in the north, where many citizens struggle to break out of the cycle of violence and poverty. Still, culture and family life remain strong throughout.

Power & Politics

Democracies in Central America are often fragile, but transfers of power in the region's most stable nation are smooth. On April 1, 2018, Costa Rica elected President Carlos Alvarado Quesada, a 38-year-old novelist, musician and former cabinet minister. The decisive victory was sweet for proponents of gay rights and for Afro-Caribbeans, who were delighted to see economist Epsy Campbell Barr become Central America's first female vice president of African descent.

In stark contrast, Nicaragua has devolved into civil unrest that's left hundreds of people dead, mostly due to moves by the country's leader, Daniel Ortega, who remains in power since he took the presidency for the second time in 2006. In 2018 Ortega attempted to reduce pension benefits, prompting clashes between hundreds of unarmed protesters and

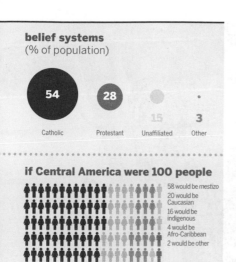

belief systems
(% of population)

54 Catholic
28 Protestant
15 Unaffiliated
3 Other

if Central America were 100 people

58 would be *mestizo*
20 would be Caucasian
16 would be indigenous
4 would be Afro-Caribbean
2 would be other

population per sq km

⭡ ≈ 25 people

Central America   USA   Europe

police and pro-government militaries, who used live bullets. Ortega rescinded the social security cut, but the crisis endured, with protesters demanding that the government be held accountable.

Poverty & Violence

Up and down the isthmus, millions of people face extreme poverty and soaring crime rates. Even the most prosperous nations (Costa Rica and Panama) have poverty rates above 20%, with a wide disparity between the richest and poorest citizens. Other countries are faring much worse, with some 59% of the population living below the poverty line in Guatemala and 61% in Honduras. Meanwhile, crime continues to plague poverty-stricken barrios and rural villages, especially in Guatemala, El Salvador and Honduras. Government corruption, gang violence and drug-cartel activity pose overwhelming challenges for citizens of these countries – the only escape often involves a perilous attempt at emigration.

US Relations

Throughout the 20th century, the USA meddled in Central American politics, helping oust democratically elected leaders and prop up military dictators aligned with US interests. The resulting civil wars and genocides sent waves of refugees to the USA, where anti-immigration policies landed some on the streets or in prisons. These places became breeding grounds for gangs such as Mara Salvatrucha (MS-13), and the USA deported members back to El Salvador, where they continue to wreak havoc.

Although US president Donald Trump's campaign promise to build a wall between Mexico and the USA has so far failed to gain traction in Congress, in 2018 his administration began enforcing a 'zero tolerance' policy toward Central Americans who crossed into the USA illegally. The government directed officials to separate asylum-seeking and illegal immigrant families, and to place adults and children in different detention facilities. A public outcry reversed the rule, but not before thousands of families were separated.

Keeping the 'Eco' in Ecotourism

Much of Central America has embraced tourism as a promise of prosperity that offers employment and investment. It's the number-one industry in both Costa Rica and Belize, and plays a smaller but increasingly significant role in Nicaragua, Honduras and Panama.

The challenge of balancing the demands of the tourist sector with its environmental impacts is an old story, and debates have raged around paving roads, building on beaches and chopping down trees. At the same time, the benefits are indisputable. Tourism provides millions of jobs, as well as a solid customer base for small-business owners. Landowners have a financial incentive to preserve forests, while farmers and indigenous communities can supplement their incomes through rural tourism.

Colombus with Native Americans, from *Le Costume Ancien et Moderne, Vol 1*, by Jules Ferrario (1815)

History

*In the pre-Columbian era, the Maya empire
stretched across the Central American isthmus.
After this heyday, the region's inhabitants endured
conquistadors and colonialism, brutal civil wars and
coups. More recently, the seven spirited nations
have aimed to overcome this legacy of violence and
establish peace and prosperity in their corner of the
planet – with decidedly mixed results.*

1100 BC
Proto-Maya settlements begin to appear in the Copán Valley. By 1000 BC, coastal settlements begin developing a hierarchical society.

AD 250–1000
The Classic period of the Maya civilization sees the construction of cities along with artistic achievements.

1502
Christopher Columbus sails down the Caribbean coastline and makes contact with indigenous inhabitants.

Relief detail from Chichén Itzá

Empires & Nations

Meet the Maya

The Maya were one of Mesoamerica's greatest pre-Columbian civilizations and for centuries their territory extended from southern Mexico to Nicaragua, and from Honduras to El Salvador. Their most noteworthy achievements included a perfected hieroglyphic writing system, precise astronomy and advanced mathematics, and they designed and built grandiose stone temples and palaces.

The Maya endured for nearly three millennia, reaching their apex between AD 250 and 900 and particularly thriving in the high plains of Guatemala and the lowlands of Belize and the Yucatán. In the 16th century, European conquistadors invaded from across the ocean, vanquishing the region and transforming Central America.

1510	**1540**	**1638**
The first permanent Spanish settlement in Central America is established in Panama (present-day Darién).	The Spanish establish the Kingdom of Guatemala, which includes Costa Rica, Nicaragua, Honduras, El Salvador and Guatemala.	British Baymen 'settle' Belize when former pirate Peter Wallace lays the foundations for a new port at the mouth of the Belize River.

Maya glyphs, Copán

★ Read about the Maya

Ancient Maya (Robert J Sharer; 2006)

Breaking the Maya Code (Michael D Coe; 1992)

Blood of Kings (Linda Schele & Mary Ellen Miller; 1986)

Maya glyphs, Copán

Meet the Conquistadors

When Columbus explored the verdant Central American isthmus in 1502, he encountered gold-accessorized natives and excitedly believed that he had found a paradise of vast riches. Two decades later, Spanish conquistadors trained their sights on Central America, in search of the fabled El Dorado.

The first permanent Spanish settlement in Central America was erected in Panama (present-day Darién) in 1510. It served as base for the Pizarro brothers, conquistadors from the Extremadura area of Spain, who trooped south to assault the Incas; and for Vasco Núñez de Balboa, who ventured west to gaze on the Pacific. Panama was also the launch site for Gil González Dávila, who sailed north to Nicaragua, where he betrayed the *cacique* (tribal leader) Nicarao and beheaded his rival conquistador, Francisco Hernández de Córdoba.

Another Extremaduran, Pedro de Alvarado, crossed the Atlantic in 1510, and his ferocity placed him second in command on the legendary march of Hernán Cortés against the Aztecs. Rumors of a jade kingdom to the south led Alvarado on a four-year campaign across Central America, slashing through the jungle and cutting down its native inhabitants. He never found the kingdom, but became military governor of Guatemala, which he tyrannized for 15 years. In his final battle against desperate natives, Alvarado's horse rolled over and killed him.

Spanish Rule

By the middle of the 16th century, the days of vainglorious conquistadors had passed, and the Spanish Crown now imposed imperial bureaucracy. Alvarado's fiefdom was reorganized into the Kingdom of Guatemala, under the Viceroy of New Spain. For most of the next 300 years, this included present-day states of Central America and Mexico's Chiapas. The capital was located in Santiago (now Antigua) in southwest Guatemala. Meanwhile, present-day Panama was also under Spanish rule, but part of the Viceroyalty of Peru, with its capital in Lima.

1821	**1853–56**	**1903–14**
Central America becomes independent from Spain and eventually joins the United Provinces of Central America.	Tennessee-born conquistador William Walker attempts to conquer Central America. He is defeated and executed by a Honduran firing squad.	Panama declares itself independent from Colombia, and canal concessions are granted to the USA.

The Crown's hold was not complete, however. In northeast Honduras (present-day Belize), upstart British squatters built a haven for pirates, smugglers and poachers, who withstood all of the king's eviction efforts.

Independence in the Americas

In 1821 the Americas wriggled free of Imperial Spain's grip. Mexico declared independence for itself, as well as for Central America. The Central American colonies then declared independence from Mexico and, with an empire up for grabs, the region descended into conflict.

The newly liberated colonies considered their fate: stay together in a United States of Central America or go their separate national ways? At first, they came up with something in between – the Central American Federation (CAF) – but it could neither field an army nor collect taxes. Accustomed to being in charge, Guatemala attempted to dominate the CAF, thus hastening the federation's demise. One by one, the constituent parts became independent nation-states.

Paradise & Plunder

New World Economy

The pre-Columbian economy rested on agriculture and trade. The Maya built terraced fields in the steep mountains, raised platforms in the swampy lowlands, and slashed and burned the thick forests. They grew corn, tubers, beans, squash and peppers. They tamed the wild fruits of the forest: papaya, mango, banana and cacao. They fished the rivers and lakes with nets – and with cormorants on a leash – and they hunted down tasty forest creatures such as peccary, deer and monkey. But the tropical terrain made grand-scale agriculture impractical, and the region was notably lacking in precious metals.

The Spanish were undeterred, and instead harnessed the region's main economic resource – people. The Crown authorized the creation of feudal-style agricultural estates, the notorious *economienda,* whereby powerful colonial overlords exploited an indigenous labor force. They produced New World luxuries for Old World aristocrats – indigo from El Salvador, cacao from Guatemala, tobacco from Chiapas. The *economienda* system, however, did not take hold in Costa Rica, the poorest region of colonial Central America, where private family farms prevailed over corporate feudal estates.

Coffee Rica

In 1843 the merchant vessel HMS *Monarch* arrived in London from Puerto Limón carrying bulging sacks of roasted red beans. The riches that Costa Rica had long promised had finally been uncovered, as the volcanic soil and moist climate of the Central Valley highlands proved ideal for coffee cultivation. The drink's quick fix made it popular with working-class

1946	1948	1960–90
The US Army's School of the Americas, which trained Latin America's worst human-rights abusers, is founded in Panama.	Costa Rica's President José Figueres abolishes the army and redirects spending toward education and healthcare.	Military crackdowns on impoverished and indigenous peoples lead to the formation of active left-wing guerrilla groups.

consumers in the industrializing north of England. Thousands of coffee saplings were quickly planted along shady hillsides in Guatemala, Nicaragua and Honduras. The Central American coffee boom was on.

Costa Rica went from the most impoverished to the wealthiest country in the region. The aroma of riches lured a wave of enterprising German immigrants to Central America. Across the region, powerful cliques of coffee barons reaped the rewards from the caffeine craze.

Banana Boom

In Costa Rica, getting coffee out to world markets required rail links from the central highlands to the coast. Meanwhile, the California gold rush prompted a Panamanian rail link between the Atlantic and Pacific. US companies undertook the railroad construction projects, both of which were disastrous due to malaria and yellow fever. Local recruits gave way to US convicts, to Chinese indentured servants, and to freed Jamaican slaves.

In Costa Rica, bananas were planted along the tracks as a cheap food source for the workers. As an experiment, would-be railroad tycoon Minor Cooper Keith shipped a few bananas to New Orleans, and he struck gold – or rather, yellow. Northern consumers went crazy for the elongated finger fruit.

By the 1900s, bananas had replaced coffee as the region's most lucrative export. The United Fruit Company converted much of Central America into a corporate fiefdom, controlling transportation, communication, postal service, labor markets and export markets – as well as more than a few politicians.

Ecotourism

In the 1980s, following a downturn in world coffee prices, an unusual alliance was formed between economic developers and environmental conservationists. If exports alone could not sustain the economy, then what about imports...of tourists?

Costa Rica led the region in launching a green revolution, establishing some 125 national parks, forest preserves and wildlife reserves. Its neighbors followed the trend, and Indiana Jones enthusiasts were soon clambering around ancient temples in the Yucatán and Guatemala. Birders flocked to Panama to glimpse nearly 1000 species of feathered fauna, and the Belize Barrier Reef was recognized as a Unesco World Heritage site.

With ecotourism, the rainforest and the reef were essentially paying for themselves, making it financially beneficial to take care of them. Tourism brought hundreds of millions of US dollars to the economy, becoming one of the region's main sources of foreign currency. Moreover, tourism profits stayed in the countries, boosting standards of living.

1972	**1980s**	**1981**
Jacques Cousteau brings publicity to the Blue Hole, boosting Belize's popularity as a destination for divers and snorkelers.	Costa Rica makes up for coffee's economic downturn with a new form of import business. Ecotourism is born.	Belize receives formal international recognition of its independence from Great Britain.

Dictatorship & Democracy

A Democratic Oasis

After independence, politics in Central America usually featured a few elite families competing for control of state patronage, through shifting alliances of army officers and coffee barons. Presidents were more often removed at gunpoint than by the ballot box. Across the region – and particularly in Costa Rica, El Salvador, Honduras and Guatemala – the polarized left and right fought for power through coups and electoral fraud.

In Costa Rica, the unsustainable situation came to a head in 1948, when economic and ethnic tensions spiraled into civil war. Armed workers battled military forces, and Nicaraguan and US forces joined the fray. Peace was restored two months – and 2000 deaths – later. Out of the chaos came a coffee grower and utopian democrat, José Figueres Ferrer, who became the unlikely leader of a temporary junta government. He taxed the wealthy, nationalized the banks and built a modern welfare state. His 1949 constitution granted voting rights to women, as well as full citizenship to black, Indian and Chinese minorities. Most extraordinarily, Figueres abolished the military, calling it a threat to democracy. His transformative regime became the foundation for Costa Rica's uniquely unarmed democracy.

Cold War in the Hot Tropics

In 1823 the USA challenged European colonialism by claiming hegemony over the Western Hemisphere with the Monroe Doctrine. By the mid-20th century, the USA was routinely acting to constrain the autonomy of Central America's nation-states, seeking to influence political choices, economic development and foreign policies.

In the 1950s Guatemala's democratically elected president, Jacobo Arbenz Guzmán, vowed to nationalize the vast unused landholdings of the United Fruit Company. Democracy be damned: United Fruit appealed to its friends in Washington; in 1954 a CIA-orchestrated coup forced President Arbenz from office. His successor, Colonel Castillo Armas, was hailed as an anti-communist hero and treated to a ticker-tape parade in New York City. Three years later, Armas was gunned down in the presidential palace; soon after United Fruit's confiscated lands were finally returned. Armas was succeeded by a series of military presidents.

More support came from the US government – in the form of money and counter-insurgency training. In 1960 left-wing guerrilla groups began to form, and the Guatemalan civil war was on. By the 1970s, radical socialists had forced military oligarchies around the region onto the defensive. In Nicaragua, the rebellious Sandinistas toppled the American-backed Somoza dictatorship. Alarmed by the Sandinistas' Soviet and Cuban ties, the USA decided it was time to intervene. The organizational details of the counter-revolution were delegated to junior officer Oliver North, who secretly aided and abetted the Contra rebels to incite civil war in Nicaragua.

1979–87	1980–92	1987
Guerrilla groups known as the Sandinistas overthrow the dictatorial Somoza regime in Nicaragua.	After years of strife, El Salvador descends into all-out civil war between a US-backed military and various guerrilla groups.	Costa Rican president Oscar Arias Sánchez wins the Nobel Peace Prize for his work on regional peace accords.

Palenque

★ **Best Destinations for History Buffs**

Chichén Itzá, Mexico (p67)

Copán, Honduras (p177)

Tikal, Guatemala (p129)

Palenque, Mexico (p81)

Panama City, Panama (p284)

The conflict polarized the region. When civil war erupted in El Salvador after the assassination of Archbishop Romero, the US pumped huge sums into the moribund military, effectively prolonging that conflict as well. Throughout the 1980s, government-sponsored death squads decimated villages, while guerrilla groups did their best to undermine elections and stifle the economy. Meanwhile, Honduras became a base for the US-sponsored covert war in Nicaragua.

The young president of Costa Rica, Oscar Arias Sánchez, was the driving force in uniting Central America around a peace plan, which finally ended the Nicaraguan war. Arias was awarded a Nobel Peace Prize.

From Colonialism to Neocolonialism

While civil wars raged around the region, two countries remained relatively peaceful, albeit under the control of greater powers.

In Belize, it was not the Spanish but rather the British who took hold, logging the forests, growing fruit and sugarcane, and dubbing the colony 'British Honduras.' While an independence movement gathered force throughout the second half of the 20th century, full independence was put off until a nagging security matter was resolved: namely, the Guatemalan constitution explicitly included Belize as part of its territorial reach. Only British troops at the border stopped the larger country from following through on that.

It was not until 1981 that Belize was at last declared an independent nation-state within the British Commonwealth. Even Guatemala recognized Belize as a sovereign nation in 1991, although to this day it maintains its territorial claim on 53% of Belize's land. In a 2018 referendum, Guatemalans voted in favor of taking the issue to the International Court of Justice, and Belize voters did the same in May 2019. Experts say the court will likely offer a final resolution in about four years' time.

Meanwhile, at the southern end of the isthmus, Panama was still a province of Colombia at the start of the 20th century. When a military junta declared Panama independent, the US government immediately recognized the sovereignty of the new country – backing it up with battleships when Colombia tried to regain control. In return, Panama granted the

1989	1996	1999
The USA invades Panama and ousts dictator Manuel Noriega, who is found guilty of drug-trafficking and money-laundering.	Peace accords are signed in Guatemala, bringing to an end the 36-year civil war, in which an estimated 200,000 people died.	The USA ends occupation of Panama by closing all of its military bases and rescinding control of the canal.

US concession to the canal, as well as a broad right of intervention into Panamanian affairs.

In the years following the completion of the canal, Panamanians became increasingly disenchanted with US intervention and occupation. As the northern giant gradually ceded its rights, the Panamanian military grew more powerful. When Manuel Noriega came to power in the 1980s, he expanded the military and brutally crushed all dissent; drug trafficking, election rigging and murder all played a role in his regime. The USA finally intervened in 1989, invading Panama City and arresting Noriega. A decade later the USA rescinded control of the canal and withdrew all troops, finally leaving Panama to negotiate its own uncertain future.

Imperfect Democracy

Today a new era of democratization has unfolded, as both right-wing and left-wing dictatorships have stepped aside to allow contested elections. Here's one auspicious sign of the times: a former Salvadoran guerrilla organization managed to transition to mainstream politics, even fielding a successful presidential candidate.

The systems are not perfect, however. In 2009 democratically elected Honduran president Manuel Zelaya was ousted by the military (on orders from the Supreme Court), and more recently, an unexpected and incredibly narrow electoral victory by President Juan Orlando Hernández sparked allegations of fraud and deadly protests. A contentious 2015 Supreme Court ruling paved the way for Hernández to be elected for a consecutive term, an event Honduras hadn't seen since military rule four decades prior.

In 2014 the Nicaraguan Congress made a similarly controversial decision to abolish term limits – just in time for President Daniel Ortega to run for his third consecutive term. He was reelected in 2016 and, after he announced plans to cut welfare benefits, violent protests erupted across the nation in 2018. Hundreds of people were killed, ostensibly by paramilitary groups. At the time of writing in 2019, the situation remained volatile and President Ortega remained in power.

A Saint for the People

In the late 20th century, a wave of 'liberation theology' washed over the region, setting populist priests against rapacious dictators. Subversive clerics were feared by the ruling class, which mobilized its coercive agents to quell the criticism. The most notorious episode in this conflict was the assassination of the Archbishop of San Salvador, Óscar A Romero, who was gunned down while saying Mass in 1980.

The heinous crime made Romero a martyr: the UN marked his death date, March 24, as the Day of Truth and Dignity for Victims of Human Rights Atrocities, and the Vatican bestowed sainthood on the bishop in 2015.

2012	**2017–18**	**2018**
Baktun 13 ends without major incidents and a new Great Cycle of the Maya Long Count calendar begins.	The Trump administration separates thousands of Central American families along the US–Mexico border.	Nicaragua descends into chaos after President Daniel Ortega announces an unpopular welfare proposal.

Participants in a Maya beauty pageant

People & Society

At the crossroads of continents, Central America has been influenced not only by its neighbors, but even more so by its European colonizers and African immigrants. With populations descended from these corners – as well as prominent indigenous groups – the region's culture is a rich and fascinating blend. Family life remains sacred, while the disparity between urban and rural lifestyles is growing.

Peoples of Central America

Central America may appear homogeneous at first glance, but this mostly Latin American region is a patchwork of European-, Amerindian- and African-descended groups – most of which have intermixed with each other. Some 78% of the regional population are in fact mestizo (Spanish-Amerindian mix) or Caucasian (European). Most of the remaining population is made up of dozens of distinct indigenous groups, from the once-mighty Maya to the barely surviving Maleku. A small but significant percentage descends from African slaves and immigrant workers.

Mestizo

Mestizos are people of mixed Spanish and indigenous Amerindian descent. They are the largest ethnic group in Central America, comprising about 58% of the regional population; they're also the largest ethnic group in every Central American country except Costa Rica. (El Salvador has the region's highest percentage of mestizos, at 86%.) Even Belize – which was not settled by the Spanish – has a large and growing mestizo population, due to the influx of refugees from neighboring countries.

While not uniform, the mestizo culture defines the region, which is predominantly Catholic and Spanish-speaking.

Caucasian

Approximately 20% of the Central American population is Caucasian – mostly of Spanish origin, descending from conquistadors and colonists who settled here, beginning in the 16th century.

Guatemala, Nicaragua and Panama all have small but still significant Caucasian populations – 12% to 18% – mostly descended from Spanish settlers. In the late 19th and early 20th centuries, the government of Nicaragua gave away land to German and French immigrants who were willing to cultivate it, which contributed to its 17% Caucasian population.

In the 20th century Central America became a refuge for alternative thinkers seeking a peaceful place to live according to beliefs that were unwelcome in North America. Belize has a small but visible population of Mennonites (of German/Dutch descent), who settled here in the 1950s and 1960s in an attempt to preserve their traditional way of life and strict moral code. A few years later, a group of Quakers fled the USA to avoid conscription into the military; they settled in Monteverde, Costa Rica, eventually founding the famous cloud-forest reserve.

Indigenous

The Maya are the most famous and populous indigenous group in Central America, but there are dozens of lesser-known Amerindian groups. These native peoples make up 16% of the overall regional population.

o **Maya** The Maya are the largest indigenous group in Central America, with an estimated population of seven million. From 1000 BC to AD 1500, the Maya civilization spanned the northern part of Central America, building great cities, undertaking elaborate rituals and engaging in violent warfare. Contemporary Maya culture does not bear much resemblance to its ancient counterpart, but it does retain some unique remnants of the heritage, including traditional clothing, religious practices and – most significantly – language. Throughout Central America, there are some 32 distinct linguistic groups that comprise the modern-day Maya population.

o **Other Indigenous Groups** In pre-Columbian Central America, the southern part of the region was inhabited by many distinct indigenous groups that were unrelated to the Maya. Dozens of them endure to this day, although they all face challenges in preserving their culture, language and identity in this era of increasing global uniformity.

Afro Central American

From their earliest arrivals in the New World, the Spanish brought African slaves to trade and to work. In the 19th century, many other peoples of African descent arrived from Jamaica and other parts of the Antilles. African laborers, both immigrants and slaves, played a crucial role in the development of the region – felling forests, building railroads and dredging canals. Today their descendants make up about 4% of the Central American population, and they are concentrated mainly on the Caribbean coast.

Central American Lifestyles

In Central America, the contrast between urban and rural lifestyles is pretty stark, with gaping disparities in opportunity, education and income. For better or for worse, some things such as family and church remain constant – though *which* church may be a subject for debate these days.

Family

The family unit in Central America remains the nucleus of life. Extended families often live near each other and socialize together. Those with relatives in positions of power – nominal or otherwise – don't hesitate to turn to them for support. Favors are graciously accepted, promptly returned and never forgotten. Despite modernizing influences – education, cable TV, contact with foreign travelers, time spent abroad – traditional family ties remain strong at all levels of society. Old-fashioned gender roles are strong too, although this is changing in Costa Rica, Nicaragua and Panama.

Religion

Religion continues to be a major force in the lives of Central Americans, though the once staunchly Catholic region is changing. Ever since the arrival of the Spanish – and with them missionaries, priests and papal decrees – Central America has been dominated by Catholics. Today more than half of the region's population practices Catholicism.

But the 20th century brought a new set of missionaries – this time evangelical Protestants from North America – commonly known as *evangelicos*. The fiery services and paradisaical promises have particular appeal among the rural poor. Nearly a third of the region's population has been wooed into joining the faith.

Urban vs Rural

Central America is characterized by a vast chasm in levels of healthcare, education, wealth and modernity. These differences often line up along the urban–rural divide. In capital cities, well-heeled residents drive high-end cars, own vacation properties and travel overseas. Meanwhile, just an hour's drive away, an indigenous family might paddle a dugout canoe and practice subsistence agriculture.

Even in the region's most prosperous countries (Costa Rica and Panama), around 20% of the population lives below the poverty line. In the poorest countries (Guatemala and Honduras), the number is more than 50%. The vast majority of the destitute live in rural areas, many representing indigenous groups. Across the region, the rural poor have significantly lower standards of living, fewer opportunities for education and less-than-adequate healthcare.

The middle and upper classes reside mainly in urban areas, especially in capital cities, where they enjoy a lifestyle that is similar to their counterparts in North America or Europe.

Garifuna drumming

BARNA TANKO/SHUTTERSTOCK ©

Arts & Culture

You probably didn't come to Central America for high culture: art museums and symphony halls are thin on the ground. To discover the richness of Central America's arts, you have to look in unexpected places – gritty dance clubs and dark alleys, rural villages and women's cooperatives. In Central America, anyone and everyone is an artist, or a musician, or a poet. Truly, art is all around you.

Street Art

Throughout Central America and Mexico, the art scene is vibrant and visible, as some of the most poignant contemporary work takes the form of street art – murals and mosaics that grace decrepit buildings and brighten city streets. Often these paintings record historic events and raise awareness of social issues, a tradition that dates from a time when a large percentage of the population was illiterate. Interestingly, street art is most vibrant in war-torn countries such as El Salvador, Guatemala and Nicaragua.

In El Salvador, the best examples are in Perquín, La Palma and Suchitoto, as well as in the capital and the villages along the Ruta de las Flores. In 1997 national icon Fernando Llort created a colorful, folkloric ceramic-tile mural entitled *Harmonia de mi pueblo*. A tribute to persevering Salvadorans and a celebration of peace, the artwork was mounted

Pottery at market in Granada

★ **Best Destinations to Shop for Indigenous Art**

Lago de Atitlán, Guatemala (p124)

Granada, Nicaragua (p211)

Palenque, Mexico (p78)

Antigua, Guatemala (p103)

Chiriquí Province, Panama (p324)

on the facade of the Catedral Metropolitana in San Salvador. Artists and residents were shocked and outraged when the local archbishop had the mural removed in 2012, without consulting the government or the artist.

Paintings cover the walls in many Nicaraguan cities, especially the Sandinista strongholds of León and Estelí. The latter is home to a new movement of *muralistas,* who use more recognizable graffiti techniques to deliver their social commentary.

Urban Maeztro is the pseudonym of a Honduran street artist who makes provocative, overtly political work, decrying the violence that pervades Tegucigalpa.

The most famous Guatemalan artist is Efraín Recinos, whose murals grace the National Music Conservatory in Guatemala City. He's also a celebrated architect and sculptor. Not exactly a street artist, Recinos was awarded Guatemala's highest honor, the Order of the Quetzal, in 1999.

Indigenous Art

Souvenir hunters will be delighted by the wealth of handicrafts and folk art that is available in Central America, much of it produced by indigenous groups in the region.

Especially in the highlands of Guatemala, the Maya weave festive, colorful clothing and textiles. The *huipil* (a women's tunic) is often a true work of art – a multicolored web of stylized animal, human, plant and mythological shapes. Many women still use the pre-Hispanic backstrap loom to make these creations.

Panama's indigenous groups produce high-quality woodcarvings, textiles, ceramics, masks and other handicrafts. The Emberá and Wounaan are renowned for their woven baskets, some of which are highly decorated with bright colors and natural motifs, made from the nahuala bush and chunga palm. The Guna are known for their *molas* (the embroidered panels used by women in their traditional dress). Ocú and Penonomé people produce superior panama hats.

In Costa Rica, indigenous crafts include intricately carved and painted masks made by the Boruca, as well as handwoven bags and linens, and colorful Chorotega pottery.

Poetry

In Central America, peasants can be poets, and poets can be politicians. Poetry is beloved throughout the region, especially in the countries that have seen the most violence and poverty – always good inspiration for verse.

Guatemala's first great literary figure was poet and Jesuit priest Rafael Landivar, whose collection of poetry was published in 1781. The literary spokesperson of the Guatemala people is Miguel Ángel Asturias (1899–1974). His masterpiece novel, *Men of Maize,* won the Nobel Prize for Literature in 1967, but before that he was a poet-diplomat and an out-spoken political commentator.

In Nicaragua, any *campesino* (farmer) can tell you who the greatest poet in history is: Rubén Darío, voice of the nation and founder of the *modernismo* literary movement. Nicaragua is also home to the peculiar cultural archetype of 'warrior poets,' folks who choose to use both the pen and the sword. The best-known example is Gioconda Belli, who was working undercover with the Sandinistas when she won the prestigious Casa de las Américas international poetry prize.

Music

At the intersection of Latin beats and Caribbean cool, there is the *música* of Central America. You'll hear calypso, reggae, soca and salsa around the region, but you'll also discover lesser-known, uniquely Central American musical genres that incorporate the best of the more mainstream styles.

The marimba is a percussion instrument that resembles a xylophone, except it's made of wood and so produces a mellower sound. The instrument is usually played by three men; there's a carnival-like quality to its sound and compositions. Marimba music is used during Maya religious ceremonies, and it's considered the national instrument in Guatemala. But it's also popular in Costa Rica and Nicaragua, where groups such as La Cuneta Son Machín have updated marimba folk music with a rocky *cumbia* (Colombian dance tunes) beat.

Musicians and linguists speculate that the name *punta,* a traditional Garifuna drumming and dance style, comes from the word *bunda,* which means 'buttocks' in many West African languages. The word derivation is not certain, but it is perhaps apt. Played at any celebration, this music inspires Garifuna peoples across Central America to get up and shake their *bunda*.

In the 1970s, Belizean musician Pen Cayetano traveled around Central America and came to the realization that Garifuna traditions were in danger of withering away. He wanted to inspire young people to embrace their own culture, so he invented a cool and contemporary genre by adding electric guitar to traditional *punta* rhythms – and *punta* rock was born. Since the 1980s, *punta* rock has become popular across the region (and across ethnic groups), especially in Belize and Honduras.

Once the music of the urban poor in Panama, reggaetón nowadays permeates all countries and social strata in Central America (and beyond). Taking cues from hip-hop, especially the rap-like vocals, this unique genre also incorporates musical influences from Jamaican dancehall, Trinidadian soca and Puerto Rican salsa. Reggaetón is wildly popular across the region, especially in Panama, Costa Rica and Guatemala.

Diving at Belize Barrier Reef (p144)

Outdoor Activities

Flanked by miles upon miles of Pacific and Caribbean coastline, lush with high-altitude forestland and tropical jungle, crisscrossed by raging rivers, and undulating with mountains and volcanoes (some active!), Central America is beyond ripe for outdoor exploration.

Diving & Snorkeling

The Caribbean coast of Central America includes miles of nearly unbroken barrier reef, making this one of the world's superlative spots for diving and snorkeling. Life under the sea is dramatic and diverse, from the fantastic coral formations and the kaleidoscopic fish that feed there to the massive (and sometimes menacing) creatures lurking in deeper waters. Mexico, Belize and Honduras offer world-class underwater viewing, but there are also snorkeling and diving opportunities further south, and the Pacific coast is also rich with life. There is no reef, but there's still plenty to see, especially from October to February when conditions are normally clearer.

Aside from the two great bodies of blue, Central America has some intriguing opportunities for inland diving. Mexico offers otherworldly dives in cenotes (freshwater limestone

sinkholes), while in Guatemala you can go high altitude diving at Lago de Atitlán. No matter where you intend to dive, don't forget your license. Equipment (for diving or snorkeling) is widely available for rent.

Diving Safety Guidelines

Before scuba diving, free diving or snorkeling, carefully consider the following points to ensure a safe and enjoyable experience.

- If diving, you'll need a current diving certification card from a recognized scuba-diving instructional agency.

- Be sure you are healthy and feel comfortable diving.

- Obtain reliable information about physical and environmental conditions at the dive site (eg from a reputable local dive operator).

- Be aware of local laws, regulations and etiquette relating to marine life and the environment.

- Dive only at sites within your realm of experience; engage the services of a competent, professionally trained dive instructor or dive master.

- Be aware that underwater conditions vary significantly depending on region, season, and even from one site to another.

★ Best Destinations for Hiking

Lago de Atitlán, Guatemala (p112)

Isla de Ometepe, Nicaragua (p218)

Bosque Nuboso Monteverde, Costa Rica (p232)

Ruta de las Flores, El Salvador (p162)

Bosque Nuboso Monteverde

Hiking

Central America's dense forests, steaming volcanoes and abundant wildlife make for great hiking. The terrain ranges from cloud forests and rainforests to tropical dry forest, including river trails and palm-lined beaches.

Most tourist-oriented parks and reserves offer ample trails that are well maintained and well marked, most of which do not require a guide. Longer-distance hikers can take their pick from several popular, multiday treks. If you really want to get off the beaten track, you can do that too (though you'll definitely want to hire a guide).

Hiking Seasons

In the rainforest (and the cloud forest, for that matter), hiking trails can be muddy. Throughout the region, trails are maintained to varying degrees. They may be reinforced with concrete blocks or wooden supports, but the mud prevails. Trails are obviously firmer and easier to navigate during the dry season, which is when travelers should plan their hiking trips (late December to April).

Hiking Safety

Remember to play it safe on the trails.

○ Bring plenty of water, extra snacks, sunblock and insect repellent.

○ Be sure to inform somebody (ie a park ranger) where you're going before you set out.

○ Always be cautious of insects, snakes and other wildlife.

Surfing

Surf's up, all across Central America. This sport's popularity is on the rise, with many places offering weeklong surf camps, hourly lessons and board rentals.

Costa Rica has the most developed scene and, arguably, the most and biggest waves. But El Salvador, Nicaragua, Panama and even Guatemala have up-and-coming surfing scenes. The waves might not be 'world-class' – at least not all of them – but they're pretty darn good. Plus, there are fewer surfers in these lesser-known spots, so you may have the breaks all to yourself.

Surfing Seasons

The surf season varies throughout the region – but there's always a wave to ride somewhere.

○ **El Salvador** Along the south-facing coastline, the months from May to August bring the biggest swells, but they also bring massive amounts of rain. Seasoned surfers claim that the tail end of the dry season (late March and early April) offers the best of both worlds, with still-glorious weather and the first southern swells.

○ **Nicaragua** The Pacific coast here sees the biggest waves from April to June, thanks to southern swells and offshore winds. The surf is dependable anytime between March and November, though. Again, the rain starts in May, so be prepared.

○ **Costa Rica and Panama** These two countries are among a select group of destinations where you can surf two oceans in one day. In both countries, the Caribbean surf season lasts from November to April, with an additional mini season in June and July. You can't really escape the rain on this coast. On the Pacific side, in Costa Rica the most consistent surf comes from the southwest between late May and August. Panama's Pacific coast peaks from April to June, with offshore winds and consistent southwesterly swells. In both cases, the surfing is reliably good anytime between February and August. Again, expect more rain (but fewer crowds) starting in May.

White-Water Rafting

Central America offers some of the best white-water rafting in the tropics, including in Guatemala, Honduras, Panama and especially Costa Rica. The Central American rivers offer everything from frothing Class IV white water to easy Class II floats. Most rivers can be run year-round, though more rain brings higher waters.

Wildlife-Watching

The unexpected appearance of a toucan, howler monkey or sloth will surely be a highlight of your trip. Central America is rife with opportunities to spot these kinds of creatures in the wild, thanks to an extensive system of protected areas throughout the region. Often the best sightings occur when you're not really looking – perhaps in your hotel's garden or on the roadside in a remote area. In short: keep your eyes peeled.

Early morning and late afternoon are the best times to watch for wildlife activity anywhere.

Hiking near Quepos (p274)

KATHRIN ZIEGLER/GETTY IMAGES ©

Survival Guide

DIRECTORY A–Z   **361**

Accessible Travel 361
Accommodations 361
Climate............................362
Customs Regulations 363
Discount Cards 363
Electricity........................363
Emergency &
Important Numbers 363
Food 364
Health..............................364

Insurance 365
Internet Access................366
Legal Matters...................366
LGBT Travelers 366
Maps................................367
Money 367
Photography 368
Safe Travel.......................368
Smoking...........................368
Telephone 368
Toilets..............................369
Tourist Information..........369

Visas................................369
Women Travelers 370

TRANSPORT   **370**

Getting There
& Away 370
Getting Around 371
Arriving in 374

LANGUAGE   **376**

Directory A–Z

Accessible Travel

Central America generally isn't well equipped for those with disabilities: services such as specially equipped phones, toilets or anything in braille are rare to the point of nonexistence. Expensive international hotels are more likely to cater to guests with disabilities than cheap hotels; air travel or prearranged transportation will be more feasible than most local buses; and off-the-beaten-track destinations will be less accessible than well-developed ones.

Belize and Costa Rica are better equipped for travelers with mobility issues than other Central American

Book Your Stay Online

For more accommodations reviews by Lonely Planet authors, check out www.lonelyplanet. com/central-america/ hotels. You'll find independent reviews, as well as recommendations on the best places to stay. Best of all, you can book online.

countries (due in part to the many elderly travelers who arrive on cruise ships). In both countries, it's possible to find hotels and attractions that can accommodate wheelchairs, especially in the most popular tourist spots. Some of Costa Rica's national parks are also wheelchair-accessible.

Accommodations

The cost of accommodations varies from country to country. Nicaragua, Honduras, El Salvador and Guatemala are the cheaper countries, while Mexico, Belize, Panama and Costa Rica (and many beach destinations) are more expensive. Features such as a private bathroom, hot water and air-con will drive up the price.

Reservations are necessary in tourist areas during peak season, particularly during Semana Santa (Holy Week, preceding Easter) and the week between Christmas and New Year, when locals are also traveling around the region.

Camping

If you plan on camping, it's best to bring your own gear. Organized campgrounds aren't common. Facilities at campgrounds vary widely, so make sure you know ahead of time if fire pits, latrines and water will be available.

Some hostels have dedicated camping areas. Some national parks and reserves (particularly in Costa Rica) also have basic camping facilities, but they can get crowded. In some places it's also feasible to ask to camp on private land.

Guesthouses & Hotels

Guesthouses are generally small, family-run lodgings. Most rooms have a fan and shared bathroom (though you may need to bring your own towel and soap). Conditions are highly variable, ranging from pleasant rooms to those with a dumpy bed, smeared mosquito remains on the walls and a leaky-faucet 'shower' down the hall.

In hotels, rooms with air-con and TV usually cost at least $20 more than a room with a fan. Breakfast is not usually included in the overnight rate.

'Hot water' can be lukewarm and working only at certain hours of the day. Be sure to inquire if your water is unexpectedly cold, as it may just be a matter of turning on the hot water heater. Beware of the electric shower – it's a cold-water showerhead juiced by an electric heating element. Don't touch it, or anything metal, while in the shower or you may get a shock.

Used toilet paper should be placed in the receptacle provided, and *not* flushed down the toilet.

Hammocks & Cabins

Sleeping in a hammock can make for a breezier night than sleeping in a stuffy room. Many beach towns have hammock rooms or areas for the same price as a dorm. *Cabañas* (or *cabinas;* cabins) provide memorable stays on the beach or in the jungle. Amenities vary – many are simple thatched-roof huts with a dirt or sand floor.

Homestays

Spanish-language schools arrange homestays in towns where the language-school scene is strong, including Antigua and Quetzaltenango (Guatemala), Granada (Nicaragua), Copán (Honduras) and Bocas del Toro (Panama). A similar option is *turismo rural* – community tourism initiatives with rural homestays.

Homestays usually offer private sleeping quarters in a local home, with bathroom facilities shared with the family. Meals are often included. It's usually an affordable room-and-board option, with the added benefit of giving you plenty of opportunities to practice your Spanish.

Hostels

Hostels are found throughout Central America and serve all ages. Many hostels offer a few private rooms in addition to dormitories with bunk beds (which generally cost around US$10 to US$20 per person). Except in Mexico, Hostelling International (HI) membership isn't particularly useful:

Climate

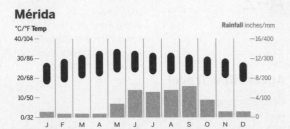

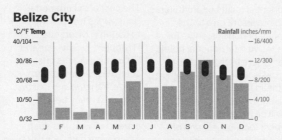

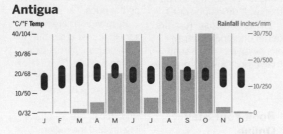

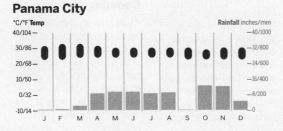

most hostels in the region are independently run.

Customs Regulations

All visitors leaving and entering a Central American country go through customs. Be prepared for bag checks at both airports and land borders. Most are just a quick gaze-and-poke, more of a formality than a search – but not always. Be polite to officials at all times.

Discount Cards

A member card from **Hostelling International** (HI; www.hihostels.com) isn't terribly useful in Central America, except in Mexico and Costa Rica, where some hostels offer minimal discounts to cardholders. Those going on to South America, however, may want to invest in the membership, as the card is more commonly accepted there.

Carriers of the **International Student Identity Card** (ISIC; www.isic.org) can get very good discounts on travel insurance, as well as discounted air tickets.

Electricity

Most countries in Central America use plug type A or B, the same as is used in the USA. In Belize you may come across type G plugs. Voltage varies between 110v and 220v.

Type A
120V/60Hz

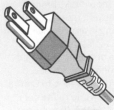

Type B
120V/60Hz

Emergency & Important Numbers

Belize

Country code	✆501
Directory assistance	✆113
International access code	✆00
Emergency	✆90, ✆911
Operator assistance	✆115

Costa Rica

Country code	✆506
International access code	✆011
Emergency	✆911
International operator	✆00

El Salvador

Country code	✆503
International access code	✆00
Ambulance	✆911
Police	✆911
Fire	✆911

Guatemala

Country code	✆502
International access code	✆00
Ambulance	✆125
Police	✆120
Proatur (24hr tourist information & assistance)	✆1500

Honduras

Country code	504
International access code	00
Emergency	911

Mexico

Country code	52
Emergency	911
International access code	00
National tourist assistance (including emergencies)	088

Nicaragua

Country code	505
International access code	00
Ambulance	128
Fire	115, from cell phones 911
Police	118

Panama

Country code	507
International operator	106
Directory assistance	102
Ambulance	455 & 107
Police	104

Food

Reservations for eating here are practically unheard of, except at high-end restaurants in the biggest tourist centers.

○ **Street food** Urban areas throughout Central America have cheap street food, served from *carritos* (carts) or food trucks. Options vary by country, but may include tacos, *pupusas* (grilled corn-meal with cheese or bean filling) or *churrasco* (BBQ meat) with rice and beans.

○ **Comedores** A simple diner serving set meals – almost every town has one. Also known as *sodas* in Costa Rica.

○ **Restaurantes** A more formal dining experience than the *comedor,* with a wider menu and probably a selection of wines and beers.

Health

The most critical health concern in Central America is mosquito-borne illnesses, including malaria, dengue and the Zika virus. All travelers should take precautions to prevent mosquito bites: strong insect repellent with DEET is essential. At the time of writing, pregnant women were advised against traveling to Central America due to the outbreak of the Zika virus.

There are no required vaccinations for Central America, except if you are coming from a yellow-fever-infected country in Africa or South America – then you must have a yellow fever vaccine. Among others recommended are typhoid, rabies and hepatitis A and B.

Visit your doctor well ahead of your trip, since most vaccines don't produce immunity until at least two weeks after they're given. Ask your doctor for an International Certificate of Vaccination (aka 'the yellow booklet'), which will list all the vaccinations you've received. This is mandatory for countries that require proof of yellow-fever vaccination.

Before You Go

Health Insurance

Most insurance providers do not cover overseas expenses, so it's strongly recommended to purchase a traveler's insurance policy that includes health coverage.

Find out in advance if your insurance plan will make payments directly to providers or reimburse you later for overseas health expenditure. If the latter, be sure to collect receipts.

If your travel insurance does not cover you for medical expenses abroad, consider buying supplemental insurance. Check lonelyplanet.com/travel-insurance for more information.

Websites

It's usually a good idea to consult the health sections of your government's travel advice website before departure. Other resources:

○ **World Health Organization** (www.who.int/ith) Publishes a superb book called *International Travel and Health,* which is revised annually and available on its website at no cost. The website lists updated risks and worldwide vaccination certificate requirements.

o **MD Travel Health** (www. mdtravelhealth.com) Provides complete travel health recommendations for every country, updated daily.

In Central America

Availability & Cost of Healthcare

Good medical care is available in most of the region's capital cities, but options are limited elsewhere. In general, private hospitals are more reliable than public facilities, which may experience significant shortages of equipment and supplies.

Many doctors and hospitals expect payment in cash, regardless of whether you have travel health insurance. If you develop a life-threatening medical problem, you'll probably want to be evacuated to a country with state-of-the-art medical care. Since this may cost tens of thousands of dollars, take out travel insurance that covers medical expenses before your trip.

US travelers can find a list of recommended doctors abroad and emergency evacuation details on the website of the **US State Department** (http://travel. state.gov). Click on International Travel, then Before You Go, then Your Health Abroad.

Many pharmacies are well supplied, but important medications may not be consistently available. Be sure to bring along adequate supplies of all prescription drugs.

Mosquito-borne Diseases

All travelers are advised to take precautions against insect-borne diseases, including malaria, chikungunya, dengue and Zika. Many of these illnesses cannot be prevented with vaccines or medication, so the most effective prevention is to avoid bug bites.

o Use an insect repellent that contains 20% or more DEET.

o Treat clothing, bedding and camping gear with permethrin, which binds tightly to clothing.

o Cover exposed skin with long sleeves, pants and hats.

o Sleep in places with screened windows or use a bed net.

Tap Water

Tap water is not safe to drink in many parts of Central America. Vigorous boiling for one minute is the most effective means of water purification. At altitudes greater than 2000m (6500ft), boil for three minutes.

Another option is to disinfect water with iodine pills. Instructions are usually enclosed and should be carefully followed. Alterna-

tively you can add 2% tincture of iodine to 1L of water (five drops to clear water, 10 drops to cloudy water) and let it stand for 30 minutes. If the water is cold, longer times may be required. The taste of iodinated water may be improved by adding vitamin C (ascorbic acid). Iodinated water should not be consumed for more than a few weeks. Pregnant women, those with a history of thyroid disease and those allergic to iodine should not drink iodinated water.

A number of water filters are on the market. Those with smaller pores (reverse osmosis filters) provide the broadest protection, but they are relatively large and also readily plugged by debris. Those that have somewhat larger pores (microstrainer filters) are ineffective against viruses, although they do remove other organisms. Manufacturers' instructions must be carefully followed.

Insurance

A travel insurance policy covering theft, loss, accidents and illness is highly recommended. Some policies compensate travelers for misrouted or lost luggage. Also check that the coverage includes worst-case scenarios: ambulances, evacuations or an emergency flight home. Some policies specifically exclude 'dangerous activities,' which can include scuba diving, motorcycling or even trekking. Be sure to read the small print.

There is a wide variety of policies available. Policies handled by student-travel organizations usually offer good value. If a policy offers lower and higher medical-expense options, the low-expenses policy should be OK for Central America – medical costs are not nearly as high here as elsewhere.

If you are robbed and need to make a claim, you must report the loss or theft to local police within 24 hours. Make a list of stolen items and their value. At the police station, you need to complete a *denuncia* (statement), a copy of which is given to you for your insurance claim.

Worldwide travel insurance is available at www.lonelyplanet.com/travel-insurance. You can buy, extend and claim online anytime – even if you're already on the road.

Internet Access

Internet access is widely available. Wi-fi is available at all but the most basic accommodations, as well as at some cafes and restaurants. Many hostels also have computers for guest use.

Internet cafes are less prevalent than they used to be; rates range from US$0.50 per hour in cities

and touristy destinations to US$6 in remote areas.

Either Alt + 64 or Alt-G + 2 is the command to get the @ symbol on Spanish-language keyboards.

Legal Matters

It is advisable (and sometimes required) to carry a passport or photo ID at all times.

Costa Rica, Guatemala and Honduras have dedicated tourist police working in the big cities. In some countries the police force has a reputation for corruption, and from time to time you may be stopped and hassled or asked for a bribe. Law enforcement is generally professional, visible and effective, though. Throughout the region, police checkpoints and vehicle searches are not uncommon.

Marijuana and cocaine are illegal everywhere in the region and penalties are severe. Reforms to drug laws in Mexico stipulate that first-time offenders are not punished for possession of a small amount of drugs for personal use. Still, it's inadvisable to carry any amount of drugs, and if you are caught you may be shaken down for a bribe. Allowable amounts are strictly enforced, and offenders will generally be arrested and prosecuted.

In many countries, you are presumed guilty until

found innocent. If you are accused of a serious crime, you will be taken to jail. In this case, your embassy will offer only limited assistance. This may include a visit from an embassy staff member to make sure your human rights have not been violated, contacting your family and putting you in touch with a lawyer (whom you must pay yourself).

LGBT Travelers

Central America can be an unwelcoming place for LGBTIQ+ travelers, but there are some bright spots. Same-sex marriage was legalized in Mexico in 2009 and in Costa Rica in 2013. The current president of Costa Rica, Carlos Alvarado Quesada, has been unusually vocal in his support for gay rights.

Advocacy groups in other Central American countries are eager to follow suit. Consensual gay sex has also been decriminalized all around the region. That said, official and unofficial harassment is possible anywhere in Central America. In general, public displays of affection will not be tolerated and gay men (and possibly women) could find themselves the target of verbal or physical abuse. Discretion is definitely the rule in Central America, especially in the countryside. Lesbians are generally less maligned than gay men, so women traveling together should encounter few, if any, problems.

Maps

The best map of the region is the fold-up color 1:1,100,000 *Central America Travel Reference Map* (US$13), produced by **International Travel Maps & Books** (www.itmb.ca) in Canada.

ITMB also publishes separate maps covering each of the Central American countries and various regions of Mexico, as well as several maps of South America.

Lonely Planet's *Central America Planning Map* gives a great overview of the region and some of its highlights.

Money

It's a good idea to always have a small amount of US dollars handy – enough to get a room, a meal and a taxi, at least – because they can be exchanged or even spent practically anywhere. It's particularly useful when crossing a border or when an ATM isn't available. Central American currencies don't always fly in the next country; plan ahead before you head to remote areas and take more than enough cash.

Getting change for bigger notes in local currency is a

daily concern. Notes worth even US$20 can sometimes be difficult to change.

ATMs

o Bring an ATM (or debit) card. ATMs are available in most cities and large towns, and are almost always the most convenient, reliable, secure and economical way of getting cash. Many ATMs are connected to the MasterCard/Cirrus or Visa/Plus networks.

o The exchange rate from ATMs is usually as good as (if not better than) that at any bank or legal money changer.

o Notify your bank of your travel plans so international transactions are not rejected.

Bargaining

It's OK to bargain in markets and at street stalls, but educate yourself first by asking around to get an idea of the pricing of different items and the specific factors that contribute to the quality of what you're bargaining for.

Black Market

The *mercado negro* (black market) – also known as *mercado paralelo* (parallel market) – is generally limited to money changers at borders, who may or may not be legal. They are known to slip in torn bills or to short-change on occasion, though they accept local currencies that banks elsewhere sometimes

don't take. Such unofficial exchange rates for the US dollar can be lower than official bank rates.

Credit Cards

o American Express, Visa and MasterCard are the most widely accepted credit cards in Central America.

o Some card companies charge a fee (from 2% to 10%) for international transactions.

o Some banks issue cash advances on major credit cards.

o Although credit cards are widely accepted, it is not always economical to use them. In Costa Rica, for example, many hotels offer a discount for cash payment.

Exchanging Money

If you insist on still using traveler's checks, or you've got foreign cash to convert, you can handle this at a bank or a *casa de cambio* (currency exchange office). Rates between the two are usually similar, but in general *casas de cambio* are quicker, less bureaucratic and open longer or on weekends. Street money changers, who may or may not be legal, will handle only cash.

Sometimes you can also change money unofficially at hotels or in shops that sell imported goods (electronics dealers are an obvious choice). Compare exchange rates and commission fees first; big cities tend to offer better rates.

Don't accept even slightly torn notes, as most locals won't when you try to use them.

Tipping

Guides Tip US$1 to US$2 per person for day tours, with more substantial tips for specialized guides.

Restaurants Tip 10% (but check first to see if it's included in the bill).

Taxis Tipping is optional but you can round up to leave extra, especially at night.

Photography

○ Always ask before photographing individuals, particularly indigenous people.

○ Paying people for a portrait is a personal decision; in most cases, subjects will tell you straight off the going rate for a photo.

○ Some tourist sites charge an additional fee for video cameras or cameras.

○ Don't photograph military installations or personnel; it may be illegal in some areas.

○ In churches, photography or the use of flashes is often prohibited.

Safe Travel

○ Parts of Honduras, El Salvador and Guatemala are plagued by high crime rates and gang activity. Visitors are rarely affected, but some have been victims of grab-and-run theft, assault, rape, carjacking and murder.

○ Capital cities tend to have the highest rates of crime.

○ Many sexual assaults occur on isolated beaches.

○ Avoid night buses (with the possible exception of Panama and Mexico), as highway robberies often happen at night.

○ Avoid drug use entirely.

○ Seek out updates from other travelers, tourist offices, police, guesthouse owners and Lonely Planet's Thorn Tree (www.lonely-planet.com/thorntree).

Smoking

Regulations vary widely from country to country. In Belize and Nicaragua, there are few restrictions, and smoking in bars and restaurants is generally permitted. In Costa Rica and Panama, it is banned in enclosed spaces, as well as outdoor public places. The other countries' laws are somewhere in between, but generally ban smoking in enclosed public areas.

Telephone

Internet cafes with net-to-phone (VOIP) service provide the cheapest way to make international calls, with rates varying between US$0.10 and US$0.50 per minute to the USA and Europe.

Government Travel Advice

The following government websites offer travel advisories and information on current hot spots.

Australian Department of Foreign Affairs (www.smarttraveller.gov.au)

Canadian Department of Foreign Affairs (www.travel.gc.ca)

Foreign Office of the Federal Republic of Germany (www.auswaertiges-amt.de/en)

Japanese Ministry of Foreign Affairs (www.mofa.go.jp)

Netherlands Ministry of Foreign Affairs (www.government.nl/ministries/ministry-of-foreign-affairs)

New Zealand Foreign Affairs & Trade (www.safetravel.govt.nz)

UK Foreign & Commonwealth Office (www.fco.gov.uk/travel)

US Department of State (www.travel.state.gov)

From traditional landlines, the most economical way of calling abroad is using phone cards purchased at kiosks or corner stores. You can also try direct-dial lines, accessed via special numbers and billed to an account at home. It is sometimes cheaper to make a collect or credit-card call to Europe or North America than to pay for the call where you are.

Many towns and cities have a telephone office with phone booths for local and international calls. Rates can be high. Avoid credit-card phones in Mexico and the black 'press button' phones in Guatemala, which charge extortionate rates.

Toilets

The toilets of Central America are fine; it's just the plumbing that has issues. Nowhere in the region should you deposit toilet paper or anything else in the toilet unless a sign specifies that it's OK to do so. Wastebaskets are generally provided.

Some public toilets have attendants who charge a small fee (US$0.10 or so) and provide paper. It's a good idea to keep a spare roll of toilet paper handy while traveling.

Viva El CA-4!

Guatemala, Honduras, El Salvador and Nicaragua's 'CA-4 Border Control' agreement allows free travel for up to 90 days within this subregion for citizens of the four countries and many foreign nationals (including residents of the USA, Canada, the UK and Australia).

On paper, at least, you should only have to pay a tourist fee once to enter these four countries. Yet border patrols may also charge you a few dollars for 'paperwork'; if they insist, you won't have much alternative but to pay.

Tourist Information

Travelers will find a tourist office in the capital city of each country; some countries have them in outlying towns as well. If you're a student, look for student travel agencies in the capital cities of Costa Rica and Panama and in Cancún, Mexico.

Check www.visitcentro america.com, which has standard tourist-board coverage of all countries.

Visas

At present citizens of the USA, EU, Canada, Australia, New Zealand and many other nations can arrive in all Central American countries (including Mexico) without arranging a visa beforehand. Check ahead from your country before planning your trip, as this may change.

Many countries charge an entry or tourist fee upon arrival – from US$5 to US$20.

Note that if you need a visa for a certain country and arrive at a land border without one, you will probably have to return to the nearest town that has a consulate and obtain a visa. Airlines will not normally let you board a plane to a country for which you don't have the necessary visa. Also, a visa in itself may not guarantee entry: in rare cases, you may still be turned back at the border if you don't have sufficient funds for your visit or an onward or return ticket.

Sufficient Funds & Onward Tickets

Having your passport checked is a routine procedure upon arrival in a country, but some officials may ask about your financial resources, either verbally or on the application form. If you lack 'sufficient funds' for your proposed visit, officials may limit the length of your stay. (US$500 per month for your planned stay is generally considered sufficient; traveler's checks, and sometimes a credit card, should qualify toward the total amount.)

Several Central American countries require you to have an onward ticket leaving the country.

Visa Extensions

Once you are inside a country, you can always apply for a visa extension at the country's immigration office *(migración)*. There's usually a limit to how many extensions you can receive; if you leave the country and reenter, your time starts over again.

Women Travelers

Women traveling solo through Central America typically find that popular perceptions overestimate

the dangers they face. The biggest adjustment is getting used to the vocal male population, many of whom hoot, hiss and whistle. Ignore this behavior and most of the time you will be simply left alone.

Of course, women should take all the normal precautions they would in any new territory or big city. Dress according to local norms to avoid unwanted attention (often this means avoiding shorts). Talk to locals to find out which areas may be dangerous. Certain bars and soccer games tend to be testosterone-fueled territory where a woman's presence will invite attention.

Locals, particularly families, will often go out of their way to help a single female traveler. Keep in mind, though, that it's more typical for Latin American women to socialize with other women, and women in Central America's more conservative societies

rarely have male friends – so befriending someone's husband can attract resentment. Socializing with men here in general is a little unusual – it's probable that they will think you want more than friendship.

In the case of sexual assault, contact your embassy and see a doctor.

Transport

Getting There & Away

Most visitors reach Central America by air or overland from Mexico. Flights, cars and tours can be booked online at lonelyplanet.com/bookings.

Air

All Central American countries have international airports. Other than flights from South America, most arriving flights go via US gateways (particularly Houston, Miami or New York's JFK) or Mexico City.

Land

It's possible to take a bus from the US or Canada into Mexico and directly into Central America. The three most convenient land bor-

---

Climate Change & Travel

Every form of transport that relies on carbon-based fuel generates CO_2, the main cause of human-induced climate change. Modern travel is dependent on airplanes, which might use less fuel per kilometer per person than most cars but travel much greater distances. The altitude at which aircraft emit gases (including CO_2) and particles also contributes to their climate change impact. Many websites offer 'carbon calculators' that allow people to estimate the carbon emissions generated by their journey and, for those who wish to do so, to offset the impact of the greenhouse gases emitted with contributions to portfolios of climate-friendly initiatives throughout the world. Lonely Planet offsets the carbon footprint of all staff and author travel.

ders between Mexico and Central America:

● The Chetumal–Corozal (Belize) border in Quintana Roo (Yucatán Peninsula).

● The Ciudad Cuauhtémoc–La Mesilla (Guatemala) border.

● The Ciudad Hidalgo–Ciudad Tecún Umán (Guatemala) border in Chiapas state (about 38km south of Tapachula).

There are no road connections between South America and Central America (via Panama). Instability in the Panama–Colombia border region, plus the difficulty of travel, have essentially made the trip over the Darién Gap an impossibility. All visitors to the Darién must register with the police.

Sea

Unless you're a yachtie or on a cruise ship, options for boat travel heading to/from the region are limited. The most popular route is taking a (shared) chartered sailboat between the Archipiélago de San Blas, Panama, and Cartagena in Colombia (US$550 per person). The five-day trip usually includes a few days on the islands and two days' transit to/from Colombia. There is also a shorter route to/from the border town of La Miel, Colombia, and nearby Sapzurro, Colombia (US$400 per person).

Blue Sailing (✐Cartagena 57-5-668-6485, USA 203-660-

Border Crossings

Border crossings in Central America are usually a straightforward, albeit stressful, affair. There are plenty of border posts, so crossing the border does not usually require going too far out of your way. Most crossings are by road (or bridge), but there are a few that involve boat travel.

International travelers are not a new sight to border guards. Remember that they will appreciate being treated with respect and being spoken to (at least a little) in Spanish.

8644; www.bluesailing.net) This company keeps the schedule for more than a dozen boats that sail between Colombia and Panama. Look online to see photos of the boats, to learn about the captains and to book the trips.

Sail Colombia Panama (✐Colombia 57-312-214-4844; www.sailcolombiapanama.com) Does sailing trips to Colombia out of Puerto Lindo, Portobelo and El Porvenir, with an option for a (pricier) private cabin.

Casa Viena (✐Cartagena 57-320-538-3619; www.casaviena.com) A Cartagena hostel that helps with boat trips to Panama.

Sailing Koala (✐Cartagena 57-322-516-3359; www.sailingkoala.com) A recommended sailing operation.

Mamallena Tours (✐Panama 507-6676-6163; www.mamallena.com) This tour company – based at the hostels of the same name in Panama City and Cartagena – organizes sailing trips between the two countries, via San Blas.

Note that cargo boats are a risky business; smuggling

is common on the Colón–Cartagena cargo route.

Getting Around

Air

Many flights connect the region, run by international carriers as well as the national airlines. Some smaller domestic airlines provide services too. Occasionally it will be necessary to change planes in the carrier's hub city (eg a Managua–Panama City flight may change planes up north in San Salvador).

Cost is an obstacle. Despite relatively short distances, individual one-way and round-trip tickets within Central America (whether bought abroad or within the region) can be expensive.

● Flights can sometimes be overbooked; reconfirm your ticket before arriving at the airport.

● Airfares can vary wildly – depending on the length

of stay, time of year and special promotions – so treat high-season fares as a rough gauge only in identifying potential routes.

• Note that San Salvador and San José are the most popular hubs. Occasionally a promotional return flight may be even cheaper than a one-way fare.

• Worthwhile domestic flights include Managua to Nicaragua's Corn Islands (about US$165 return), which saves a two-day bus/boat trip each way. Flights within Panama and Costa Rica can also be cheap.

Bicycle

Long-distance cycling in the region can be dangerous, as few drivers are accustomed to sharing narrow streets in cities, or often-shoulderless two-lane highways, with bicycles. That said, cycling is on an upswing, with mountain rides and coffee-plantation tours (including guide and bike) available all over Central America.

You can rent bicycles in several cities and traveler hangouts, such as San Cristóbal de Las Casas (Mexico), Flores (Guatemala), Granada (Nicaragua), La Fortuna (Costa Rica) and Panama City. There are many mountain-bike tours available (notably in cooler locales such as Guatemala's highlands and San Cristóbal de Las Casas). Consider the seasons if you're planning to cycle a lot. The dry season (roughly December to April)

should spare you from getting soaked.

If you're planning to cycle across borders, keep a document proving your ownership of the bike handy for immigration officials.

Check out **El Pedalero** (www.elpedalero.com) to read cyclist Gareth Collingwood's adventures and tips on cycling around Latin America.

Boat

Traveling by boat is a common way to get around the region, including several border crossings.

• Travelers between Palenque, Mexico, and Flores, Guatemala, cross the Río Usumacinta near Frontera Corozal, Mexico, and Bethel, Guatemala.

• There is a regular water taxi between Punta Gorda, Belize, and Puerto Barrios (and sometimes Lívingston), Guatemala.

• Newer weekly boat services make trips between Placencia, Belize, and Puerto Cortes, Honduras, and Belize City and Puerto Cortes (via Dangriga, Belize).

• There's a river border crossing between San Carlos, Nicaragua, and Los Chiles, Costa Rica, though nowadays most folks use the new bridge at Las Tablillas.

Key domestic water journeys include the ride down the Río Dulce in Guatemala, or down the Río Escondidas to Bluefields, Nicaragua,

and then out to the Corn Islands in the Caribbean.

Other Caribbean islands reached by boat include the Bay Islands in Honduras; Caye Caulker and Ambergris Caye in Belize; and Cozumel and Isla Mujeres in Mexico. And of course, the Panama Canal is one of the world's most important waterways, connecting the Caribbean and the Pacific.

Bus

Some of the most memorable moments of your trip will come from bus rides. Bus service is well developed throughout the region, though not always comfortable. While some buses are air-conditioned with reserved seats that may recline, many others are colorfully repainted former US school buses (aka 'chicken buses'), with a liberal policy toward lugging merchandise (though it's unlikely you'll have to share your seat with a chicken).

Avoid night buses throughout the region (with the possible exception of Mexico and Panama), as these have been popular targets for highway robbers.

First-class and some 2nd-class buses depart on scheduled times from a *terminal de autobuses* (long-distance bus station); others leave from parking-lot bus terminals once they are full (these stop to collect more passengers all along the way – so you're likely to be able to get a lift from the highway if need be). Be aware that many cities have more than one bus station. Bus companies can have their own terminals as well. Departure frequency varies.

Luggage may be stored in a lower compartment or piled on the roof of the bus. Keep an eye on your luggage if you can, particularly on the easily accessible racks in a packed bus. Always keep your valuables tucked away on your person. Watch out for pickpockets on crowded buses and in bus stations.

In some places, travel agents run private shuttle services (mostly vans with air-con) to popular destinations. They're more comfortable and more expensive than public buses.

Colectivos & Minibuses

Connecting hub towns with smaller ones on short-haul trips is an array of minibuses (called *rapidito* in Honduras, *chiva* in Panama, and *colectivo* in Costa Rica and Mexico). When available, these are cheaper than 1st-class buses and run frequently. The catch: they also make frequent stops and the driver rarely considers them full.

Car & Motorcycle

A drive through Central America will likely offer an amazing trip, but it's unlikely to save you money. In addition to fees, there's

paperwork, tolls, parking concerns and other red tape. Border crossings are a particular hassle. You'll also need to be prepared to stop for passport checks at military checkpoints. Also, highway robberies aren't unknown, so avoid driving at night.

To drive in Central America, you must have a valid driver's license from your home country or an International Driving Permit (IDP), which is issued by automobile associations worldwide.

Be prepared for police checkpoints – always stop and have your papers handy.

Hire & Fuel

Central America is relatively easy to explore by private vehicle. This option would be more popular if it weren't for the cost (rental, insurance and fuel). Rentals range from about US$15 per day in Nicaragua to US$55 per day in Belize, but 4WD vehicles are more expensive (generally US$30 to US$80). If your goal in renting a car is to reach some otherwise unreachable areas (such as isolated beaches south of Tulum in Mexico and around Costa Rica's Península de Nicoya), it's worth paying for a 4WD: paved roads only go so far.

○ At the time of research, the price of gas ranged from about US$0.87 (in Panama)

to US$2.99 (in Belize) per liter.

○ In many cases it's cheaper to arrange (even same-day) rentals with major car-rental agencies on their websites.

○ To rent a car, you'll need a passport and a driver's license.

○ Some agencies rent to those 21 and over; others to only those 25 and over.

○ All of Central America drives on the right-hand side of the road.

○ Rented cars are usually not allowed to leave the country – though Budget, for example, allows travel from Guatemala to Mexico, Honduras and El Salvador, with some restrictions.

○ Scooters and bigger motorcycles are available in some places, the latter usually costing about the same price as a compact car.

Insurance

Mandatory insurance is a huge add-on to the cost of car rental in most Central American countries, and your insurance policy back home is not accepted here. The (usually) mandatory Collision Damage Waiver (CDW) can double your daily rate, while many companies will give a hard sell for more expensive comprehensive insurance. If your credit card provides insurance on car rentals, be sure to bring the documentation to prove it; in most cases, you'll still have to pay for the CDW.

Arriving in...

Belize

Philip Goldson International Airport (Belize City) Many hotels and resorts offer airport shuttles. Taxis into town cost BZ$50 for one to two passengers and BZ$60 for three to four passengers. No public buses serve the facility.

Main Bus Terminal (Belize City) Long-distance buses from Mexico arrive at the main bus terminal, which is a short distance from downtown Belize City – although walking is not recommended. Taxis wait outside the terminal and charge BZ$7 to downtown hotels or the water-taxi terminals.

International Departures Dock (San Pedro) Boat services from Mexico arrive at this facility in downtown San Pedro. Collective minivan taxis meet boats and charge BZ$7 around town. Rates to hotels outside the center are negotiable.

Costa Rica

Aeropuerto Internacional Juan Santamaría (San José) Buses (about US$1.50) from the airport to central San José run hourly all day. Taxis charge from US$30 and depart from the official stand; the trip takes 20 minutes to an hour. Interbus runs between the airport and San José accommodations (US$17 per adult, children under two free if sharing a seat). Many rental-car agencies have desks at the airport, but it's advisable to book ahead.

El Salvador

Monseñor Óscar Arnulfo Romero International Airport (San Salvador) Shuttles operated by Taxis Acacya leave the airport at 7am, 8am, noon, 1pm, 5pm and 6pm (US$5 per person; 45 minutes). Buses run to the city center every 60 minutes, but it can be stressful finding the location, especially with luggage. Taxis cost about US$30 to US$35 (45 minutes) and are plentiful, but negotiate beforehand. Hotels arrange pick-ups.

Tica Bus Terminal (San Salvador) The most popular long-distance buses arrive in safe and fashionable Zona Rosa. From here, taxis can take you anywhere in the capital for US$10 or so.

Guatemala

Aeropuerto Internacional La Aurora (Guatemala City) Authorized taxis wait out the front of departures. Buy a coupon (Q80 for Zona 1, Q70 for Zona 10 or 13) at the booth before the exit. Shuttle buses to Antigua (Q80) wait out the front, too – just listen for someone yelling 'Antigua, Antigua.'

Aeropuerto Internacional Mundo Maya (Santa Elena) Taxis wait outside, charging Q60 to downtown Flores or Santa Elena. For Tikal or El Remate, go out to the main road and hail a passing minibus.

Honduras

Palmerola International Airport (Comayagua) Honduras's new airport, due to be completed in 2019, is near Comayagua (20 minutes) and Tegucigalpa

(1½ hours), and there should be transportation options to both.

Toncontín International Airport (Tegucigalpa) It's possible to get taxis from outside the terminal, but a safer option is to ask your hotel to arrange for a transfer to meet you. This service should cost between L200 and L3050.

Ramón Villeda Morales International Airport (San Pedro Sula) A prearranged transfer from the airport to your hotel is the best option (L200 to L300).

Juan Manuel Gálvez International Airport (Roatán) Most lodging options will arrange transfers for you *Colectivo* taxis will cost around L50 to West End, a private taxi around L150.

Mexico's Yucatán & Chiapas

Aeropuerto Internacional de Cancún (Cancún) Green Line shuttles and Super Shuttle charge US$50 per person to Ciudad Cancún or the Zona Hotelera. ADO buses (M$72) go to the downtown bus station. Regular taxis charge M$650.

Aeropuerto Internacional de Mérida (Mérida) Curbside taxis charge M$200 per carload to downtown. Buses (M$8) do not enter the airport; catch one on the main road if you don't mind walking.

Cozumel International Airport (Isla Cozumel) Shared shuttles from the airport into town cost about M$70. For hotels on the island's north and south ends, they charge M$150 to M$200.

Ángel Albino Corzo International Airport (Tuxtla Gutiérrez) Minibuses run between Tuxtla Gutiérrez's airport and

San Cristobal de las Casas' bus terminal.

Nicaragua

Managua International Airport (Managua) Official taxis inside the airport meet all incoming flights and charge around US$20 to US$25 to most local destinations. During the day, more-economical licensed collective taxis wait outside the domestic terminal. If you're heading out of Managua, it's possible to book

a pick-up with a private shuttle service.

Panama

Tocumen International Airport (Panama City) From the airport it's 40-minute trip downtown by taxi (from US$30). During daylight hours local buses depart every 15 minutes for Albrook Bus Terminal (US$1.25, one hour), near Albrook regional airport, and other destinations.

Panamá Pacífico International Airport (Panama City) Located 12km southwest of Panama City. Viva Air Colombia airline began using this small airport, the former US Howard Air Force Base, in 2014. A taxi will cost about US$6.

Aeropuerto Enrique Malek (David, Chiriquí Province) Receives frequent flights to and from San José (Costa Rica). The 5km trip into town by taxi costs US$5 .

Language

You can read our pronunciation guides below as if they were English and you'll be understood just fine. And if you pronounce 'kh' in our guides as a throaty sound and remember to roll the 'r,' you'll even sound like a real Costa Rican.

To enhance your trip with a phrasebook, visit **lonelyplanet.com**. Lonely Planet iPhone phrasebooks are available through the Apple App store.

Basics

Hello.
Hola.   o·la
How are you?
¿Cómo está? (pol)   ko·mo es·ta
¿Cómo estás? (inf)   ko·mo es·tas
I'm fine, thanks.
Bien, gracias.   byen gra·syas
Excuse me. (to get attention)
Con permiso.   kon per·mee·so
Yes./No.
Sí./No.   see/no
Thank you.
Gracias.   gra·syas
You're welcome./That's fine.
Con mucho gusto.   kon moo·cho goo·sto
Goodbye./See you later.
Adiós./Nos vemos.   a·dyos/nos ve·mos
Do you speak English?
¿Habla inglés? (pol)   a·bla een·gles
¿Hablas inglés? (inf)   a·blas een·gles
I don't understand.
No entiendo.   no en·tyen·do
How much is this?
¿Cuánto cuesta?   kwan·to kwes·ta
Can you reduce the price a little?
¿Podría bajarle el   po·dree·a ba·khar·le
el precio?   el pre·syo

Accommodations

I'd like to make a booking.
Quisiera reservar   kee·sye·ra re·ser·var
una habitación.   oo·na a·bee·ta·syon

Do you have a room available?
¿Tiene una habitación?   tye·ne oo·na a·bee·ta·syon
How much is it per night?
¿Cuánto es por noche?   kwan·to es por no·che

Eating & Drinking

I'd like ..., please.
Quisiera . . . , por favor.   kee·sye·ra . . . por fa·vor
That was delicious!
¡Estuvo delicioso!   es·too·vo de·lee·syo·so
Bring the bill/check, please.
La cuenta, por favor.   la kwen·ta por fa·vor
I'm allergic to ...
Soy alérgico/a al . . . (m/f) soy a·ler·khee·ko/a al . . .

I don't eat ...
No como . . .   no ko·mo . . .
   chicken   pollo   po·yo
   fish   pescado   pes·ka·do
   (red) meat carne (roja)   kar·ne (ro·kha)

Emergencies

I'm ill.
Estoy enfermo/a. (m/f)   es·toy en·fer·mo/a
Help!
¡Socorro!   so·ko·ro
Call a doctor!
¡Llame a un doctor!   ya·me a oon dok·tor
Call the police!
¡Llame a la policía!   ya·me a la po·lee·see·a

Directions

Where's a/the ...?
¿Dónde está . . . ?   don·de es·ta . . .
   bank
   el banco   el ban·ko
   ... embassy
   la embajada de . . .   la em·ba·kha·da de . . .
   market
   el mercado   el mer·ka·do
   museum
   el museo   el moo·se·o
   restaurant
   un restaurante   oon res·tow·ran·te
   toilet
   el baño   el ba·nyo

Behind the Scenes

Acknowledgments

Chichén Itzá illustrations pp68-9 and Tikal pp130-1 by Michael Weldon.

Climate map data adapted from Peel MC, Finlayson BL & McMahon TA (2007) 'Updated World Map of the Köppen-Geiger Climate Classification', *Hydrology and Earth System Sciences*, 11, 163–344.

This Book

This 1st edition of Lonely Planet's *Best of Central America* guidebook was curated and researched by Ashley Harrell and researched and written by Ashley, Isabel Albiston, Ray Bartlett, Celeste Brash, Stuart Butler, Paul Clammer, Steve Fallon, Anna Kaminski, Brian Kluepfel and Carolyn McCarthy.

This guidebook was produced by the following:

Destination Editors Alicia Johnson, Sarah Stocking

Senior Product Editor Saralinda Turner

Regional Senior Cartographer Corey Hutchison

Product Editors Grace Dobell, Bruce Evans

Book Designer Virginia Moreno

Assisting Editors Janet Austin, James Bainbridge, Judith Bamber, Michelle Bennett, Katie Connolly, Samantha Cook, Peter Cruttenden, Andrea Dobbin, Emma Gibbs, Carly Hall, Gabrielle Innes, Lou McGregor, Alison Morris, Lauren O'Connell, Christopher Pitts, Gabrielle Stefanos, Ross Taylor, Fionnuala Twomey, Simon Williamson

Assistant Cartographer Rachel Imeson

Cover Researcher Naomi Parker

Thanks to Bailey Freeman, Martine Power, Kirsten Rawlings

Send Us Your Feedback

We love to hear from travelers – your comments keep us on our toes and help make our books better. Our well-traveled team reads every word on what you loved or loathed about this book. Although we cannot reply individually to postal submissions, we always guarantee that your feedback goes straight to the appropriate authors, in time for the next edition. Each person who sends us information is thanked in the next edition, the most useful submissions are rewarded with a selection of digital PDF chapters.

Visit lonelyplanet.com/contact to submit your updates and suggestions or to ask for help. Our award-winning website also features inspirational travel stories, news and discussions.

Note: We may edit, reproduce and incorporate your comments in Lonely Planet products such as guidebooks, websites and digital products, so let us know if you don't want your comments reproduced or your name acknowledged. For a copy of our privacy policy visit lonelyplanet.com/privacy.

Index

A

accessible travel 361

accommodations 39, 361-3, *see also individual locations*

bookings 361

language 376

activities 25, 26, 356-9, *see also individual activities, locations*

Ahuachapán 170-1

air travel 370, 371-2

airports 374-5

Alvarado, Pedro de 344

Ambergris Caye 150-5

animals, *see individual species*

Antigua 18, 90-111, **91**, **100-1**

accommodations 91

activities 92-3, 102

drinking & nightlife 108-10

entertainment 110

food 104-8

history 107

itineraries 90, 96-7, **96-7**

money 111

shopping 103-4, 109

sights 98-102

tours 102-3

travel to/from 91, 111

travel within 111

walking tours 96-7, **96-7**

Apaneca 165, 168-9

archaeological sites 24

Chichén Itzá 21, 64-77, **68-9**

Convento de Capuchinas 99

Copán 17, 176-9

Dzibilchatún 53

Iglesia y Convento de Santo Domingo 98

La Piedra Pintada de Caldera 332

Rastrajon 183

Tikal 11, 126-33, **130-1**

Uaxactún 134-5

Uxmal 48-51

Yaxhá 139

art galleries, *see* galleries

arts 171, 353-5

Ataco 165, 170

ATMs 367

B

bananas 346

bargaining 367

bathrooms 369

bats 242, 321

Bay Islands 12, 184-95, **185**

beach parties 157

beaches

Boca del Drago 314

Parque Nacional Manuel Antonio 270-1

Playa Bluff 314

Playa Espadilla Sur 270

Playa Larga 320

Playa Manuel Antonio 271

Playa Santa Cruz 225-6

Playa Santo Domingo 225-6

Punta Catedral 270-1

Red Frog Beach 321

Secret Beach 154

beer 336

Belize 141-59

Belize Barrier Reef 144-7

bicycle travel, *see* cycling

birdwatching

Bocas del Toro 314

Boquete 333

Bosque Nuboso Monteverde 235, 242, 248

Copán 180

La Fortuna 258-9

Panama 292-3, 301

Parque Nacional Manuel Antonio 273

Parque Nacional Volcán Baru 327, 329

Pipeline Road 293

Yucatán & Chiapas 76

black market 367

Blue Hole 148-9

boat travel 371, 372

Bocas del Toro 7, 310-23, **311**, **316**

Bocas Town 314-19

books 31

Boquete 332-7, **334**

border crossings 368, 370-1

Bosque Nuboso Monteverde 15, 232-5

bus travel 372-3

butterflies 241, 300

C

cabins 362

camping 361

canoeing, *see* kayaking & canoeing

canopy tours

Apaneca 169

Boquete 333

El Castillo 265

La Fortuna 259

Manuel Antonio 279

Monteverde 238-9

Tikal 133

canyoning 243, 260

capuchins 19, 272

car rental 373

car travel 373

Casco Viejo 286-7, 299

casinos 309

Catarina 205

cathedrals, *see* churches & cathedrals

caves, *see also* cenotes

Cuevas de Ak'tun Kan 136

Nivida Bat Cave 321

Caye Caulker 155-9, **156**

cell phones 22
cenotes 52-3
  Cenote Santa Barbara 53
  Cenote Suytun 75
  Cenote X'Kekén y Samulá 74-5
  Cenote Xlacah 53
  Cenote Zací 75-6
  Cenotes de Cuzamá 52
Central American squirrel monkeys 273
changing money 367
Chiapas, see Yucatán & Chiapas
Chichén Itzá 21, 64-77, **65**, **68-9**
children, travel with 38-9
Chiriquí Province 17, 324-37, **325**
chocolate 208, 237, 258, 321
churches & cathedrals
  Catedral de Nuestra Señora de la Asunción 300
  Catedral de San Ildefonso 56
  Catedral de San Servasio 74
  Catedral de Santiago 99
  Convento y Museo San Francisco 208
  Iglesia de la Candelaria 74
  Iglesia de San José 299
  Iglesia de Xalteva 209
  Iglesia La Merced 208
  Iglesia Merced 98-9
  Iglesia y Convento de Santo Domingo 98
  Nuestra Señora de Asunción 171
  Templo de San Bernardino 74
climate 22, 28-30, 362, **22**
climate change 370
climbing, see volcano climbing
coatis 272
coffee 25, 337, 344-5
  Copán 183
  Flower Route 164-5
  Granada 209
  La Fortuna 258

Mérida 62
Panajachel 124
coffee farm tours
  Antigua 102-3
  Chiriquí Province 330-1
  Flower Route 165
  Lago de Atitlán 121
  Monteverde 236-7
  Volcán Mombacho 200-1
  Yucatán & Chiapas 62
colectivos 373
community tours 201
conquistadors 344
cooking courses
  Antigua 102
  Belize 150
  Granada 211
  La Fortuna 265
  Mérida 47
Copán 17, 174-83, **175**
  accommodations 175
  history 178-9
  itineraries 174
  tours 180
  travel to/from 175
Copán Ruinas 180-3, **181**
Cortés, Hernán 344
Costa Rica 229-81
costs 23
courses, see also cooking courses, Spanish language courses, individual locations
  pottery 211
  salsa 92-3
  surfing 313
credit cards 367
currencies 22
customs regulations 363
cycling
  Bocas del Toro 317
  Granada 214
  Isla de Ometepe 221
  La Fortuna 260, 264
  Lago de Atitlán 121

Mérida 56
Panama City 301

D

Diriá 202-3
Diriomo 202-3
discount cards 363
diving & snorkeling 356-7
  Bay Islands 186-9
  Belize Barrier Reef 145-7
  Blue Hole 148-9
  Bocas del Toro 315, 321
  Isla Taboga 295
  Panama City 301
  responsible diving & snorkeling 147
  safety 357
drinking & nightlife 27, see also individual locations
  language 376
driving tours 166-7, **166-7**
Dzibilchaltún 53

E

Earth Lodge 111
ecotourism 341, 346
El Castillo 264-5
El Panchán 87
El Remate 138-9
El Salvador 161-71
  arts 171
electricity 363
emergencies 363-4
  language 376
entertainment 27, see also individual locations
environmental issues 370
events, see festivals & events

F

family 352
family travel 38-9
farmstays 221, 227

Ferrer, José Figueres 347
festivals & events 28-30
  Filthy Fridays 318
  Panama Jazz Festival 287
  Semana Santa 104
films 31
Finca Mystica 227
fishing 274
Flores 136-8, **137**
food 26, 364, *see also individual
  locations*
  language 376
free diving 195
frogs 241-2
fuel 373

G

galleries, *see also* museums
  Casa Cakchiquel 120
  La Galería 120
  Memorias Frágiles 180
gardens, *see* parks & gardens
Garifuna music 355
gay travelers 278, 366-7
geisha coffee 331
Granada 16, 198-215, **210**
  accommodations 199
  courses 211
  drinking & nightlife 213
  food 212-13
  itineraries 198, 206-7, **206-7**
  shopping 211-12
  sights 200-5, 208-9
  tours 209-11
  travel to/from 199, 213-14
  travel within 214
  walking tours 206-7,
    206-7
Green Acres
  Chocolate Farm 321
green iguanas 273
Guatemala 89-139
guesthouses 361

H

Hacienda San Lucas 183
hammocks 58, 362
handicrafts 124, 202
health 38-9, 364-5
hiking 358
  Boquete 333
  Bosque Nuboso Monteverde
    234
  Isla de Ometepe 218-20
  Lago de Atitlán 119
  Monteverde 242
  Parque Nacional Manuel
    Antonio 271
  Parque Nacional
    Volcán Arenal 254-5
  Parque Nacional
    Volcán Barú 326
  Reserva Natural Volcán Mom-
    bacho 200-1
  safety 358
history 24, 342-9, *see also
  individual locations*
homestays 362
Honduras 173-95
horseback riding
  Copán 180
  Isla de Ometepe 221, 227
  La Fortuna 259-60
  Monteverde 243-4
  Parque Nacional
    Volcán Arenal 255
hostels 362-3
hot springs 256-7
  Aguas Termales de Calera 201
  Baldi Hot Springs 257
  Eco Termales Hot Spring 256
  Paradise Hot Springs 256-7
  Springs Resort & Spa 257
  Tabacón Hot Springs 257
hotels 361
howler monkeys 272
hummingbirds 273, 292
hyperbaric chambers 145

I

iguanas 191, 273
indigenous art 354
insurance 364, 365-6, 373
internet access 366
internet resources, *see* websites
Isla Bastimentos 313, 320-2
Isla Carenero 313, 322
Isla Colón 312, 314-19
Isla de Ometepe 8, 216-27, **222**
  accommodations 217
  activities 218-21
  itineraries 216
  orientation 225
  travel to/from 217
Isla San Cristóbal 322
Isla Taboga 294
Isletas de Granada 212
itineraries 32-7, **32-3**, **34**, **36-7**
  see also individual locations

J

jade 109
jazz 287
Jocotenango 111
Juayúa 168

K

kayaking & canoeing
  Isla de Ometepe 220-1, 225
  Isletas de Granada 212
  La Fortuna 258, 260
  Panama 291
  Parque Nacional Manuel
    Antonio 271
kitesurfing
  Caye Caulker 155-6
  Isla de Ometepe 221, 226

L

La Fortuna 258-64
Lago de Atitlán 4, 112-25, **113**
Lago de Yojoa 183

language 376, *see also* Spanish
  language courses
legal matters 366
LGBT travelers 278, 366-7
lifestyle 352

M

malaria 365
Manuel Antonio 19, 266-81, **267**
maps 367
marine reserves
  Bacalar Chico National Park &
    Marine Reserve 147
  Hol Chan Marine Reserve 145
  Parque Nacional Marino Isla
    Bastimentos 320
markets
  Antigua 103, 104
  Ataco 170
  Mérida 47, 55-6
  Panajachel 124
  Panama City 304
  Quepos 276
  Valladolid 74
Masatepe 205
Maya history 343, 344
Maya people 351
Mérida 8, 42-63, **43, 54**
  accommodations 43
  activities 56
  drinking & nightlife 61-3
  food 46-7, 58-61
  history 57
  itineraries 42
  money 62
  museums 44-5
  safety 62
  shopping 57-8
  sights 44-5, 48-53, 55-6
  tourist information 62
  tours 56-7
  travel to/from 43, 63
  travel within 63
Mexico 41-87

mobile phones 22
money 22, 23, 367-8
monkeys 19, 272, 273
Monteverde 230-49, **240**
  accommodations 231
  activities 238-9, 242
  courses 242-3
  drinking & nightlife 246
  food 244-6
  itineraries 230
  money 247
  shopping 246
  sights 232-7, 241-2
  tours 243-4
  travel to/from 231, 247-8
Monteverde Cloud Forest,
  see Bosque Nuboso
  Monteverde
motorcycle travel 373
Moyogalpa 223-5
museums
  BioMuseo 300-1
  Casa de los Venados 74
  Casa K'inich 180
  Centro Cultural
    La Azotea 99-102
  Gran Museo del
    Mundo Maya 44
  Mi Museo 208-9
  Museo de Arqueología
    Maya 180
  Museo de Arte
    Comtemporáneo 300
  Museo de Arte Popular
    de Yucatán 45
  Museo de Chocolate 208
  Museo de la
    Ciudad (Mérida) 45
  Museo de San Roque 74
  Museo del Canal
    Interoceánico 299
  Museo Digital de Copán 181
  Museo Fernando García
    Ponce-Macay 45
  Museo Lítico 133
  Museo Numismástico 226

  Museo Precolombino 226
  Museo Santa Bárbara 136
  Museo Sylvanus G Morley 133
  Museos El Ceibo 226
  Palacio Cantón 44-5
music 31, 287, 355

N

national parks & nature
  reserves, *see also* marine
  reserves
  Bacalar Chico National Park &
    Marine Reserve 147
  Bosque Eterno
    de los Niños 241
  Bosque Nuboso
    Monteverde 15, 232-5
  Ecocentro Danaus 258
  Mirador El Silencio 258
  Panama Rainforest Discovery
    Center 292-3
  Parque Nacional Manuel
    Antonio 19, 268-73
  Parque Nacional
    Volcán Arenal 252-5
  Parque Nacional
    Volcán Barú 326-9
  Reserva Natural Atitlán 120
  Reserva Natural Volcán
    Mombacho 200-1
  Reserva Santa Elena 242
Nicaragua 197-227
  politics 213
nightlife, *see* drinking & nightlife
Niquinohomo 205
Noriega, Manuel 349
Northern Cayes 6, 142-59, **143**
notable buildings
  Arco de Santa Catalina 98
  Ayuntamiento 74
  Palacio de Gobierno 55
  Palacio de los Capitanes
    Generales 99
  Quinta Montes Molina 55
  Teatro Nacional 299

O

Ortega, Daniel 349

P

Palenque 14, 78-87
  accommodations 79
  food 86-7
  history 80-1
  itineraries 78
  money 87
  safety 87
  travel to/from 79, 87
  travel within 87
Panajachel 120-5, **122**
Panama 283-337
Panama Canal 288-91
Panama City 13, 284-309, **285**, **298**, **302**
  accommodations 285
  activities 301
  drinking & nightlife 307-8
  entertainment 308
  food 304-7
  history 286
  itineraries 284, 296-7, **296-7**
  money 309
  shopping 303-4
  sights 286-95, 299-301
  tours 301-3
  travel to/from 285, 309
  travel within 309
  walking tours 296-7, **296-7**
Panama Rainforest Discovery Center 292-3
paragliding 120-1
parks & gardens
  Carambola Botanical Gardens 191
  El Explorador 333
  Finca Los Monos Botanical Garden 314
  Parque Central (Antigua) 98
  Parque Natural Metropolitano 299

Parque Santa Lucía 55
Parque Nacional Manuel Antonio 19, 268-73
Parque Nacional Volcán Arenal 252-5
Parque Nacional Volcán Barú 326-9
people 350-2
Perez, Danilo 287
photography 368
planning 22-3
  budgeting 23
  calendar of events 28-30
  itineraries 32-7, **32-3**, **34**, **36-7**
  travel seasons 22, 28-30
  travel with children 38-9
Playa Santo Domingo 225-6
poetry 354-5
politics 340-1
population 341
pottery 203-5, 211, 214-15
poverty 341
Pueblos Blancos 202-5

Q

Quepos 274-8, **275**
quetzals 248, 329

R

rafting 359
  Boquete 333
  La Fortuna 258
  Manuel Antonio 279
  Quepos 274
religion 169, 341, 352
Roatán 191-3, **190**
Romero, Archbishop Óscar 169, 348, 349
Ruta de las Flores 20, 162-71, **163**, **166-7**

S

safety 368

diving 357
government travel advice 367
hiking 358
Salcoatitán 170
salsa 92-3
San Juan de Oriente 203-5, 214-5
San Juan La Laguna 115
San Marcos La Laguna 116-17
San Pedro 150-5, **151**
San Pedro La Laguna 114-15
Sandino, General Augusto César 205
Santa Cruz La Laguna 117
Santa Elena (Costa Rica) 41-8, **240**
Santa Elena (Guatemala) 136-8
Santiago Atitlán 116
Semana Santa 104-5
Sendero Los Quetzales 327-8
shopping 26, see also individual locations
sloths 272-3
smoking 368
snorkeling, see diving & snorkeling
souvenirs 27, 124
Spanish language courses
  Antigua 92-3
  Boquete 335
  Granada 211
  Lago de Atitlán 115
  Mérida 60
  Monteverde 242-3
  Panajachel 123
  Panama City 306
standup paddleboarding
  Caye Caulker 157
  Granada 209-10
  Lago de Atitlán 121
  Quepos 274
street art 353-4
street food 364
submersible rides 191
surfing 358-9

Bocas del Toro 312-13
courses 313
Manuel Antonio 279
swimming
Chichén Itzá 74-6
Isla de Ometepe 220

T

Tea & Chocolate Place 180
telephone services 22, 368-9
Tikal 11, 126-33, **127**, **130-1**
time 22
tipping 368
toilets 369
tourist information 369
tours, *see also* canopy tours, community tours
Antigua 102-3
Bocas del Toro 317, 321
Bosque Nuboso Monteverde 235
Caye Caulker 156-7
Chichén Itzá 76
Chiriquí Province 330, 333-5
Copán 180
Granada 209-11
La Fortuna 258-60
Lago de Atitlán 121
Mérida 56-7
Monteverde 243-4
Northern Cayes 150, 156-7
Panajachel 121
Panama Canal 291
Panama City 301-3
Parque Nacional Volcán Arenal 255
Quepos 274
Tikal 136
travel to/from Central America 370

travel within Central America 23, 371-5
Tzununá 117
Tz'utujil oil painting 117

U

Uaxactún 134-5
Utila 188, 193-5
Uxmal 48-51

V

Valladolid 74-7, **75**
visas 22, 369-70
Volcán Arenal 10, 250-65, **251**
Volcán Maderas 219, 226-7
Volcán Mombacho 200-1
Volcán San Pedro 118-19
volcano climbing 119
volcanoes 94-5
Volcán Acatenango 94-5
Volcán Agua 95
Volcán Arenal 10, 250-65
Volcán Barú 326-9
Volcán Concepción 218-19
Volcán Maderas 219, 226-7
Volcán Mombacho 200-1
Volcán Pacaya 95
Volcán San Pedro 118-19
volunteering
El Remate 139
Isla de Ometepe 221, 223

W

walking tours
Antigua 96-7, **96-7**
Granada 206-7, **206-7**
Panama City 296-7, **296-7**
water 365
waterfalls

Cascada San Ramón 226-7
Catarata Río Fortuna 260
Ruta de las Seite Cascadas 168
weather 22, 28-30, 362, **22**
websites 23, 364-5
whale sharks 188-9
whale-watching 295
wildlife reserves & sanctuaries
Arch's Iguana Farm 191
Bat Jungle 242
Bosque Nuboso Monteverde 15, 232-5
Butterfly Garden 241
Greentique Wildlife Refuge 278-9
Mariposario Metropolitano 300
Ranario 241-2
wildlife-watching 24, 359
Bosque Nuboso Monteverde 235
Isla de Ometepe 226
Parque Nacional Manuel Antonio 272-3
women travelers 370

Y

Yaxná 139
yoga
Bocas del Toro 315
Northern Cayes 150, 155
Panama City 301
Yucatán & Chiapas 41-87

Z

zika 365
ziplining, *see* canopy tours

Symbols & Map Key

Look for these symbols to quickly identify listings:

- ◉ Sights
- ⊕ Activities
- ⊜ Courses
- ◉ Tours
- ✪ Festivals & Events
- ◈ Eating
- ⊕ Drinking
- ✪ Entertainment
- 🔒 Shopping
- ❶ Information & Transport

These symbols and abbreviations give vital information for each listing:

- ✐ Sustainable or green recommendation
- **FREE** No payment required

- ☑ Telephone number
- ⊙ Opening hours
- ℗ Parking
- ⊖ Nonsmoking
- ✳ Air-conditioning
- @ Internet access
- 📶 Wi-fi access
- ☀ Swimming pool
- 🚌 Bus
- ⛴ Ferry
- 🚋 Tram
- 🚃 Train
- 🍴 English-language menu
- 🥗 Vegetarian selection
- ♦ Family-friendly

Find your best experiences with these Great For... icons.

- 🖼 Art & Culture
- 🏖 Beaches
- 💳 Budget
- ☕ Cafe/Coffee
- 🚲 Cycling
- ↪ Detour
- 🍷 Drinking
- 🎫 Entertainment
- 🎆 Events
- 👪 Family Travel
- 🍽 Food & Drink
- 📕 History
- 💬 Local Life
- 🐦 Nature & Wildlife
- 📷 Photo Op
- 🔭 Scenery
- 🛍 Shopping
- 🎟 Short Trip
- 🏀 Sport
- 🚶 Walking
- ❄ Winter Travel

Sights

- 🏖 Beach
- 🐦 Bird Sanctuary
- 🛕 Buddhist
- 🏰 Castle/Palace
- ✝ Christian
- 🕍 Confucian
- 🕉 Hindu
- ☪ Islamic
- 卍 Jain
- ✡ Jewish
- 🗿 Monument
- 🏛 Museum/Gallery/ Historic Building
- 🏚 Ruin
- ⛩ Shinto
- 🪯 Sikh
- ☯ Taoist
- 🍇 Winery/Vineyard
- 🦁 Zoo/Wildlife Sanctuary
- ◉ Other Sight

Points of Interest

- 🏄 Bodysurfing
- ⛺ Camping
- ☕ Cafe
- 🛶 Canoeing/Kayaking
- • Course/Tour
- 🤿 Diving
- 🍸 Drinking & Nightlife
- ✕ Eating
- 🎭 Entertainment
- ♨ Sento Hot Baths/ Onsen
- 🛍 Shopping
- ⛷ Skiing
- 🛏 Sleeping
- 🤿 Snorkelling
- 🏄 Surfing
- 🏊 Swimming/Pool
- 🚶 Walking
- 🏄 Windsurfing
- ✦ Other Activity

Information

- 💲 Bank
- 🏛 Embassy/Consulate
- ➕ Hospital/Medical
- @ Internet
- 👮 Police
- ✉ Post Office
- 📞 Telephone
- 🚻 Toilet
- ❶ Tourist Information
- • Other Information

Geographic

- 🏖 Beach
- ⊷ Gate
- 🛖 Hut/Shelter
- 🗼 Lighthouse
- 🔭 Lookout
- ▲ Mountain/Volcano
- 🌴 Oasis
- 🌳 Park
-)(Pass
- 🌳 Picnic Area
- 💧 Waterfall

Transport

- ✈ Airport
- Ⓑ BART station
- ⊕ Border crossing
- Ⓣ Boston T station
- 🚌 Bus
- ⊕ Cable car/Funicular
- ⊸ Cycling
- ⊖ Ferry
- Ⓜ Metro/MRT station
- ⊕ Monorail
- ℗ Parking
- ⊕ Petrol station
- Ⓢ Subway/S-Bahn/ Skytrain station
- 🚕 Taxi
- ⊕ Train station/Railway
- ⊷⊷ Tram
- Ⓤ Underground/ U-Bahn station
- • Other Transport

Celeste Brash

Like many California natives, Celeste now lives in Portland, Oregon. She arrived, however, after 15 years in French Polynesia, a year and a half in Southeast Asia and a stint teaching English as a second language (in an American accent) in Brighton, England – among other things. She's been writing guidebooks for Lonely Planet since 2005, and her travel articles have appeared in publications from BBC Travel to National Geographic. She's currently writing a book about her five years on a remote pearl farm in the Tuamotu Atolls.

Stuart Butler

Stuart has been writing for Lonely Planet for a decade. In addition to guidebook writing, he writes about conservation and environmental issues, wildlife watching and hiking. As a photographer, he was a finalist in both the 2015 and 2016 Travel Photographer of the Year Awards. When not on the road for Lonely Planet he lives on the beautiful beaches of Southwest France with his wife and two children.

His website is at www.stuartbutlerjour nalist.com

Paul Clammer

Paul Clammer has worked as a molecular biologist, tour leader and travel writer. Since 2003 he has worked as a guidebook author for Lonely Planet, contributing to over 25 Lonely Planet titles, covering destinations in South and Central Asia, West and North Africa and the Caribbean. In recent years he's lived in Morocco, Jordan, Haiti and Fiji, as well as his native England. Find him online at paulclammer.com or on Twitter as @paulclammer.

Steve Fallon

A native of Boston, Massachusetts, Steve graduated from Georgetown University with a Bachelor of Science in modern languages. After working for several years for an American daily newspaper and earning a master's degree in journalism, his fascination with the 'new' Asia led him to Hong Kong, where he lived for over a dozen years, working for a variety of media and running his own travel bookshop. Steve lived in Budapest for three years before moving to London in 1994. He has written or contributed to more than 100 Lonely Planet titles. Steve is a qualified London Blue Badge Tourist Guide. Visit his website on www.steveslondon.com.

Anna Kaminski

Originally from the Soviet Union, Anna grew up in Cambridge, UK. She graduated from the University of Warwick with a degree in Comparative American Studies, a background in the history, culture and literature of the Americas and the Caribbean, and an enduring love of Latin America. Her restless wanderings led her to settle briefly in Oaxaca and Bangkok, and her flirtation with criminal law saw her volunteering as a lawyer's assistant in the courts, ghettos and prisons of Kingson, Jamaica. Anna has contributed to almost 30 Lonely Planet titles. When not on the road, Anna calls London home.

Brian Kluepfel

Brian had lived in three states and seven different residences by the time he was nine, and just kept moving, making stops in Berkeley, Bolivia, the Bronx and the 'burbs further down the line. His journalistic work across the Americas has ranged from the Copa America soccer tournament in Paraguay to an accordion festival in Quebec. Brian's titles for Lonely Planet include *Venezuela*, *Costa Rica*, *Belize & Guatemala*, *Bolivia* and *Ecuador*.

Carolyn McCarthy

Carolyn McCarthy specializes in travel, culture and adventure in the Americas. She has written for *National Geographic*, *Outside*, *BBC Magazine*, *Sierra Magazine*, *Boston Globe* and other publications. A former Fulbright fellow and Banff Mountain Grant recipient, she has documented life in the most remote corners of Latin America. Carolyn has contributed to 40 guidebooks and anthologies for Lonely Planet, including *Colorado*, *USA*, *Argentina*, *Chile*, *Trekking in the Patagonian Andes*, *Panama*, *Peru* and *USA National Parks* guides. For more information, visit www.carolynmccarthy.org or follow her Instagram travels @mccarthyoffmap.

Our Story

A beat-up old car, a few dollars in the pocket and a sense of adventure. In 1972 that's all Tony and Maureen Wheeler needed for the trip of a lifetime – across Europe and Asia overland to Australia. It took several months, and at the end – broke but inspired – they sat at their kitchen table writing and stapling together their first travel guide, *Across Asia on the Cheap*. Within a week they'd sold 1500 copies. Lonely Planet was born.

Today, Lonely Planet has offices in Franklin, London, Melbourne, Oakland, Dublin, Beijing, and Delhi, with more than 600 staff and writers. We share Tony's belief that 'a great guidebook should do three things: inform, educate and amuse'.

Our Writers

Ashley Harrell

After a brief stint selling day spa coupons door-to-door in South Florida, Ashley decided she'd rather be a writer. She went to journalism grad school, convinced a newspaper to hire her, and starting covering wildlife, crime and tourism, sometimes all in the same story. Fueling her zest for storytelling and the unknown, she traveled widely and moved often, from a tiny NYC apartment to a vast California ranch to a jungle cabin in Costa Rica, where she started writing for Lonely Planet.

Isabel Albiston

After six years working for the *Daily Telegraph* in London, Isabel left to spend more time on the road. A job as writer for a magazine in Sydney, Australia, was followed by a four-month overland trip across Asia and five years living and working in Buenos Aires, Argentina. Isabel started writing for Lonely Planet in 2014 and has contributed to 12 guidebooks. She's currently based in Ireland.

Ray Bartlett

Ray has been travel writing for nearly two decades, covering Japan, Korea, Mexico, Tanzania, Guatemala, Indonesia and many parts of the United States for top-industry publishers, newspapers and magazines. His acclaimed debut novel, *Sunsets of Tulum*, set in Yucatán, was a Midwest Book Review 2016 Fiction pick. Follow him on Facebook (@RayBartlettAuthor), Twitter (@kaisoradotcom), Instagram (@kaisoradotcom), or contact him via www.kaisora.com. Ray currently divides his time between homes in the USA, Japan and Mexico.

More Writers

STAY IN TOUCH LONELYPLANET.COM/CONTACT

AUSTRALIA The Malt Store, Level 3, 551 Swanston St, Carlton, Victoria 3053 ☏03 8379 8000, fax 03 8379 8111

IRELAND Digital Depot, Roe Lane (off Thomas St), Digital Hub, Dublin 8, D08 TCV4, Ireland

USA 124 Linden Street, Oakland, CA 94607 ☏510 250 6400, toll free 800 275 8555, fax 510 893 8572

UK 240 Blackfriars Road, London SE1 8NW ☏020 3771 5100, fax 020 3771 5101

 twitter.com/ lonelyplanet facebook.com/ lonelyplanet instagram.com/ lonelyplanet youtube.com/ lonelyplanet lonelyplanet.com/ newsletter